Lecture Notes in Computer Science 10522

Commenced Publication in 1973
Founding and Former Series Editors:
Gerhard Goos, Juris Hartmanis, and Jan van Leeuwen

More information about this series at http://www.springer.com/series/7408

Mehdi Dastani · Marjan Sirjani (Eds.)

Fundamentals of Software Engineering

7th International Conference, FSEN 2017
Tehran, Iran, April 26–28, 2017
Revised Selected Papers

Springer

Editors
Mehdi Dastani
Utrecht University
Utrecht
The Netherlands

Marjan Sirjani 🆔
Mälardalen University
Västerås
Sweden

and

Reykjavik University
Reykjavik
Iceland

ISSN 0302-9743   ISSN 1611-3349   (electronic)
Lecture Notes in Computer Science
ISBN 978-3-319-68971-5   ISBN 978-3-319-68972-2   (eBook)
DOI 10.1007/978-3-319-68972-2

Library of Congress Control Number: 2017956059

LNCS Sublibrary: SL2 – Programming and Software Engineering

Printed on acid-free paper

This Springer imprint is published by Springer Nature
The registered company is Springer International Publishing AG
The registered company address is: Gewerbestrasse 11, 6330 Cham, Switzerland

Preface

The present volume contains the proceedings of the 7th IPM International Conference on Fundamentals of Software Engineering (FSEN), held in Tehran, Iran, April 26–28, 2017. This event was organized by the School of Computer Science at the Institute for Research in Fundamental Sciences (IPM) in Iran. The topics of interest in FSEN span over all aspects of formal methods, especially those related to advancing the application of formal methods in software industry and promoting their integration with practical engineering techniques. The program committee of FSEN 2017 consisted of 41 top researchers from 17 countries. We received a total of 49 submissions from 27 countries, out of which we accepted 16 regular papers and two posters. Each submission was reviewed by at least three independent reviewers, for its quality, originality, contribution, clarity of presentation, and its relevance to the conference topics.

Three distinguished keynote speakers, Thomas Henzinger, Philippa Gardner, and Leon van der Torre, delivered their lectures at FSEN 2017.

We thank the Institute for Research in Fundamental Sciences (IPM), Tehran, Iran, for their financial support and local organization of FSEN 2017. We also thank the members of the Program Committee for their time, effort, and excellent contributions to making FSEN a quality conference. We thank Hossein Hojjat as our publicity chair, and Ali Jafari for his help in preparing this volume. Last but not least, our thanks go to our authors and conference participants, without whose submissions and participation FSEN would not have been possible.

August 2017

Mehdi Dastani
Marjan Sirjani

Organization

Program Committee

Mohammad Abdollahi Azgomi	Iran University of Science and Technology, Iran
Erika Abraham	RWTH Aachen University, Germany
Gul Agha	University of Illinois at Urbana-Champaign, USA
Christel Baier	Technical University of Dresden, Germany
Ezio Bartocci	TU Wien, Austria
Marcello Bonsangue	Leiden University, The Netherlands
Mario Bravetti	University of Bologna, Italy
Michael Butler	University of Southampton, UK
Mehdi Dastani	Utrecht University, The Netherlands
Erik De Vink	Technische Universiteit Eindhoven, The Netherlands
Wan Fokkink	Vrije Universiteit Amsterdam, The Netherlands
Adrian Francalanza	University of Malta, Malta
Masahiro Fujita	University of Tokyo, Japan
Maurizio Gabbrielli	University of Bologna, Italy
Fatemeh Ghassemi	University of Tehran, Iran
Jan Friso Groote	Eindhoven University of Technology, The Netherlands
Kim Guldstrand Larsen	Aalborg University, Denmark
Hassan Haghighi	Shahid Beheshti University, Iran
Philipp Haller	KTH Royal Institute of Technology, Sweden
Holger Hermanns	Saarland University, Germany
Hossein Hojjat	Rochester Institute of Technology, USA
Mohammad Izadi	Sharif University of Technology, Iran
Einar Broch Johnsen	University of Oslo, Norway
Joost-Pieter Katoen	RWTH Aachen University, Germany
Narges Khakpour	Linnaeus University, Sweden
Ramtin Khosravi	University of Tehran, Iran
Natallia Kokash	Leiden University, The Netherlands
Eva Kühn	Vienna University of Technology, Austria
Zhiming Liu	Southwest University, China
Mieke Massink	CNR-ISTI, Italy
Hassan Mirian Hosseinabadi	Sharif University of Technology, Iran
Ugo Montanari	Università di Pisa, Italy
Peter Mosses	Swansea University, UK
Mohammadreza Mousavi	Halmstad University, Sweden
Ali Movaghar	Sharif University of Technology, Iran
Meriem Ouederni	IRIT/INP Toulouse/ENSEEIHT, France

Wishnu Prasetya   Universiteit Utrecht, The Netherlands
Jose Proenca   University of Minho, Portugal
Wolfgang Reisig   Humboldt-Universität zu Berlin, Germany
Philipp Ruemmer   Uppsala University, Sweden
Gwen Salaün   University of Grenoble Alpes, France
Cesar Sanchez   IMDEA Software Institute, Spain
Ina Schaefer   Technische Universität Braunschweig, Germany
Wendelin Serwe   Inria Rhône-Alpes/CONVECS, France
Alexandra Silva   University College London, UK
Marjan Sirjani   Malardalen University, Reykjavik University,
                               Sweden/Iceland
Meng Sun   Peking University, China
Carolyn Talcott   SRI International, USA
Danny Weyns   Linnaeus University, Sweden
Peter Ölveczky   University of Oslo, Norway

Additional Reviewers

Al-Brashdi, Ahmed   Lachmann, Remo
Baghoolizadeh, Shirin   Lanese, Ivan
Barbon, Gianluca   Li, Yi
Bliudze, Simon   Lity, Sascha
Bruintjes, Harold   Liu, Tong
Bruni, Roberto   Lorber, Florian
Bubel, Richard   Mahdieh, Mostafa
Cassar, Ian   Mohaqeqi, Morteza
Castiglioni, Valentina   Padovani, Luca
Chrszon, Philipp   Pun, Ka I
Ciancia, Vincenzo   Radschek, Sophie Therese
Craß, Stefan   Rezazadeh, Abdolbaghi
Dan, Li   Rivadeh, Mehran
Dardha, Ornela   Schwayer, Matthias
Elaheh Habibi, Saleh Hafez Qorani   Taromirad, Masoumeh
Gkolfi, Anastasia   Ter Beek, Maurice H.
Grech, Neville   Tuosto, Emilio
Habibi, Elahe   Varshosaz, Mahsa
Haller, Philipp   Wang, Shuling
He, Nannan   Winter, Joost
Jansen, Nils   Wunderlich, Sascha
Kunze, Sebastian

Contents

Implementing Open Call-by-Value

Beniamino Accattoli[1] and Giulio Guerrieri[2(⊠)]

[1] INRIA, UMR 7161, LIX, École Polytechnique, Palaiseau, France
beniamino.accattoli@inria.fr
[2] Department of Computer Science, University of Oxford, Oxford, UK
giulio.guerrieri@cs.ox.ac.uk

Abstract. The theory of the call-by-value λ-calculus relies on weak evaluation and closed terms, that are natural hypotheses in the study of programming languages. To model proof assistants, however, strong evaluation and open terms are required. Open call-by-value is the intermediate setting of weak evaluation with open terms, on top of which Grégoire and Leroy designed the abstract machine of Coq. This paper provides a theory of abstract machines for open call-by-value. The literature contains machines that are either simple but inefficient, as they have an exponential overhead, or efficient but heavy, as they rely on a labelling of environments and a technical optimization. We introduce a machine that is simple and efficient: it does not use labels and it implements open call-by-value within a bilinear overhead. Moreover, we provide a new fine understanding of how different optimizations impact on the complexity of the overhead.

This work is part of a wider research effort, the COCA HOLA project
https://sites.google.com/site/beniaminoaccattoli/coca-hola.

1   Introduction

The λ-calculus is the computational model behind functional programming languages and proof assistants. A charming feature is that its definition is based on just one *macro-step* computational rule, *β-reduction*, and does not rest on any notion of machine or automaton. Compilers and proof assistants however are concrete tools that have to implement the λ-calculus in some way—a problem clearly arises. There is a huge gap between the abstract mathematical setting of the calculus and the technical intricacies of an actual implementation. This is why the issue is studied via intermediate *abstract machines*, that are implementation schemes with *micro-step* operations and without too many concrete details.

Closed and Strong λ-Calculus. Functional programming languages are based on a simplified form of λ-calculus, that we like to call *closed λ-calculus*, with two important restrictions. First, evaluation is *weak*, *i.e.* it does not evaluate function

M. Dastani and M. Sirjani (Eds.): FSEN 2017, LNCS 10522, pp. 1–19, 2017.
DOI: 10.1007/978-3-319-68972-2_1

bodies. Second, terms are *closed*, that is, they have no free variables. The theory of the closed λ-calculus is much simpler than the general one.

Proof assistants based on the λ-calculus usually require the power of the full theory. Evaluation is then *strong, i.e.* unrestricted, and the distinction between open and closed terms no longer makes sense, because evaluation has to deal with the issues of open terms even if terms are closed, when it enters function bodies. We refer to this setting as the *strong λ-calculus*.

Historically, the study of strong and closed λ-calculi have followed orthogonal approaches. Theoretical studies rather dealt with the strong λ-calculus, and it is only since the seminal work of Abramsky and Ong [1] that theoreticians started to take the closed case seriously. Dually, practical studies mostly ignored strong evaluation, with the notable exception of Crégut [13] (1990) and some very recent works [3,6,19]. Strong evaluation is nonetheless essential in the implementation of proof assistants or higher-order logic programming, typically for type-checking with dependent types as in the Edinburgh Logical Framework or the Calculus of Constructions, as well as for unification in simply typed frameworks like λ-prolog.

Open Call-by-Value. In a very recent work [8], we advocated the relevance of the *open λ-calculus*, a framework in between the closed and the strong ones, where evaluation is *weak* but terms may be *open*. Its key property is that the strong case can be described as the iteration of the open one into function bodies. The same cannot be done with the closed λ-calculus because—as already pointed out—entering into function bodies requires to deal with (locally) open terms.

The open λ-calculus did not emerge before because most theoretical studies focus on the *call-by-name* strong λ-calculus, and in call-by-name the distinction open/closed does not play an important role. Such a distinction, instead, is delicate for *call-by-value* evaluation (function's arguments are evaluated before being passed to the function), where Plotkin's original operational semantics [22] is not adequate for open terms. This issue is discussed at length in [8], where four extensions of Plotkin's semantics to open terms are compared and shown to be equivalent. That paper then introduces the expression *Open Call-by-Value* (shortened *Open CbV*) to refer to them as a whole, as well as *Closed CbV* and *Strong CbV* to concisely refer to the closed and strong call-by-value λ-calculus.

The Fireball Calculus. The simplest presentation of Open CbV is the *fireball calculus* λ_{fire}, obtained from the CbV λ-calculus by generalizing values into *fireballs*. Dynamically, β-redexes are allowed to fire only when the argument is a fireball (*fireball* is a pun on *fire-able*). The fireball calculus was introduced without a name by Paolini and Ronchi Della Rocca [21,23], then rediscovered independently first by Leroy and Grégoire [20], and then by Accattoli and Sacerdoti Coen [2]. Notably, on closed terms, λ_{fire} *coincides* with Plotkin's (Closed) CbV λ-calculus.

Coq by Levels. In [20] (2002) Leroy and Grégoire used the fireball calculus λ_{fire} to improve the implementation of the Coq proof assistant. In fact, Coq rests on Strong CbV, but Leroy and Grégoire design an abstract machine for the fireball calculus (*i.e.* Open CbV) and then use it to evaluate Strong CbV *by levels*: the machine is first executed at top level (that is, out of all abstractions), and then re-launched recursively under abstractions. Their study is itself formalized in Coq, but it lacks an estimation of the efficiency of the machine.

In order to continue our story some basic facts about cost models and abstract machines have to be recalled (see [4] for a gentle tutorial).

Interlude 1: Size Explosion. It is well-known that λ-calculi suffer from a degeneracy called *size explosion*: there are families of terms whose size is linear in n, that evaluate in n β-steps, and whose result has size exponential in n. The problem is that the number of β-steps, the natural candidate as a time cost model, then seems not to be a reasonable cost model, because it does not even account for the time to write down the result of a computation—the *macro-step* character of β-reduction seems to forbid to count 1 for each step. This is a problem that affects all λ-calculi and all evaluation strategies.

Interlude 2: Reasonable Cost Models and Abstract Machines. Despite size explosion, surprisingly, the number of β-steps often *is* a reasonable cost model—so one can indeed count 1 for each β-step. There are no paradoxes: λ-calculi can be simulated in alternative formalisms employing some form of sharing, such as abstract machines. These settings manage compact representations of terms via *micro-step* operations and produce compact representations of the result, avoiding size explosion. Showing that a certain λ-calculus is reasonable usually is done by simulating it with a *reasonable* abstract machine, *i.e.* a machine implementable with overhead polynomial in the number of β-steps in the calculus. The design of a reasonable abstract machine depends very much on the kind of λ-calculus to be implemented, as different calculi admit different forms of size explosion and/or require more sophisticated forms of sharing. For strategies in the closed λ-calculus it is enough to use the ordinary technology for abstract machines, as first shown by Blelloch and Greiner [12], and then by Sands, Gustavsson, and Moran [24], and, with other techniques, by combining the results in Dal Lago and Martini's [15] and [14]. The case of the strong λ-calculus is subtler, and a more sophisticated form of sharing is necessary, as first shown by Accattoli and Dal Lago [7]. The topic of this paper is the study of reasonable machines for the intermediate case of Open CbV.

Fireballs are Reasonable. In [2] Accattoli and Sacerdoti Coen study Open CbV from the point of view of cost models. Their work provides 3 contributions:

1. *Open Size Explosion*: they show that Open CbV is subtler than Closed CbV by exhibiting a form of size explosions that is not possible in Closed CbV, making Open CbV closer to Strong CbV rather than to Closed CbV;
2. *Fireballs are Reasonable*: they show that the number of β-steps in the fireball calculus is nonetheless a reasonable cost model by exhibiting a reasonable abstract machine, called GLAMOUr, improving on Leroy and Grégoire's machine in [20] (see the conclusions in Sect. 7 for more on their machine);

3. *And Even Efficient*: they optimize the GLAMOUr into the Unchaining GLA-MOUr, whose overhead is bilinear (*i.e.* linear in the number of β-steps *and* the size of the initial term), that is the best possible overhead.

This Paper. Here we present two machines, the Easy GLAMOUr and Fast GLA-MOUr, that are proved to be correct implementations of Open CbV (precisely, of the right-to-left evaluation strategy in λ_{fire}) and to have a polynomial and bilinear overhead, respectively. Their study refines the results of [2] along three axes:

1. *Simpler Machines*: both the GLAMOUr and the Unchaining GLAMOUr of [2] are sophisticated machines resting on a labeling of terms. The unchaining optimizations of the second machine is also quite heavy. Both the Easy GLA-MOUr and the Fast GLAMOUr, instead, do not need labels and the Fast GLAMOUr is bilinear with no need of the unchaining optimization.
2. *Simpler Analyses*: the correctness and complexity analyses of the (Unchaining) GLAMOUr are developed in [2] via an informative but complex decomposition via explicit substitutions, by means of the distillation methodology [5]. Here, instead, we decode the Easy and Fast GLAMOUr directly to the fireball calculus, that turns out to be much simpler. Moreover, the complexity analysis of the Fast GLAMOUr, surprisingly, turns out to be straightforward.
3. *Modular Decomposition of the Overhead*: we provide a fine analysis of how different optimizations impact on the complexity of the overhead of abstract machines for Open CbV. In particular, it turns out that one of the optimizations considered essential in [2], namely *substituting abstractions on-demand*, is not mandatory for reasonable machines—the Easy GLAMOUr does not implement it and yet it is reasonable. We show, however, that this is true only as long as one stays *inside* Open CbV because the optimization is instead mandatory for Strong CbV (seen by Grégoire and Leroy as Open CbV *by levels*). To our knowledge substituting abstractions on-demand is an optimization introduced in [7] and currently no proof assistant implements it. Said differently, our work shows that the technology currently in use in proof assistants is, at least theoretically, unreasonable.

Summing up, this paper does not improve the known bound on the overhead of abstract machines for Open CbV, as the one obtained in [2] is already optimal. Its contributions instead are a simplification and a finer understanding of the subtleties of implementing Open CbV: we introduce simpler abstract machines whose complexity analyses are elementary and carry a new modular view of how different optimizations impact on the complexity of the overhead.

In particular, while [2] shows that Open CbV is subtler than Closed CbV, here we show that Open CbV is simpler than Strong CbV, and that defining Strong CbV as iterated Open CbV, as done by Grégoire and Leroy in [20], may introduce an explosion of the overhead, if done naively.

A longer version of this paper is available on Arxiv [9]. It contains two Appendices, one with a glossary of rewriting theory and one with omitted proofs.

2   The Fireball Calculus λ_{fire} and Open Size Explosion

In this section we introduce the fireball calculus, the presentation of Open CbV we work with in this paper, and show the example of size explosion peculiar to the open setting. Alternative presentations of Open CbV can be found in [8].

Terms	$t, u, s, r ::= x \mid \lambda x.t \mid tu$
Fireballs	$f, f', f'' ::= \lambda x.t \mid i$
Inert Terms	$i, i', i'' ::= x f_1 \dots f_n \qquad n \geq 0$
Evaluation Contexts	$E ::= \langle \cdot \rangle \mid tE \mid Et$

RULE AT TOP LEVEL	CONTEXTUAL CLOSURE	
$(\lambda x.t)(\lambda y.u) \mapsto_{\beta_\lambda} t\{x \leftarrow \lambda y.u\}$	$E\langle t \rangle \to_{\beta_\lambda} E\langle u \rangle$	if $t \mapsto_{\beta_\lambda} u$
$(\lambda x.t)i \mapsto_{\beta_i} t\{x \leftarrow i\}$	$E\langle t \rangle \to_{\beta_i} E\langle u \rangle$	if $t \mapsto_{\beta_i} u$

Reduction	$\to_{\beta_f} := \to_{\beta_\lambda} \cup \to_{\beta_i}$

Fig. 1. The Fireball Calculus λ_{fire}

The Fireball Calculus. The fireball calculus λ_{fire} is defined in Fig. 1. The idea is that the values of the call-by-value λ-calculus, given by abstractions and variables, are generalized to *fireballs*, by extending variables to more general *inert terms*. Actually fireballs (noted $f, f', \dots$) and inert terms (noted $i, i', \dots$) are defined by mutual induction (in Fig. 1). For instance, $\lambda x.y$ is a fireball as an abstraction, while x, $y(\lambda x.x)$, xy, and $(z(\lambda x.x))(zz)(\lambda y.(zy))$ are fireballs as inert terms.

The main feature of inert terms is that they are open, normal, and when plugged in a context they cannot create a redex, whence the name (they are not so-called *neutral terms* because they might have β-redexes under abstractions). In Grégoire and Leroy's presentation [20], inert terms are called *accumulators* and fireballs are simply called *values*.

Terms are always identified up to α-equivalence and the set of free variables of a term t is denoted by $\mathtt{fv}(t)$. We use $t\{x \leftarrow u\}$ for the term obtained by the capture-avoiding substitution of u for each free occurrence of x in t.

Evaluation is given by *call-by-fireball* β-reduction $\to_{\beta_f}$: the β-rule can fire, *lighting up* the argument, only if the argument is a fireball (*fireball* is a catchier version of *fire-able term*). We actually distinguish two sub-rules: one that *lights up* abstractions, noted $\to_{\beta_\lambda}$, and one that *lights up* inert terms, noted $\to_{\beta_i}$ (see Fig. 1). Note that evaluation is *weak* (*i.e.* it does not reduce under abstractions).

Properties of the Calculus. A famous key property of Closed CbV (whose evaluation is exactly $\to_{\beta_\lambda}$) is *harmony*: given a closed term t, either it diverges or it evaluates to an abstraction, *i.e.* t is β_λ-normal iff t is an abstraction. The fireball calculus satisfies an analogous property in the *open* setting by replacing abstractions with fireballs (Proposition 1.1). Moreover, the fireball calculus is a conservative extension of Closed CbV: on closed terms it collapses on Closed CbV (Proposition 1.2). No other presentation of Open CbV has these properties.

Proposition 1 (Distinctive Properties of λ_{fire}). *Let t be a term.*

1. Open Harmony: t is β_f-normal iff t is a fireball.
2. Conservative Open Extension: $t \to_{\beta_f} u$ iff $t \to_{\beta_\lambda} u$ whenever t is closed.

The rewriting rules of λ_{fire} have also many good operational properties, studied in [8] and summarized in the following proposition.

Proposition 2 (Operational Properties of λ_{fire}, [8]). *The reduction $\to_{\beta_f}$ is strongly confluent, and all β_f-normalizing derivations d (if any) from a term t have the same length $|d|_{\beta_f}$, the same number $|d|_{\beta_\lambda}$ of β_λ-steps, and the same number $|d|_{\beta_i}$ of β_i-steps.*

Right-to-Left Evaluation. As expected from a *calculus*, the evaluation rule $\to_{\beta_f}$ of λ_{fire} is *non-deterministic*, because in the case of an application there is no fixed order in the evaluation of the left and right subterms. Abstract machines however implement *deterministic* strategies. We then fix a deterministic strategy (which fires β_f-redexes from right to left and is the one implemented by the machines of the next sections). By Proposition 2, the choice of the strategy does not impact on existence of a result, nor on the result itself or on the number of steps to reach it. It does impact however on the design of the machine, which selects β_f-redexes from right to left.

The *right-to-left evaluation strategy* $\to_{\mathsf{r}\beta_f}$ is defined by closing the root rules $\mapsto_{\beta_\lambda}$ and $\mapsto_{\beta_i}$ in Fig. 1 by *right contexts*, a special kind of evaluation contexts defined by $R ::= \langle \cdot \rangle \mid tR \mid Rf$. The next lemma ensures our definition is correct.

Lemma 3 (Properties of $\to_{\mathsf{r}\beta_f}$). *Let t be a term.*

1. Completeness: t has $\to_{\beta_f}$-redex iff t has a $\to_{\mathsf{r}\beta_f}$-redex.
2. Determinism: t has at most one $\to_{\mathsf{r}\beta_f}$-redex.

Example 4. Let $t := (\lambda z.z(yz))\lambda x.x$. Then, $t \to_{\mathsf{r}\beta_f} (\lambda x.x)(y \lambda x.x) \to_{\mathsf{r}\beta_f} y \lambda x.x$, where the final term $y \lambda x.x$ is a fireball (and β_f-normal).

Open Size Explosion. Fireballs are delicate, they easily *explode*. The simplest instance of *open size explosion* (not existing in Closed CbV) is a variation over the famous looping term $\omega := (\lambda x.xx)(\lambda x.xx) \to_{\beta_\lambda} \omega \to_{\beta_\lambda} \ldots$. In ω there is an infinite sequence of duplications. In the size exploding family there is a sequence of n nested duplications. We define two families, the family $\{t_n\}_{n \in \mathbb{N}}$ of size exploding terms and the family $\{i_n\}_{n \in \mathbb{N}}$ of results of evaluating $\{t_n\}_{n \in \mathbb{N}}$:

$$t_0 := y \qquad t_{n+1} := (\lambda x.xx)t_n \qquad\qquad i_0 := y \qquad i_{n+1} := i_n i_n$$

We use $|t|$ for the size of a term t, *i.e.* the number of symbols to write it.

Proposition 5 (Open Size Explosion, [2]). *Let $n \in \mathbb{N}$. Then $t_n \to_{\beta_i}^n i_n$, moreover $|t_n| = O(n)$, $|i_n| = \Omega(2^n)$, and i_n is an inert term.*

Circumventing Open Size Explosion. Abstract machines implementing the substitution of inert terms, such as the one described by Grégoire and Leroy in [20] are unreasonable because for the term t_n of the size exploding family they compute the full result i_n. The machines of the next sections are reasonable because they avoid the substitution of inert terms, that is justified by the following lemma.

Lemma 6 (Inert Substitutions Can Be Avoided). *Let t, u be terms and i be an inert term. Then, $t \rightarrow_{\beta_f} u$ iff $t\{x \leftarrow i\} \rightarrow_{\beta_f} u\{x \leftarrow i\}$.*

Lemma 6 states that substitution of inerts terms for variables cannot create redexes, which is why it can be avoided. With general terms, instead, only direction $\Rightarrow$ holds, because substitution can create redexes, as in $(xy)\{x \leftarrow \lambda z.z\} = (\lambda z.z)y$. Direction $\Leftarrow$ is distinctive of inert terms, of which it justifies the name.

3   Preliminaries on Abstract Machines, Implementations, and Complexity Analyses

- An abstract machine M is given by *states*, noted s, and *transitions* between them, noted $\rightsquigarrow_M$; as usual, the reflexive-transitive closure of $\rightsquigarrow_M$ is noted $\rightsquigarrow_M^*$;
- A state is given by the *code under evaluation* plus some *data-structures*;
- The code under evaluation, as well as the other pieces of code scattered in the data-structures, are λ-terms *not considered modulo α-equivalence*;
- Codes are overlined, to stress the different treatment of α-equivalence;
- A code $\bar{t}$ is *well-named* if x may occur only in $\bar{u}$ (if at all) for every sub-code $\lambda x.\bar{u}$ of $\bar{t}$;
- A state s is *initial* if its code is well-named and its data-structures are empty;
- Therefore, there is a bijection $\cdot^\circ$ (up to α) between terms and initial states, called *compilation*, sending a term t to the initial state t° on a well-named code α-equivalent to t;
- An *execution* is a finite (possibly empty) sequence of transitions $t_0^\circ \rightsquigarrow_M^* s$ from an initial state t_0° obtained by compiling an (initial) term t_0;
- A state s is *reachable* if it can be obtained as the end state of an execution;
- A state s is *final* if it is reachable and no transitions apply to s;
- A machine comes with a map $\underline{\cdot}$ from states to terms, called *decoding*, that on initial states is the inverse (up to α) of compilation, *i.e.* $\underline{t^\circ} = t$ for any term t;
- Transitions of a machine M are divided into *β-transitions*, denoted by $\rightsquigarrow_\beta$, which are meant to be mapped to β-reduction steps by the decoding, while the remaining *overhead transitions*, denoted by $\rightsquigarrow_\circ$, are mapped to equalities;
- We use $|\rho|$ for the length of an execution ρ, and $|\rho|_\beta$ for the number of β-transitions in ρ.

Implementations. For every machine one has to prove that it correctly implements the strategy in the λ-calculus it was conceived for. Our notion, tuned towards complexity analyses, requires a perfect match between the number of β-steps of the strategy and the number of β-transitions of the machine execution.

Definition 7 (Machine Implementation). *A machine* M *implements a strategy* $\to$ *on* λ-*terms via a decoding* $\underline{\cdot}$ *when given a* λ-*term* t *the following holds:*

1. *Executions to Derivations: for any* M-*execution* $\rho\colon t^{\circ} \leadsto_{\mathsf{M}}^{*} s$ *there exists a* $\to$-*derivation* $d\colon t \to^{*} \underline{s}$.
2. *Derivations to Executions: for every* $\to$-*derivation* $d\colon t \to^{*} u$ *there exists a* M-*execution* $\rho\colon t^{\circ} \leadsto_{\mathsf{M}}^{*} s$ *such that* $\underline{s} = u$.
3. β-*Matching: in both previous points the number* $|\rho|_{\beta}$ *of* β-*transitions in* ρ *is exactly the length* $|d|$ *of the derivation* d, *i.e.* $|d| = |\rho|_{\beta}$.

Sufficient Condition for Implementations. The proofs of implementation theorems tend to follow always the same structure, based on a few abstract properties collected here into the notion of implementation system.

Definition 8 (Implementation System). *A machine* M, *a strategy* $\to$, *and a decoding* $\underline{\cdot}$ *form an* implementation system *if the following conditions hold:*

1. β-*Projection:* $s \leadsto_{\beta} s'$ *implies* $\underline{s} \to \underline{s'}$;
2. *Overhead Transparency:* $s \leadsto_{\mathrm{o}} s'$ *implies* $\underline{s} = \underline{s'}$;
3. *Overhead Transitions Terminate:* $\leadsto_{\mathrm{o}}$ *terminates;*
4. *Determinism: both* M *and* $\to$ *are deterministic;*
5. *Progress:* M *final states decode to* $\to$-*normal terms.*

Theorem 9 (Sufficient Condition for Implementations). *Let* $(\mathsf{M}, \to, \underline{\cdot})$ *be an* implementation system. *Then,* M *implements* $\to$ *via* $\underline{\cdot}$.

The proof of Theorem 9 is a clean and abstract generalization of the concrete reasoning already at work in [2–5] for specific abstract machines and strategies.

Parameters for Complexity Analyses. By the *derivations-to-executions* part of the implementation (Point 2 in Definition 7), given a derivation $d\colon t_0 \to^{n} u$ there is a shortest execution $\rho\colon t_0^{\circ} \leadsto_{\mathsf{M}}^{*} s$ such that $\underline{s} = u$. Determining *the complexity of a machine* M amounts to bound the complexity of a concrete implementation of ρ on a RAM model, as a function of two fundamental parameters:

1. *Input:* the size $|t_0|$ of the initial term t_0 of the derivation d;
2. β-*Steps/Transitions:* the length $n = |d|$ of the derivation d, that coincides with the number $|\rho|_{\beta}$ of β-transitions in ρ by the β-matching requirement for implementations (Point 3 in Definition 7).

A machine is *reasonable* if its complexity is polynomial in $|t_0|$ and $|\rho|_{\beta}$, and it is *efficient* if it is linear in both parameters. So, a strategy is reasonable (resp. efficient) if there is a reasonable (resp. efficient) machine implementing it. In Sects. 4–5 we study a reasonable machine implementing right-to-left evaluation $\to_{\mathrm{x}\beta_f}$ in λ_{fire}, thus showing that it is a reasonable strategy. In Sect. 6 we optimize the machine to make it efficient. By Proposition 2, this implies that *every* strategy in λ_{fire} is efficient.

Recipe for Complexity Analyses. For the complexity analysis on a machine M, overhead transitions $\leadsto_o$ are further separated into two classes:

1. *Substitution Transitions* $\leadsto_s$: they are in charge of the substitution process;
2. *Commutative Transitions* $\leadsto_c$: they are in charge of searching for the next β or substitution redex to reduce.

Then, the estimation of the complexity of a machine is done in three steps:

1. *Number of Transitions*: bounding the length of the execution ρ, by bounding the number of overhead transitions. This part splits into two subparts:
   i. *Substitution vs. β*: bounding the number $|\rho|_s$ of substitution transitions in ρ using the number of β-transitions;
   ii. *Commutative vs.* Substitution: bounding the number $|\rho|_c$ of commutative transitions in ρ using the size of the input and $|\rho|_s$; the latter—by the previous point—induces a bound with respect to β-transitions.
2. *Cost of Single Transitions*: bounding the cost of concretely implementing a single transition of M. Here it is usually necessary to go beyond the abstract level, making some (high-level) assumption on how codes and data-structure are concretely represented. Commutative transitions are designed on purpose to have constant cost. Each substitution transition has a cost linear in the size of the initial term thanks to an invariant (to be proved) ensuring that only subterms of the initial term are duplicated and substituted along an execution. Each β-transition has a cost either constant or linear in the input.
3. *Complexity of the Overhead*: obtaining the total bound by composing the first two points, that is, by taking the number of each kind of transition times the cost of implementing it, and summing over all kinds of transitions.

(Linear) Logical Reading. Let us mention that our partitioning of transitions into β, substitution, and commutative ones admits a proof-theoretical view, as machine transitions can be seen as cut-elimination steps [5,11]. Commutative transitions correspond to commutative cases, while β and substitution are principal cases. Moreover, in linear logic the β transition corresponds to the multiplicative case while the substitution transition to the exponential one. See [5] for more details.

4   Easy GLAMOUr

In this section we introduce the Easy GLAMOUr, a simplified version of the GLAMOUr machine from [2]: unlike the latter, the Easy GLAMOUr does not need any labeling of codes to provide a reasonable implementation.

With respect to the literature on abstract machines for CbV, our machines are unusual in two respects. First, and more importantly, they use a single *global* environment instead of *closures* and *local environments*. Global environments are used in a minority of works [2,3,5,6,16,17,24] and induce simpler, more abstract machines where α-equivalence is pushed to the meta-level (in the operation $\overline{t}^\alpha$

$$\phi ::= \lambda x.\overline{u}@\epsilon \mid x@\pi$$
$$\pi ::= \epsilon \mid \phi : \pi \qquad E ::= \epsilon \mid [x{\leftarrow}\phi]:E$$
$$D ::= \epsilon \mid D:\overline{t}\Diamond\pi \qquad s := (D,\overline{t},\pi,E)$$

$$\underline{\epsilon} := \langle\cdot\rangle \qquad t{\downarrow}_\epsilon := t \quad t{\downarrow}_{[x{\leftarrow}\phi]E} := t\{x{\leftarrow}\phi\}{\downarrow}_E$$
$$\underline{\phi:\pi} := \langle\langle\cdot\rangle\underline{\phi}\rangle\underline{\pi} \qquad C_s := \underline{D}\langle\underline{\pi}\rangle{\downarrow}_E$$
$$\underline{\overline{t}@\pi} := \langle t\rangle\underline{\pi} \qquad \underline{s} := \underline{D}\langle\langle\overline{t}\rangle\underline{\pi}\rangle{\downarrow}_E = C_s\langle\overline{t}{\downarrow}_E\rangle$$
$$\underline{D:\overline{t}\Diamond\pi} := \underline{D}\langle\langle\overline{t}\langle\cdot\rangle\rangle\underline{\pi}\rangle \qquad \text{where } s = (D,\overline{t},\pi,E)$$

Dump	Code	Stack	Global Env		Dump	Code	Stack	Global Env
D	$\overline{t}\overline{u}$	π	E	$\leadsto_{c_1}$	$D:\overline{t}\Diamond\pi$	$\overline{u}$	ϵ	E
$D:\overline{t}\Diamond\pi$	$\lambda x.\overline{u}$	ϵ	E	$\leadsto_{c_2}$	D	$\overline{t}$	$\lambda x.\overline{u}@\epsilon : \pi$	E
$D:\overline{t}\Diamond\pi$	x	π'	E	$\leadsto_{c_3}$	D	$\overline{t}$	$x@\pi' : \pi$	E
							if $E(x)=\bot$ or $E(x)=y@\pi''$	
D	$\lambda x.\overline{t}$	$\phi:\pi$	E	$\leadsto_\beta$	D	$\overline{t}$	π	$[x{\leftarrow}\phi]E$
D	x	π	$E_1[x{\leftarrow}\lambda y.\overline{u}@\epsilon]E_2$	$\leadsto_s$	D	$(\lambda y.\overline{u})^\alpha$	π	$E_1[x{\leftarrow}\lambda y.\overline{u}@\epsilon]E_2$

where $(\lambda y.\overline{u})^\alpha$ is any well-named code α-equivalent to $\lambda y.\overline{u}$ such that its
bound names are fresh with respect to those in D, π and $E_1[x{\leftarrow}\lambda y.\overline{u}@\epsilon]E_2$.

Fig. 2. Easy GLAMOUr machine: data-structures (stacks π, dumps D, global env. E, states s), unfolding $t{\downarrow}_E$, decoding $\underline{\cdot}$ (stacks are decoded to contexts in postfix notation for plugging, *i.e.* we write $\langle\overline{t}\rangle\underline{\pi}$ rather than $\underline{\pi}\langle\overline{t}\rangle$), and transitions.

in $\leadsto_s$ in Figs. 2 and 3). This on-the-fly α-renaming is harmless with respect to complexity analyses, see also discussions in [4,5]. Second, argument stacks contain pairs of a code and a stack, to implement some of the machine transitions in constant time.

Background. GLAMOUr stands for *Useful* (*i.e.* optimized to be *reasonable*) *Open* (reducing open terms) *Global* (using a single global environment) LAM, and LAM stands for *Leroy Abstract Machine*, an ordinary machine implementing right-to-left Closed CbV, defined in [5]. In [2] the study of the GLAMOUr was done according to the distillation approach of [5], *i.e.* by decoding the machine towards a λ-calculus with explicit substitutions. Here we do not follow the distillation approach, we decode directly to λ_{fire}, which is simpler.

Machine Components. The Easy GLAMOUr is defined in Fig. 2. A machine state s is a quadruple $(D,\overline{t},\pi,E)$ given by:

- *Code $\overline{t}$*: a term not considered up to α-equivalence, which is why it is overlined.
- *Argument Stack π*: it contains the arguments of the current code. Note that stacks items ϕ are pairs $x@\pi$ and $\lambda x.\overline{u}@\epsilon$. These pairs allow to implement some of the transitions in constant time. The pair $x@\pi$ codes the term $\langle x\rangle\underline{\pi}$ (defined in Fig. 2—the decoding is explained below) that would be obtained by putting x in the context obtained by decoding the argument stack π. The pair $\lambda x.\overline{u}@\epsilon$ is used to inject abstractions into pairs, so that items ϕ can be uniformly seen as pairs $\overline{t}@\pi$ of a code $\overline{t}$ and a stack π.
- *Dump D*: a second stack, that together with the argument stack π is used to walk through the code and search for the next redex to reduce. The dump is extended with an entry $\overline{t}\Diamond\pi$ every time evaluation enters in the right subterm $\overline{u}$ of an application $\overline{t}\overline{u}$. The entry saves the left part $\overline{t}$ of the application and

the current stack π, to restore them when the evaluation of the right subterm $\overline{u}$ is over. The dump D and the stack π decode to an evaluation context.
- *Global Environment E*: a list of explicit (*i.e.* delayed) substitutions storing the β-redexes encountered so far. It is used to implement micro-step evaluation (*i.e.* the substitution for one variable occurrence at a time). We write $E(x) = \bot$ if in E there is no entry of the form $[x \leftarrow \phi]$. Often $[x \leftarrow \phi]E$ stands for $[x \leftarrow \phi] : E$.

Transitions. In the Easy GLAMOUr there is one β-transition whereas overhead transitions are divided up into substitution and commutative transitions.

- *β-Transition $\leadsto_\beta$*: it morally fires a $\to_{r\beta_f}$-redex, the one corresponding to $(\lambda x.\overline{t})\phi$, except that it puts a new delayed substitution $[x \leftarrow \phi]$ in the environment instead of doing the meta-level substitution $\overline{t}\{x \leftarrow \phi\}$ of the argument ϕ for the (free) occurrences of the variable x in the body $\overline{t}$ of the abstraction;
- *Substitution Transition $\leadsto_s$*: it substitutes the variable occurrence under evaluation with a (properly α-renamed copy of a) code from the environment. It is a micro-step variant of meta-level substitution. It is invisible on λ_{fire} because the decoding produces the term obtained by meta-level substitution, and so the micro work done by $\leadsto_s$ cannot be observed at the coarser granularity of λ_{fire}.
- *Commutative Transitions $\leadsto_c$*: they locate and expose the next redex according to the right-to-left strategy, by rearranging the data-structures. They are invisible on the calculus. The commutative rule $\leadsto_{c_1}$ forces evaluation to be right-to-left on applications: the machine processes first the right subterm $\overline{u}$, saving the left sub-term $\overline{t}$ on the dump together with its current stack π. The role of $\leadsto_{c_2}$ and $\leadsto_{c_3}$ is to backtrack to the entry on top of the dump. When the right subterm, *i.e.* the pair $\overline{t}@\pi$ of current code and stack, is finally in normal form, it is pushed on the stack and the machine backtracks.

O for Open: note condition $E(x) = \bot$ in $\leadsto_{c_3}$—that is how the Easy GLA-MOUr handles open terms. *U for Useful*: note condition $E(x) = y@\pi''$ in $\leadsto_{c_3}$—inert terms are never substituted, according to Lemma 6. Removing the useful side-condition one recovers Grégoire and Leroy's machine [20]. Note that terms substituted by $\leadsto_s$ are always abstractions and never variables—this fact will play a role in Sect. 6. *Garbage Collection*: it is here simply ignored, or, more precisely, it is encapsulated at the meta-level, in the decoding function. It is well-known that this is harmless for the study of time complexity.

Compiling, Decoding and Invariants. A term t is compiled to the machine *initial state* $t^\circ = (\epsilon, \overline{t}, \epsilon, \epsilon)$, where $\overline{t}$ is a well-named term α-equivalent to t. Conversely, every machine state s decodes to a term $\underline{s}$ (see the top right part of Fig. 2), having the shape $C_s\langle \overline{t}{\downarrow}_E \rangle$, where $\overline{t}{\downarrow}_E$ is a λ-term, obtained by applying to the code the meta-level substitution ${\downarrow}_E$ induced by the global environment E, and C_s is an evaluation context, obtained by decoding the stack π and the dump D and then applying ${\downarrow}_E$. Note that, to improve readability, stacks are decoded to contexts in postfix notation for plugging, *i.e.* we write $\langle \bar{t} \rangle \underline{\pi}$ rather than $\underline{\pi} \langle \bar{t} \rangle$ because π is a context that puts arguments in front of $\bar{t}$.

Example 10. To have a glimpse of how the Easy GLAMOUr works, let us show how it implements the derivation $t := (\lambda z.z(yz))\lambda x.x \to^2_{\mathtt{r}\beta_f} y \lambda x.x$ of Example 4:

Dump	Code	Stack	Global Environment	
ϵ	$(\lambda z.z(yz))\lambda x.x$	ϵ	ϵ	$\rightsquigarrow_{c_1}$
$\lambda z.z(yz)\Diamond\epsilon$	$\lambda x.x$	ϵ	ϵ	$\rightsquigarrow_{c_2}$
ϵ	$\lambda z.z(yz)$	$\lambda x.x@\epsilon$	ϵ	$\rightsquigarrow_{\beta}$
ϵ	$z(yz)$	ϵ	$[z\leftarrow\lambda x.x@\epsilon]$	$\rightsquigarrow_{c_1}$
$z\Diamond\epsilon$	yz	ϵ	$[z\leftarrow\lambda x.x@\epsilon]$	$\rightsquigarrow_{c_1}$
$z\Diamond\epsilon : y\Diamond\epsilon$	z	ϵ	$[z\leftarrow\lambda x.x@\epsilon]$	$\rightsquigarrow_{s}$
$z\Diamond\epsilon : y\Diamond\epsilon$	$\lambda x'.x'$	ϵ	$[z\leftarrow\lambda x.x@\epsilon]$	$\rightsquigarrow_{c_2}$
$z\Diamond\epsilon$	y	$\lambda x'.x'@\epsilon$	$[z\leftarrow\lambda x.x@\epsilon]$	$\rightsquigarrow_{c_3}$
ϵ	z	$y@(\lambda x'.x'@\epsilon)$	$[z\leftarrow\lambda x.x@\epsilon]$	$\rightsquigarrow_{s}$
ϵ	$\lambda x''.x''$	$y@(\lambda x'.x'@\epsilon)$	$[z\leftarrow\lambda x.x@\epsilon]$	$\rightsquigarrow_{\beta}$
ϵ	x''	ϵ	$[x''\leftarrow y@(\lambda x'.x'@\epsilon)] : [z\leftarrow\lambda x.x@\epsilon]$	

Note that the initial state is the compilation of the term t, the final state decodes to the term $y \lambda x.x$, and the two β-transitions in the execution correspond to the two $\to_{\mathtt{r}\beta_f}$-steps in the derivation considered in Example 4.

The study of the Easy GLAMOUr machine relies on the following invariants.

Lemma 11 (Easy GLAMOUr Qualitative Invariants). *Let $s = (D, \bar{t}, \pi, E)$ be a reachable state of an Easy GLAMOUr execution. Then:*

1. *Name:*
    i. *Explicit Substitution: if $E = E'[x \leftarrow \bar{u}]E''$ then x is fresh wrt $\bar{u}$ and E'';*
    ii. *Abstraction: if $\lambda x.\bar{u}$ is a subterm of $D, \bar{t}, \pi$ or E, x may occur only in $\bar{u}$;*
2. *Fireball Item: $\underline{\phi}$ and $\underline{\phi}{\downarrow}_E$ are inert terms if $\phi = x@\pi'$, and abstractions otherwise, for every item ϕ in π, in E, and in every stack in D;*
3. *Contextual Decoding: $C_s = \underline{D}\langle\underline{\pi}\rangle{\downarrow}_E$ is a right context.*

Implementation Theorem. The invariants are used to prove the implementation theorem by proving that the hypotheses of Theorem 9 hold, that is, that the Easy GLAMOUr, $\to_{\mathtt{r}\beta_f}$ and $\underline{\cdot}$ form an implementation system.

Theorem 12 (Easy GLAMOUr Implementation). *The Easy GLAMOUr implements right-to-left evaluation $\to_{\mathtt{r}\beta_f}$ in λ_{fire} (via the decoding $\underline{\cdot}$).*

5 Complexity Analysis of the Easy GLAMOUr

The analysis of the Easy GLAMOUr is done according to the recipe given at the end of Sect. 3. The result (see Theorem 17 below) is that the Easy GLAMOUr is linear in the number $|\rho|_\beta$ of β-steps/transitions and quadratic in the size $|t_0|$ of the initial term t_0, *i.e.* its overhead has complexity $O((1 + |\rho|_\beta) \cdot |t_0|^2)$.

The analysis relies on a quantitative invariant, the crucial *subterm invariant*, ensuring that $\rightsquigarrow_s$ duplicates only subterms of the initial term, so that the cost of duplications is connected to one of the two parameters for complexity analyses.

Lemma 13 (Subterm Invariant). *Let* $\rho\colon t_0^\circ \rightsquigarrow^* (D, \bar{t}, \pi, E)$ *be an Easy GLA-MOUr execution. Every subterm* $\lambda x.\bar{u}$ *of* D, $\bar{t}$, π, *or* E *is a subterm of* t_0.

Intuition About Complexity Bounds. The number $|\rho|_{\mathsf{s}}$ of substitution transitions $\rightsquigarrow_{\mathsf{s}}$ depends on both parameters for complexity analyses, the number $|\rho|_\beta$ of β-transitions *and* the size $|t_0|$ of the initial term. Dependence on $|\rho|_\beta$ is standard, and appears in every machine [2,3,5,6,12,24]—sometimes it is quadratic, here it is linear, in Sect. 6 we come back to this point. Dependence on $|t_0|$ is also always present, but usually only for *the cost* of a single $\rightsquigarrow_{\mathsf{s}}$ transition, since only subterms of t_0 are duplicated, as ensured by the subterm invariant. For the Easy GLAMOUr, instead, also *the number* of $\rightsquigarrow_{\mathsf{s}}$ transitions depends on $|t_0|$: this is a side-effect of dealing with open terms. Since both the cost and the number of $\rightsquigarrow_{\mathsf{s}}$ transitions depend linearly on $|t_0|$, the overall contribution of $\rightsquigarrow_{\mathsf{s}}$ transitions to the overhead in a implementation of ρ on RAM depends quadratically on $|t_0|$.

The following family of terms shows the dependence on $|t_0|$ in isolation (*i.e.*, with no dependence on $|\rho|_\beta$). Let $r_n := \lambda x.(\ldots((y\,x)x)\ldots)x$ and consider:
$$u_n := r_n r_n = (\lambda x.(\ldots((y\,x)x)\ldots)x)r_n \to_{\beta_\lambda} (\ldots((y\,r_n)r_n)\ldots)r_n \,. \qquad (1)$$

Forgetting about commutative transitions, the Easy GLAMOUr would evaluate u_n with one β-transition $\rightsquigarrow_\beta$ and n substitution transitions $\rightsquigarrow_{\mathsf{s}}$, each one duplicating r_n, whose size (as well as the size of the initial term u_n) is linear in n.

The number $|\rho|_{\mathsf{c}}$ of commutative transitions $\rightsquigarrow_{\mathsf{c}}$, roughly, is linear in the amount of code involved in the evaluation process. This amount is given by the initial code plus the code produced by duplications, which is bounded by the number of substitution transitions times the size of the initial term. The number of commutative transitions is then $O((1 + |\rho|_\beta) \cdot |t_0|^2)$. Since each one has constant cost, this is also a bound to their overall cost in a implementation of ρ on RAM.

Number of Transitions 1: Substitution vs. β Transitions. The number $|\rho|_{\mathsf{s}}$ of substitution transitions is proven (see Corollary 15 below) to be bilinear, *i.e.* linear in $|t_0|$ and $|\rho|_\beta$, by means of a measure $|\cdot|_{\mathsf{free}}$ such that $|t|_{\mathsf{free}} \leq |t|$ for any term t.

The *free size* $|\cdot|_{\mathsf{free}}$ of a code counts the number of free variable occurrences that are not under abstractions. It is defined and extended to states as follows:

$$
\begin{aligned}
|x|_{\mathsf{free}} &:= 1 & |\epsilon|_{\mathsf{free}} &:= 0 \\
|\lambda y.\bar{u}|_{\mathsf{free}} &:= 0 & |\phi : \pi|_{\mathsf{free}} &:= |\phi|_{\mathsf{free}} + |\pi|_{\mathsf{free}} \\
|\bar{t}u|_{\mathsf{free}} &:= |t|_{\mathsf{free}} + |u|_{\mathsf{free}} & |D : (\bar{t}, \pi)|_{\mathsf{free}} &:= |t|_{\mathsf{free}} + |\pi|_{\mathsf{free}} + |D|_{\mathsf{free}}
\end{aligned}
$$

$$|(D, \bar{t}, \pi, E)|_{\mathsf{free}} := |D|_{\mathsf{free}} + |\bar{t}|_{\mathsf{free}} + |\pi|_{\mathsf{free}}.$$

Lemma 14 (Free Occurrences Invariant). *Let $\rho \colon t_0^\circ \leadsto^* s$ be an Easy GLA-MOUr execution. Then, $|s|_{\mathsf{free}} \leq |t_0|_{\mathsf{free}} + |t_0| \cdot |\rho|_\beta - |\rho|_\mathsf{s}$.*

Corollary 15 (Bilinear Number of Substitution Transitions). *Let $\rho \colon t_0^\circ \leadsto^* s$ be an Easy GLAMOUr execution. Then, $|\rho|_\mathsf{s} \leq (1 + |\rho|_\beta) \cdot |t_0|$.*

Number of Transitions 2: Commutative vs. Substitution Transitions. The bound on the number $|\rho|_\mathsf{c}$ of commutative transitions is found by means of a (different) measure $|s|_\mathsf{c}$ on states. The bound is linear in $|t_0|$ and in $|\rho|_\mathsf{s}$, which means—by applying the result just obtained in Corollary 15—*quadratic* in $|t_0|$ and linear in $|\rho|_\beta$.

The *commutative size* of a state is defined as $|(D, \overline{t}, \pi, E)|_\mathsf{c} := |\overline{t}| + \Sigma_{\overline{u} \lozenge \pi' \in D} |\overline{u}|$, where $|\overline{t}|$ is the usual size of codes (and terms).

Lemma 16 (Number of Commutative Transitions). *Let $\rho \colon t_0^\circ \leadsto^* s$ be an Easy GLAMOUr execution. Then, $|\rho|_\mathsf{c} \leq |\rho|_\mathsf{c} + |s|_\mathsf{c} \leq (1 + |\rho|_\mathsf{s}) \cdot |t_0| \in O((1 + |\rho|_\beta) \cdot |t_0|^2)$.*

Cost of Single Transitions. We need to make some hypotheses on how the Easy GLAMOUr is going to be itself implemented on RAM:

1. *Variable (Occurrences) and Environment Entries*: a variable is a memory location, a variable occurrence is a reference to it, and an environment entry $[x \leftarrow \phi]$ is the fact that the location associated to x contains ϕ.
2. *Random Access to Global Environments*: the environment E can be accessed in $O(1)$ (in $\leadsto_\mathsf{s}$) by just following the reference given by the variable occurrence under evaluation, with no need to access E sequentially, thus ignoring its list structure (used only to ease the definition of the decoding).

With these hypotheses it is clear that β and commutative transitions can be implemented in $O(1)$. The substitution transition $\leadsto_\mathsf{s}$ needs to copy a code from the environment (the renaming $\overline{t}^\alpha$) and can be implemented in $O(|t_0|)$, since the subterm to copy is a subterm of t_0 by the subterm invariant (Lemma 13) and the environment can be accessed in $O(1)$.

Summing Up. By putting together the bounds on the number of transitions with the cost of single transitions we obtain the overhead of the machine.

Theorem 17 (Easy GLAMOUr Overhead Bound). *Let $\rho \colon t_0^\circ \leadsto^* s$ be an Easy GLAMOUr execution. Then ρ is implementable on RAM in $O((1 + |\rho|_\beta) \cdot |t_0|^2)$, i.e. linear in the number of β-transitions (aka the length of the derivation $d \colon t_0 \to^*_{\mathtt{r}\beta_f} \underline{s}$ implemented by ρ) and quadratic in the size of the initial term t_0.*

6   Fast GLAMOUr

In this section we optimize the Easy GLAMOUr, obtaining a machine, the Fast GLAMOUr, whose dependence on the size of the initial term is linear, instead of quadratic, providing a bilinear—thus optimal—overhead (see Theorem 21 below and compare it with Theorem 17 on the Easy GLAMOUr). We invite the reader to go back to Eq. (1), where the quadratic dependence was explained. Note that in that example the substitutions of r_n do not create β_f-redexes, and so they are useless. The Fast GLAMOUr avoids these useless substitutions and it implements the example with no substitutions at all.

Optimization: Abstractions On-Demand. The difference between the Easy GLA-MOUr and the machines in [2] is that, whenever the former encounters a variable occurrence x bound to an abstraction $\lambda y.\bar{t}$ in the environment, it replaces x with $\lambda y.\bar{t}$, while the latter are more parsimonious. They implement an optimization that we call *substituting abstractions on-demand*: x is replaced by $\lambda y.\bar{t}$ only if this is useful to obtain a β-redex, that is, only if the argument stack is non-empty. The Fast GLAMOUr, defined in Fig. 3, upgrades the Easy GLAMOUr with *substitutions of abstractions on-demand*—note the new side-condition for $\leadsto_{c_3}$ and the non-empty stack in $\leadsto_s$.

Dump	Code	Stack	Global Env		Dump	Code	Stack	Global Env
D	$\bar{t}\bar{u}$	π	E	$\leadsto_{c_1}$	$D:\bar{t}\Diamond\pi$	$\bar{u}$	ϵ	E
$D:\bar{t}\Diamond\pi$	$\lambda x.\bar{u}$	ϵ	E	$\leadsto_{c_2}$	D	$\bar{t}$	$\lambda x.\bar{u}@\epsilon : \pi$	E
$D:\bar{t}\Diamond\pi$	x	π'	E	$\leadsto_{c_3}$	D	$\bar{t}$	$x@\pi':\pi$	E
			if $E(x) = \bot$ or $E(x) = y@\pi''$ or $(E(x) = \lambda y.\bar{u}@\epsilon$ and $\pi' = \epsilon)$					
D	$\lambda x.\bar{t}$	$y@\epsilon:\pi$	E	$\leadsto_{\beta_1}$	D	$\bar{t}\{x\leftarrow y\}$	π	E
D	$\lambda x.\bar{t}$	$\phi:\pi$	E	$\leadsto_{\beta_2}$	D	$\bar{t}$	π	$[x\leftarrow\phi]E$
								if $\phi \neq y@\epsilon$
D	x	$\phi:\pi$	$E_1[x\leftarrow\lambda y.\bar{u}@\epsilon]E_2$	$\leadsto_s$	D	$(\lambda y.\bar{u})^\alpha$	$\phi:\pi$	$E_1[x\leftarrow\lambda y.\bar{u}@\epsilon]E_2$

Fig. 3. Fast GLAMOUr (data-structures, decoding, and $(\lambda y.\bar{u})^\alpha$ defined as in Fig. 2).

Abstractions On-Demand and the Substitution of Variables. The new optimization however has a consequence. To explain it, let us recall the role of another optimization, *no substitution of variables*. In the Easy GLAMOUr, abstractions are at depth 1 in the environment: there cannot be chains of renamings, *i.e.* of substitutions of variables for variable, ending in abstractions (so, there cannot be chains like $[x\leftarrow y@\epsilon][y\leftarrow z@\epsilon][z\leftarrow\lambda z'.\bar{t}@\epsilon])$. This property implies that the overhead is linear in $|\rho|_\beta$ and it is induced by the fact that variables cannot be substituted. If variables can be substituted then the overhead becomes quadratic in $|\rho|_\beta$—this is what happens in the GLAMOUr machine in [2]. The relationship between *substituting variables* and a linear/quadratic overhead is studied in-depth in [10].

Now, because the Fast GLAMOUr substitutes abstractions on-demand, variable occurrences that are not applied are not substituted by abstractions. The question becomes what to do when the code is an abstraction $\lambda x.\bar{t}$ and the top of the stack argument ϕ is a simple variable occurrence $\phi = y@\epsilon$ (potentially bound to an abstraction in the environment E) because if one admits that $[x\leftarrow y@\epsilon]$ is added to E then the depth of abstractions in the environment may be arbitrary and so the dependence on $|\rho|_\beta$ may be quadratic, as in the GLAMOUr. There are two possible solutions to this issue. The complex one, given by the Unchaining GLAMOUr in [2], is to add labels and a further unchaining optimization. The simple one is to split the β-transition in two, handling this situation with a new rule that renames x as y in the code $\bar{t}$ without touching the environment—this exactly what the Fast GLAMOUr does with $\leadsto_{\beta_1}$ and $\leadsto_{\beta_2}$. The consequence is that abstractions stay at depth 1 in E, and so the overhead is indeed bilinear.

The simple solution is taken from Sands, Gustavsson, and Moran's [24], where they use it on a call-by-name machine. Actually, it repeatedly appears in the literature on abstract machines often with reference to space consumption and *space leaks*, for instance in Wand's [26], Friedman et al.'s [18], and Sestoft's [25].

Fast GLAMOUr. The machine is in Fig. 3 (note the two kinds of β-transitions). Its data-structures, compiling and decoding are exactly as for the Easy GLAMOUr.

Example 18. Let us now show how the derivation $t := (\lambda z.z(yz))\lambda x.x \rightarrow_{r\beta_f}^2 y\,\lambda x.x$ of Example 4 is implemented by the Fast GLAMOUr. The execution is similar to that of the Easy GLAMOUr in Example 10, since they implement the same derivation and hence have the same initial state. In particular, the first five transitions in the Fast GLAMOUr (omitted here) are the same as in the Easy GLAMOUr (see Example 10 and replace $\leadsto_\beta$ with $\leadsto_{\beta_2}$). Then, the Fast GLAMOUr executes:

Dump	Code	Stack	Global Environment	
$z\Diamond\epsilon : y\Diamond\epsilon$	z	ϵ	$[z\leftarrow\lambda x.x@\epsilon]$	$\leadsto_{c_3}$
$z\Diamond\epsilon$	y	$z@\epsilon$	$[z\leftarrow\lambda x.x@\epsilon]$	$\leadsto_{c_3}$
ϵ	z	$y@(z@\epsilon)$	$[z\leftarrow\lambda x.x@\epsilon]$	$\leadsto_{s}$
ϵ	$\lambda x''.x''$	$y@(z@\epsilon)$	$[z\leftarrow\lambda x.x@\epsilon]$	$\leadsto_{\beta_2}$
ϵ	x''	ϵ	$[x''\leftarrow y@(z@\epsilon)] : [z\leftarrow\lambda x.x@\epsilon]$	

The Fast GLAMOUr executes only one substitution transition (the Easy GLAMOUr takes two) since the replacement of z with $\lambda x.x$ from the environment is *on-demand* (*i.e.* useful to obtain a β-redex) only for the first occurrence of z in $z(yz)$.

The Fast GLAMOUr satisfies the same invariants (the qualitative ones—the *fireball item* is slightly different—as well as the subterm one, see [9]) and also forms an implementation system with respect to $\rightarrow_{r\beta_f}$ and $\,\underline{\cdot}\,$. Therefore,

Theorem 19 (Fast GLAMOUr Implementation). *The Fast GLAMOUr implements right-to-left evaluation $\rightarrow_{r\beta_f}$ in λ_{fire} (via the decoding $\underline{\cdot}$).*

Complexity Analysis. What changes is the complexity analysis, that, surprisingly, is simpler. First, we focus on *the number* of overhead transitions. The *substitution vs β transitions* part is simply trivial. Note that a substitution transition $\leadsto_s$ is always immediately followed by a β-transition, because substitutions are done only *on-demand*—therefore, $|\rho|_s \leq |\rho|_\beta + 1$. It is easy to remove the $+1$: executions must have a $\leadsto_{\beta_2}$ transition before any substitution one, otherwise the environment is empty and no substitutions are possible—thus $|\rho|_{\mathsf{s}} \leq |\rho|_{\beta}$.

For the *commutative vs substitution transitions* the exact same measure and the same reasoning of the Easy GLAMOUr provide the same bound, namely $|\rho|_{\mathsf{c}} \leq (1+|\rho|_{\mathsf{s}}) \cdot |t_0|$. What improves is the dependence of commutative transitions on β ones (obtained by substituting the bound for substitution transitions), that is now linear because so is that of substitutions—so, $|\rho|_{\mathsf{c}} \leq (1 + |\rho|_{\beta}) \cdot |t_0|$.

Lemma 20 (Number of Overhead Transitions). *Let* $\rho\colon t_0^{\circ} \leadsto^* s$ *be a Fast GLAMOUr execution. Then,*

1. *Substitution vs β Transitions:* $|\rho|_{\mathsf{s}} \leq |\rho|_{\beta}$.
2. *Commutative vs Substitution Transitions:* $|\rho|_{\mathsf{c}} \leq (1+|\rho|_{\mathsf{s}}) \cdot |t_0| \leq (1+|\rho|_{\beta}) \cdot |t_0|$.

Cost of Single Transitions and Global Overhead. For the cost of single transitions, note that $\leadsto_{\mathsf{c}_1}, \leadsto_{\mathsf{c}_2}, \leadsto_{\mathsf{c}_3}$ and $\leadsto_{\beta_2}$ have (evidently) cost $O(1)$ while $\leadsto_{\mathsf{s}}$ and $\leadsto_{\beta_1}$ have cost $O(|t_0|)$ by the subterm invariant. Then we can conclude with

Theorem 21 (Fast GLAMOUr Bilinear Overhead). *Let* $\rho\colon t_0^{\circ} \leadsto^* s$ *be a Fast GLAMOUr execution. Then ρ is implementable on RAM in $O((1 + |\rho|_{\beta}) \cdot |t_0|)$, i.e. linear in the number of β-transitions (aka the length of the derivation $d\colon t_0 \to^*_{\mathsf{r}\beta_f} s$ implemented by ρ) and the size of the initial term.*

7   Conclusions

Modular Overhead. The overhead of implementing Open CbV is measured with respect to the size $|t_0|$ of the initial term and the number n of β-steps. We showed that its complexity depends crucially on three choices about substitution.

The first is whether to substitute inert terms that are not variables. If they are substituted, as in Grégoire and Leroy's machine [20], then the overhead is exponential in $|t_0|$ because of open size explosion (Proposition 5) and the implementation is then unreasonable. If they are not substituted, as in the machines studied here and in [2], then the overhead is polynomial.

The other two parameters are whether to substitute variables, and whether abstractions are substituted whenever or only *on-demand*, and they give rise to the following table of machines and reasonable overheads:

	Sub of Abs Whenever	Sub of Abs On-Demand
Sub of Variables	Slow GLAMOUr $O((1+n^2) \cdot |t_0|^2)$	GLAMOUr $O((1+n^2) \cdot |t_0|)$
No Sub of Variables	Easy GLAMOUr $O((1+n) \cdot |t_0|^2)$	Fast / Unchaining GLAMOUr $O((1+n) \cdot |t_0|)$

The Slow GLAMOUr has been omitted for lack of space, because it is slow and involved, as it requires the labeling mechanism of the (Unchaining) GLAMOUr developed in [2]. It is somewhat surprising that the Fast GLAMOUr presented here has the best overhead and it is also the easiest to analyze.

Abstractions On-Demand: Open CbV is simpler than Strong CbV. We explained that Grégoire and Leroy's machine for Coq as described in [20] is unreasonable. Its actual implementation, on the contrary, does not substitute non-variable inert terms, so it is reasonable for Open CbV. None of the versions, however, substitutes abstractions on-demand (nor, to our knowledge, does any other implementation), despite the fact that it is a necessary optimization in order to have a reasonable implementation of Strong CbV, as we now show. Consider the following size exploding family (obtained by applying s_n to the identity $I := \lambda x.x$), from [4]:

$$s_1 := \lambda x.\lambda y.(yxx) \quad s_{n+1} := \lambda x.(s_n(\lambda y.(yxx))) \qquad r_0 := I \quad r_{n+1} := \lambda y.(yr_nr_n)$$

Proposition 22 (Abstraction Size Explosion). *Let $n > 0$. Then $s_nI \to_{\beta_\lambda}^n$ r_n. Moreover, $|s_nI| = O(n)$, $|r_n| = \Omega(2^n)$, s_nI is closed, and r_n is normal.*

The evaluation of s_nI produces 2^n non-applied copies of I (in r_n), so a strong evaluator not substituting abstractions on-demand must have an exponential overhead. Note that evaluation is weak but the 2^n copies of I are substituted under abstraction: this is why machines for Closed and Open CbV can be reasonable without substituting abstractions on-demand.

The Danger of Iterating Open CbV Naively. The size exploding example in Proposition 22 also shows that iterating reasonable machines for Open CbV is subtle, as it may induce unreasonable machines for Strong CbV, if done naively. Evaluating Strong CbV by iterating the Easy GLAMOUr (that does not substitute abstractions on-demand), indeed, induces an exponential overhead, while iterating the Fast GLAMOUr provides an efficient implementation.

Acknowledgements. This work has been partially funded by the ANR JCJC grant COCA HOLA (ANR-16-CE40-004-01).

References

1. Abramsky, S., Ong, C.L.: Full abstraction in the lazy lambda calculus. Inf. Comput. **105**(2), 159–267 (1993)
2. Accattoli, B., Sacerdoti Coen, C.: On the relative usefulness of fireballs. In: LICS 2015, pp. 141–155 (2015)
3. Accattoli, B.: The useful MAM, a reasonable implementation of the strong λ-Calculus. In: Väänänen, J., Hirvonen, Å., de Queiroz, R. (eds.) WoLLIC 2016. LNCS, vol. 9803, pp. 1–21. Springer, Heidelberg (2016). doi:10.1007/978-3-662-52921-8_1
4. Accattoli, B.: The complexity of abstract machines. In: WPTE 2016 (invited paper), pp. 1–15 (2017)
5. Accattoli, B., Barenbaum, P., Mazza, D.: Distilling abstract machines. In: ICFP 2014, pp. 363–376 (2014)

6. Accattoli, B., Barenbaum, P., Mazza, D.: A strong distillery. In: Feng, X., Park, S. (eds.) APLAS 2015. LNCS, vol. 9458, pp. 231–250. Springer, Cham (2015). doi:10. 1007/978-3-319-26529-2_13
7. Accattoli, B., Dal Lago, U.: Beta reduction is invariant, indeed. In: CSL-LICS 2014. pp. 8:1–8:10 (2014)
8. Accattoli, B., Guerrieri, G.: Open call-by-value. In: Igarashi, A. (ed.) APLAS 2016, LNCS, vol. 10017, pp. 206–226. Springer, Cham (2016). doi:10.1007/ 978-3-319-47958-3_12
9. Accattoli, B., Guerrieri, G.: Implementing Open Call-by-Value (Extended Version). CoRR abs/1701.08186 (2017). https://arxiv.org/abs/1701.08186
10. Accattoli, B., Sacerdoti Coen, C.: On the value of variables. In: Kohlenbach, U., Barceló, P., Queiroz, R. (eds.) WoLLIC 2014. LNCS, vol. 8652, pp. 36–50. Springer, Heidelberg (2014). doi:10.1007/978-3-662-44145-9_3
11. Ariola, Z.M., Bohannon, A., Sabry, A.: Sequent calculi and abstract machines. ACM Trans. Program. Lang. Syst. **31**(4), 13:1–13:48 (2009)
12. Blelloch, G.E., Greiner, J.: A provable time and space efficient implementation of NESL. In: ICFP 1996, pp. 213–225 (1996)
13. Crégut, P.: An abstract machine for lambda-terms normalization. In: LISP and Functional Programming, pp. 333–340 (1990)
14. Dal Lago, U., Martini, S.: Derivational complexity is an invariant cost model. In: Eekelen, M., Shkaravska, O. (eds.) FOPARA 2009. LNCS, vol. 6324, pp. 100–113. Springer, Heidelberg (2010). doi:10.1007/978-3-642-15331-0_7
15. Dal Lago, U., Martini, S.: On constructor rewrite systems and the lambda-calculus. In: Albers, S., Marchetti-Spaccamela, A., Matias, Y., Nikoletseas, S., Thomas, W. (eds.) ICALP 2009. LNCS, vol. 5556, pp. 163–174. Springer, Heidelberg (2009). doi:10.1007/978-3-642-02930-1_14
16. Danvy, O., Zerny, I.: A synthetic operational account of call-by-need evaluation. In: PPDP, pp. 97–108 (2013)
17. Fernández, M., Siafakas, N.: New developments in environment machines. Electr. Notes Theor. Comput. Sci. **237**, 57–73 (2009)
18. Friedman, D.P., Ghuloum, A., Siek, J.G., Winebarger, O.L.: Improving the lazy Krivine machine. Higher-Order Symbolic Comput. **20**(3), 271–293 (2007)
19. García-Pérez, Á., Nogueira, P., Moreno-Navarro, J.J.: Deriving the full-reducing Krivine machine from the small-step operational semantics of normal order. In: PPDP, pp. 85–96 (2013)
20. Grégoire, B., Leroy, X.: A compiled implementation of strong reduction. In: ICFP 2002, pp. 235–246 (2002)
21. Paolini, L., Ronchi Della Rocca, S.: Call-by-value Solvability. ITA **33**(6), 507–534 (1999)
22. Plotkin, G.D.: Call-by-name, call-by-value and the lambda-calculus. Theor. Comput. Sci. **1**(2), 125–159 (1975)
23. Ronchi Della Rocca, S., Paolini, L.: The Parametric λ-Calculus - A Metamodel for Computation. Springer, Berlin (2004)
24. Sands, D., Gustavsson, J., Moran, A.: Lambda calculi and linear speedups. In: Mogensen, T.Æ., Schmidt, D.A., Sudborough, I.H. (eds.) The Essence of Computation. LNCS, vol. 2566, pp. 60–82. Springer, Heidelberg (2002). doi:10.1007/ 3-540-36377-7_4
25. Sestoft, P.: Deriving a lazy abstract machine. J. Funct. Program. **7**(3), 231–264 (1997)
26. Wand, M.: On the correctness of the Krivine machine. Higher-Order Symbolic Comput. **20**(3), 231–235 (2007)

Debugging of Concurrent Systems Using Counterexample Analysis

Gianluca Barbon[1]([⊠]), Vincent Leroy[2], and Gwen Salaün[1]

[1] Institute of Engineering, Univ. Grenoble Alpes, CNRS,
Grenoble INP, Inria, LIG, F-38000 Grenoble, France
gianluca.barbon@inria.fr
[2] Institute of Engineering, Univ. Grenoble Alpes, CNRS,
Grenoble INP, LIG, F-38000 Grenoble, France

Abstract. Model checking is an established technique for automatically verifying that a model satisfies a given temporal property. When the model violates the property, the model checker returns a counterexample, which is a sequence of actions leading to a state where the property is not satisfied. Understanding this counterexample for debugging the specification is a complicated task for several reasons: (i) the counterexample can contain hundreds of actions, (ii) the debugging task is mostly achieved manually, and (iii) the counterexample does not give any clue on the state of the system (*e.g.*, parallelism or data expressions) when the error occurs. This paper presents a new approach that improves the usability of model checking by simplifying the comprehension of counterexamples. Our solution aims at keeping only actions in counterexamples that are relevant for debugging purposes. To do so, we first extract in the model all the counterexamples. Second, we define an analysis algorithm that identifies actions that make the behaviour skip from incorrect to correct behaviours, making these actions relevant from a debugging perspective. Our approach is fully automated by a tool that we implemented and applied on real-world case studies from various application areas for evaluation purposes.

1 Introduction

Concurrent and distributed applications are used in various domains, such as cyber-physical systems, software and middleware technologies, Service Oriented Computing, cloud computing, or the Internet of Things. The design and development of these applications is complex and cannot be achieved without introducing subtle bugs, which are defects of the software that prevent the correct behaviour of the system. The process of finding and resolving bugs is commonly called *debugging*. This process is a challenging task for a developer, since it is difficult for a human being to understand the behaviour of all the possible executions of this kind of systems, and bugs can be hidden inside parallel behaviours. There is a need for automatic techniques that can help the developer in detecting and understanding those bugs.

Published by Springer International Publishing AG 2017. All Rights Reserved
M. Dastani and M. Sirjani (Eds.): FSEN 2017, LNCS 10522, pp. 20–34, 2017.
DOI: 10.1007/978-3-319-68972-2_2

Model checking [8] is an established technique for verifying concurrent systems. It takes as input a model and a property. A model describes all the possible behaviours of a concurrent program and is produced from a specification of the system. In this paper, we adopt Labelled Transition Systems (LTS) as model description language. A property represents the requirements of the system and is usually expressed with a temporal logic. Given a model and a property, a model checker verifies whether the model satisfies the property. When the model violates the property, the model checker returns a counterexample, which is a sequence of actions leading to a state where the property is not satisfied.

Although model checking techniques automatically find bugs in concurrent systems, it is still difficult to interpret the returned counterexamples for several reasons: (i) the counterexample can contain hundreds (even thousands) of actions, (ii) the debugging task is mostly achieved manually (satisfactory automatic debugging techniques do not yet exist), and (iii) the counterexample does not give any clue on the state of the system (*e.g.*, parallelism or data expressions) when the error occurs.

This work aims at developing a new approach for simplifying the comprehension of counterexamples and thus favouring usability of model checking techniques. In order to do this, we propose a method to produce all the counterexamples from a given model and to compare them with the correct behaviours of the model to better identify actions that caused the bug. The goal of our approach is to return as result an abstraction of counterexamples, which contains only those actions.

More precisely, we define a method that first extracts all the counterexamples from the original model containing all the executions. This procedure is able to collect all the counterexamples in a new LTS, maintaining a correspondence with the original model. Second, we define an analysis algorithm that identifies actions at the frontier between the new LTS and the original one. The frontier represents the area where counterexamples and correct behaviours, that share a common prefix, split in different paths. Actions at the frontier are relevant since they are responsible for the choice between a correct behaviour and a counterexample. We have implemented our approach in a tool and validated it on a set of real-world case studies from various application areas. Our experiments show that our approach is able to reduce the size of counterexamples by keeping only relevant actions at the frontier, and thus making the debugging process easier.

The rest of this paper is organized as follows. Section 2 introduces LTS models and model checking notions. Section 3 presents our counterexample abstraction techniques, including the generation of the LTS containing all the counterexamples and the process for identifying relevant actions in counterexamples. In Sect. 4, we describe our implementation and we apply it on real-word examples. Section 5 presents related work while Sect. 6 concludes this paper.

2 Preliminaries

In this work, we adopt *Labelled Transition Systems (LTS)* as behavioural models of concurrent programs. An LTS consists of states and labelled transitions connecting these states.

Definition 1 *(LTS). An LTS is a tuple $M = (S, s^0, \Sigma, T)$ where S is a finite set of states; $s^0 \in S$ is the initial state; Σ is a finite set of labels; $T \subseteq S \times \Sigma \times S$ is a finite set of transitions.*

A transition is represented as $s \xrightarrow{l} s' \in T$, where $l \in \Sigma$. An LTS is produced from a higher-level specification of the system described with a process algebra for instance. Specifications can be compiled into an LTS using specific compilers. In this work, we use LNT as specification language [7] and compilers from the CADP toolbox [11] for obtaining LTSs from LNT specifications (see Sect. 4 for more details). However, our approach is generic in the sense that it applies on LTSs produced from any specification language and any compiler/verification tool. An LTS can be viewed as all possible executions of a system. One specific execution is called a *trace*.

Definition 2 *(Trace). Given an LTS $M = (S, s^0, \Sigma, T)$, a trace of size $n \in \mathbb{N}$ is a sequence of labels $l_1, l_2, \ldots, l_n \in \Sigma$ such that $s^0 \xrightarrow{l_1} s_1 \in T, s_1 \xrightarrow{l_2} s_2 \in T, \ldots, s_{n-1} \xrightarrow{l_n} s_n \in T$. The set of all traces of M is written as $t(M)$.*

Note that $t(M)$ is prefix closed. One may not be interested in all traces of an LTS, but only in a subset of them. To this aim, we introduce a particular label δ, called *final label*, which marks the end of a trace, similarly to the notion of accepting state in language automata. This leads to the concept of *final trace*.

Definition 3 *(Final Trace). Given an LTS $M = (S, s^0, \Sigma, T)$, and a label δ, called final label, a final trace is a trace $l_1, l_2, \ldots, l_n \in \Sigma$ such that $s^0 \xrightarrow{l_1} s_1 \in T, s_1 \xrightarrow{l_2} s_2 \in T, \ldots, s_{n-1} \xrightarrow{l_n} s_n \in T, l_1, l_2, \ldots, l_n \neq \delta$ and there exists a final transition $s_n \xrightarrow{\delta} s_{n+1}$. The set of final traces of M is written as $t_\delta(M)$.*

Note that the final transition characterized by δ does not occur in the final traces and that $t_\delta(M) \subseteq t(M)$. Moreover, if M has no final label then $t_\delta(M) = \emptyset$.

Model checking consists in verifying that an LTS model satisfies a given temporal property φ, which specifies some expected requirement of the system. Temporal properties are usually divided into two main families: *safety* and *liveness* properties [2]. In this work, we focus on safety properties, which are widely used in the verification of real-world systems. Safety properties state that "*something bad never happens*". A safety property is usually formalised using a temporal logic (we use MCL [16] in Sect. 4). It can be semantically characterized by an infinite set of traces t_φ, corresponding to the traces that violate the property φ in an LTS. If the LTS model does not satisfy the property, the model checker returns a *counterexample*, which is one of the traces characterised by t_φ.

Definition 4 *(Counterexample). Given an LTS $M = (S, s^0, \Sigma, T)$ and a property φ, a counterexample is any trace which belongs to $t(M) \cap t_\varphi$.*

Our solution for counterexample analysis presented in the next section relies on a state matching algorithm, which takes its foundation into the notion of preorder simulation between two LTSs [19].

Definition 5 *(Simulation Relation). Given two LTSs $M_1 = (S_1, s_1^0, \Sigma_1, T_1)$ and $M_2 = (S_2, s_2^0, \Sigma_2, T_2)$, the simulation relation $\sqsubseteq$ between M_1 and M_2 is the largest relation in $S_1 \times S_2$ such that $s_1 \sqsubseteq s_2$ iff $\forall s_1 \xrightarrow{l} s_1' \in T_1$ there exists $s_2 \xrightarrow{l} s_2' \in T_2$ such that $s_1' \sqsubseteq s_2'$. M_1 is simulated by M_2 iff $s_1^0 \sqsubseteq s_2^0$.*

3   Counterexample Analysis

In this section, we describe our approach to simplify counterexamples. We first introduce the procedure to build an LTS containing all counterexamples (*counterexample LTS*), given a model of the system (*full LTS*) and a temporal property. We then present a technique to match all states of the counterexample LTS with states of the full LTS. This step allows us to identify transitions at the *frontier* between the counterexample and the full LTS. The frontier is the area where traces, that share a common prefix in the two LTSs, split in different paths. We define a notion of *neighbourhood* to extract sets of relevant transitions at the frontier and a procedure to collect the set of all neighbourhoods. Finally, by keeping transitions in these neighbourhoods, we are able to provide an abstraction of a given counterexample. To sum up, our approach consists of the four following steps, that we detail in the rest of this section:

1. Counterexample LTS generation
2. States matching
3. States comparison
4. Counterexample abstraction

3.1   Counterexample LTS Generation

The full LTS (M_F) is given as input in our approach and is a model representing all possible executions of a system. Given such an LTS and a safety property, our goal in this subsection is to generate the LTS containing all counterexamples (M_C).

Definition 6 *(Counterexample LTS). Given a full LTS $M_F = (S_F, s_F^0, \Sigma_F, T_F)$, where $\delta \notin \Sigma_F$, and a safety property φ, a counterexample LTS M_C is an LTS such that $t_\delta(M_C) = t(M_F) \cap t_\varphi$, i.e., a counterexample LTS is a finite representation of the set of all traces of the full LTS that violate the property φ.*

We use the set of final traces $t_\delta(M_C)$ instead of $t(M_C)$ since $t(M_C)$ is prefix closed, but prefixes of counterexamples that belongs to $t(M_C)$ are not counterexamples. Moreover, traces in the counterexample LTS share prefixes with correct traces in the full LTS. Given a full LTS M_F and a safety property φ, the procedure for the generation of the counterexample LTS consists of the following steps:

1. Conversion of the φ formula describing the property into an LTS called M_φ, using the technique that allows the encoding of a formula into a graph

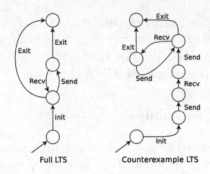

Fig. 1. Full LTS and counterexample LTS

described in [12]. M_φ is a finite representation of t_φ, using final transitions, such that $t_\delta(M_\varphi) = t_\varphi \cap \Sigma_F^*$, where Σ_F is the set of labels occurring in M_F. In this step, we also apply the subset construction algorithm defined in [1] in order to determinise M_φ. We finally reduce the size of M_φ without changing its behaviour, performing a minimisation based on strong bisimulation [17]. Those two transformations keep the set of final traces of M_φ unchanged. The LTS M_φ obtained in this way is the minimal one that is deterministic and accepts all the execution sequences that violates φ.

2. Synchronous product between M_F and M_φ with synchronisation on all the labels of Σ_F (thus excluding the final label δ). The result of this product is an LTS whose final traces belong to $t(M_F) \cap t_\delta(M_\varphi)$, thus it contains all the traces of the LTS M_F that violate the formula φ. Note that $t(M_F) \cap t_\delta(M_\varphi) = t(M_F) \cap t_\varphi$, because $t(M_F) \subseteq \Sigma_F^*$ and $t_\delta(M_\varphi) = t_\varphi \cap \Sigma_F^*$.

3. Pruning of the useless transitions generated during the previous step. In particular, we use the pruning algorithm proposed in [15] to remove the traces produced by the synchronous product that are not the prefix of any final trace.

Proposition: *The LTS M_C obtained by this procedure is a counterexample LTS for M_F and φ.*

Let us illustrate this algorithm on the example given in Fig. 1. The full LTS on the left hand side represents a model of a simple protocol that performs send and receive actions in a loop. The counterexample LTS on the right hand side is generated with a property φ stating that *no more than one send action is allowed*. Note that final transitions characterised by the δ label are not made explicit in the examples.

3.2   States Matching

We now need to match each state belonging to the counterexample LTS with the states from the full LTS. To do this, we define a matching relation between each state of the two LTSs, by relying on the simulation relation introduced in

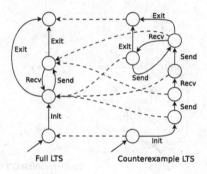

Fig. 2. States matching

Sect. 2. In our context, we want to build such a relation between M_C and M_F, where a state $x \in S_C$ matches a state $y \in S_F$ when the first is simulated by the latter, that is, when $x \sqsubseteq y$. Since the LTS that contains the incorrect behaviours is extracted from the full LTS, the full LTS always simulates the counterexample LTS. The algorithm that we have implemented to build the simulation between M_C and M_F relies on well-known graph traversal algorithms. More precisely, it relies on Breadth-First Search (BFS) to explore the graph. The algorithm is capable of performing backtracking steps in case it cannot match some states (this may happen due to nondeterministic behaviours present in both LTSs).

Let us consider again the example described in Fig. 1. Each state of the counterexample LTS on the right hand side of the picture matches a state of the full LTS on the left hand side as shown in Fig. 2. Note that multiple states of the counterexample LTS may correspond to a single state of the full LTS. In the example of Fig. 2, the property φ has become unsatisfied after several iterations of the loop composed of *Send* and *Recv* actions, so that loop has been partially rolled out in the counterexample LTS, resulting in a correspondence of several states of the counterexample LTS to a single state of the full LTS.

It may also occur that a single state of the counterexample LTS may correspond to multiple states of the full LTS. For instance, the example given in Fig. 3 shows a full LTS and a counterexample LTS produced with a property that avoids *Recv* actions after a *Send* action. Thus, there exists a correspondence of more than one state of the full LTS with a single state of the counterexample LTS. In this specific case, the counterexample LTS can be described using a single trace, since the two states with an exiting *Send* transition after the *Init* transition simulate only one state in the counterexample LTS.

3.3 States Comparison

The result of the matching algorithm is then analysed in order to compare transitions outgoing from similar states in both LTSs. This comparison aims at identifying transitions that originate from matched states, and that appear in the full LTS but not in the counterexample LTS. We call this kind of transition a *correct transition*.

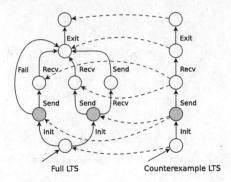

Fig. 3. Multiple matching

Definition 7 *(Correct Transition). Given an LTS $M_F = (S_F, s_F^0, \Sigma_F, T_F)$, a property φ, the counterexample LTS $M_C = (S_C, s_C^0, \Sigma_C, T_C)$ obtained from M_F and φ, and given two states $s \in S_F$ and $s' \in S_C$, such that $s' \sqsubseteq s$, we call a transition $s \xrightarrow{l} s'' \in T_F$ a correct transition if there is no transition $s' \xrightarrow{l} s''' \in T_C$ such that $s''' \sqsubseteq s''$.*

A correct transition is preceded by incoming transitions that are common to the correct and incorrect behaviours. We call these transitions *relevant predecessors*. Correct transitions allow us to introduce the notion of *frontier*. The frontier is a set of states at the border between the counterexample LTS and the rest of the full LTS, where for two matched states, there exists a correct transition in the full LTS.

Definition 8 *(Frontier). Given an LTS $M_F = (S_F, s_F^0, \Sigma_F, T_F)$, a property φ, the counterexample LTS $M_C = (S_C, s_C^0, \Sigma_C, T_C)$ obtained from M_F and φ, the frontier is the set of states $S_{fr} \subseteq S_F$ such that for each $s \in S_{fr}$, there exists $s' \in S_C$, such that $s' \sqsubseteq s$ and there exists a correct transition $s \xrightarrow{l} s'' \in T_F$.*

A given state in the frontier allows us in a second step to identify a *neighbourhood* in the corresponding counterexample LTS, which consists of all incoming and outgoing transitions of that state.

Definition 9 *(Neighbourhood). Given an LTS $M_F = (S_F, s_F^0, \Sigma_F, T_F)$, a property φ, the counterexample LTS $M_C = (S_C, s_C^0, \Sigma_C, T_C)$, two states $s \in S_{fr}$ and $s' \in S_C$ such that $s' \sqsubseteq s$, the neighbourhood of state s' is the set of transitions $T_{nb} \subseteq T_C$ such that for each $t \in T_{nb}$, either $t = s'' \xrightarrow{l} s' \in T_C$ or $t = s' \xrightarrow{l} s'' \in T_C$.*

Let us illustrate these notions on an example. Figure 4 shows a piece of a full LTS and the corresponding counterexample LTS. The full LTS on the left hand side of the figure represents a state that is at the frontier, thus it has been matched by a state of the counterexample LTS on the right hand side and it has correct transitions outgoing from it. The incoming and outgoing transitions for this state in the counterexample LTS correspond to the neighbourhood.

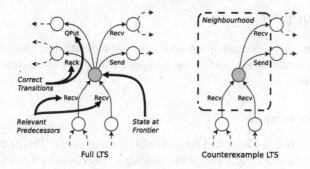

Fig. 4. Example of neighbourhood

3.4 Counterexample Abstraction

The final goal is to abstract a counterexample of the model in order to highlight the source of the bug and thus favour the comprehension of its cause. Given the counterexample LTS M_C, produced from a model M_F and a property φ, where neighbourhoods have been identified in the previous subsection, and a counterexample c_e, produced from M_F and φ, the procedure for the counterexample abstraction consists of the following steps:

1. Matching between states of c_e with states of M_C.
2. Identification of states in c_e that are matched to states in M_C, which belong to a neighbourhood.
3. Suppression of actions in c_e, which do not represent incoming or outgoing transitions of a neighbourhood.

For illustration purposes, let us consider the counterexample, produced by a model checker from a model M and a property φ, given on the top side of Fig. 5. Once the set of neighbourhoods in the counterexample LTS is computed using M and φ, we are able to locate sub-sequences of actions corresponding to transitions in the neighbourhoods. We finally remove all the remaining actions to obtain the simplified counterexample shown on the bottom side of the figure. We will comment on the relevance and benefit of these results on real-world examples in the next section.

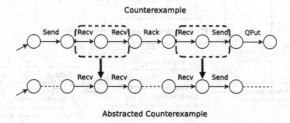

Fig. 5. Counterexample abstraction

4   Tool Support

In this section, we successively present the implementation of our approach, illustrate it on a case study, and present experimental results on examples found in the literature.

4.1   Implementation

Our tool is depicted in Fig. 6 and consists of two main parts. The first one implements the counterexample LTS generation step described in Sect. 3.1. It relies on the CADP toolbox [11], which enables one to specify and analyse concurrent systems using model and equivalence checking techniques. We particularly make use of the LNT value passing process algebra [7] for specifying systems, of the BCG binary format for representing LTSs, and of the MCL mu-calculus logic [16] for describing safety temporal properties. The LNT specification is automatically transformed into an LTS model in BCG format (the full LTS in Sect. 3) using CADP compilers. The CADP model checker (Evaluator [16]) takes as input an MCL property and an input specification/model (LNT or LTS), and returns a verdict (true or false + a counterexample if the property is violated). The computation of the counterexample LTS is achieved by a script we wrote using SVL [10], a scripting language that allows one to interface with tools provided in the CADP toolbox. This script calls several tools: a specific option of Evaluator for building an LTS from a formula following the algorithm in [12]; EXP.OPEN for building LTS products; Reductor for minimizing LTSs; Scrutator [15] for removing spurious traces in LTSs.

The second part of our tool implements the algorithms for state matching (2), state comparison (3) and counterexample abstraction (4), described from Sects. 3.2 to 3.4. This part of the tool has been implemented in Java and

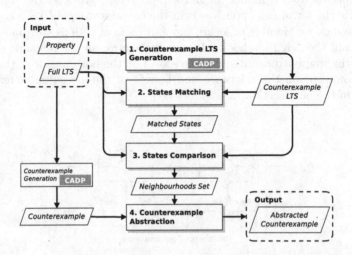

Fig. 6. Overview of the tool support

consists of about 2,500 lines of code. The tool takes as input the files containing the full and the counterexample LTS, converted into an intermediate ASCII format called AUT (provided by CADP), and stores them in memory using a Java graph modelling library. The matching step (2) is based on a BFS graph search algorithm in order to build the simulation relation between the two LTSs. The state matching is then stored into a map, used by the state comparison step (3) to analyse outgoing transitions for each association of states between the two LTSs. This allows us to retrieve the set of neighbourhoods. Finally, the counterexample abstraction step (4) first produces the shortest counterexample from the full LTS and the property by using the Evaluator model checker, and second performs the counterexample reduction by locating and keeping actions that correspond to neighbourhoods. The result retrieved by our tool consists of the shortest counterexample abstracted in the form of a list of sub-sequences of actions, accompanied by the list of all neighbourhoods.

4.2   Case Study

We now describe an example taken from a real-world case study [20]. The example models a sanitary agency that aims at supporting elderly citizens in receiving sanitary agency assistance from the public administration. The model involves four different participants: (i) a citizen who requests services such as transportation or meal; the request can be accepted or refused by the agency; (ii) a sanitary agency that manages citizens' requests and provides public fee payment; (iii) a bank that manages fees and performs payments; (iv) a cooperative that receives requests from the sanitary agency, receives payments from the bank, and provides transportations and meal services. Figure 7 gives the LTS model for each participant. We assume in this example that the participants interact together asynchronously by exchanging messages via FIFO buffers.

For illustration purposes, we use an MCL safety property, which indicates that the payment of a transportation service to the transportation cooperative cannot occur after submission of a request by a citizen to the sanitary agency:

[true* . 'REQUEST_EM' . true* . 'PAYMENTT_EM' . true*] false

We applied our tool to the sanitary agency model with the aforementioned property. Our tool was able to identify seven neighbourhoods in the couterexample LTS. The shortest counterexample involves three neighbourhoods, and this allows us to reduce its size from 19 actions to only 6 actions. Figure 8 shows (from left to right) the full LTS of the sanitary agency model, the shortest counterexample, and the three neighbourhoods (+ correct transitions) for this counterexample. The neighbourhoods and corresponding extracted actions are relevant in the sense that they precisely identify choices that lead to the incorrect behaviour. In particular, they identify the two causes of the property violation and those causes can be observed on the shortest counterexample. The first cause of violation is emphasized by the first neighbourhood and occurs when the citizen request is accepted. In that case, the refusal of the request is a correct transition and leads to a part of the LTS where the property is not violated. Indeed,

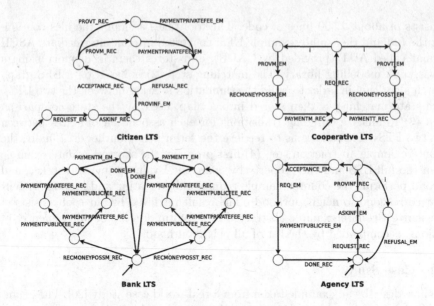

Fig. 7. LTS models for the sanitary agency

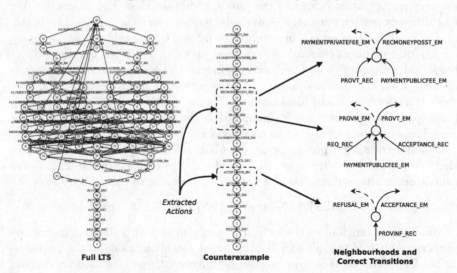

Fig. 8. Sanitary agency: full LTS and shortest counterexample

when a citizen request is refused by the sanitary agency, the execution skips the part of the system behaviour where the transportation service and payment appear. The two next neighbourhoods pinpoint the second reason of property violation. They show that actions RECMONEYPOST_EM and PROVT_EM have been performed, which correspond to triggering the request for payment of the transportation service, that is not permitted by the property.

Our solution thus allows the developer to identify the cause of the property violation by identifying specific actions in counterexamples via the notion of neighbourhood. It is worth stressing that, since our approach applies on the counterexample LTS and computes all the neighbourhoods, the returned solution is able to pinpoint all the causes of the property violation, as we have shown with the example above.

4.3 Experimental Results

We carried out experiments on about 20 real-world examples found in the literature. For each example, we use as input an LNT specification or an LTS model as well as a safety property. Table 1 summarizes the results for some of these experiments. The first two columns contain the name of the model, the reference to the corresponding article, and the property. The third and fourth columns show the size of the full and the counterexample LTSs, respectively, in terms of number of states, transitions and labels. The following columns give the number of identified neighbourhoods, the size of the shortest (retrieved with breadth first search techniques) and of the abstracted counterexample, respectively. Finally, the last two columns detail the execution time for the counterexample LTS production, and for the matching and comparison algorithms (in seconds).

Table 1. Experimental results

Example	φ	L_F (s/t/l)	L_C (s/t/l)	$|N|$	$|Ce|$	$|Ce_r|$	t_{L_C}	t_N
sanitary agency [20]	φ_{sa1}	227/492/31	226/485/31	6	17	2	6.3 s	0.3 s
sanitary agency [20]	φ_{sa2}	142/291/31	492/943/31	18	64	6	5.7 s	0.2 s
ssh protocol [14]	φ_{sp1}	23/25/23	20/20/19	2	14	3	4.9 s	0.2 s
ssh protocol [14]	φ_{sp2}	23/25/23	35/35/19	4	29	7	4.8 s	0.1 s
client supplier [6]	φ_{cs1}	35/45/26	29/33/24	3	18	5	4.6 s	0.1s
client supplier [6]	φ_{cs2}	35/45/26	25/25/24	4	19	6	4.9 s	0.1s
client supplier [6]	φ_{cs3}	35/46/26	33/41/24	2	15	2	4.8 s	0.2s
train station [21]	φ_{ts}	39/66/18	26/34/18	1	6	2	5.2 s	0.2 s
selfconfig [22]	φ_{ac}	314/810/27	159/355/27	30	14	5	5.6 s	0.3 s
online stock broker [9]	φ_{osb}	1331/2770/13	2653/5562/13	61	23	23	4.9 s	0.7 s

First of all, we can see a clear gain in length between the original counterexample and the abstracted one, which keeps only relevant actions using our approach. There is one case (online stock broker, last row) in which our solution was not able to reduce the counterexample. This may occur in specific cases when the counterexample (the shortest here) does not exhibit any actions corresponding to transitions in a neighbourhood. In that particular situation, our abstraction techniques cannot help the developer in the identification of the cause of the property violation.

As far as computation time is concerned, the table shows that, for these examples, the time for producing counterexample LTSs is slightly longer than the time for computing the matching/comparison algorithms, which is very low (less than a second). The script for counterexample LTS computation is longer because it calls several CADP tools in sequence, which takes time.

5   Related Work

In this section, we survey related papers providing techniques for supporting the debugging of specifications and programs. LocFaults [5] is a flow-driven and constraint-based approach for error localization. It takes as input a faulty program for which a counterexample and a postcondition are provided. This approach makes use of constraint based bounded model checking combined with a minimal correction set notion to locate errors in the faulty program. This work focuses on programs with numerical statements and relies on a constraint programming framework allowing the combination of Boolean and numerical constraints. In addition, the authors do not explicitly describe the capacity of their solution for analysing concurrent programs.

Concurrency is explicitly taken into account in [3,4]. In [3], the authors choose the Halpern and Pearl model to define causality checking. In particular, they analyse traces of counterexamples generated by bounded model checking to localise errors in hardware systems. In [4], sequential pattern mining is applied to execution traces for revealing unforeseen interleavings that may be a source of error, through the adoption of the well-known mining algorithm CloSpan [24]. This work deals with various typical issues in the analysis of concurrent models, for instance the problem of increasing length of traces and the introduction of spurious patterns when abstraction methods are used. CloSpan is also adopted in [13], where the authors applied sequential pattern mining to traces of counterexamples generated from a model using the SPIN model checker. By doing so, they are able to reveal unforeseen interleavings that may be a source of error. The approach presented in [13] is able to analyse concurrent systems and to extract sequences of events for identifying bugs, thus representing one of the closest results to our work. Reasoning on traces as achieved in [3,4,13] induces several issues. The handling of looping behaviours is non-trivial and may result in the generation of infinite traces or of an infinite number of traces. Coverage is another problem, since a high number of traces does not guarantee to produce all the relevant behaviours for analysis purposes. As a result, we decided to work on the debugging of LTS models, which represent in a finite way all possible behaviours of the system.

Another solution for localization of faults in failing programs consists in using testing techniques. As an example, [18] presents a mutation-based fault localization approach and suggests the use of a sufficient mutant set to locate effectively the faulty statements. This mutation analysis approach applies on C programs under validation using testing techniques whereas we focus on formal specifications and models being analysed using model checking techniques. In [23], the authors propose a new approach for debugging value-passing process algebra through coverage analysis. The authors define several coverage notions before showing how to instrument the specification without affecting original behaviours. This approach helps one to find errors such as ill-formed decisions or dead code, but does not help to understand why a property is violated during analysis using model checking techniques.

6 Conclusion

In this paper, we have proposed a new method for debugging concurrent systems based on the analysis of counterexamples produced by model checking techniques. First, we have defined a procedure to obtain an LTS containing all the counterexamples given a full LTS and a safety property. Second, we have introduced the notion of neighbourhoods corresponding to the junction of correct and erroneous transitions in the LTS, as well as an algorithm for computing them by comparing the full LTS and the LTS consisting of all counterexamples. Finally, we have implemented our approach as a tool and evaluated it on real-world case studies, showing the advantage of the counterexample abstraction in practice when adopting the neighbourhood approach.

As far as future improvements are concerned, a first perspective of this work is to extend our approach to focus on probabilistic specifications and models, and refine our LTS analysis techniques for handling those models. Another perspective is to increase the scope of system requirements that we can take into account. Indeed, although safety properties already allow us to define most requirements for real-world systems, we would like to consider liveness properties as well. Finally, we plan to investigate the introduction of code colouring in the specification by highlighting code portions that correspond to the source of the problem according to our approach.

Acknowledgements. We would like to thank Frédéric Lang and Radu Mateescu for their valuable suggestions to improve the paper.

References

1. Aho, A.V., Sethi, R., Ullman, J.D.: Compilers: Principles, Techniques, and Tools. Addison-Wesley, Reading (1986)
2. Baier, C., Katoen, J.: Principles of Model Checking. MIT Press, Cambridge (2008)
3. Beer, A., Heidinger, S., Kühne, U., Leitner-Fischer, F., Leue, S.: Symbolic causality checking using bounded model checking. In: Fischer, B., Geldenhuys, J. (eds.) SPIN 2015. LNCS, vol. 9232, pp. 203–221. Springer, Cham (2015). doi:10.1007/978-3-319-23404-5_14
4. Befrouei, M.T., Wang, C., Weissenbacher, G.: Abstraction and mining of traces to explain concurrency bugs. In: Bonakdarpour, B., Smolka, S.A. (eds.) RV 2014. LNCS, vol. 8734, pp. 162–177. Springer, Cham (2014). doi:10.1007/978-3-319-11164-3_14
5. Bekkouche, M., Collavizza, H., Rueher, M.: LocFaults: a new flow-driven and constraint-based error localization approach. In: Proceedings of SAC 2015. ACM (2015)

6. Cámara, J., Martín, J.A., Salaün, G., Canal, C., Pimentel, E.: Semi-automatic specification of behavioural service adaptation contracts. Electr. Notes Theor. Comput. Sci. **264**(1), 19–34 (2010)
7. Champelovier, D., Clerc, X., Garavel, H., Guerte, Y., Lang, F., McKinty, C., Powazny, V., Serwe, W., Smeding, G.: Reference Manual of the LOTOS NT to LOTOS Translator (Version 6.1). INRIA/VASY, 131 p. (2014)
8. Clarke, E.M., Grumberg, O., Peled, D.A.: Model Checking. MIT Press, Cambridge (2001)
9. Fu, X., Bultan, T., Su, J.: Conversation protocols: a formalism for specification and verification of reactive electronic services. Theor. Comput. Sci. **328**(1–2), 19–37 (2004)
10. Garavel, H., Lang, F.: SVL: a scripting language for compositional verification. In: Proceedings of FORTE 2001. IIFIP, vol. 197. Kluwer (2001)
11. Garavel, H., Lang, F., Mateescu, R., Serwe, W.: CADP 2011: a toolbox for the construction and analysis of distributed processes. STTT **15**(2), 89–107 (2013)
12. Lang, F., Mateescu, R.: Partial model checking using networks of labelled transition systems and boole an equation systems. Log. Methods Comput. Sci. **9**(4), 1–32 (2013)
13. Leue, S., Befrouei, M.T.: Mining sequential patterns to explain concurrent counterexamples. In: Bartocci, E., Ramakrishnan, C.R. (eds.) SPIN 2013. LNCS, vol. 7976, pp. 264–281. Springer, Heidelberg (2013). doi:10.1007/978-3-642-39176-7_17
14. Martín, J.A., Pimentel, E.: Contracts for security adaptation. J. Log. Algebraic Program. **80**(3–5), 154–179 (2011)
15. Mateescu, R., Poizat, P., Salaün, G.: Adaptation of service protocols using process algebra and on-the-fly reduction techniques. IEEE Trans. Softw. Eng. **38**(4), 755–777 (2012)
16. Mateescu, R., Thivolle, D.: A model checking language for concurrent value-passing systems. In: Cuellar, J., Maibaum, T., Sere, K. (eds.) FM 2008. LNCS, vol. 5014, pp. 148–164. Springer, Heidelberg (2008). doi:10.1007/978-3-540-68237-0_12
17. Milner, R.: Communication and Concurrency. Prentice Hall, Upper Saddle River (1989)
18. Papadakis, M., Traon, Y.L.: Effective fault localization via mutation analysis: a selective mutation approach. In: Proceedings of SAC 2014. ACM (2014)
19. Park, D.: Concurrency and automata on infinite sequences. In: Deussen, P. (ed.) GI-TCS 1981. LNCS, vol. 104, pp. 167–183. Springer, Heidelberg (1981). doi:10.1007/BFb0017309
20. Salaün, G., Bordeaux, L., Schaerf, M.: Describing and reasoning on web services using process algebra. In: Proceedings of ICWS 2004. IEEE Computer Society (2004)
21. Salaün, G., Bultan, T., Roohi, N.: Realizability of choreographies using process algebra encodings. IEEE Trans. Serv. Comput. **5**(3), 290–304 (2012)
22. Salaün, G., Etchevers, X., De Palma, N., Boyer, F., Coupaye, T.: Verification of a self-configuration protocol for distributed applications in the cloud. In: Cámara, J., de Lemos, R., Ghezzi, C., Lopes, A. (eds.) Assurances for Self-Adaptive Systems. LNCS, vol. 7740, pp. 60–79. Springer, Heidelberg (2013). doi:10.1007/978-3-642-36249-1_3
23. Salaün, G., Ye, L.: Debugging process algebra specifications. In: D'Souza, D., Lal, A., Larsen, K.G. (eds.) VMCAI 2015. LNCS, vol. 8931, pp. 245–262. Springer, Heidelberg (2015). doi:10.1007/978-3-662-46081-8_14
24. Yan, X., Han, J., Afshar, R.: CloSpan: mining closed sequential patterns in large databases. In: Proceedings of SDM 2003. SIAM (2003)

Bisimilarity of Open Terms in Stream GSOS

Filippo Bonchi[1], Matias David Lee[1], and Jurriaan Rot[2(✉)]

[1] Univ Lyon, ENS de Lyon, CNRS, UCB Lyon 1, LIP, Lyon, France
{filippo.bonchi,matias-david.lee}@ens-lyon.fr
[2] Radboud University, Nijmegen, The Netherlands
jrot@cs.ru.nl

Abstract. Stream GSOS is a specification format for operations and calculi on infinite sequences. The notion of bisimilarity provides a canonical proof technique for equivalence of closed terms in such specifications. In this paper, we focus on *open terms*, which may contain variables, and which are equivalent whenever they denote the same stream for every possible instantiation of the variables. Our main contribution is to capture equivalence of open terms as bisimilarity on certain Mealy machines, providing a concrete proof technique. Moreover, we introduce an enhancement of this technique, called bisimulation up-to substitutions, and show how to combine it with other up-to techniques to obtain a powerful method for proving equivalence of open terms.

1 Introduction

Structural operational semantics (SOS) can be considered the de facto standard to define programming languages and process calculi. The SOS framework relies on defining a *specification* consisting of a set of operation symbols, a set of labels or actions and a set of inference rules. The inference rules describe the behaviour of each operation, typically depending on the behaviour of the parameters. The semantics is then defined in terms of a labelled transition system over *(closed) terms* constructed from the operation symbols. *Bisimilarity* of closed terms ($\sim$) provides a canonical notion of behavioural equivalence.

It is also interesting to study equivalence of *open terms*, for instance to express properties of program constructors, like the commutativity of a non-deterministic choice operator. The latter can be formalised as the equation $\mathcal{X} + \mathcal{Y} = \mathcal{Y} + \mathcal{X}$, where the left and right hand sides are terms with variables $\mathcal{X}, \mathcal{Y}$. Equivalence of open terms ($\sim_o$) is usually based on $\sim$: for all open terms t_1, t_2

$$t_1 \sim_o t_2 \text{ iff for all closed substitutions } \phi, \ \phi(t_1) \sim \phi(t_2). \tag{1}$$

The research leading to these results has received funding from the European Research Council (FP7/2007-2013, grant agreement nr. 320571); as well as from the LABEX MILYON (ANR-10-LABX-0070, ANR-11-IDEX-0007), the project PACE (ANR-12IS02001) and the project REPAS (ANR-16-CE25-0011).

Published by Springer International Publishing AG 2017. All Rights Reserved
M. Dastani and M. Sirjani (Eds.): FSEN 2017, LNCS 10522, pp. 35–50, 2017.
DOI: 10.1007/978-3-319-68972-2_3

The main problem of such a definition is the quantification over all substitutions: one would like to have an alternative characterisation, possibly amenable to the coinduction proof principle. This issue has been investigated in several works, like [1,3,7,11,13,15,20].

$$(a)\quad \frac{}{n \xrightarrow{n} 0} \qquad \frac{x \xrightarrow{n} x' \quad y \xrightarrow{m} y'}{x \oplus y \xrightarrow{n+m} x' \oplus y'} \qquad \frac{x \xrightarrow{n} x' \quad y \xrightarrow{m} y'}{x \otimes y \xrightarrow{n \times m} (n \otimes y') \oplus (x' \otimes y)}$$

$$(b)\quad \frac{}{n \xrightarrow{n} 0} \qquad \frac{x \xrightarrow{n} x' \quad y \xrightarrow{m} y'}{x \oplus y \xrightarrow{n+m} x' \oplus y'} \qquad \frac{x \xrightarrow{n} x' \quad y \xrightarrow{m} y'}{x \otimes y \xrightarrow{n \times m} (n \otimes y') \oplus (x' \otimes m.y')} \qquad \frac{x \xrightarrow{m} x'}{n.x \xrightarrow{n} m.x'}$$

$$(c)\quad \frac{}{n \xrightarrow{b|n} 0} \qquad \frac{x \xrightarrow{b|n} x' \quad y \xrightarrow{b|m} y'}{x \oplus y \xrightarrow{b|n+m} x' \oplus y'} \qquad \frac{x \xrightarrow{b|n} x' \quad y \xrightarrow{b|m} y'}{x \otimes y \xrightarrow{b|n \times m} (n \otimes y') \oplus (x' \otimes m.y')} \qquad \frac{x \xrightarrow{b|m} x'}{n.x \xrightarrow{b|n} m.x'}$$

$$(d)\quad \frac{}{\mathcal{X} \xrightarrow{\varsigma|\varsigma(\mathcal{X})} \mathcal{X}} \qquad \frac{}{n \xrightarrow{\varsigma|n} 0} \qquad \cdots \qquad \frac{x \xrightarrow{\varsigma|n} x' \quad y \xrightarrow{\varsigma|m} y'}{x \otimes y \xrightarrow{\varsigma|n \times m} (n \otimes y') \oplus (x' \otimes m.y')} \qquad \frac{x \xrightarrow{\varsigma|m} x'}{n.x \xrightarrow{\varsigma|n} m.x'}$$

Fig. 1. A stream GSOS specification (a) is transformed first into a monadic specification (b), then in a Mealy specification (c) and finally in a specification for open terms (d). In these rules, n and m range over real numbers, b over an arbitrary set B, $\mathcal{X}$ over variables and ς over substitutions of variables into reals.

In this paper, we continue this line of research, focusing on the simpler setting of *streams*, which are infinite sequences over a fixed data type. More precisely, we consider stream languages specified in the *stream GSOS format* [10], a syntactic rule format enforcing several interesting properties. We show how to transform a stream specification into a *Mealy machine* specification that defines the operational semantics of open terms. Moreover, a notion of bisimulation – arising in a canonical way from the theory of coalgebras [16] – exactly characterises $\sim_o$ as defined in (1).

Our approach can be illustrated by taking as running example the fragment of the stream calculus [18] presented in Fig. 1(a). The first step is to transform a stream GSOS specification (Sect. 2) into a *monadic* one (Sect. 3). In this variant of GSOS specifications, no variable in the source of the conclusion appears in the target of the conclusion. For example, in the stream specification in Fig. 1(a), the rule associated to $\otimes$ is not monadic. The corresponding monadic specification is illustrated in Fig. 1(b). Notice this process requires the inclusion of a family of prefix operators (on the right of Fig. 1(b)) that satisfy the imposed restriction.

The second step – based on [8] – is to compute the *pointwise extension* of the obtained specification (Sect. 4). Intuitively, we transform a specification of streams with outputs in a set A into a specification of Mealy machines with inputs in an arbitrary set B and outputs in A, by replacing each transition $\xrightarrow{a}$ (for $a \in A$) with a transition $\xrightarrow{b|a}$ for each input $b \in B$. See Fig. 1(c).

In the last step (Sect. 5), we fix $B = \mathcal{V} \to A$, the set of functions assigning outputs values in A to variables in $\mathcal{V}$. To get the semantics of open terms, it only remains to specify the behaviours of variables in $\mathcal{V}$. This is done with the leftmost rule in Fig. 1(d).

As a result of this process, we obtain a notion of bisimilarity over open terms, which coincides with behavioural equivalence of all closed instances, and provides a concrete proof technique for equivalence of open terms. By relating open terms rather than all its possible instances, this novel technique often enables to use *finite* relations, while standard bisimulation techniques usually require relations of infinite size on closed terms. In Sect. 6 we further enhance this novel proof technique by studying *bisimulation up-to* [14]. We combine known up-to techniques with a novel one which we call *bisimulation up-to substitutions*.

2 Preliminaries

We define the two basic models that form the focus of this paper: stream systems, that generate infinite sequences (streams), and Mealy machines, that generate output streams given input streams.

Definition 2.1. *A* stream system *with outputs in a set A is a pair $(X, \langle o, d \rangle)$ where X is a set of states and $\langle o, d \rangle \colon X \to A \times X$ is a function, which maps a state $x \in X$ to both an output value $o(x) \in A$ and to a next state $d(x) \in X$. We write $x \xrightarrow{a} y$ whenever $o(x) = a$ and $d(x) = y$.*

Definition 2.2. *A* Mealy machine *with inputs in a set B and outputs in a set A is a pair (X, m) where X is a set of states and $m \colon X \to (A \times X)^B$ is a function assigning to each $x \in X$ a map $m(x) = \langle o_x, d_x \rangle \colon B \to A \times X$. For all inputs $b \in B$, $o_x(b) \in A$ represents an output and $d_x(b) \in X$ a next state. We write $x \xrightarrow{b|a} y$ whenever $o_x(b) = a$ and $d_x(b) = y$.*

We recall the notion of *bisimulation* for both models.

Definition 2.3. *Let $(X, \langle o, d \rangle)$ be a stream system. A relation $\mathcal{R} \subseteq X \times X$ is a bisimulation if for all $(x, y) \in \mathcal{R}$, $o(x) = o(y)$ and $(d(x), d(y)) \in \mathcal{R}$.*

Definition 2.4. *Let (X, m) be a Mealy machine. A relation $\mathcal{R} \subseteq X \times X$ is a bisimulation if for all $(x, y) \in \mathcal{R}$ and $b \in B$, $o_x(b) = o_y(b)$ and $(d_x(b), d_y(b)) \in \mathcal{R}$.*

For both kind of systems, we say that x and y are *bisimilar*, notation $x \sim y$, if there is a bisimulation $\mathcal{R}$ s.t. $x \mathcal{R} y$.

Stream systems and Mealy machines, as well as the associated notions of bisimulation, are instances of the theory of *coalgebras* [16]. Coalgebras provide a suitable mathematical framework to study state-based systems and their semantics at a high level of generality. In the current paper, the theory of coalgebras underlies and enables our main results.

Definition 2.5. *Given a functor* $F\colon Set \to Set$, *an* F-*coalgebra is a pair* (X, d), *where* X *is a set (called the carrier) and* $d\colon X \to FX$ *is a function (called the structure). An* F-*coalgebra morphism from* $d\colon X \to FX$ *to* $d'\colon Y \to FY$ *is a map* $h\colon X \to Y$ *such that* $Fh \circ d = d' \circ h$.

Stream systems and Mealy machines are F-coalgebras for the functors $FX = A \times X$ and $FX = (A \times X)^B$, respectively.

The semantics of systems modelled as coalgebras for a functor F is provided by the notion of *final coalgebra*. A coalgebra $\zeta\colon Z \to FZ$ is called *final* if for every F-coalgebra $d\colon X \to FX$ there is a unique morphism $[\![-]\!]\colon X \to Z$ such that $[\![-]\!]$ is a morphism from d to ζ. We call $[\![-]\!]$ the *coinductive extension* of d.

Intuitively, a final coalgebra $\zeta\colon Z \to FZ$ defines all possible behaviours of F-coalgebras, and $[\![-]\!]$ assigns behaviour to all states $x, y \in X$. This motivates to define x and y to be *behaviourally equivalent* iff $[\![x]\!] = [\![y]\!]$. Under the condition that F preserves weak pullbacks, behavioural equivalence coincides with bisimilarity, i.e., $x \sim y$ iff $[\![x]\!] = [\![y]\!]$ (see [16]). This condition is satisfied by (the functors for) stream systems and Mealy machines. In the sequel, by $\sim$ we hence refer both to bisimilarity and behavioural equivalence.

Final coalgebras for stream systems and Mealy machines will be pivotal for our exposition. We briefly recall them, following [9,16]. The set A^ω of streams over A carries a final coalgebra for the functor $FX = A \times X$. For every stream system $\langle o, d \rangle\colon X \to A \times X$, the coinductive extension $[\![-]\!]\colon X \to A^\omega$ assigns to a state $x \in X$ the stream $a_0 a_1 a_2 \ldots$ whenever $x \xrightarrow{a_0} x_1 \xrightarrow{a_1} x_2 \xrightarrow{a_2} \ldots$

Recalling a final coalgebra for Mealy machines requires some more care. Given a stream $\beta \in B^\omega$, we write $\beta\!\upharpoonright_n$ for the prefix of β of length n. A function $\mathfrak{c}\colon B^\omega \to A^\omega$ is *causal* if for all $n \in \mathbb{N}$ and all $\beta, \beta' \in B^\omega$: $\beta\!\upharpoonright_n = \beta'\!\upharpoonright_n$ entails $\mathfrak{c}(\beta)\!\upharpoonright_n = \mathfrak{c}(\beta')\!\upharpoonright_n$. The set $\Gamma(B^\omega, A^\omega) = \{\mathfrak{c}\colon B^\omega \to A^\omega \mid \mathfrak{c} \text{ is causal}\}$ carries a final coalgebra for the functor $FX = (A \times X)^B$. For every Mealy machine $m\colon X \to (A \times X)^B$, the coinductive extension $[\![-]\!]\colon X \to \Gamma(B^\omega, A^\omega)$ assigns to each state $x \in X$ and each input stream $b_0 b_1 b_2 \cdots \in B^\omega$ the output stream $a_0 a_1 a_2 \cdots \in A^\omega$ whenever $x \xrightarrow{b_0 | a_0} x_1 \xrightarrow{b_1 | a_1} x_2 \xrightarrow{b_2 | a_2} \ldots$

2.1 System Specifications

Different kinds of transition systems, like stream systems or Mealy machines, can be specified by means of algebraic specification languages. The syntax is given by an *algebraic signature* Σ, namely a collection of operation symbols $\{f_i \mid i \in I\}$ where each operator f_i has a (finite) arity $n_i \in \mathbb{N}$. For a set X, $T_\Sigma X$ denotes the set of Σ-terms with variables over X. The set of closed Σ-terms is denoted by $T_\Sigma \emptyset$. We omit the subscript when Σ is clear from the context.

A standard way to define the operational semantics of these languages is by means of structural operational semantics (SOS) [12]. In this approach, the semantics of each of the operators is described by syntactic rules, and the behaviour of a composite system is given in terms of the behaviour of its components. We recall *stream GSOS* [10], a specification format for stream systems.

Definition 2.6. *A stream GSOS rule* r *for a signature* Σ *and a set* A *is a rule*

$$\frac{x_1 \xrightarrow{a_1} x_1' \quad \cdots \quad x_n \xrightarrow{a_n} x_n'}{f(x_1, \ldots, x_n) \xrightarrow{a} t} \tag{2}$$

where $f \in \Sigma$ *with arity* n, $x_1, \ldots, x_n, x_1', \ldots, x_n'$ *are pairwise distinct variables,* t *is a term built over variables* $\{x_1, \ldots, x_n, x_1', \ldots, x_n'\}$ *and* $a, a_1, \ldots, a_n \in A$. *We say that* r *is triggered by* $(a_1, \ldots, a_n) \in A^n$.

A stream GSOS specification is a tuple (Σ, A, R) *where* Σ *is a signature,* A *is a set of actions and* R *is a set of stream GSOS rules for* Σ *and* A *s.t. for each* $f \in \Sigma$ *of arity* n *and each tuple* $(a_1, \ldots, a_n) \in A^n$, *there is only one rule* $r \in R$ *for* f *that is triggered by* $(a_1, \ldots, a_n)$.

A stream GSOS specification allows us to extend any given stream system $\langle o, d \rangle : X \to A \times X$ to a stream system $\overline{\langle o, d \rangle} : TX \to A \times TX$, by induction: the base case is given by $\langle o, d \rangle$, and the inductive cases by the specification. This construction can be defined formally in terms of proof trees, or by coalgebraic means; we adopt the latter approach, which is recalled later in this section.

There are two important uses of the above construction: (A) applying it to the (unique) stream system carried by the empty set $\emptyset$ yields a stream system over closed terms, i.e., of the form $T\emptyset \to A \times T\emptyset$; (B) applying the construction to the final coalgebra yields a stream system of the form $TA^\omega \to A \times TA^\omega$. The coinductive extension $[\![-]\!] : TA^\omega \to A^\omega$ of this stream system is, intuitively, the interpretation of the operations in Σ on streams in A^ω.

$$\frac{}{a \xrightarrow{a} a} \, \forall a \in A \qquad \frac{x \xrightarrow{a} x' \quad y \xrightarrow{b} y'}{\mathsf{alt}(x, y) \xrightarrow{a} \mathsf{alt}(y', x')} \, \forall a, b \in A$$

Fig. 2. The GSOS-rules of our running example   **Fig. 3.** A stream system

Example 2.1. Let (Σ, A, R) be a stream GSOS specification where the signature Σ consists of constants $\{\mathsf{a} \mid a \in A\}$ and a binary operation alt. The set R contains the rules in Fig. 2. For an instance of (A), the term $\mathsf{alt}(\mathsf{a}, \mathsf{alt}(\mathsf{b}, \mathsf{c})) \in T\emptyset$ defines the stream system depicted in Fig. 3. For an instance of (B), the operation $\mathsf{alt} : A^\omega \times A^\omega \to A^\omega$ maps streams $a_0 a_1 a_2 \ldots, b_0 b_1 b_2 \ldots$ to $a_0 b_1 a_2 b_2 \ldots$.

Example 2.2. We now consider the specification $(\Sigma, \mathbb{R}, R)$ which is the fragment of the *stream calculus* [17,18] consisting of the constants $n \in \mathbb{R}$ and the binary operators *sum* $\oplus$ and *(convolution) product* $\otimes$. The set R is defined in Fig. 1(a). For an example of (A), consider $n \oplus m \xrightarrow{n+m} 0 \oplus 0 \xrightarrow{0} 0 \oplus 0 \xrightarrow{0} \ldots$. For (B), the induced operation $\oplus : \mathbb{R}^\omega \times \mathbb{R}^\omega \to \mathbb{R}^\omega$ is the pointwise sum of streams, i.e., it maps any two streams $n_0 n_1 \ldots, m_0 m_1 \ldots$ to $(n_0 + m_0)(n_1 + m_1) \ldots$.

Definition 2.7. *We say that a stream GSOS rule r as in (2) is* monadic *if t is a term built over variables $\{x'_1, \ldots, x'_n\}$. A stream GSOS specification is* monadic *if all its rules are monadic.*

The specification of Example 2.1 satisfies the monadic stream GSOS format, while the one of Example 2.2 does not since, in the rules for $\otimes$, the variable y occurs in the arriving state of the conclusion.

The notions introduced above for stream GSOS, as well as the analogous ones for standard (labeled transition systems) GSOS [5], can be reformulated in an abstract framework – the so-called *abstract GSOS* [10,19] – that will be pivotal for the proof of our main result.

In this setting, signatures are represented by *polynomial functors*: a signature Σ corresponds to the polynomial functor $\Sigma X = \coprod_{i \in I} X^{n_i}$. For instance, the signature Σ in Example 2.1 corresponds to the functor $\Sigma X = A + (X \times X)$, while the signature of Example 2.2 corresponds to the functor $\Sigma X = \mathbb{R} + (X \times X) + (X \times X)$. Models of a signature are seen as algebras for the corresponding functor.

Definition 2.8. *Given a functor $F\colon Set \to Set$, an* F-algebra *is a pair (X, d), where X is the* carrier *set and $d\colon FX \to X$ is a function. An algebra homomorphism* from an F-algebra (X, d) to an F-algebra (Y, d') *is a map $h\colon X \to Y$ such that $h \circ d = d' \circ Fh$.*

Particularly interesting are *initial algebras*: an F-algebra is called initial if there exists a unique algebra homomorphism from it to every F-algebra. For a functor corresponding to a signature Σ, the initial algebra is $(T\emptyset, \kappa)$ where $\kappa\colon \Sigma T\emptyset \to T\emptyset$ maps, for each $i \in I$, the tuple of closed terms $t_1, \ldots t_{n_i}$ to the closed term $f_i(t_1, \ldots t_{n_i})$. For every set X, we can define in a similar way $\kappa_X\colon \Sigma TX \to TX$. The *free monad over* Σ consists of the endofunctor $T\colon Set \to Set$, mapping every set X to TX, together with the natural transformations $\eta\colon Id \Longrightarrow T$ (interpretation of variables as terms) and $\mu\colon TT \Longrightarrow T$ (glueing terms built of terms). Given an algebra $\sigma\colon \Sigma Y \to Y$, for any function $f\colon X \to Y$ there is a unique algebra homomorphism $f^\dagger\colon TX \to Y$ from (TX, κ_X) to (Y, σ). In particular, the identity function $id\colon X \to X$ induces a unique algebra homomorphism from TX to X, which we denote by $\sigma^\sharp\colon TX \to X$; this is the interpretation of terms in σ.

Definition 2.9. *An* abstract GSOS specification *(of Σ over F) is a natural transformation $\lambda\colon \Sigma(Id \times F) \Longrightarrow FT$. A* monadic abstract GSOS specification *(in short, monadic specification) is a natural transformation $\lambda\colon \Sigma F \Longrightarrow FT$.*

By instantiating the functor F in the above definition to the functor for streams ($FX = A \times X$) one obtains all and only the stream GSOS specifications. Instead, by taking the functor for Mealy machines ($FX = (A \times X)^B$) one obtains the Mealy GSOS format [10]: for the sake of brevity, we do not report the concrete definition here but this notion will be important in Sect. 5 where, to deal with open terms, we transform stream specifications into Mealy GSOS specifications.

Example 2.3. For every set X, the rules in Example 2.1 define a function λ_X : $A + (A \times X) \times (A \times X) \to (A \times T_\Sigma X)$ as follows: each $a \in A$ is mapped to (a, a) and each pair $(a, x'), (b, y') \in (A \times X) \times (A \times X)$ is mapped to $(a, \mathsf{alt}(y', x'))$ [10].

We focus on monadic distributive laws for most of the paper, and since they are slightly simpler than abstract GSOS specifications, we only recall the relevant concepts for monadic distributive laws. However, we note that the concepts below can be extended to abstract GSOS specifications; see, e.g., [4, 10] for details.

A monadic abstract GSOS specification induces a distributive law $\rho \colon TF \Longrightarrow FT$. This distributive law allows us to extend any F-coalgebra $d \colon X \to FX$ to an F-coalgebra on terms:

$$TX \xrightarrow{Td} TFX \xrightarrow{\rho_X} FTX$$

This construction generalises and formalises the aforementioned extension of stream systems to terms by means of a stream GSOS specification. In particular, (A) the unique coalgebra on the empty set $! \colon \emptyset \to F\emptyset$ yields an F-coalgebra on closed terms $T\emptyset \to FT\emptyset$. If F has a final coalgebra (Z, ζ), the unique morphism $[\![-]\!]_c \colon T\emptyset \to Z$ defines the *semantics of closed terms*.

$$
\begin{array}{ccccc}
T\emptyset & \xrightarrow{T!} & TF\emptyset & \xrightarrow{\rho_\emptyset} & FT\emptyset \\
{\scriptstyle [\![-]\!]_c} \downarrow & & (A) & & \downarrow {\scriptstyle F[\![-]\!]_c} \\
Z & & \xrightarrow{\ \ \ \zeta\ \ \ } & & FZ
\end{array}
\qquad
\begin{array}{ccccc}
TZ & \xrightarrow{T\zeta} & TFZ & \xrightarrow{\rho_Z} & FTZ \\
{\scriptstyle [\![-]\!]_a} \downarrow & & (B) & & \downarrow {\scriptstyle F[\![-]\!]_a} \\
Z & & \xrightarrow{\ \ \ \zeta\ \ \ } & & FZ
\end{array}
$$

Further (B), the final coalgebra (Z, ζ) yields a coalgebra on TZ. By finality, we then obtain a T-algebra over the final F-coalgebra, which we denote by $[\![-]\!]_a \colon TZ \to Z$ and we call it the *abstract semantics*. We define the *algebra induced by* λ as the Σ-algebra $\sigma \colon \Sigma Z \to Z$ given by

$$\Sigma Z \xrightarrow{\Sigma \eta_Z} \Sigma T Z \xrightarrow{\kappa_Z} TZ \xrightarrow{[\![-]\!]_a} Z \, . \tag{3}$$

3 Making Arbitrary Stream GSOS Specifications Monadic

The results presented in the next section are restricted to monadic specifications, but one can prove them for arbitrary GSOS specifications by exploiting some auxiliary operators, introduced in [8] with the name of *buffer*. Theorem 6.1 in Sect. 6 only holds for monadic GSOS specifications. This does not restrict the applicability of our approach: as we show below, arbitrary stream GSOS specifications can be turned into monadic ones.

Let (Σ, A, R) be a stream GSOS specification. The extended signature $\tilde{\Sigma}$ is given by $\{\tilde{f} \mid f \in \Sigma\} \cup \{a._- \mid a \in A\}$. The set of rules $\tilde{R}$ is defined as follows:

– For all $a, b \in A$, $\tilde{R}$ contains the following rule

$$\frac{x \xrightarrow{b} x'}{a.x \xrightarrow{a} b.x'} \tag{4}$$

– For each rule $r = \dfrac{x_1 \xrightarrow{a_1} x_1' \quad \cdots \quad x_n \xrightarrow{a_n} x_n'}{f(x_1,\ldots,x_n) \xrightarrow{a} t(x_1,\ldots,x_n,x_1',\ldots,x_n')} \in R$, the set $\tilde{R}$ contains

$$\tilde{r} = \frac{x_1 \xrightarrow{a_1} x_1' \quad \cdots \quad x_n \xrightarrow{a_n} x_n'}{\tilde{f}(x_1,\ldots,x_n) \xrightarrow{a} \tilde{t}(a_1.x_1',\ldots,a_n.x_n',x_1',\ldots,x_n')} \tag{5}$$

where $\tilde{t}$ is the term obtained from t by replacing each $g \in \Sigma$ by $\tilde{g} \in \tilde{\Sigma}$.

The specification $(\tilde{\Sigma}, A, \tilde{R})$ is now monadic and preserves the original semantics as stated by the following result.

Theorem 3.1. *Let (Σ, A, R) be a stream GSOS specification and $(\tilde{\Sigma}, A, \tilde{R})$ be the corresponding monadic one. Then, for all $t \in T_\Sigma \emptyset$, $t \sim \tilde{t}$.*

Example 3.1. Consider the non-monadic specification in Example 2.2. The corresponding monadic specification consists of the rules in Fig. 1(b) where, to keep the notation light, we used operation symbols f rather than $\tilde{f}$.

4   Pointwise Extensions of Monadic GSOS Specifications

The first step to deal with the semantics of open terms induced by a stream GSOS specification is to transform the latter into a Mealy GSOS specification. We follow the approach in [8] which is defined for arbitrary GSOS but, as motivated in Sect. 3, we restrict our attention to monadic specifications.

Let (Σ, A, R) be a monadic stream GSOS specification and B some input alphabet. The corresponding monadic Mealy GSOS specification is a tuple $(\Sigma, A, B, \overline{R})$, where $\overline{R}$ is the least set of Mealy rules which contains, for each stream GSOS rule $r = \dfrac{x_1 \xrightarrow{a_1} x_1' \quad \cdots \quad x_n \xrightarrow{a_n} x_n'}{f(x_1,\ldots,x_n) \xrightarrow{a} t(x_1',\ldots,x_n')} \in R$ and $b \in B$, the Mealy rule $\overline{r}_b$ defined by

$$\overline{r}_b = \frac{x_1 \xrightarrow{b|a_1} x_1' \quad \cdots \quad x_n \xrightarrow{b|a_n} x_n'}{f(x_1,\ldots,x_n) \xrightarrow{b|a} t(x_1',\ldots,x_n')} \tag{6}$$

An example of this construction is shown in Fig. 1(c).

Recall from Sect. 2 that any abstract GSOS specification induces a Σ-algebra on the final F-coalgebra. Let $\sigma \colon \Sigma A^\omega \to A^\omega$ be the algebra induced by the stream specification and $\overline{\sigma} \colon \Sigma \Gamma(B^\omega, A^\omega) \to \Gamma(B^\omega, A^\omega)$ the one induced by the corresponding Mealy specification. Theorem 4.1, at the end of this section, informs us that $\overline{\sigma}$ is the *pointwise extension* of σ.

Definition 4.1. *Let* $g: (A^\omega)^n \to A^\omega$ *and* $\bar{g}: (\Gamma(B^\omega, A^\omega))^n \to \Gamma(B^\omega, A^\omega)$ *be two functions. We say that* $\bar{g}$ *is the* pointwise extension *of* g *iff for all* $c_1, \ldots, c_n \in \Gamma(B^\omega, A^\omega)$ *and* $\beta \in B^\omega$, $\bar{g}(c_1, \ldots, c_n)(\beta) = g(c_1(\beta), \ldots, c_n(\beta))$. *This notion is lifted in the obvious way to* Σ-*algebras for an arbitrary signature* Σ.

Example 4.1. Recall the operation $\oplus: A^\omega \times A^\omega \to A^\omega$ from Example 2.2 that arises from the specification in Fig. 1(a) (it is easy to see that the same operation also arises from the monadic specification in Fig. 1(b)). Its pointwise extension $\bar{\oplus}: \Gamma(B^\omega, \mathbb{R}^\omega) \times \Gamma(B^\omega, \mathbb{R}^\omega) \to \Gamma(B^\omega, \mathbb{R}^\omega)$ is defined for all $c_1, c_2 \in \Gamma(B^\omega, \mathbb{R}^\omega)$ and $\beta \in B^\omega$ as $(c_1 \bar{\oplus} c_2)(\beta) = c_1(\beta) \oplus c_2(\beta)$. Theorem 4.1 tells us that $\bar{\oplus}$ arises from the corresponding Mealy GSOS specification (Fig. 1(c)).

In [8], the construction in (6) is generalised from stream specifications to arbitrary abstract GSOS. The key categorical tool is the notion of *costrength* for an endofunctor $F: Set \to Set$. Given two sets B and X, we first define $\epsilon^b: X^B \to X$ as $\epsilon^b(f) = f(b)$ for all $b \in B$. Then, $cs^F_{B,X}: F(X^B) \to (FX)^B$ is a natural map in B and X, given by $cs^F_{B,X}(t)(b) = (F\epsilon^b)(t)$.

Now, given a monadic specification $\lambda: \Sigma F \Longrightarrow FT$, we define $\bar{\lambda}: \Sigma(F^B) \Longrightarrow (FT)^B$ as the natural transformation that is defined for all sets X by

$$\Sigma(FX)^B \xrightarrow{\;cs^\Sigma_{B,FX}\;} (\Sigma FX)^B \xrightarrow{\;\lambda^B_X\;} (FTX)^B \; . \tag{7}$$

Observe that $\bar{\lambda}$ is also a monadic specification, but for the functor F^B rather than the functor F. The reader can easily check that for F being the stream functor $FX = A \times X$, the resulting $\bar{\lambda}$ is indeed the Mealy specification corresponding to λ as defined in (6).

It is worth to note that the construction of $\bar{\lambda}$ for an arbitrary abstract GSOS $\lambda: \Sigma(Id \times F) \Longrightarrow FT$, rather than a monadic one, would not work as in (7). The solution devised in [8] consists of introducing some auxiliary operators as already discussed in Sect. 3. The following result has been proved in [8] for arbitrary abstract GSOS, with these auxiliary operators. Our formulation is restricted to monadic specifications.

Theorem 4.1. *Let* F *be a functor with a final coalgebra* (Z, ζ), *and let* $(\bar{Z}, \bar{\zeta})$ *be a final* F^B-*coalgebra. Let* $\lambda: \Sigma F \Longrightarrow FT$ *be a monadic distributive law, and* $\sigma: \Sigma Z \to Z$ *the algebra induced by it. The algebra* $\bar{\sigma}: \Sigma\bar{Z} \to \bar{Z}$ *induced by* $\bar{\lambda}$ *is a pointwise extension of* σ.

In the theorem above, the notion of pointwise extension should be understood as a generalisation of Definition 4.1 to arbitrary final F and F^B-coalgebras. This generalised notion, that has been introduced in [8], will not play a role for our paper where F is fixed to be the stream functor $FX = A \times X$.

5   Mealy Machines over Open Terms

We now consider the problem of defining a semantics for the set of open terms TV for a fixed set of variables V. Our approach is based on the results in the previous sections: we transform a monadic GSOS specification for streams with outputs in A into a Mealy machine with inputs in $A^{\mathcal{V}}$ and outputs in A, i.e., a coalgebra for the functor $FX = (A \times X)^{A^{\mathcal{V}}}$. The coinductive extension of this Mealy machine provides the open semantics: for each open term $t \in T\mathcal{V}$ and variable assignment $\psi \colon \mathcal{V} \to A^{\omega}$, it gives an appropriate output stream in A^{ω}. This is computed in a stepwise manner: for an input $\varsigma \colon \mathcal{V} \to A$, representing "one step" of a variable assignment ψ, we obtain one step of the output stream.

We start by defining a Mealy machine $c \colon \mathcal{V} \to (A \times \mathcal{V})^{A^{\mathcal{V}}}$ on the set of variables $\mathcal{V}$ as on the left below, for all $\mathcal{X} \in \mathcal{V}$ and $\varsigma \in A^{\mathcal{V}}$:

$$c(\mathcal{X})(\varsigma) = (\varsigma(\mathcal{X}), \mathcal{X}) \qquad \mathcal{X} \overset{\curvearrowright}{} \varsigma|\varsigma(\mathcal{X}) \tag{8}$$

Concretely, this machine has variables as states and for each $\varsigma \colon \mathcal{V} \to A$ a self-loop, as depicted on the right. Now, let $\lambda \colon \Sigma(A \times -) \Rightarrow A \times T$ be a monadic stream specification and $\bar{\lambda} \colon \Sigma((A\times-)^{A^{\mathcal{V}}}) \Rightarrow (A \times T(-))^{A^{\mathcal{V}}}$ be the induced Mealy specification, as defined in (7). As mentioned in Sect. 2, $\bar{\lambda}$ defines a distributive law $\rho \colon T((A \times -)^{A^{\mathcal{V}}}) \Rightarrow (A \times T(-))^{A^{\mathcal{V}}}$, which allows to extend c (see (8)) to a coalgebra $m_{\lambda} \colon T\mathcal{V} \to (A \times T\mathcal{V})^{A^{\mathcal{V}}}$, given by

$$T\mathcal{V} \xrightarrow{\ Tc\ } T(A \times \mathcal{V})^{A^{\mathcal{V}}} \xrightarrow{\ \rho_{\mathcal{V}}\ } (A \times T\mathcal{V})^{A^{\mathcal{V}}}. \tag{9}$$

This is the Mealy machine of interest.

Example 5.1. Consider the stream specification λ of the operation alt, given in Example 2.1. The states of the Mealy machine m_{λ} are the open terms $T\mathcal{V}$. The transitions of terms are defined by the set of rules

$$\frac{}{\mathsf{a} \xrightarrow{\varsigma|a} \mathsf{a}} \qquad \frac{x \xrightarrow{\varsigma|a} x' \quad y \xrightarrow{\varsigma|b} y'}{\mathsf{alt}(x,y) \xrightarrow{\varsigma|a} \mathsf{alt}(y',x')} \qquad \text{for all } \varsigma \colon \mathcal{V} \to A \text{ and } a,b \in A$$

together with the transitions for the variables as in (8). For instance, for each $\mathcal{X}, \mathcal{Y}, \mathcal{Z} \in \mathcal{V}$ and all $\varsigma, \varsigma' \colon \mathcal{V} \to A$, we have the following transitions in m_{λ}:

$$\mathsf{alt}(\mathcal{X}, \mathsf{alt}(\mathcal{Y}, \mathcal{Z}))$$
$$\varsigma|\varsigma(\mathcal{X}) \Big(\qquad \Big) \varsigma'|\varsigma'(\mathcal{Z})$$
$$\mathsf{alt}(\mathsf{alt}(\mathcal{Z}, \mathcal{Y}), \mathcal{X})$$

Example 5.2. For the fragment of the stream calculus introduced in Example 2.2, the Mealy machine over open terms is defined by the rules in Fig. 1(d). Below we draw the Mealy machines of some open terms that will be useful later.

$$\begin{array}{cccc}
\varsigma|\varsigma(\mathcal{X})+\varsigma(\mathcal{Y}) & \varsigma|\varsigma(\mathcal{Y})+\varsigma(\mathcal{X}) & \varsigma|(\varsigma(\mathcal{X})+\varsigma(\mathcal{Y}))+\varsigma(\mathcal{Z}) & \varsigma|\varsigma(\mathcal{X})+(\varsigma(\mathcal{Y})+\varsigma(\mathcal{Z})) \\
\curvearrowright & \curvearrowright & \curvearrowright & \curvearrowright \\
\mathcal{X} \oplus \mathcal{Y} & \mathcal{Y} \oplus \mathcal{X} & (\mathcal{X} \oplus \mathcal{Y}) \oplus \mathcal{Z} & \mathcal{X} \oplus (\mathcal{Y} \oplus \mathcal{Z})
\end{array}$$

We define the open semantics below by the coinductive extension of m_λ. Let $\tilde{\Gamma} = \Gamma((A^\mathcal{V})^\omega, A^\omega)$ be the set of causal functions $\mathfrak{c}: (A^\mathcal{V})^\omega \to A^\omega$, which is the carrier of the final coalgebra for the functor $FX = (A \times X)^{A^\mathcal{V}}$. Notice that a function $\mathfrak{c}: (A^\mathcal{V})^\omega \to A^\omega$ can equivalently be presented as a function $\tilde{\mathfrak{c}}: (A^\omega)^\mathcal{V} \to A^\omega$ (swapping the arguments in the domain). Given such a function $\mathfrak{c}: (A^\mathcal{V})^\omega \to A^\omega$ and a function $\psi: \mathcal{V} \to A^\omega$, in the sequel, we sometimes abuse of notation by writing $\mathfrak{c}(\psi)$ where we formally mean $\tilde{\mathfrak{c}}(\psi)$.

Definition 5.1. *Let $\lambda: \Sigma(A \times -) \Rightarrow A \times T$ be a monadic stream GSOS specification. The* open semantics *of λ is the coinductive extension $[\![-]\!]_o: T\mathcal{V} \to \tilde{\Gamma}$ of the Mealy machine $m_\lambda: T\mathcal{V} \to (A \times T\mathcal{V})^{A^\mathcal{V}}$ defined in (9).*

Behavioural equivalence of open terms can now be checked by means of bisimulations on Mealy machines (Definition 2.4). We define *open bisimilarity*, denoted by $\sim_o$, as the greatest bisimulation on m_λ. Obviously, for all open terms $t_1, t_2 \in T\mathcal{V}$ it holds that $t_1 \sim_o t_2$ iff $[\![t_1]\!]_o = [\![t_2]\!]_o$. The following result provides another useful characterisation of $[\![-]\!]_o$.

Lemma 5.1. *Let λ be a monadic stream GSOS specification, with induced algebra $\sigma: \Sigma A^\omega \to A^\omega$. Let $\bar{\lambda}$ be the corresponding Mealy specification, with induced algebra $\bar{\sigma}: \Sigma\tilde{\Gamma} \to \tilde{\Gamma}$. Then the open semantics $[\![-]\!]_o$ is the unique homomorphism making the diagram below commute:*

$$
\begin{array}{ccc}
\Sigma T\mathcal{V} & \xrightarrow{\ \Sigma[\![-]\!]_o\ } & \Sigma\tilde{\Gamma} \\[2pt]
{\scriptstyle \kappa_\mathcal{V}}\downarrow & & \downarrow{\scriptstyle \bar{\sigma}} \\[2pt]
T\mathcal{V} & \xrightarrow{\ [\![-]\!]_o\ } & \tilde{\Gamma} \\[2pt]
{\scriptstyle \eta_\mathcal{V}}\uparrow & \nearrow{\scriptstyle proj} & \\[2pt]
\mathcal{V} & &
\end{array}
\qquad (10)
$$

where η and κ are defined by initiality (Sect. 2), and for each $\mathcal{X} \in \mathcal{V}$ and $\psi: \mathcal{V} \to A^\omega$, $proj(\mathcal{X})(\psi) = \psi(\mathcal{X})$.

Observe that, by virtue of Theorem 4.1, the algebra $\bar{\sigma}$ is the pointwise extension of σ. This fact will be useful in the next section to relate $\sim_o$ with bisimilarity on the original stream system.

5.1 Abstract, Open and Closed Semantics

Recall from Sect. 2 the abstract semantics $[\![-]\!]_a: TA^\omega \to A^\omega$ arising as in (B) from a monadic stream specification λ. The following proposition is the key to prove Theorem 5.1 relating open bisimilarity and abstract semantics.

Proposition 5.1. *Let $[\![-]\!]_a$ and $[\![-]\!]_o$ be the abstract and open semantics respectively of a monadic stream GSOS specification λ. For any $t \in T\mathcal{V}$, $\psi: \mathcal{V} \to A^\omega$:*

$$[\![t]\!]_o(\psi) = [\![(T\psi)(t)]\!]_a.$$

As a simple consequence, we obtain the following characterization of $\sim_o$.

Theorem 5.1. *For all $t_1, t_2 \in TV$, $[\![t_1]\!]_o = [\![t_2]\!]_o$ iff for all $\psi\colon V \to A^\omega$: $[\![T\psi(t_1)]\!]_a = [\![T\psi(t_2)]\!]_a$.*

This is one of the main results of this paper: $T\psi(t_1)$ and $T\psi(t_2)$ are expressions in TA^ω built from symbols of the signature Σ and streams $\alpha_1, \ldots \alpha_n \in A^\omega$. By checking $t_1 \sim_o t_2$ one can prove that the two expressions are equivalent for all possible streams $\alpha_1, \ldots \alpha_n \in A^\omega$.

Example 5.3. By using the Mealy machine m_λ in Example 5.1, the relation

$$R = \{(\mathsf{alt}(\mathcal{X}, \mathsf{alt}(\mathcal{Y}, \mathcal{Z})), \mathsf{alt}(\mathcal{X}, \mathsf{alt}(\mathcal{W}, \mathcal{Z}))), (\mathsf{alt}(\mathsf{alt}(\mathcal{Z}, \mathcal{Y}), \mathcal{X}), \mathsf{alt}(\mathsf{alt}(\mathcal{Z}, \mathcal{W}), \mathcal{X}))\}$$

is easily verified to be a bisimulation (Definition 2.4). In particular this shows that $[\![\mathsf{alt}(\mathcal{X}, \mathsf{alt}(\mathcal{Y}, \mathcal{Z}))]\!]_o = [\![\mathsf{alt}(\mathcal{X}, \mathsf{alt}(\mathcal{W}, \mathcal{Z}))]\!]_o$. By Theorem 5.1, we have that $[\![T\psi(\mathsf{alt}(\mathcal{X}, \mathsf{alt}(\mathcal{Y}, \mathcal{Z})))]\!]_a = [\![T\psi(\mathsf{alt}(\mathcal{X}, \mathsf{alt}(\mathcal{W}, \mathcal{Z})))]\!]_a$ for all $\psi\colon V \to A^\omega$, i.e.,

$$\mathsf{alt}(\alpha_1, \mathsf{alt}(\alpha_2, \alpha_3)) \sim \mathsf{alt}(\alpha_1, \mathsf{alt}(\alpha_4; \alpha_3)) \text{ for all } \alpha_1, \alpha_2, \alpha_3, \alpha_4 \in A^\omega.$$

The above law can be understood as an equivalence of program schemes stating that one can always replace the stream α_2 by an arbitrary stream α_4, without changing the result.

Example 5.4. By using the Mealy machines in Example 5.2, it is easy to check that both $\{((\mathcal{X} \oplus \mathcal{Y}) \oplus \mathcal{Z}, \mathcal{X} \oplus (\mathcal{Y} \oplus \mathcal{Z}))\}$ and $\{(\mathcal{X} \oplus \mathcal{Y}, \mathcal{Y} \oplus \mathcal{X})\}$ are bisimulations. This means that $[\![(\mathcal{X} \oplus \mathcal{Y}) \oplus \mathcal{Z}]\!]_o = [\![\mathcal{X} \oplus (\mathcal{Y} \oplus \mathcal{Z})]\!]_o$ and $[\![\mathcal{X} \oplus \mathcal{Y}]\!]_o = [\![\mathcal{Y} \oplus \mathcal{X}]\!]_o$. By Theorem 5.1 we obtain associativity and commutativity of $\oplus$:

$$(\alpha_1 \oplus \alpha_2) \oplus \alpha_3 \sim \alpha_1 \oplus (\alpha_2 \oplus \alpha_3) \text{ and } \alpha_1 \oplus \alpha_2 \sim \alpha_2 \oplus \alpha_1 \text{ for all } \alpha_1, \alpha_2, \alpha_3 \in A^\omega.$$

Example 5.5. In a similar way, one can check that $\{((a+b).(\mathcal{X} \oplus \mathcal{Y}), a.\mathcal{X} \oplus b.\mathcal{Y}) \mid a, b \in \mathbb{R}\}$ is a bisimulation. This means that $[\![(a+b).(\mathcal{X} \oplus \mathcal{Y})]\!]_o = [\![a.\mathcal{X} \oplus b.\mathcal{Y}]\!]_o$ for all $a, b \in \mathbb{R}$ and, using again Theorem 5.1, we conclude that $(a+b).(\alpha_1 \oplus \alpha_2) \sim a.\alpha_1 \oplus b.\alpha_2$ for all $\alpha_1, \alpha_2 \in A^\omega$.

Often, equivalence of open terms is defined by relying on the equivalence of closed terms: two open terms are equivalent iff under all possible closed substitutions, the resulting closed terms are equivalent. For $\sim_o$, this property does not follow immediately by Theorem 5.1, where variables range over streams, i.e., elements of the final coalgebra. One could assume that all the behaviours of the final coalgebra are denoted by some term, however this restriction would rule out most of the languages we are aware of: in particular, the stream calculus that can express only the so-called rational streams [18].

The following theorem, that is the second main result of this paper, only requires that the stream GSOS specification is sufficiently expressive to describe arbitrary finite prefixes. We use that any closed substitution $\phi\colon V \to T\emptyset$ defines $\phi^\dagger\colon TV \to T\emptyset$ (see Sect. 2.1).

Theorem 5.2. *Suppose* $\lambda\colon \Sigma(A \times -) \Rightarrow A \times T_\Sigma$ *is a monadic stream GSOS specification which contains, for each* $a \in A$, *the prefix operator* $a.-$ *as specified in (4) in Sect. 3. Further, assume* $T\emptyset$ *is non-empty.*

Let $[\![-]\!]_c$ *and* $[\![-]\!]_o$ *be the closed and open semantics respectively of* λ. *Then for all* $t_1, t_2 \in TV$: $[\![t_1]\!]_o = [\![t_2]\!]_o$ *iff* $[\![\phi^\dagger(t_1)]\!]_c = [\![\phi^\dagger(t_2)]\!]_c$ *for all* $\phi\colon V \to T\emptyset$.

Example 5.6. The specification in Fig. 2 does not include the prefix operator, therefore it does not meet the assumptions of Theorem 5.2. Instead, the monadic GSOS specification in Fig. 1(b) contains the prefix. Recall from Example 5.5 that $(a + b).(\mathcal{X} \oplus \mathcal{Y}) \sim_o a.\mathcal{X} \oplus b.\mathcal{Y}$. Using Theorem 5.2, we can conclude that $(a + b).(t_1 \oplus t_2) \sim a.t_1 \oplus b.t_2$ for all $t_1, t_2 \in T\emptyset$.

6 Bisimulation Up-To Substitutions

In the previous section, we have shown that bisimulations on Mealy machines can be used to prove equivalences of open terms specified in the stream GSOS format. In this section we introduce *up-to substitutions*, an enhancement of the bisimulation proof method that allows to deal with smaller, often finite, relations. We also show that up-to substitutions can be effectively combined with other well-known up-to techniques such as up-to bisimilarity and up-to context.

Intuitively, in a bisimulation up-to substitutions $\mathcal{R}$, the states reached by a pair of states do not need to be related by $\mathcal{R}$, but rather by $\theta(\mathcal{R})$, for some substitution $\theta\colon V \to TV$. We give a concrete example. Suppose we extend the stream calculus of Example 2.2 with the operators f and g defined by the rules in Fig. 4. In Fig. 5, we have the pointwise extensions of these new operators. It should be clear that $f(\mathcal{X}) \sim g(\mathcal{X})$. To try to formally prove $f(\mathcal{X}) \sim g(\mathcal{X})$, consider the relation $\mathcal{R} = \{(f(\mathcal{X}), g(\mathcal{X}))\}$. For all $\varsigma\colon V \to A$, there are transitions $f(\mathcal{X}) \xrightarrow{\varsigma|\varsigma(\mathcal{X})} f(\mathcal{X} \oplus \mathcal{X})$ and $g(\mathcal{X}) \xrightarrow{\varsigma|\varsigma(\mathcal{X})} g(\mathcal{X} \oplus \mathcal{X})$. The outputs of both transitions coincide but the reached states are not in $\mathcal{R}$, hence $\mathcal{R}$ is not a bisimulation. However it is a bisimulation up-to substitutions, since the arriving states are related by $\theta(\mathcal{R})$, for some substitution θ mapping $\mathcal{X}$ to $\mathcal{X} \oplus \mathcal{X}$. In fact, without this technique, any bisimulation relating $f(\mathcal{X})$ and $g(\mathcal{X})$ should contain infinitely many pairs.

$$\frac{x \xrightarrow{a} x'}{f(x) \xrightarrow{a} f(x' \oplus x')} \qquad \frac{x \xrightarrow{a} x'}{g(x) \xrightarrow{a} g(x' \oplus x')} \qquad\qquad \frac{x \xrightarrow{\varsigma|a} x'}{f(x) \xrightarrow{\varsigma|a} f(x' \oplus x')} \qquad \frac{x \xrightarrow{\varsigma|a} x'}{g(x) \xrightarrow{\varsigma|a} g(x' \oplus x')}$$

Fig. 4. f and g, operators over streams   **Fig. 5.** Pointwise extensions of f and g.

In order to prove the soundness of this technique, as well as the fact that it can be safely combined with other known up-to techniques, we need to recall some notions of the theory of up-to techniques in lattices from [14]. Given a

Mealy machine (X, m), we consider the lattice $(\mathcal{P}(X \times X), \subseteq)$ of relations over X, ordered by inclusion, and the monotone map $\mathbf{b} \colon \mathcal{P}(X \times X) \to \mathcal{P}(X \times X)$ defined for all $\mathcal{R} \subseteq X \times X$ as

$$\mathbf{b}(\mathcal{R}) = \{(s, t) \in X \times X \mid \forall b \in B, o_s(b) = o_t(b) \text{ and } d_s(b) \, \mathcal{R} \, d_t(b)\}. \tag{11}$$

It is easy to see that post fixed points of $\mathbf{b}$, i.e., relations $\mathcal{R}$ such that $\mathcal{R} \subseteq \mathbf{b}(\mathcal{R})$, are exactly bisimulations for Mealy machines (Definition 2.4) and that its greatest fixed point is $\sim$.

For a monotone map $\mathbf{f} \colon \mathcal{P}(X \times X) \to \mathcal{P}(X \times X)$, a *bisimulation up-to* $\mathbf{f}$ is a relation $\mathcal{R}$ such that $\mathcal{R} \subseteq \mathbf{bf}(\mathcal{R})$. We say that $\mathbf{f}$ is *compatible with* $\mathbf{b}$ if $\mathbf{fb}(\mathcal{R}) \subseteq \mathbf{bf}(\mathcal{R})$ for all relations $\mathcal{R}$. Two results in [14] are pivotal for us: first, if $\mathbf{f}$ is compatible and $\mathcal{R} \subseteq \mathbf{bf}(\mathcal{R})$ then $\mathcal{R} \subseteq \sim$; second if $\mathbf{f}_1$ and $\mathbf{f}_2$ are compatible with $\mathbf{b}$ then $\mathbf{f}_1 \circ \mathbf{f}_2$ is compatible with $\mathbf{b}$. The first result informs us that bisimilarity can be proved by means of bisimulations up-to $\mathbf{f}$, whenever $\mathbf{f}$ is compatible. The second result states that compatible up-to techniques can be composed.

We now consider up-to techniques for the Mealy machine over open terms $(T\mathcal{V}, m_\lambda)$ as defined in Sect. 5. Recall that bisimilarity over this machine is called open bisimilarity, denoted by $\sim_o$. Up-to substitutions is the monotone function $(-)_{\forall \theta} \colon \mathcal{P}(T\mathcal{V} \times T\mathcal{V}) \to \mathcal{P}(T\mathcal{V} \times T\mathcal{V})$ mapping every $\mathcal{R} \subseteq T\mathcal{V} \times T\mathcal{V}$ to

$$(\mathcal{R})_{\forall \theta} = \{(\theta(t_1), \theta(t_2)) \mid \theta \colon \mathcal{V} \to T\mathcal{V} \text{ and } t_1 \, \mathcal{R} \, t_2\}.$$

Similarly, we define up-to context as the monotone function mapping every relation $\mathcal{R} \subseteq T\mathcal{V} \times T\mathcal{V}$ to its contextual closure $\mathcal{C}(\mathcal{R})$ and up-to (open) bisimilarity as the function mapping $\mathcal{R}$ to $\sim_o \mathcal{R} \sim_o = \{(t_1, t_2) \mid \exists t_1', t_2' \text{ s.t. } t_1 \sim_o t_1' \, \mathcal{R} \, t_2' \sim_o t_2\}$.

Compatibility with $\mathbf{b}$ of up-to context and up-to bisimilarity hold immediately by the results in [6]. For the novel technique, up-to substitutions, we have:

Theorem 6.1. *The function* $(-)_{\forall \theta}$ *is compatible with* $\mathbf{b}$.

As a consequence of the above theorem and the results in [14], up-to substitutions can be used in combination with up-to bisimilarity and up-to context (as well as any another compatible up-to technique) to prove open bisimilarity. We will show this in the next, concluding example, for which a last remark is useful: the theory in [14] also ensures that if $\mathbf{f}$ is compatible with $\mathbf{b}$, then $\mathbf{f}(\sim) \subseteq \sim$. By Theorem 6.1, this means that $(\sim_o)_{\forall \theta} \subseteq \sim_o$. The same obviously holds for the contextual closure: $\mathcal{C}(\sim_o) \subseteq \sim_o$.

Example 6.1. We prove that the convolution product $\otimes$ distributes over the sum $\oplus$, i.e., $\alpha_1 \otimes (\alpha_2 \oplus \alpha_3) \sim (\alpha_1 \otimes \alpha_2) \oplus (\alpha_1 \otimes \alpha_3)$ for all streams $\alpha_1, \alpha_2, \alpha_3 \in \mathbb{R}^\omega$. By Theorems 5.1 and 6.1, to prove our statement it is enough to show that $\mathcal{R} = \{(\mathcal{X} \otimes (\mathcal{Y} \oplus \mathcal{Z}), (\mathcal{X} \otimes \mathcal{Y}) \oplus (\mathcal{X} \otimes \mathcal{Z}))\}$ is a bisimulation up-to $\sim_o \mathcal{C}(\sim_o (-)_{\forall \theta} \sim_o) \sim_o$.

By rules in Fig. 1(d), for all $\varsigma \colon \mathcal{V} \to \mathbb{R}$, the transitions of the open terms are

- $\mathcal{X} \otimes (\mathcal{Y} \oplus \mathcal{Z}) \xrightarrow{\varsigma | \varsigma(\mathcal{X}) \times (\varsigma(\mathcal{Y}) + \varsigma(\mathcal{Z}))} (\varsigma(\mathcal{X}) \otimes (\mathcal{Y} \oplus \mathcal{Z})) \oplus (\mathcal{X} \otimes (\varsigma(\mathcal{Y}) + \varsigma(\mathcal{Z})).(\mathcal{Y} \oplus \mathcal{Z}))$
- $(\mathcal{X} \otimes \mathcal{Y}) \oplus (\mathcal{X} \otimes \mathcal{Z}) \xrightarrow{\varsigma | \varsigma(\mathcal{X}) \times \varsigma(\mathcal{Y}) + \varsigma(\mathcal{X}) \times \varsigma(\mathcal{Z})}$
  $((\varsigma(\mathcal{X}) \otimes \mathcal{Y}) \oplus (\mathcal{X} \otimes \varsigma(\mathcal{Y}).\mathcal{Y})) \oplus ((\varsigma(\mathcal{X}) \otimes \mathcal{Z}) \oplus (\mathcal{X} \otimes \varsigma(\mathcal{Z}).\mathcal{Z}))$

For the outputs, it is evident that $\varsigma(\mathcal{X}) \times (\varsigma(\mathcal{Y}) + \varsigma(\mathcal{Z})) = \varsigma(\mathcal{X}) \times \varsigma(\mathcal{Y}) + \varsigma(\mathcal{X}) \times \varsigma(\mathcal{Z})$. For the arriving states we need a few steps, where for all $\varsigma: V \to \mathbb{R}$ and $\mathcal{X} \in V$, $\varsigma(\mathcal{X})$ denotes either a real number (used as a prefix) or a constant of the syntax (Example 2.2).

(a) $\mathcal{X} \otimes (\varsigma(\mathcal{Y}).\mathcal{Y} \oplus \varsigma(\mathcal{Z}).\mathcal{Z}) \; \mathcal{R}_{\forall\theta} \; (\mathcal{X} \otimes \varsigma(\mathcal{Y}).\mathcal{Y}) \oplus (\mathcal{X} \otimes \varsigma(\mathcal{Z}).\mathcal{Z})$.

(b) By Example 5.5 and $\mathcal{C}(\sim_o) \subseteq \sim_o$, we have that:
$\mathcal{X} \otimes (\varsigma(\mathcal{Y}) + \varsigma(\mathcal{Z})).(\mathcal{Y} \oplus \mathcal{Z}) \sim_o \mathcal{X} \otimes (\varsigma(\mathcal{Y}).\mathcal{Y} \oplus \varsigma(\mathcal{Z}).\mathcal{Z})$.

(c) By (b) and (a):
$\mathcal{X} \otimes (\varsigma(\mathcal{Y}) + \varsigma(\mathcal{Z})).(\mathcal{Y} \oplus \mathcal{Z}) \sim_o \mathcal{R}_{\forall\theta} \sim_o (\mathcal{X} \otimes \varsigma(\mathcal{Y}).\mathcal{Y}) \oplus (\mathcal{X} \otimes \varsigma(\mathcal{Z}).\mathcal{Z})$.

(d) $\varsigma(\mathcal{X}) \otimes (\mathcal{Y} \oplus \mathcal{Z}) \; \mathcal{R}_{\forall\theta} \; (\varsigma(\mathcal{X}) \otimes \mathcal{Y}) \oplus (\varsigma(\mathcal{X}) \otimes \mathcal{Z})$.

(e) Using (d) and (c) with context $\mathcal{C} = \_ \oplus \_$:
$(\varsigma(\mathcal{X}) \otimes (\mathcal{Y} \oplus \mathcal{Z})) \oplus (\mathcal{X} \otimes (\varsigma(\mathcal{Y}) + \varsigma(\mathcal{Z})).(\mathcal{Y} \oplus \mathcal{Z}))$
$\mathcal{C}(\sim_o \mathcal{R}_{\forall\theta} \sim_o) \; ((\varsigma(\mathcal{X}) \otimes \mathcal{Y}) \oplus (\varsigma(\mathcal{X}) \otimes \mathcal{Z})) \oplus ((\mathcal{X} \otimes \varsigma(\mathcal{Y}).\mathcal{Y}) \oplus (\mathcal{X} \otimes \varsigma(\mathcal{Z}).\mathcal{Z}))$.

(f) By Example 5.4 (associativity and commutativity of $\oplus$) and $(\sim_o)_{\forall\rho} \subseteq \sim_o$:
$((\varsigma(\mathcal{X}) \otimes \mathcal{Y}) \oplus (\varsigma(\mathcal{X}) \oplus \mathcal{Z})) \oplus ((\mathcal{X} \otimes \varsigma(\mathcal{Y}).\mathcal{Y}) \oplus (\mathcal{X} \otimes \varsigma(\mathcal{Z})).\mathcal{Z}))$
$\sim_o ((\varsigma(\mathcal{X}) \otimes \mathcal{Y}) \oplus (\mathcal{X} \otimes \varsigma(\mathcal{Y}).\mathcal{Y})) \oplus ((\varsigma(\mathcal{X}) \otimes \mathcal{Z}) \oplus (\mathcal{X} \otimes \varsigma(\mathcal{Z}).\mathcal{Z}))$.

(g) By (e) and (f):
$(\varsigma(\mathcal{X}) \otimes (\mathcal{Y} \oplus \mathcal{Z})) \oplus (\mathcal{X} \times (\varsigma(\mathcal{Y}) + \varsigma(\mathcal{Z})).(\mathcal{Y} \oplus \mathcal{Z}))$
$\sim_o \mathcal{C}(\sim_o \mathcal{R}_{\forall\theta} \sim_o) \sim_o ((\varsigma(\mathcal{X}) \otimes \mathcal{Y}) \oplus (\mathcal{X} \otimes \varsigma(\mathcal{Y}).\mathcal{Y})) \oplus ((\varsigma(\mathcal{X}) \otimes \mathcal{Z}) \oplus (\mathcal{X} \otimes \varsigma(\mathcal{Z}).\mathcal{Z}))$.

7   Final Remarks

In this paper we have studied the semantics of open terms specified in the stream GSOS format. Our recipe consists in translating the stream specification into a Mealy specification giving semantics to all open terms. Remarkably, this semantics equates two open terms if and only if they are equivalent under all possible interpretations of variables as streams (Theorem 5.1) or under the interpretation of variables as closed terms (Theorem 5.2). Furthermore, semantic equivalence can be checked by means of the bisimulation proof method enhanced with a technique called up-to substitutions (Theorem 6.1).

Our work can be considered as a first step toward a (co)algebraic understanding of the semantics of open terms in the general setting of abstract GSOS [10,19]. While our approach exploits several peculiarities of the final coalgebra for stream systems, several intermediate results hold in the general setting: for instance, the construction in Sect. 3 transforming arbitrary stream GSOS specifications into monadic ones, seems to hold for arbitrary abstract GSOS. Another promising clue in this direction comes from the way we specified the semantics of variables in Sect. 5: it is reminiscent of the technique adopted in [2] for dealing with open terms of process calculi denoting labeled transition systems.

References

1. Aceto, L., Cimini, M., Ingólfsdóttir, A.: Proving the validity of equations in GSOS languages using rule-matching bisimilarity. MSCS **22**(2), 291–331 (2012)
2. Aceto, L., Fokkink, W., Ingolfsdottir, A., Luttik, B.: Finite equational bases in process algebra: results and open questions. In: Middeldorp, A., van Oostrom, V., van Raamsdonk, F., de Vrijer, R. (eds.) Processes, Terms and Cycles: Steps on the Road to Infinity. LNCS, vol. 3838, pp. 338–367. Springer, Heidelberg (2005). doi:10.1007/11601548_18
3. Baldan, P., Bracciali, A., Bruni, R.: A semantic framework for open processes. Theor. Comput. Sci. **389**(3), 446–483 (2007)
4. Bartels, F.: On generalised coinduction and probabilistic specification formats. Ph.D. thesis, CWI, Amsterdam (2004)
5. Bloom, B., Istrail, S., Meyer, A.R.: Bisimulation can't be traced. J. ACM **42**(1), 232–268 (1995)
6. Bonchi, F., Petrisan, D., Pous, D., Rot, J.: A general account of coinduction up-to. Acta Informatica **54**(2), 127–190 (2017)
7. de Simone, R.: Higher-level synchronising devices in Meije-SCCS. Theor. Comput. Sci. **37**, 245–267 (1985)
8. Hansen, H.H., Klin, B.: Pointwise extensions of GSOS-defined operations. Math. Struct. Comput. Sci. **21**(2), 321–361 (2011)
9. Hansen, H.H., Rutten, J.J.M.M.: Symbolic synthesis of mealy machines from arithmetic bitstream functions. Sci. Ann. Comp. Sci. **20**, 97–130 (2010)
10. Klin, B.: Bialgebras for structural operational semantics: an introduction. Theor. Comput. Sci. **412**(38), 5043–5069 (2011)
11. Lucanu, D., Goriac, E.-I., Caltais, G., Roşu, G.: CIRC: a behavioral verification tool based on circular coinduction. In: Kurz, A., Lenisa, M., Tarlecki, A. (eds.) CALCO 2009. LNCS, vol. 5728, pp. 433–442. Springer, Heidelberg (2009). doi:10.1007/978-3-642-03741-2_30
12. Mousavi, M., Reniers, M., Groote, J.: SOS formats and meta-theory: 20 years after. Theor. Comput. Sci. **373**(3), 238–272 (2007)
13. Popescu, A., Gunter, E.L.: Incremental pattern-based coinduction for process algebra and its isabelle formalization. In: Ong, L. (ed.) FoSSaCS 2010. LNCS, vol. 6014, pp. 109–127. Springer, Heidelberg (2010). doi:10.1007/978-3-642-12032-9_9
14. Pous, D., Sangiorgi, D.: Enhancements of the bisimulation proof method. In: Advanced Topics in Bisimulation and Coinduction, Cambridge (2012)
15. Rensink, A.: Bisimilarity of open terms. Inf. Comput. **156**(1–2), 345–385 (2000)
16. Rutten, J.: Universal coalgebra: a theory of systems. TCS **249**(1), 3–80 (2000)
17. Rutten, J.: Elements of stream calculus (an extensive exercise in coinduction). ENTCS **45**, 358–423 (2001)
18. Rutten, J.: A tutorial on coinductive stream calculus and signal flow graphs. TCS **343**(3), 443–481 (2005)
19. Turi, D., Plotkin, G.D.: Towards a mathematical operational semantics. In: Proceedings of the LICS 1997, pp. 280–291 (1997)
20. Zantema, H., Endrullis, J.: Proving equality of streams automatically. In: Proceedings of RTA 2011, Novi Sad, Serbia, pp. 393–408 (2011)

Composing Families of Timed Automata

Guillermina Cledou[1,2]([✉]), José Proença[1,2], and Luis Soares Barbosa[1,2]

[1] HASLab, INESCTEC, Braga, Portugal
mgc@inesctec.pt, {jose.proenca,lsb}@di.uminho.pt
[2] Universidade do Minho, Braga, Portugal

Abstract. Featured Timed Automata (FTA) is a formalism that enables the verification of an entire Software Product Line (SPL), by capturing its behavior in a single model instead of product-by-product. However, it disregards compositional aspects inherent to SPL development. This paper introduces Interface FTA (IFTA), which extends FTA with variable interfaces that restrict the way automata can be composed, and with support for transitions with atomic multiple actions, simplifying the design. To support modular composition, a set of Reo connectors are modelled as IFTA. This separation of concerns increases reusability of functionality across products, and simplifies modelling, maintainability, and extension of SPLs. We show how IFTA can be easily translated into FTA and into networks of Timed Automata supported by UPPAAL. We illustrate this with a case study from the electronic government domain.

Keywords: Software Product Lines · Featured Timed Automata · Compositionality

1 Introduction

Software product lines (SPLs) enable the definition of families of systems where all members share a high percentage of common features while they differ in others. Among several formalisms developed to support SPLs, Featured Timed Automata (FTA) [5] model families of real-time systems in a single model. This enables the verification of the entire SPL instead of product-by-product.

G. Cledou—Supported by the European Regional Development Fund (ERDF) through the Operational Programme for Competitiveness and Internationalisation (COMPETE 2020), and by National Funds through the Portuguese funding agency, FCT, within project POCI-01-0145-FEDER-016826 and FCT grant PD/BD/52238/2013.

J. Proenca—Supported by FCT under grant SFRH/BPD/91908/2012.

L. Barbosa—Supported by the project SMARTEGOV: Harnessing EGOV for Smart Governance (Foundations, Methods, Tools)/NORTE-01-0145-FEDER-000037, supported by Norte Portugal Regional Operational Programme (NORTE 2020), under the PORTUGAL 2020 Partnership Agreement, through the European Regional Development Fund (ERDF).

M. Dastani and M. Sirjani (Eds.): FSEN 2017, LNCS 10522, pp. 51–66, 2017.
DOI: 10.1007/978-3-319-68972-2_4

However, FTA still need more modular and compositional techniques well suited to SPL-based development.

To address this issue, this paper proposes Interface FTA (IFTA), a mechanism enriching FTA with (1) interfaces that restrict the way multiple automata interact, and (2) transitions labelled with multiple actions that simplify the design. Interfaces are synchronisation actions that can be linked with interfaces from other automata when composing automata in parallel. IFTA can be composed by combining their feature models and linking interfaces, imposing new restrictions over them. The resulting IFTA can be exported to the UPPAAL real-time model checker to verify temporal properties, using either a network of parallel automata in UPPAAL, or by flattening the composed automata into a single one. The latter is better suited for IFTA with many multiple actions.

We illustrate the applicability of IFTA with a case study from the electronic government (e-government) domain, in particular, a family of licensing services. This services are present in most local governments, who are responsible for assessing requests and issuing licenses of various types. E.g., for providing public transport services, driving, construction, etc. Such services comprise a number of common functionality while they differ in a number of features, mostly due to specific local regulations.

The rest of this paper is structured as follows. Section 2 presents some background on FTA. Section 3 introduces IFTA. Section 4 presents a set of Reo connectors modeled as IFTA. Section 5 discusses a prototype tool to specify and manipulate IFTA. Section 6 presents the case study. Section 7 discusses related work, and Sect. 8 concludes.

2   Featured Timed Automata

This work builds on top of *Featured Timed Automata* (FTA) an extension to *Timed Automata*, introduced by Cordy et al. [5] to verify real-time systems parameterised by a variability model. This section provides an overview of FTA and their semantics, based on Cordy et al.

Informally, a Featured Timed Automaton is an automaton whose *edges* are enriched with *clocks*, *clock constraints* (CC), *synchronisation actions*, and *feature expressions* (FE). A *clock* $c \in C$ is a logical entity that captures the (continuous and dense) time that has passed since it was last reset. When a timed automaton evolves over time, all clocks are incremented simultaneously. A *clock constraint* is a logic condition over the value of a clock. A *synchronisation action* $a \in A$ is used to coordinate automata in parallel; an edge with an action a can only be taken when its dual action in a neighbor automaton is also on an edge that can be taken simultaneously. Finally, a *feature expression* (FE) is a logical constraint over a set of *features*. Each of these features denotes a unit of variability; by selecting a desired combination of features one can map an FTA into a Timed Automaton.

Figure 1 exemplifies a simple FTA with two locations, ℓ_0 and ℓ_1, with a clock c and two features cf and mk, standing for the support for brewing *coffee* and for

Fig. 1. Example of a Featured Timed Automata over the features cf and mk.

including *milk* in the coffee. Initially the automaton is in location ℓ_0, and it can evolve either by waiting for time to pass (incrementing the clock c) or by taking one of its two transitions to ℓ_1. The top transition, for example, is labelled by the action *coffee* and is only active when the feature cf is present. Taking this transition triggers the reset of the clock c back to 0, evolving to the state ℓ_1. Here it can again wait for the time to pass, but for at most 5 time units, determined by the invariant $c \leq 5$ in ℓ_1. The transition labelled with *brew* has a different guard: a clock constraint $c \geq 2$ that allows this transition to be taken only when the clock c is greater than 2. Finally, the lower expression [$fm = mk \rightarrow cf$] defines the *feature model*. I.e., how the features relate to each other. In this case the mk feature can only be selected when the cf feature is also selected.

We now formalize clock constraints, feature expressions, and the definition of FTA and its semantics.

Definition 1 (Clock Constraints (CC), valuation, and satisfaction). *A clock constraint over a set of clocks C, written $g \in CC(C)$ is defined by*

$$g ::= c < n \mid c \leq n \mid c = n \mid c > n \mid c \geq n \mid g \wedge g \mid \top \qquad \text{(clock constraint)}$$

where $c \in C$, and $n \in \mathbb{N}$.

A clock valuation η for a set of clocks C is a function $\eta \colon C \to \mathbb{R}_{\geq 0}$ that assigns each clock $c \in C$ to its current value ηc. We use $\mathbb{R}^C$ to refer to the set of all clock valuations over a set of clocks C. Let $\eta_0(c) = 0$ for all $c \in C$ be the initial clock valuation that sets to 0 all clocks in C. We use $\eta + d$, $d \in \mathbb{R}_{\geq 0}$, to denote the clock assignment that maps all $c \in C$ to $\eta(c) + d$, and let $[r \mapsto 0]\eta$, $r \subseteq C$, be the clock assignment that maps all clocks in r to 0 and agrees with η for all other clocks in $C \setminus r$.

The satisfaction of a clock constraint g by a clock valuation η, written $\eta \models g$, is defined as follows

$$
\begin{aligned}
\eta &\models \top && always \\
\eta &\models c \,\square\, n && if\ \eta(c) \,\square\, n \\
\eta &\models g_1 \wedge g_2 && if\ \eta \models g_1 \wedge \eta \models g_2
\end{aligned}
\qquad \text{(clock satisfaction)}
$$

where $\square \in \{<, \leq, =, >, \geq\}$.

Definition 2 (Feature Expressions (FE) and satisfaction). *A feature expression φ over a set of features F, written $\varphi \in FE(F)$, is defined by*

$$\varphi ::= f \mid \varphi \wedge \varphi \mid \varphi \vee \varphi \mid \neg \varphi \mid \top \qquad \text{(feature expression)}$$

where $f \in F$ is a feature. The other logical connectives can be encoded as usual: $\bot = \neg \top$; $\varphi_1 \rightarrow \varphi_2 = \neg \varphi_1 \vee \varphi_2$; and $\varphi_1 \leftrightarrow \varphi_2 = (\varphi_1 \rightarrow \varphi_2) \wedge (\varphi_2 \rightarrow \varphi_1)$.

Given a feature selection $FS \subseteq F$ over a set of features F, and a feature expression $\varphi \in FE(F)$, FS satisfies φ, noted $FS \models \varphi$, if

$$
\begin{array}{lll}
FS \models \top & \text{always} & \\
FS \models f & \Leftrightarrow f \in FS & \\
FS \models \varphi_1 \Diamond \varphi_2 & \Leftrightarrow FS \models \varphi_1 \Diamond FS \models \varphi_2 & \text{(FE satisfaction)} \\
FS \models \neg \varphi & \Leftrightarrow FS \not\models \varphi &
\end{array}
$$

where $\Diamond \in \{\wedge, \vee\}$.

Definition 3 (Featured Timed Automata (FTA) [5]**).** *An FTA is a tuple $\mathcal{A} = (L, L_0, A, C, F, E, Inv, fm, \gamma)$ where L is a finite set of locations, $L_0 \subseteq L$ is the set of initial locations, A is a finite set of synchronisation actions, C is a finite set of clocks, F is a finite set of features, E is a finite set of edges, $E \subseteq L \times CC(C) \times A \times 2^C \times L$, $Inv : L \rightarrow CC(C)$ is the invariant, a partial function that assigns CCs to locations, $fm \in FE(F)$ is a feature model defined as a Boolean formula over features in F, and $\gamma : E \rightarrow FE(F)$ is a total function that assigns feature expressions to edges.*

The semantics of FTA is given in terms of Featured Transition Systems (FTSs) [4]. An FTS extends Labelled Transition Systems with a set of features F, a feature model fm, and a total function γ that assigns FE to transitions.

Definition 4 (Semantics of FTA). *Let $\mathcal{A} = (L, L_0, A, C, F, E, Inv, fm, \gamma)$ be an FTA. The semantics of $\mathcal{A}$ is defined as an FTS $\langle S, S_0, A, T, F, fm, \gamma' \rangle$, where $S \subseteq L \times \mathbb{R}^C$ is the set of states, $S_0 = \{\langle \ell_0, \eta_0 \rangle \mid \ell_0 \in L_0\}$ is the set of initial states, $T \subseteq S \times (A \cup \mathbb{R}_{\geq 0}) \times S$ is the transition relation, with $(s_1, \alpha, s_2) \in T$, and $\gamma' : T \rightarrow FE(F)$ is a total function that assigns feature expressions to transitions. The transition relation and γ are defined as follows.*

$$\langle \ell, \eta \rangle \xrightarrow[\top]{d} \langle \ell, \eta + d \rangle \quad \text{if } \eta \models Inv(\ell) \text{ and } (\eta + d) \models Inv(\ell), \quad \text{for } d \in \mathbb{R}_{\geq 0} \quad (1)$$

$$\langle \ell, \eta \rangle \xrightarrow[\varphi]{a} \langle \ell', \eta' \rangle \qquad \text{if } \exists \ell \xrightarrow[\varphi]{g,a,r} \ell' \in E \quad s.t. \; \eta \models g, \; \eta \models Inv(l),$$

$$\eta' = [r \mapsto 0]\eta, \quad \text{and} \; \eta' \models Inv(\ell') \quad (2)$$

where $s_1 \xrightarrow[\varphi]{\alpha} s_2$ means that $(s_1, \alpha, s_2) \in T$ and $\gamma(s_1, \alpha, s_2) = \varphi$, for any $s_1, s_2 \in S$.

Notation: We write $L_{\mathcal{A}}$, $L_{0,\mathcal{A}}$, $A_{\mathcal{A}}$, etc., to denote the locations, initial locations, actions, etc., of an FTA $\mathcal{A}$, respectively. We write $\ell_1 \xrightarrow{cc,a,c}_{\mathcal{A}} \ell_2$ to denote that $(\ell_1, cc, a, c, \ell_2) \in E_{\mathcal{A}}$, and use $\ell_1 \xrightarrow[\varphi]{cc,a,c}_{\mathcal{A}} \ell_2$ to express that $\gamma_{\mathcal{A}}(\ell_1, cc, a, c, \ell_2) = \varphi$. We omit the subscript whenever automaton $\mathcal{A}$ is clear from the context. We use an analogous notation for elements of an FTS.

3 Interface Featured Timed Automata

Multiple FTAs can be composed and executed in parallel, using *synchronising actions* to synchronise edges from different parallel automata. This section introduces *interfaces* to FTA that: (1) makes this implicit notion of communication more explicit, and (2) allows multiple actions to be executed atomically in a transition. Synchronisation actions are lifted to so-called *ports*, which correspond to actions that can be linked with actions from other automata. Hence composition of IFTA is made by linking ports and by combining their variability models.

Definition 5 (Interface Featured Timed Automata). *An IFTA is a tuple $\mathcal{A} = (L, l_0, A, C, F, E, Inv, fm, \gamma)$ where L, C, F, Inv, fm, γ are defined as in Featured Timed Automata, there exists only one initial location l_0, $A = I \uplus O \uplus H$ is a finite set of actions, where I is a set of input ports, O is a set of output ports, and H is a set of hidden (internal) actions, and edges in E contain sets of actions instead of single actions ($E \subseteq L \times CC(C) \times \underline{\mathbf{2}}^A \times \mathbf{2}^C \times L$).*

We call *interface* of an IFTA $\mathcal{A}$ the set $\mathbb{P}_{\mathcal{A}} = I_{\mathcal{A}} \uplus O_{\mathcal{A}}$ of all input and output ports of an automaton. Given a port $p \in \mathbb{P}$ we write $p?$ and $p!$ to denote that p is an input or output port, respectively, following the same conventions as UPPAAL for actions, and write p instead of $\{p\}$ when clear from context. The lifting of actions into sets of actions will be relevant for the composition of automata. **Notation:** we use i, i_1, etc., and o, o_1, etc. to refer specifically to input and output ports of an IFTA, respectively. For any IFTA $\mathcal{A}$ it is possible to infer a feature expression for each action $a \in A_{\mathcal{A}}$ based on the feature expressions of the edges in which a appears. Intuitively, this feature expression determines the set of products requiring a.

Definition 6 (Feature Expression of an Action). *Given an IFTA $\mathcal{A}$, the feature expression of any action a is the disjunction of the feature expressions of all of its associated edges, defined as*

$$\widehat{\Gamma}_{\mathcal{A}}(a) = \bigvee \{\gamma_{\mathcal{A}}(\ell \xrightarrow{g,\omega,r}_{\mathcal{A}} \ell') \mid a \in \omega\} \qquad \text{(FE of an action)}$$

We say an IFTA $\mathcal{A}$ is *grounded*, if it has a total function associating a feature expression to each action $a \in A_{\mathcal{A}}$ that indicates the set of products where a was originally designed to be present in. Given an IFTA $\mathcal{A}$ we can construct a *grounded* $\mathcal{A}$ by incorporating a function Γ such that,

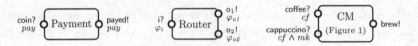

Fig. 2. Representation of 3 IFTA, depicting their interfaces (blue) and associated feature expressions. (Color figure online)

$\mathcal{A} = (L_\mathcal{A}, l_{0_\mathcal{A}}, A_\mathcal{A}, C_\mathcal{A}, Inv_\mathcal{A}, F_\mathcal{A}, fm_\mathcal{A}, \gamma_\mathcal{A}, \Gamma)$, where $\Gamma : A_\mathcal{A} \to FE(F_\mathcal{A})$ assigns a feature expression to each action of $\mathcal{A}$, and is constructed based on $\widehat{\Gamma}_\mathcal{A}$. From now on when referring to an IFTA we assume it is a grounded IFTA.

Figure 2 depicts the interfaces of 3 different IFTA. The leftmost is a payment machine that receives actions representing coins and publishes actions confirming the payment, whose actions are dependent on a feature called *pay*. The rightmost is the coffee machine from Fig. 1. Finally, the middle one depicts a connector *Router* that could be used to *combine* the payment and the coffee machines. This notion of *combining* IFTA is the core contribution of this work: how to reason about the modular composition of timed systems with variable interfaces. For example, let us assume the previous IFTA are connected by linking actions as follows: (payed,i), (o_1, coffee), and (o_2, cappuccino). In a real coffee machine, after a payment, the machine should allow to select only beverages supported, i.e., if the machine does not support cappuccino the user should not be able to select it and be charged. Similarly, the composed system here should not allow to derive a product with o_2 if cappuccino is not present. To achieve this, we need to impose additional restriction on the variability model of the composed system, since as it will be shown later in this section, combining the feature models of the composed IFTA through logical conjunction is not enough.

The semantics of IFTA is given in terms of FTSs, similarly to the semantics of FTA with the difference that transitions are now labelled with sets of actions. We formalize this as follows.

Definition 7 (Semantics of IFTA). *Let $\mathcal{A}$ be an IFTA, its semantics is an FTS $\mathcal{F} = (S, s_0, A, T, F, fm, \gamma)$, where S, A, F, fm, and γ are defined as in Definition 4, $s_0 = \langle \ell_0, \eta_0 \rangle$ is now the only initial state, and $T \subseteq S \times (2^A \cup \mathbb{R}_{\geq 0}) \times S$ now supports transitions labelled with sets of actions.*

We now introduce two operations: *product* and *synchronisation*, which are used to define the composition of IFTA. The *product* operation for IFTA, unlike the classical product of timed automata, is defined over IFTA with disjoint sets of actions, clocks and features, performing their transitions in an interleaving fashion.

Definition 8 (Product of IFTA). *Given two IFTA $\mathcal{A}_1$ and $\mathcal{A}_2$, with disjoint actions, clocks and features, the product of $\mathcal{A}_1$ and $\mathcal{A}_2$, denoted $\mathcal{A}_1 \times \mathcal{A}_2$, is*

$$\mathcal{A} = (L_1 \times L_2, \ell_{0_1} \times \ell_{0_2}, A, C_1 \cup C_2, F_1 \cup F_2, E, Inv, fm_1 \wedge fm_2, \gamma, \Gamma)$$

where A, E, Inv, γ and Γ are defined as follows

- $A = I \uplus O \uplus H$, where $I = I_1 \cup I_2$, $O = O_1 \cup O_2$, and $H = H_1 \cup H_2$.
- E and γ are defined by the rules below, for any $\omega_1 \subseteq A_1$, $\omega_2 \subseteq A_2$.

$$\frac{\ell_1 \xrightarrow[\varphi_1]{g_1,\omega_1,r_1}_1 \ell_1'}{\langle \ell_1, \ell_2 \rangle \xrightarrow[\varphi_1]{g_1,\omega_1,r_1} \langle \ell_1', \ell_2 \rangle} \qquad \frac{\ell_2 \xrightarrow[\varphi_2]{g_2,\omega_2,r_2}_2 \ell_2'}{\langle \ell_1, \ell_2 \rangle \xrightarrow[\varphi_2]{g_2,\omega_2,r_2} \langle \ell_1, \ell_2' \rangle}$$

$$\frac{\ell_1 \xrightarrow[\varphi_1]{g_1,\omega_1,r_1}_1 \ell_1' \quad \ell_2 \xrightarrow[\varphi_2]{g_2,\omega_2,r_2}_2 \ell_2'}{\langle \ell_1, \ell_2 \rangle \xrightarrow[\varphi_1 \wedge \varphi_2]{g_1 \wedge g_2,\omega_1 \cup \omega_2,r_1 \cup r_2} \langle \ell_1', \ell_2' \rangle}$$

- $Inv(\ell_1, \ell_2) = Inv_1(\ell_1) \wedge Inv_2(\ell_2)$.
- $\forall_{a \in \mathbb{P}_A} \cdot \Gamma(a) = \Gamma_i(a)$ if $a \in A_i$, for $i = 1, 2$.

The *synchronisation* operation over an IFTA $\mathcal{A}$ connects and synchronises two actions a and b from $A_\mathcal{A}$. The resulting automaton has transitions without neither a and b, nor both a and b. The latter become internal transitions.

Definition 9 (Synchronisation). *Given an IFTA $\mathcal{A} = (L, \ell_0, A, C, F, E, Inv, fm, \gamma, \Gamma)$ and two actions $a, b \in A$, the synchronisation of a and b is given by $\Delta_{a,b}(\mathcal{A}) = (L, \ell_0, A', C, F, E', Inv, fm', \gamma, \Gamma)$ where A', E' and fm' are defined as follows*

- $A = I' \uplus O' \uplus H'$, where $I' = I \setminus \{a.b\}$, $O' = O \setminus \{a.b\}$, and $H' = H \cup \{a.b\}$.
- $E' = \{\ell \xrightarrow{g,\omega,r} \ell' \in E \mid a \notin \omega \text{ and } b \notin \omega\} \cup$
  $\{\ell \xrightarrow{g,\omega\setminus\{a,b\},r} \ell' \mid \ell \xrightarrow{g,\omega,r} \ell' \in E \text{ and } a \in \omega \text{ and } b \in \omega\}$
- $fm' = fm \wedge (\Gamma_\mathcal{A}(a) \leftrightarrow \Gamma_\mathcal{A}(b))$.

Together, the product and the synchronisation can be used to obtain in a *compositional* way, a complex IFTA modelling SPLs built out of primitive IFTA.

Definition 10 (Composition of IFTA). *Given two disjoint IFTA, $\mathcal{A}_1$ and $\mathcal{A}_2$, and a set of bindings $\{(a_1, b_1), \ldots, (a_n, b_n)\}$, where $a_k \in \mathbb{P}_1$, $b_k \in \mathbb{P}_2$, and such that $(a_k, b_k) \in I_1 \times O_2$ or $(a_k, b_k) \in I_2 \times O_1$, for $1 \leq k \leq n$, the composition of $\mathcal{A}_1$ and $\mathcal{A}_2$ is defined as $\mathcal{A}_1 \bowtie_{(a_1,b_1),\ldots,(a_n,b_n)} \mathcal{A}_2 = \Delta_{a_1,b_1} \cdots \Delta_{a_n,b_n}(\mathcal{A}_1 \times \mathcal{A}_2)$.*

Figure 3 exemplifies the composition of the coffee machine (CM) and Router IFTA from Fig. 2. The resulting IFTA combines the feature models of the CM and Router, imposing additional restrictions given by the binded ports, E.g., the binding (o_1, coffee) imposes that o_1 will be present, if and only if, coffee is present, which depends on the feature expressions of each port, I.e., $(f_i \wedge f_{o1}) \leftrightarrow cf$. In the composed IFTA, transitions with binded actions transition together, while transitions labelled with non-binded actions can transition independently or together. Combining their feature models only through logical conjunction allows $\{cf, f_{o_2}, f_i, f_{o_1}\}$ as a valid feature selection. In such scenario, we could derive a product that can issue o_2 but that can not be captured by cappuccino.

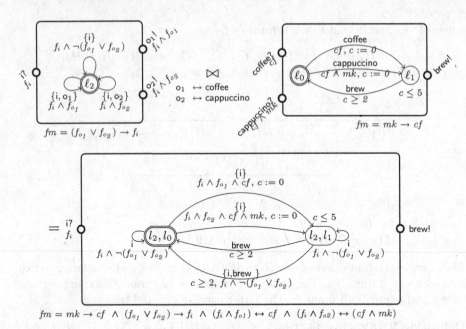

Fig. 3. Composition of a Router IFTA (top left) with the CM IFTA (top right) by binding ports (o_1,coffee) and (o_2,cappuccino), yielding the IFTA below.

In terms of methods calls in a programming language, the derive product will have a call to a method that does not exists, leading to an error.

To study properties of IFTA operations, we define the notion of IFTA equivalence in terms of bisimulation over their underlying FTSs. We formally introduce the notion of timed bisimulation adapted to FTSs.

Definition 11 (Timed Bisimulation). *Given two FTSs $\mathcal{F}_1$ and $\mathcal{F}_2$, we say $\mathcal{R} \subseteq S_1 \times S_2$ is a bisimulation, if and only if, for all possible feature selections $FS \in \mathbf{2}^{F_1 \cup F_2}$, $FS \models fm_1 \Leftrightarrow FS \models fm_2$ and for all $(s_1, s_2) \in R$ we have:*

- *$\forall\, t = s_1 \xrightarrow{\alpha}_1 s_1'$, $\alpha \in \mathbf{2}^A \cup \mathbb{R}_{\geq 0}$, $\exists\, t' = s_2 \xrightarrow{\alpha}_2 s_2'$ s.t. $(s_1', s_2') \in \mathcal{R}$ and $FS \models \gamma_1(t) \Leftrightarrow FS \models \gamma_2(t')$,*
- *$\forall\, t' = s_2 \xrightarrow{\alpha}_2 s_2'$, $\alpha \in \mathbf{2}^A \cup \mathbb{R}_{\geq 0}$, $\exists\, t = s_1 \xrightarrow{\alpha}_1 s_1'$ s.t. $(s_1', s_2') \in \mathcal{R}$ and $FS \models \gamma_1(t) \Leftrightarrow FS \models \gamma_2(t')$*

where $A = A_1 \cup A_2$.

Two states $s_1 \in S_1$ and $s_2 \in S_2$ are bisimilar, written $s_1 \sim s_2$, if there exists a bisimulation relation containing the pair (s_1, s_2). Given two IFTA $\mathcal{A}_1$ and $\mathcal{A}_2$, we say they are bisimilar, written $\mathcal{A}_1 \sim \mathcal{A}_2$, if there exists a bisimulation relation containing the initial states of their corresponding FTSs.

Proposition 1 (Product is commutative and associative). *Given two IFTA $\mathcal{A}_1$ and $\mathcal{A}_2$ with disjoint set of actions and clocks, $\mathcal{A}_1 \times \mathcal{A}_2 \sim \mathcal{A}_2 \times \mathcal{A}_1$, and $\mathcal{A}_1 \times (\mathcal{A}_2 \times \mathcal{A}_3) \sim (\mathcal{A}_1 \times \mathcal{A}_2) \times \mathcal{A}_3$.*

The proof follows trivially by definition of product and FTSs, and because $\cup$ and $\wedge$ are associative and commutative.

The *synchronisation* operation is commutative, and it interacts well with *product*. The following proposition captures these properties.

Proposition 2 (Synchronisation commutativity). *Given two IFTA $\mathcal{A}_1$ and $\mathcal{A}_2$, the following properties hold:*

1. $\Delta_{a,b}\Delta_{c,d}\mathcal{A}_1 \sim \Delta_{c,d}\Delta_{a,b}\mathcal{A}_1$, *if $a, b, c, d \in A_1$, a, b, c, d different actions.*
2. $(\Delta_{a,b}\mathcal{A}_1) \times \mathcal{A}_2 \sim \Delta_{a,b}(\mathcal{A}_1 \times \mathcal{A}_2)$, *if $a, b \in A_1$ and $A_1 \cap A_2 = \emptyset$.*

Both proof follow trivially by definition of product, synchronization and FTSs.

4   Reo Connectors as IFTA

Reo is a channel-based exogenous coordination language where complex coordinators, called connectors, are compositionally built out of simpler ones, called channels [2]. Exogenous coordination facilitates anonymous communication of components. Each connector has a set of input and output ports, and a formal semantics of how data flows from the inputs to the outputs. We abstract from the notion of data and rather concentrate on how execution of actions associated to input ports enables execution of actions associated to output ports.

Table 1 shows examples of basic Reo connectors and their corresponding IFTA. For example, $Merger(i_1, i_2, o)$ synchronises each input port, separately, with the output port, i.e. each i_k executes simultaneously with o for $k = 1, 2$; and $FIFO1(i, o)$ introduces the notion of delay by executing its input while transitions to a state where time can pass, enabling the execution of its output without time restrictions.

Modelling Reo connectors as IFTA enables them with variable behavior based on the presence of ports connected through synchronisation to their ports. Thus, we can use them to coordinate components with variable interfaces. We associate a feature f_a to each port a of a connector and define its behavior in terms of these features. Table 1 shows Reo basic connectors as IFTA with variable behavior. Bold edges represent the standard behavior of the corresponding Reo connector, and thinner edges model variable behavior. For example, the *Merger* connector supports the standard behavior, indicated by the transitions $\ell_0 \xrightarrow{\{i_k, o\}} \ell_0$, $k = 1, 2$ and the corresponding feature expression $f_k \wedge f_o$; and a variable behavior, in which both inputs can execute independently at any time if o is not present, indicated by transitions $\ell_0 \xrightarrow{\{i_k\}} \ell_0$, $k = 1, 2$ and the corresponding feature expression $f_k \wedge \neg f_o$.

The *Sync* connector behaves as the *identity* when composed with other automata. The following proposition captures this property.

Proposition 3 (*Sync* behaves as identity). *Given an IFTA $\mathcal{A}$ and a Sync connector, $\Delta_{i,a}(\mathcal{A} \times Sync(i, o)) \sim \mathcal{A}[o/a]$ with the following updates*

Table 1. Examples of basic Reo connectors and their corresponding IFTA.

Connector	IFTA	Connector	IFTA
$i \longrightarrow o$ *Sync*	$\{i,o\}$ f_{io} ℓ_0 $fm = T$	$i_1 \rightarrow \leftarrow i_2$ *SyncDrain*	$\{i_2\}$ $\neg f_{i_1} \wedge f_{i_2}$ ℓ_0 $\{i_1, i_2\}$ $f_{i_1} \wedge f_{i_2}$ $\{i_1\}$ $f_{i_1} \wedge \neg f_{i_2}$ $fm = T$
$i \longrightarrow\!\square\!\longrightarrow o$ *FIFO1*	$\{i\}$ $f_i \wedge f_o$ $\ell_0 \quad \ell_1$ $\{o\}$ $f_i \wedge f_o$ $fm = f_o \rightarrow f_i$	i_1 $i_2 \longrightarrow o$ *Merger*	$\{i_2, o\}$ $f_{i_2} \wedge f_o$ $\{i_1\}$ $f_{i_1} \wedge \neg f_o$ ℓ_0 $\{i_2\}$ $f_{i_2} \wedge \neg f_o$ $\{i_1, o\}$ $f_{i_1} \wedge f_o$ $fm = f_o \rightarrow (f_{i_1} \vee f_{i_2})$
$i \longrightarrow\!\oplus\! \begin{smallmatrix} o_1 \\ \\ o_2 \end{smallmatrix}$ *Router*	$\{i_1\}$ $f_i \wedge \neg f_{o_1} \wedge \neg f_{o_2}$ ℓ_0 $\{i, o_2\}$ $f_i \wedge f_{o_2}$ $\{i, o_1\}$ $f_i \wedge f_{o_1}$ $fm = (f_{o_1} \vee f_{o_2}) \rightarrow f_i$	$i \longrightarrow \begin{smallmatrix} o_1 \\ \\ o_2 \end{smallmatrix}$ *Replicator*	$\{i\}$ $f_i \wedge \neg f_{o_1} \wedge \neg f_{o_2}$ $\{i, o_2\}$ $f_i \wedge \neg f_{o_1} \wedge f_{o_2}$ ℓ_0 $\{i, o_1, o_2\}$ $f_i \wedge f_{o_1} \wedge f_{o_2}$ $\{i, o_1\}$ $f_i \wedge f_{o_1} \wedge \neg f_{o_2}$ $fm = (f_{o_1} \vee f_{o_2}) \rightarrow f_i$

- $fm_{A[o/a]} = fm_A \wedge (f_{io} \leftrightarrow \Gamma_A(a))$
- $\gamma_{A[o/a]}(\ell \xrightarrow{g,\omega,r}_{A[o/a]} \ell') = \gamma_A(\ell \xrightarrow{g,\omega[a/o],r}_A \ell') \wedge f_{io}$, if $o \in \omega$
- $F_{A[o/a]} = F_A \cup \{f_{io}\}$
- $\Gamma_{A[o/a]}(o) = \Gamma_{Sync}(o)$

if $\{i, o\} \not\subseteq A_A$, and $a \in A_A$. $A[o/a]$ is A with all occurrences of a replaced by o.

Proof. First for simplicity, let $A_S = (A \times Sync(i, o))$, and $A' = \Delta_{i,a}(A_S)$. Lets note that the set of edges in A' is defined as follows

$$E_{A'} = \{(\ell_1, \ell_0) \xrightarrow{g,\omega,r}_{A_S} (\ell'_1, \ell_0) \qquad | \, i \notin \omega \text{ and } a \notin \omega\} \cup \qquad (1)$$

$$\{(\ell_1, \ell_0) \xrightarrow{g, \omega \setminus \{i,a\}, r} (\ell'_1, \ell_0) \qquad | \, (\ell_1, \ell_0) \xrightarrow{g,\omega,r}_{A_S} (\ell'_1, \ell_0)$$
$$\text{and } i \in \omega \text{ and } a \in \omega\} \qquad (2)$$

where ℓ_0 is the initial and only location of *Sync*. Let $\mathcal{F}_1$ and $\mathcal{F}_2$ be the underlying FTS of A' and $A[o/a]$, and note that $\mathcal{R} = \{(\langle(\ell_1, \ell_0), \eta\rangle, \langle\ell_1, \eta\rangle) \mid \ell_1 \in S_{A[o/a]}\}$ is a bisimulation between states of $\mathcal{F}_1$ and $\mathcal{F}_2$. Let $(\langle(\ell_1, \ell_0), \eta\rangle, \langle\ell_1, \eta\rangle) \in \mathcal{R}$.

The proof for delay transitions follows trivially from the fact that $Inv(\ell_1, \ell_0) = Inv(\ell_1)$ for all $\ell_1 \in S_{\mathcal{A}[o/a]}$.

Lets consider any action transition $\langle(\ell_1, \ell_0), \eta\rangle \xrightarrow{\omega} \langle(\ell_1', \ell_0), \eta'\rangle \in T_{\mathcal{F}_1}$. If it comes from an edge in (1), then $\exists\, \ell_1 \xrightarrow{g,\omega,r} \ell_1' \in E_{\mathcal{A}}$ s.t. $a \notin \omega$, thus $\exists\, \langle \ell_1, \eta\rangle \xrightarrow{\omega} \langle\ell_1', \eta'\rangle \in T_{\mathcal{F}_2}$; if it comes from (2), then $\exists\, \ell_1 \xrightarrow{g,\omega_1,r} \ell_1' \in E_{\mathcal{A}}$ s.t. $a \in \omega_1$, thus $\exists\, \langle \ell_1, \eta\rangle \xrightarrow{\omega_1[o/a]} \langle\ell_1', \eta'\rangle \in T_{\mathcal{F}_2}$, where $\omega = \omega_1 \cup \{i, o\} \setminus \{i, a\} = \omega[o/a]$. Conversely, if $\exists\, \langle \ell_1, \eta\rangle \xrightarrow{\omega} \langle\ell_1', \eta'\rangle \in T_{\mathcal{F}_2}$ and $o \notin \omega$, then $\exists\, (\ell_1, \ell_0) \xrightarrow{g,\omega,r} (\ell_1', \ell_0) \in E_{\mathcal{A}_S}$ s.t. $i \notin \omega \wedge a \notin \omega$, thus $\exists\, \langle(\ell_1, \ell_0), \eta\rangle \xrightarrow{\omega} \langle(\ell_1', \ell_0), \eta'\rangle \in T_{\mathcal{F}_1}$; if $o \in \omega$, then $\exists\, (\ell_1, \ell_0) \xrightarrow{g,\omega_1 \cup \{o\} \setminus \{a\},r} (\ell_1', \ell_0) \in E_{\mathcal{A}'}$, such that $\omega = \omega_1[o/a] = \omega_1 \cup \{o\} \setminus \{a\}$, thus $\exists\, \langle(\ell_1, \ell_0), \eta \xrightarrow{\omega} \langle(\ell_1', \ell_0), \eta'\rangle\rangle \in T_{\mathcal{F}_1}$.

In both cases, we have $\gamma_{\mathcal{F}_1}(\langle(\ell_1, \ell_0), \eta\rangle \xrightarrow{\omega} \langle(\ell_1', \ell_0), \eta'\rangle) = \gamma_{\mathcal{F}_2}(\langle\ell_1, \eta\rangle \xrightarrow{\omega} \langle\ell_1', \eta'\rangle)$. Furthermore, $fm'_{\mathcal{A}} = fm_{\mathcal{A}[o/a]}$. □

5 Implementation

We developed a prototype tool in Scala[1] consisting of a small Domain Specific Language (DSL) to specify (networks of) (N)IFTA and manipulate them. Although we do not provide the formal definitions and semantics due to space constraints, informally, a network of any kind of automata is a set of automata parallel composed ($\|$) and synchronised over a set of shared actions.

Main features supported by the DSL include: (1) specification of (N)IFTA, (2) composition, product and synchronisation over IFTA, (3) conversion of NIFTA to networks of FTA (NFTA) with committed states (CS), and (4) conversion of NFTA to UPPAAL networks of TA (NTA) with features. Listing 1.1 shows how the *router* connector from Table 1 can be specified using the DSL. A comprehensive list of functionality and more examples, including the case study from Sect. 6 can be found in the tool's repository (see footnote 1).

```
val router = newifta ++ (
    0 --> 0 by "i,o1"    when "vi" && "vo1",
    0 --> 0 by "i,o2"    when "vi" && "vo2",
    0 --> 0 by "i"       when "vi" && not("vo1" || "vo2")
) get "i" pub "o1,o2" when ("vo1" || "vo2") --> "vi"
```

Listing 1.1. Example specification of a router connector using the Scala DSL.

A NIFTA can be converted into a NFTA with committed states, which in turn can be converted into a network of UPPAAL TA, through a stepwise conversion, as follows. **NIFTA to NFTA.** Informally, this is achieved by converting each transition with set of actions into to a set of transitions with single actions. All transitions in this set must execute atomically (committed states between them) and support all combinations of execution of the actions. **NFTA to UPPAAL NTA.** First, the NFTA obtained in the previous step is translated into a network of UPPAAL TA, where features are encoded as Boolean variables, and transition's feature expressions as logical guards over Boolean variables. Second, the

---

[1] https://github.com/haslab/ifta.

feature model of the network is solved using a SAT solver to find the set of valid feature selections. This set is encoded as a TA with an initial committed location and outgoing transitions to new locations for each element in the set. Each transition initializes the set of variables of a valid feature selection. The initial committed state ensures a feature selection is made before any other transition is taken.

When translating IFTA to FTA with committed states, the complexity of the model grows quickly. For example, the IFTA of a simple replicator with 3 output ports consists of a location and 8 transitions, while its corresponding FTA consists of 23 locations and 38 transitions. Without any support for composing variable connectors, modelling all possible cases is error prone and it quickly becomes unmanageable. This simplicity in design achieved through multi-action transitions leads to a more efficient approach to translate IFTA to UPPAAL TA, in particular by using the composition of IFTA. The IFTA resulting from composing a network of IFTA, can be simply converted to an FTA by flattening the set of actions in to a single action, and later into an UPPAAL TA.

6   Case Study: Licensing Services in E-Government

This section presents a case study of using IFTA to model a family of public licensing services. All services in the family support submissions and assessment of licensing requests. Some services, in addition, require a fee before submitting (pa), others allow appeals on rejected requests (apl), or both. Furthermore, services that require a fee can support credit card (cc) or PayPal payments (pp), or both. Functionality is divided in components and provided as follows. Each component can be visualized in Fig. 4. We omit the explicit illustration of interfaces and rather use the notation ?,! to indicate whether an action corresponds to an input or output, respectively. In addition, we use the same action name in two different automata to indicate pairs of actions to be linked. The feature model, also omitted, is initially $\top$ for each of these IFTA.

App - Models licenses requests. An applicant must submit the required documents (subdocs), and pay a fee (payapp) if pa is present, before submitting (submit). If the request is accepted (accept) or considered incomplete (incomplete), the request is closed. If it is rejected (reject) and it is not possible to appeal ($\neg apl$), the request is closed, otherwise a clock ($tapl$) is reseted to track the appeal window time. The applicant has 31 days to appeal ($Inv_{App}(\ell_5)$), otherwise the request is canceled (cancelapp) and closed. If an appeal is submitted (appeal), it can be rejected or accepted, and the request is closed.

CC and *PP* - Handle payments through credit cards and PayPal, respectively. If a user requests to pay by credit card (paycc) or PayPal (paypp), a clock is reset to track payment elapsed time ($tocc$ and $topp$). The user has 1 day ($Inv_{CC}(\ell_1)$ and $Inv_{PP}(\ell_1)$) to proceed with the payment which can result in success (paidcc and paidpp) or cancellation (cancelcc and cancelpp).

Appeal - Handles appeal requests. When an appeal is received (appeal), a clock is reseted to track the appeal submission elapsed time (tas). Authorities have 20 days ($Inv_{Appeal}(\ell_1)$) to start assessing the request (assessapl).

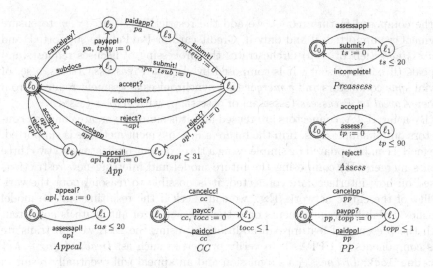

Fig. 4. IFTA modelling domain functionality.

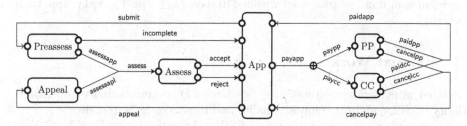

Fig. 5. IFTA for a family of Licensing Services

Preassess - Checks if a request contains all required documents. When a request is received (submit), a clock is reseted to track the submission elapsed time (ts). Authorities have 20 days ($Inv_{Preasses}(\ell_1)$) to check the completeness of the documents and notify whether it is incomplete (incomplete) or ready to assessed (assessapp).

Assess - Analyzes requests. When a request is ready to be assessed (assess), a clock is reseted to track the processing elapsed time (tp). Authorities have 90 days to make a decision of weather accept it (accept) or reject it (reject).

We use a set of Reo connectors to integrate these IFTA. The final integrated model can be seen in Fig. 5. For simplicity, we omit the feature expressions associated to ports and the resulting feature model. Broadly, we can identify two new components in this figure: *Payment* - (right of *App*) Orchestrates payment requests based on the presence of payment methods. It is composed by components *CC*, *PP*, and a set of connectors. A *router* synchronises payment requests (payapp) with payment by *CC* or *PayPal* (paypp or paycc). A *merger* synchronises the successful response (paidpp or paidcc), while other *merger* synchronises the cancellation response (cancelpp or cancelcc) from either *CC* or *PP*. On top of the composed feature model, we add the restriction $pa \leftrightarrow cc \vee pp$ to ensure payment is supported, if and only if, Credit card or PayPal are supported; and *Processing* - (left of *App*) Orchestrates the processing of licenses requests and appeals (if apl is present). It is composed by *Appeal, Preassess, Assess*, a set of trivial *sync* connectors and a *merger* that synchronises assessment requests from either *Appeal* or *Preassess* (assessapl or assessapp) with *Assess* (assess).

By using IFTA, connectors are reused and it is simple to create complex connectors out of simple ones. If in the future a new payment methods is supported, the model can be updated by simple using a three output replicator and two three inputs mergers. By composing the future model and inferring new restrictions based on how interfaces are connected, it is possible to reason about the variability of the entire network, E.g., we can check if the resulting feature model satisfies variability requirements or if the interaction of automata is consistent with the presence of features. In addition, by using the DSL we can translate this components to UPPAAL to verify properties such as: *Deadlock free* – A[] not deadlock; *Liveness* – a submission and an appeal will eventually result in an answer (App.ℓ_4 --> App.ℓ_0 and App.ℓ_6 --> App.ℓ_0, respectively); *Safety* – a submission must be processed within 110 days (A[] App.ℓ_4 imply App.tsub <=110).

7   Related Work

Related work is discussed following two lines: (1) compositionality and modularity of SPLs, and (2) compositionality and interfaces for automata.

Compositionality and modularity of SPLs. An extension to Petri Nets, Feature Nets (FNs) [11] enables specifying the behavior of an SPL in a single model, and supports composition of FNs by applying deltas FNs to core FNs. An extension to CCS process calculus consisting on a modular approach to modelling and verifying variability of SPLs based on DeltaCCS [9]. A compositional approach for verification of software product lines [10] where new features and variability may be added incrementally, specified as finite state machines with variability information.

Interfaces and compositionality of automata. Interface automata [1] use input interfaces to support incremental design and independent implementability of components, allowing compatibility checking of interfaces for partial system descriptions, without knowing the interfaces of all components, and separate refinement of compatible interfaces, respectively. [6] presents a specification theory for I/O TA supporting refinement, consistency checking, logical and structural composition, and quotient of specifications. In [8] Modal I/O automata are used to construct a behavioral variability theory for SPL development and can serve to verify if certain requirements can be satisfied from a set of existing assets. [7] proposes a formal integration model based on Hierarchical TA for real time systems, with different component composition techniques. [3] presents a compositional specification theory to reason about components that interact by synchronisation of I/O actions.

8   Conclusions

This paper introduced IFTA, a formalism for modelling SPL in a modular and compositional manner, which extends FTA with variable interfaces to restrict the way automata can be composed, and with multi-action transitions that simplify the design. A set of Reo connectors were modeled as IFTA and used to orchestrate the way various automata connect. We discussed a prototype tool to specify and manipulate IFTA, which takes advantage of IFTA composition to translate them into TA that can be verified using the UPPAAL model checker.

Delegating coordination aspects to connectors enables separation of concerns. Each automata can be designed to be modular and cohesive, facilitating the maintenance, adaptability, and extension of an SPL. In particular, by facilitating compositional reasoning when replacing components, E.g., when checking for a refinement relation, as well as enabling changes in the coordination mechanisms without affecting core domain functionality. Using bare FTA for designing variable connectors, can be error prone and it quickly becomes unmanageable. IFTA simplifies this design by enabling the modeling of automata in isolation and composing them by explicitly linking interfaces and combining their feature models.

Future work includes studying an implementation relation, I.e, refinement, to reason about how to safely replace an IFTA with a more detailed one in a compose environment.

References

1. de Alfaro, L., Henzinger, T.A.: Interface automata. SIGSOFT Softw. Eng. Notes **26**(5), 109–120 (2001). http://doi.acm.org/10.1145/503271.503226
2. Arbab, F.: Reo: a channel-based coordination model for component composition. Math. Struct. Comp. Sci. **14**(3), 329–366 (2004). http://dx.doi.org/10.1017/S0960129504004153
3. Chen, T., Chilton, C., Jonsson, B., Kwiatkowska, M.: A compositional specification theory for component behaviours. In: Seidl, H. (ed.) ESOP 2012. LNCS, vol. 7211, pp. 148–168. Springer, Heidelberg (2012). doi:10.1007/978-3-642-28869-2_8
4. Classen, A., Heymans, P., Schobbens, P.Y., Legay, A.: Symbolic model checking of software product lines. International Conference on Software Engineering, ICSE, pp. 321–330 (2011). http://dl.acm.org/citation.cfm?id=1985838
5. Cordy, M., Schobbens, P.Y., Heymans, P., Legay, A.: Behavioural modelling and verification of real-time software product lines. In: Proceedings of the 16th International Software Product Line Conference, SPLC 2012, vol. 1. pp. 66–75. ACM, New York (2012). http://doi.acm.org/10.1145/2362536.2362549
6. David, A., Larsen, K.G., Legay, A., Nyman, U., Wasowski, A.: Timed i/o automata: a complete specification theory for real-time systems. In: Proceedings of the 13th ACM International Conference on Hybrid Systems: Computation and Control, HSCC 2010, pp. 91–100. ACM, New York (2010). http://doi.acm.org/10.1145/1755952.1755967
7. Jin, X., Ma, H., Gu, Z.: Real-time component composition using hierarchical timed automata. In: Seventh International Conference on Quality Software (QSIC 2007), pp. 90–99, October 2007

8. Larsen, K.G., Nyman, U., Wąsowski, A.: Modal I/O automata for interface and product line theories. In: De Nicola, R. (ed.) ESOP 2007. LNCS, vol. 4421, pp. 64–79. Springer, Heidelberg (2007). doi:10.1007/978-3-540-71316-6_6
9. Lochau, M., Mennicke, S., Baller, H., Ribbeck, L.: Incremental model checking of delta-oriented software product lines. J. Logic Algebraic Program. **85**(1, Part 2), 245–267 (2016). http://dx.doi.org/10.1016/j.jlamp.2015.09.004, Formal Methods for Software Product Line Engineering
10. Millo, J.-V., Ramesh, S., Krishna, S.N., Narwane, G.K.: Compositional verification of software product lines. In: Johnsen, E.B., Petre, L. (eds.) IFM 2013. LNCS, vol. 7940, pp. 109–123. Springer, Heidelberg (2013). doi:10.1007/978-3-642-38613-8_8
11. Muschevici, R., Proença, J., Clarke, D.: Feature nets: behavioural modelling of software product lines. Softw. Syst. Model. **15**(4), 1181–1206 (2016). http://dx.doi.org/10.1007/s10270-015-0475-z

A Formal Model for Multi SPLs

Ferruccio Damiani[✉], Michael Lienhardt, and Luca Paolini

University of Torino, Torino, Italy
{ferruccio.damiani,michael.lienhardt,luca.paolini}@unito.it

Abstract. A Software Product Line (SPL) is a family of similar programs generated from a common artifact base. A Multi SPL (MPL) is a set of interdependent SPLs that are typically managed and developed in a decentralized fashion. Delta-Oriented Programming (DOP) is a flexible and modular approach to implement SPLs. This paper presents new concepts that extend DOP to support the implementation of MPLs. These extensions aim to accommodate compositional analyses. They are presented by means of a core calculus for delta-oriented MPLs of Java programs. Suitability for MPL compositional analyses is demonstrated by compositional reuse of existing SPL analysis techniques.

1 Introduction

Highly-configurable software systems can be described as *Software Product Lines* (SPLs). An SPL is a family of similar programs, called *variants*, that have a well-documented variability and are generated from a common artifact base [2,7,19]. An SPL consists of: (i) a *feature model* defining the set of variants in terms of *features* (each feature represents an abstract description of functionality and each variant is identified by a set of features, called a *product*); (ii) an *artifact base* providing language dependent reusable code artifacts that are used to build the variants; and (iii) *configuration knowledge* which connects feature model and artifact base by defining how to derive variants from the code artifacts given the products (thus inducing a mapping from products to variants, called the *generator* of the SPL).

Delta-Oriented Programming (DOP) [2, Sect. 6.6.1], [21] is a flexible and modular approach to implement SPLs. The artifact base of a delta-oriented SPL consists of a *base program* (that might be empty) and of a set of *delta modules* (*deltas* for short), which are containers of modifications to a program (e.g., for Java programs, a delta can add, remove or modify classes and interfaces). The configuration knowledge of a delta-oriented SPL defines the generator by associating to each delta an *activation condition* over the features (i.e., a set of products) and

---

This work has been partially supported by: EU Horizon 2020 project HyVar (www.hyvar-project.eu), GA No. 644298; ICT COST Action IC1402 ARVI (www.cost-arvi.eu); and Ateneo/CSP D16D15000360005 project RunVar (runvar-project.di.unito.it).

M. Dastani and M. Sirjani (Eds.): FSEN 2017, LNCS 10522, pp. 67–83, 2017.
DOI: 10.1007/978-3-319-68972-2_5

specifying an *application ordering* between deltas. DOP supports the automatic generation of variants based on a selection of features: once a user selects a product, the corresponding variant is derived by applying the deltas with a satisfied activation condition to the base program according to the application ordering. Moreover, DOP is a generalization of *Feature-Oriented Programming* (FOP) [2, Sect. 6.1], [4] a previously proposed approach to implement SPLs where deltas correspond one-to-one to features and do not contain remove operations.

Modern software systems often out-grow the scale of SPLs by involving the notion of *Multi SPLs* (MPLs), i.e., sets of interdependent SPLs that need to be managed in a decentralized fashion by multiple teams and stakeholders [13]. There are two main motivations to build such MPLs: either to structure a complex SPL into more manageable modules, or to reuse existing SPLs into a bigger project. In this paper we give, to the best of our knowledge, the first formal model of MPLs that spans feature model, artifact base and configuration knowledge. Our model is constructed around the concepts of *SPL signature*, *Dependent SPL* and *SPL composition*. It builds on recent work done by Schröter et al. [24] on compositional analysis of feature models, and on the delta-oriented programming core calculus IFΔJ by Bettini et al. [5], which is extended here to enable the construction of MPLs. The main achievement of our model is the ability to modularly compose and analyze SPLs by means of Dependent SPLs, which are SPLs with explicit dependencies, modeled by SPL signatures, that can be filled by SPLs (or Dependent SPLs) satisfying the given signatures.

Section 2 provides some background. Section 3 formalizes the main concepts proposed in the paper by introducing the IMPERATIVE FEATHERWEIGHT MULTI DELTA JAVA (IFMΔJ) calculus, which extends IFΔJ to implement MPLs. Section 4 illustrates how the concepts of SPL signature, dependent SPL, and SPL composition support compositionality of existing SPL analysis, like feature model analysis or type checking. Section 5 discusses related work.

2   Background and Running Example

2.1   IFΔJ: A Formal Foundation for Delta-Oriented SPLs

IFΔJ [5] is a core calculus for delta-oriented SPLs where variants are written in IFJ (an imperative version of FJ [14]). The abstract syntax of IFJ is given in Fig. 1 (explanations are given in the caption)—following [14], we use the overline notation for (possibly empty) sequences of elements: for instance $\bar{e}$ stands for a sequence of expressions. The empty sequence is denoted by $\emptyset$. Type system, operational semantics, and type soundness for IFJ are given in [5].

The abstract syntax of IFΔJ SPLs is given in Fig. 2 (explanations are given in the caption). The deltas in the artifact base must have distinct names, the class operations in a delta must act on distinct classes, and the attribute operations in a class operation must act on distinct attributes. In IFΔJ there is no concrete syntax for the feature model and the configuration knowledge. As usual, to simplify the formalization, we represent feature models $\mathcal{M}$ as pairs (set of features, set of products) and configuration knowledges $\mathcal{K}$ as pairs (mapping from deltas to activation conditions, delta application ordering).

$$
\begin{array}{llr}
P & ::= \overline{CD} & \text{Program} \\
CD & ::= \textbf{class } \texttt{C} \textbf{ extends } \texttt{C} \ \{ \ \overline{AD} \ \} & \text{Class Declaration} \\
AD & ::= FD \mid MD & \text{Attribute (Field or Method) Declaration} \\
FD & ::= \texttt{C f} & \text{Field Declaration} \\
MH & ::= \texttt{C m}(\overline{\texttt{C x}}) & \text{Method Header} \\
MD & ::= MH \ \{\textbf{return } e; \} & \text{Method Declaration} \\
e & ::= \texttt{x} \mid e.\texttt{f} \mid e.\texttt{m}(\overline{e}) \mid \textbf{new } \texttt{C}() \mid (\texttt{C})e \mid e.\texttt{f} = e \mid \textbf{null} & \text{Expression}
\end{array}
$$

Fig. 1. Syntax of IFJ. A program P is a sequence of class declarations $\overline{CD}$. A class declaration comprises the name $\texttt{C}$ of the class, the name of the superclass (which must always be specified, even if it is the built-in class $\texttt{Object}$), and a list of attribute (field or method) declarations $\overline{AD}$. Variables $\texttt{x}$ include the special variable **this** (implicitly bound in any method declaration MD), which may not be used as the name of a method's formal parameter. All fields and methods are public, there is no field shadowing, there is no method overloading, and each class is assumed to have an implicit constructor that initialized all fields to **null**. The subtyping relation $<:$ on classes, which is the reflexive and transitive closure of the immediate subclass relation (given by the **extends** clauses in class declarations), is supposed to be acyclic.

$$
\begin{array}{llr}
LD & ::= \textbf{line } \texttt{L} \ \{\mathcal{M} \ \mathcal{K} \ AB\} & \text{SPL Delaration} \\
AB & ::= P \ \overline{DD} & \text{Artifact Base} \\
DD & ::= \textbf{delta } \texttt{d} \ \{ \ \overline{CO} \ \} & \text{Delta Declaration} \\
CO & ::= \textbf{adds } CD \mid \textbf{removes } \texttt{C} \mid \textbf{modifies } \texttt{C} \ [\textbf{extends } \texttt{C}'] \ \{ \ \overline{AO} \ \} & \text{Class Operation} \\
AO & ::= \textbf{adds } AD \mid \textbf{removes } \texttt{a} \mid \textbf{modifies } MD & \text{Attribute Operation}
\end{array}
$$

Fig. 2. Syntax of IFΔJ SPLs. An SPL declaration comprises the name $\texttt{L}$ of the product line, a feature model $\mathcal{M}$, configuration knowledge $\mathcal{K}$, and an artifact base AB. The artifact base comprises a (possibly empty) IFJ program P, and a set of deltas $\overline{DD}$. A delta declaration DD comprises the name $\texttt{d}$ of the delta and class operations $\overline{CO}$ representing the transformations performed when the delta is applied to an IFJ program. A class operation can add, remove, or modify a class. A class can be modified by (possibly) changing its super class and performing attribute operations $\overline{AO}$ on its body. An *attribute name* $\texttt{a}$ is either a field name $\texttt{f}$ or a method name $\texttt{m}$. An attribute operation can add or remove fields and methods, and modify the implementation of a method by replacing its body. The new body may call the special method $\texttt{original}$, which is implicitly bound to the previous implementation of the method and may not be used as the name of a method.

Definition 1 (Feature model). *A* feature model $\mathcal{M}_x$ *is a pair* $(\mathcal{F}_x, \mathcal{P}_x)$ *where* $\mathcal{F}_x$ *is a set of features and* $\mathcal{P}_x \subseteq 2^{\mathcal{F}_x}$ *is a set of products.* $\mathcal{M}_\emptyset = (\emptyset, \emptyset)$ *is the* empty *feature model.*

Definition 2 (Configuration knowledge). *A* configuration knowledge $\mathcal{K}_x$ *is a pair* $(\alpha_x, <_x)$ *where* α_x *is a map that associates to each delta declaration the set of products that activate it (the activation condition), and* $<_x$ *is an ordering between deltas (the application ordering).*

These representations simplify stating and proving results independently from implementation details. However, they do not scale well in actual implementations.

In the examples, we represent feature models also as feature diagrams (which are diagrams that illustrate feature dependencies by organizing features in a tree structure with cross tree-constraints) or as propositional formulas Φ where variables are feature names f (see, e.g., [3] for a discussion on other possible representations):

$$\Phi ::= \textbf{true} \mid f \mid \Phi \Rightarrow \Phi \mid \neg\Phi \mid \Phi \wedge \Phi \mid \Phi \vee \Phi$$

To avoid over-specification, the ordering $<_x$ may be partial. We assume *unambiguity* of the SPL, i.e., for each product, any total ordering of the activated deltas that respects $<_x$ generates the same variant (see [5, 18] for effective means to ensure unambiguity). In examples, we represent activation conditions as propositional formulas (see above) and application orderings as total orderings on a partition of the set of delta names.

Feature model, configuration knowledge and artifact base of an SPL named L are denoted by $\mathcal{M}_L = (\mathcal{F}_L, \mathcal{P}_L)$, $\mathcal{K}_L = (\alpha_L, <_L)$ and AB_L, respectively. In order to define the generator $\mathcal{G}_L$ of an SPL L, we first introduce the auxiliary notions of delta applicability and delta application. A delta d is *applicable* to a program P iff each class to be added does not exist; each class to be removed or modified exists; and (for every class-modify operation): each method or field to be added does not exist; each method or field to be removed exists; each method to be modified exists and has the same header specified in the method-modify operation. If d is applicable to P, then the *application* of d to P is the program, denoted by $d(P)$, obtained from P by applying all the operations in d—otherwise $d(P)$ is undefined.

Definition 3 (Generator of an SPL [5]). *The* generator *of* L, *denoted by* $\mathcal{G}_L$, *is the mapping that associates each product p of* L *to the IFJ program* $d_n(\cdots d_1(P) \cdots)$, *where P is the base program of* L *and* $d_1 \ldots, d_n$ $(n \geq 0)$ *are the deltas of* L *activated by p, listed according to the application order.*

The generator $\mathcal{G}_L$ may be partial since, for some product of L, a delta DD_i ($1 \leq i \leq n$) may not be applicable to the intermediate variant $DD_{i-1}(\cdots DD_1(P) \cdots)$ thus making $\mathcal{G}_L$ undefined for that product.

The running example of this paper is based on bank accounts. Figure 3 illustrates an SPL of capital accounts (CapitalAccount, on the left) and an SPL of financial accounts (FinancialAccount, on the right)—explanations are given in the caption. To make the example more readable, in the artifact bases we use Java syntax for field initialization, primitive data types, strings and sequential composition—encoding in IFΔJ syntax is straightforward (see [5]).

Remark 1 (Base program and empty product). In order to simplify the presentation, the formal definitions in the rest of this document assume that: (i) the base program is always the empty program; (ii) no delta d is activated by the empty product (i.e., $\emptyset \notin \alpha_L(d)$ for all d); and (iii) $\mathcal{G}_L(\emptyset) = \emptyset$, even when $\emptyset$ is not a product. Note that these assumptions are not restrictive. In particular, the base program of any SPL L can be always encoded as an extra delta (the *base* delta) with distinguished name d_L such that $\alpha_L(d_L) = \mathcal{P}_L$ and d_L is the minimum according to $<_L$.

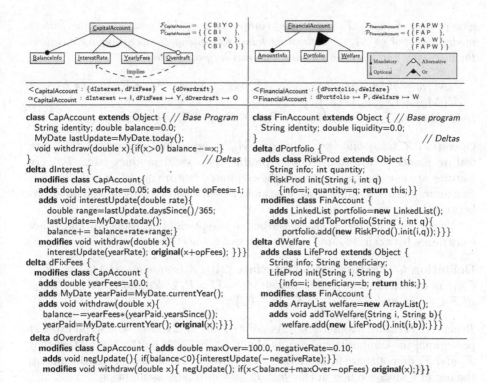

Fig. 3. Left: CapitalAccount SPL: feature model $\mathcal{M}_{\mathrm{CapitalAccount}}$ (top), configuration knowledge $\mathcal{K}_{\mathrm{CapitalAccount}}$ (middle), and artifact base $AB_{\mathrm{CapitalAccount}}$ (bottom). This SPL provides a class `CapAccount` for money managing bank accounts. The mandatory feature BalanceInfo provides some basic fields (`identity`, `balance` and `lastUpdate`) and a method `withdraw` (method `deposit`, which is similar, is omitted). InterestRate and YearlyFees provide two alternative bank-policies: one and only one of them, must be selected. The former manages accrued interests and operation-fees (applied to each withdraw), the second manages fixed fees per year (and no bank interests). The optional feature Overdraft, which allows to withdraw more money than that available, requires feature InterestRate in order to apply a negative interest. **Right:** FinancialAccount SPL: $\mathcal{M}_{\mathrm{FinancialAccount}}$ (top), $\mathcal{K}_{\mathrm{FinancialAccount}}$ (middle), and $AB_{\mathrm{FinancialAccount}}$ (bottom). This SPL provides a class `FinAccount` for investment product managing bank accounts. The mandatory feature AmountInfo provides basic fields (`identity`, `liquidity`). It must be flanked by at least one feature between Portfolio and Welfare. The latter provides a list of welfare products. The former provides a list of financial products.

2.2 Feature Model Composition and Feature Model Interfaces

Recently, Schröter et al. [24] considered a notion of feature model composition through aggregation (i.e., by inclusion of one feature model into another feature model [20]) and proposed to use it in combination with a notion of feature model interface in order to support compositional analyses of feature models.

Definition 4 (Feature model composition [24]). *Let* $\mathcal{M}_x = (\mathcal{F}_x, \mathcal{P}_x)$, $\mathcal{M}_y = (\mathcal{F}_y, \mathcal{P}_y)$, *and* $\mathcal{M}_{Glue} = (\mathcal{F}_{Glue}, \mathcal{P}_{Glue})$ *be feature models that satisfy the* glue-proviso $\mathcal{F}_{Glue} \subseteq \mathcal{F}_x \cup \mathcal{F}_y$. The composition of $\mathcal{M}_x$ and $\mathcal{M}_y$ is the feature model, denoted as $\mathcal{M}_{x/y}$, defined as follows by using composition operation $\circ$, the auxiliary join operation $\bullet$, and the auxiliary operation $\mathcal{R}$:

$$\mathcal{M}_{x/y} = \circ(\mathcal{M}_x, \mathcal{M}_y, \mathcal{M}_{Glue}) = \mathcal{M}_x \circ_{\mathcal{M}_{Glue}} \mathcal{M}_y = (\mathcal{M}_x \bullet \mathcal{R}(\mathcal{M}_y)) \bullet \mathcal{M}_{Glue}$$
$$\mathcal{R}(\mathcal{M}_y) = (\mathcal{F}_y, \mathcal{P}_y \cup \{\emptyset\})$$
$$\mathcal{M}_x \bullet \mathcal{M}_y = (\mathcal{F}_x \cup \mathcal{F}_y, \{p \cup q \mid p \in \mathcal{P}_x, q \in \mathcal{P}_y, p \cap \mathcal{F}_y = q \cap \mathcal{F}_x\})$$

Operation $\mathcal{R}$ takes one feature model $\mathcal{M}_y$ as input and converts it to a new feature model in which the empty product is a valid product (thus $\mathcal{P}_y$ core features are not necessarily core in the composed feature model). Operation $\bullet$ is similar to a cross product from relational algebra and creates all combinations between both product sets.

The feature model $\mathcal{M}_{Glue}$ describes a parent-child relationship and other constraints between $\mathcal{M}_x$ and $\mathcal{M}_y$ in order to connect them.

Definition 5 (Feature model interface [24]). *A feature model* $\mathcal{M}_{Int} = (\mathcal{F}_{Int}, \mathcal{P}_{Int})$ *is an interface of feature model* $\mathcal{M}_x = (\mathcal{F}_x, \mathcal{P}_x)$, *denoted as* $\mathcal{M}_{Int} \preceq \mathcal{M}_x$, *iff* $\mathcal{F}_{Int} \subseteq \mathcal{F}_x$ *and* $\mathcal{P}_{Int} = \{p \cap \mathcal{F}_{Int} \mid p \in \mathcal{P}_x\}$.

Remark 2 (Feature disjointness). As pointed out in [24, Sect. 4.1, second to last paragraph] the compositional results about $\circ$ "are based on the assumption that $\mathcal{F}_x$ and $\mathcal{F}_y$ do not share features (i.e. $\mathcal{F}_x \cap \mathcal{F}_y = \emptyset$)". In the rest of this document, the use of $\circ$ always relies on this *feature disjointedness* assumption.

3   IFMΔJ: A Core Calculus for MPLs

The example presented in Fig. 3 introduces two SPLs, CapitalAccount and FinancialAccount, describing two kinds of bank accounts: it would make perfect sense to combine these two SPLs in order to obtain an SPL describing a bank account with functionalities described in both SPLs.

In a first approach, one could define a new SPL DualAccount that uses (i.e., depends on) the two bank account SPLs presented in Fig. 3 to define a new class that implements the different features defined in the two SPLs. We call an SPL with such dependencies a *Dependent SPL*. However, such an approach is not satisfactory as it couples too strongly DualAccount to its SPLs: DualAccount is set to use the CapitalAccount and FinancialAccount SPLs and cannot change even if a more efficient implementation of these SPLs comes up. To deal with this issue, we introduce the notion of *SPL signature* which is used to specify the APIs on which a Dependent SPL depends; then any SPL that implements such signature can fulfill the dependencies of a Dependent SPL.

Hence, our approach to define the DualAccount Dependent SPL follows the structure presented on the right:

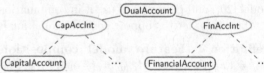

DualAccount depends on two SPL signatures: CapAcclnt specifies the API requested by DualAccount for the capital account backend implementation, while FinAcclnt specifies the API requested by DualAccount for the financial account implementation. Then these two signatures are implemented by CapitalAccount and FinancialAccount respectively, and possibly other SPLs.

We structure the presentation of our model as follows: first we introduce the concept of SPL signature (SPLS) and formally define when an SPL implements an SPL signature; second we define the notion of Dependent SPL (DPL) as we just presented; and finally, we demonstrate how to generate the variants of a DPL.

3.1 SPL Signatures

An *SPL signature* (SPLS) describes the API of an SPL and is structured like an SPL with a feature model, configuration knowledge, and an artifact base. Its difference with an SPL lies in the fact that its artifact base does not include the implementation of methods. Figure 4 (middle) gives the abstract syntax of SPLSs which uses *program signatures*, presented in Fig. 4 (top), to construct their artifact bases. A program signature is a program deprived of method bodies. An SPLS declaration LS comprises the name Z of the SPLS, a feature model $\mathcal{M}$, configuration knowledge $\mathcal{K}$ and an *artifact base signature ABS* which, in turn, comprises a program signature PS and a set of delta signatures $\overline{DS}$—a *delta signature DS* is a delta deprived of method-modifies operations and method bodies.

An SPL L implements an SPLS Z when all the declarations in Z are implemented in L. I.e., when all the products of Z can be extended in a product of L and for each variant of Z, all of its declared elements are implemented in the corresponding variant of L. We first define the *generator* of an SPLS (in order

$PS ::= \overline{CS}$	Program Signature
$CS ::= $ **class** C **extends** C $\{ \overline{AS} \}$	Class Signature
$AS ::= FD \mid MH$	Attribute (Field or Method) Signature

$LS \quad ::= $ **sig** Z $\{\mathcal{M} \, \mathcal{K} \, ABS\}$	SPL Signature Declaration
$ABS ::= PS \, \overline{DS}$	AB Signature
$DS \quad ::= $ **delta** d $\{ \overline{COS} \}$	Delta Signature
$COS ::= $ **adds** $CS \mid$ **removes** C $\mid$ **modifies** C [**extends** C'] $\{ \overline{AOS} \}$	CO Signature
$AOS ::= $ **adds** $AS \mid$ **removes** a	AO Signature

$LD \quad ::= $ **line** L $(\overline{Z})$ $\{\mathcal{M}_{Main} \; \mathcal{M}_{Glue} \; \mathcal{K} \, AB\}$	Dependent SPL Delaration

Fig. 4. Syntax of IFMΔJ. Program signatures (top). SPL signature declarations (middle). Dependent SPL declarations (bottom)—the extensions with respect to IFΔJ SPLs (given in Fig. 2, with the syntax of artifact bases AB) are highlighted in grey.

to define what are its variants and their declaration), and then present the definition of the *interface* relation, defining when an SPL implements an SPLS.

Definition 6 (Generator of an SPLS). *The* generator *of an SPLS* Z, *denoted by* $\mathcal{G}_Z$, *is a mapping from products to program signatures defined similarly to the generator of an SPL (see Definition 3).*

Definition 7 (Program interface). *A program signature* PS_{Int} *is an* interface *of program* P, *denoted as* $PS_{Int} \preceq P$, *iff* PS_{Int} *is obtained from* P *by dropping some class or attributes, the body of the remaining methods and by replacing some* **extends** C *clause by* **extends** C' *where* C' *is a superclass of* C.

Definition 8 (SPL interface). *An SPLS* Z_{Int} *is an* interface *of an SPL* L, *denoted as* $Z_{Int} \preceq L$, *iff: (i)* $\mathcal{M}_{Z_{Int}} \preceq \mathcal{M}_L$; *and (ii) the generators* $\mathcal{G}_{Z_{Int}}$ *and* $\mathcal{G}_L$ *are total and for each* $p \in \mathcal{P}_L$, $\mathcal{G}_{Z_{Int}}(p \cap \mathcal{F}_{Z_{Int}}) \preceq \mathcal{G}_L(p)$.

We say that an SPL L *implements* an SPLS Z when Z is an interface of L.

Figure 5 represents an interface of SPL CapitalAccount (CapAccInt, on the left) and an interface of SPL FinancialAccount (FinAccInt, on the right), explanations are given in the caption.

3.2 Dependent SPLs

A *Dependent SPL* (DPL) is an SPL extended with dependencies modeled by SPLSs. The abstract syntax of IFMΔJ DPLs is given in Fig. 4 (bottom). A

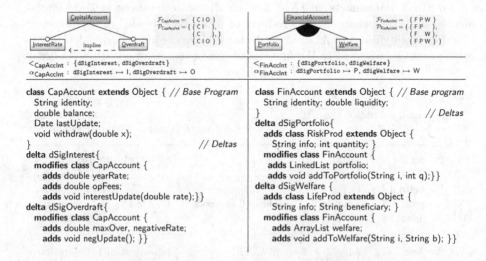

Fig. 5. Left: CapAccInt SPLS: $\mathcal{M}_{\mathsf{CapAccInt}}$ (top), $\mathcal{K}_{\mathsf{CapAccInt}}$ (middle), and $AB_{\mathsf{CapAccInt}}$ (bottom). This SPLS is an interface of the CapitalAccount SPL if Fig. 3 (left). It hides features BalanceInfo and YearlyFees. **Right:** FinAccInt SPLS: $\mathcal{M}_{\mathsf{FinAccInt}}$ (top), $\mathcal{K}_{\mathsf{FinAccInt}}$ (middle), and $AB_{\mathsf{FinAccInt}}$ (bottom). This SPLS is an interface of the FinancialAccount SPL of Fig. 3 (right). It hides feature AmountInfo.

DPL declaration comprises the name L of the DPL, a sequence of SPLS names $\overline{Z} = Z_1, \ldots, Z_n$ specifying its dependencies, a pair of feature models $\mathcal{M}_{Main}$ and $\mathcal{M}_{Glue}$, configuration knowledge $\mathcal{K}$ and an artifact base AB. The two feature models $\mathcal{M}_{Main}$ and $\mathcal{M}_{Glue}$ structure the actual feature model $\mathcal{M}_L$ of L in two parts: $\mathcal{M}_{Main}$ describes the part of $\mathcal{M}_L$ that is local to L, while $\mathcal{M}_{Glue}$ states how the features of $\mathcal{M}_L$ are related with the features of L's dependencies. Formally, the feature model of L is defined as a composition of $\mathcal{M}_{Main}$ and the feature models $\mathcal{M}_{Z_1}, \ldots, \mathcal{M}_{Z_n}$, glued together with $\mathcal{M}_{Glue}$: $\mathcal{M}_L = \mathcal{M}_{Main/\overline{Z}} = \mathcal{M}_{Main} \circ \mathcal{M}_{Glue} \mathcal{M}_{\overline{Z}}$ where $\mathcal{M}_{\overline{Z}} = \mathcal{R}(\mathcal{M}_{Z_1}) \bullet \cdots \bullet \mathcal{R}(\mathcal{M}_{Z_n})$. Lemma 1 below guarantees that the order of $Z_1, \ldots, Z_n$ is immaterial.

Lemma 1 (Join operation). *The join operation* $\bullet$ *is associative and commutative, with* $\mathcal{M}_{Id} = \mathcal{R}(\mathcal{M}_{\emptyset}) = \mathcal{R}((\emptyset, \emptyset)) = (\emptyset, \{\emptyset\})$ *as identity.*

Figure 6 presents the DPL DualAccount with dependencies CapAccInt and FinAccInt —explanations are given in the caption.

Remark 3 (DPL conservatively extends SPL). In order to ensure that the concept of DPL is a conservative extension of the concept of SPL (cf. Sect. 2.1), we assume that if a DPL L has no dependencies (i.e., $\overline{Z} = \emptyset$) then $\mathcal{M}_{Glue} = \mathcal{M}_{Id}$ (cf. Lemma 1). Therefore: (i) any DPL L without dependencies can be seen as an SPL with feature model $\mathcal{M}_L = \mathcal{M}_{Main}$; and (ii) any SPL L can be seen as a DPL with $\mathcal{M}_{Main} = \mathcal{M}_L$ and $\mathcal{M}_{Glue} = \mathcal{M}_{Id}$.

Definition 9 (Multi Software Product Lines). *A* Multi Software Product Line *(MPL) is a set of SPL Signatures and Dependent SPLs.*

Sanity Conditions. To simplify the manipulation of our model in the rest of the document, we give here a set of standard sanity conditions that are supposed to be satisfied by the MPLs that we consider in this paper. First, we suppose that all the DPL and SPLS names used in an MPL are declared exactly once in the MPL. Second, we suppose that a DPL depends *only once* on an SPLS, i.e., the list of dependencies ($\overline{Z}$) in the DPL syntax does not contain duplicates. Finally, we suppose that a class can only be declared and modified by at most one DPL in an MPL. Note that class disjointness enforces a boundary between different DPLs and rules out class name clashes between variants of different DPLs. Moreover, without loss of generality, we assume that the scope of the name of a delta is limited to the DPL or SPLS that contain its declaration (i.e., each delta name may belong to a unique DPL or SPLS).

3.3   DPLs Composition

The concept of *DPL-SPLs composition* formalizes composition of software product lines through aggregation by means of the concepts of DPL and SPL interface

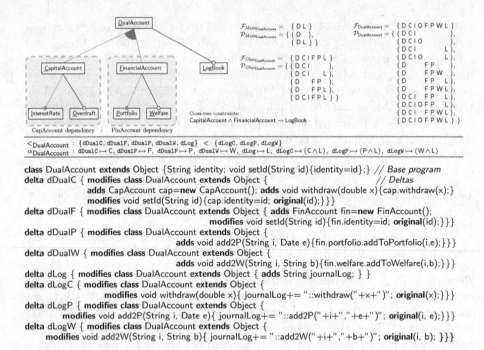

$\mathcal{F}_{Main_{DualAccount}} = \{D\ L\}$
$\mathcal{P}_{Main_{DualAccount}} = \{\{D\quad\},\{D\ L\}\}$

$\mathcal{F}_{DualAccount} = \{D\ C\ I\ O\ F\ P\ W\ L\}$
$\mathcal{P}_{DualAccount} = \{\{D\ C\ I\qquad\},$
$\{D\ C\ I\qquad\},$
$\{D\ C\ I\ O\qquad\},$
$\{D\ C\ I\qquad L\},$
$\{D\ C\ I\ O\qquad L\},$

$\mathcal{F}_{Glue_{DualAccount}} = \{D\ C\ I\ F\ P\ L\}$
$\mathcal{P}_{Glue_{DualAccount}} = \{\{D\ C\ I\qquad\},$
$\{D\ C\ I\qquad L\},$
$\{D\quad F\ P\quad\},$
$\{D\quad F\ P\ L\},$
$\{D\ C\ I\ F\ P\ L\}\}$

$\{D\qquad F\ P\qquad\},$
$\{D\qquad F\ P\ W\quad\},$
$\{D\qquad F\ P\qquad L\},$
$\{D\qquad F\ P\ W\ L\},$
$\{D\ C\ I\ O\ F\ P\qquad L\},$
$\{D\ C\ I\qquad F\ P\ W\ L\},$
$\{D\ C\ I\ O\ F\ P\ W\ L\}\}$

Cross-tree constraints:
CapitalAccount ∧ FinancialAccount → LogBook

$<_{DualAccount}$: {dDualC, dDualF, dDualP, dDualW, dLog} < {dLogC, dLogP, dLogW}
$\alpha_{DualAccount}$: dDualC ↦ C, dDualF ↦ F, dDualP ↦ P, dDualW ↦ W, dLog ↦ L, dLogC ↦ (C∧L), dLogP ↦ (P∧L), dLogW ↦ (W∧L)

```
class DualAccount extends Object {String identity; void setId(String id){identity=id};} // Base program
delta dDualC { modifies class DualAccount extends Object {                                    // Deltas
                    adds CapAccount cap=new CapAccount(); adds void withdraw(double x){cap.withdraw(x);}
                    modifies void setId(String id){cap.identity=id; original(id);}}}
delta dDualF { modifies class DualAccount extends Object { adds FinAccount fin=new FinAccount();
                                    modifies void setId(String id){fin.identity=id; original(id);}}}
delta dDualP { modifies class DualAccount extends Object {
                            adds void add2P(String i, Date e){fin.portfolio.addToPortfolio(i,e);}}}
delta dDualW { modifies class DualAccount extends Object {
                            adds void add2W(String i, String b){fin.welfare.addToWelfare(i,b);}}}
delta dLog { modifies class DualAccount extends Object { adds String journalLog; } }
delta dLogC { modifies class DualAccount extends Object {
                    modifies void withdraw(double x){ journalLog+= "::withdraw("+x+")"; original(x);}}}
delta dLogP { modifies class DualAccount extends Object {
                modifies void add2P(String i, Date e){ journalLog+= "::add2P("+i+","+e+")"; original(i, e);}}}
delta dLogW { modifies class DualAccount extends Object {
                modifies void add2W(String i, String b){ journalLog+= "::add2W("+i+","+b+")"; original(i, b); }}}
```

Fig. 6. DualAccount DPL is declared as:

line   DualAccount(CapAccInt,FinAccInt) $\{\mathcal{M}_{Main_{DualAccount}} \mathcal{M}_{Glue_{DualAccount}} \mathcal{K}_{DualAccount} \mathcal{AB}_{DualAccount}\}$.
It has feature model $\mathcal{M}_{DualAccount} = \mathcal{M}_{Main_{DualAccount}}/CapAccInt,FinAccInt =$
$\mathcal{M}_{Main_{DualAccount}} \circ \mathcal{M}_{Glue_{DualAccount}} \mathcal{M}_{CapAccInt,FinAccInt}$ (depicted as a feature diagram at
the top of the figure); configuration knowledge $\mathcal{K}_{DualAccount}$ (middle); and artifact
base $\mathcal{AB}_{DualAccount}$ (bottom). It provides a class **DualAccount** that combines two
bank accounts that satisfy the dependencies CapAccInt and FinAccInt (given in
Fig. 5), respectively. The feature model $\mathcal{M}_{DualAccount}$ is the composition of four feature
models. (i) The feature model $\mathcal{M}_{Main_{DualAccount}}$, which comprises the mandatory feature
DualAccount and the optional feature LogBook (that ensures that transactions are
traced). (ii)-(iii) The feature models of the dependencies CapAccInt and FinAccInt
(given in Fig. 5). (iv) The feature model $\mathcal{M}_{Glue_{DualAccount}}$, which has features DualAccount, LogBook, CapitalAccount,FinancialAccount, InterestRate, Portfolio and expresses
the constraints FinancialAccount ∨ CapitalAccount, CapitalAccount → InterestRate
FinancialAccount → Portfolio (represented by the parts colored in red of the feature
diagram) and CapitalAccount ∧ FinancialAccount → LogBook (represented by the
cross-tree constraint, also colored in red). The dashed rectangles depict the feature
diagrams representing the feature model obtained from $\mathcal{M}_{CapAccInt}$ and $\mathcal{M}_{FinAccInt}$ by
adding the constraints provided by the feature model $\mathcal{M}_{Glue_{DualAccount}}$, respectively.
(color figure online)

(i.e., by inclusion of some SPLs into a DPL to fulfill its dependencies)—thus
extending the concept of feature model composition to encompass the configuration knowledge and the artifact base.

Definition 10 (DPL-SPLs composition). *Let* L *be a DPL with dependencies* $\overline{Z} = Z_1, ..., Z_n$ $(n \geq 0)$ *and* $\overline{L} = L_1, ..., L_n$ *be SPLs such that* $Z_i \preceq L_i$ $(1 \leq i \leq n)$. *The composition of* L *with* $\overline{L}$ *is the SPL (cf. Remark 3)* $L_0 = L(\overline{L})$ *such that:*[1]

- $\mathcal{M}_{Main_{L_0}} = \mathcal{M}_{Main_L/\overline{L}} = \mathcal{M}_{Main_L} \circ_{\mathcal{M}_{Glue_L}} \mathcal{M}_{\overline{L}}$;
- $\mathcal{K}_{L_0} = (\alpha_{L_0}, <_{L_0}) = (\alpha'_L \cup (\bigcup_{i \in \{1,...,n\}} \alpha'_{L_i}), <_L \cup (\bigcup_{i \in \{1,...,n\}} <_{L_i}))$ *where*
  - $\alpha'_L(d) = \{p \in \mathcal{P}_{L_0} \mid p \cap \mathcal{F}_L \in \alpha_L(d)\}$ *for all deltas* d *of* L;
  - $\alpha'_{L_i}(d) = \{p \in \mathcal{P}_{L_0} \mid p \cap \mathcal{F}_{L_i} \in \alpha_{L_i}(d)\}$ *for all deltas* d *of* L_i;
- $AB_{L_0} = AB_L \cup (\bigcup_{i \in \{1,...,n\}} AB_{L_i})$; *and*
- $\mathcal{M}_{Glue_{L_0}} = \mathcal{M}_{Id}$.

Note that, if L has no dependencies (i.e., $n = 0$), then $\mathcal{G}_{L(\overline{L})} = \mathcal{G}_{L(\emptyset)} = \mathcal{G}_L$ (so, $L(\overline{L})$ and L have the same variants). For example, the DPL DualAccount can be composed with the SPLs CapitalAccount and FinancialAccount to obtain the SPL DualAccount(CapitalAccount,FinancialAccount).

The following theorems shed light on DPL-SPLs composition. Theorem 1 states that the variants of the composed SPL $L(\overline{L})$ can be generated by building the composed feature model $\mathcal{M}_{L(\overline{L})}$ and then using the generators of the DPL L and of the SPLs $\overline{L}$—thus, there is no need to actually build the whole $L(\overline{L})$. Theorem 2 states that fulfilling the dependencies of a DPL preserves the set of implemented interfaces.

Theorem 1 (Generator of the composed product line). *Let* $L_0 = L(\overline{L})$. *For each product* $p \in \mathcal{P}_{L_0}$, $\mathcal{G}_{L_0}(p) = \mathcal{G}_L(p \cap \mathcal{F}_L) \cup (\bigcup_{L_i \in \overline{L}} \mathcal{G}_{L_i}(p \cap \mathcal{F}_{L_i}))$.

Theorem 2 (DPL-SPLs composition preserves interfacing). *Let* Z *be an SPLS,* L *be a DPL with dependencies* $\overline{Z} = Z_1, ..., Z_n$ $(n \geq 0)$, *and* $\overline{L} = L_1, ..., L_n$ *be SPLs. If* $Z \preceq L$ *and* $Z_i \preceq L_i$ $(1 \leq i \leq n)$, *then* $Z \preceq L(\overline{L})$.

In the following, we show that composition can also be done between DPLs: we just need to define the *interface* relation on DPLs and then extend the DPL-SPLs composition to DPL-DPL as well.

Definition 11 (DPL interface). *An SPLS* Z_{Int} *is an* interface *of an DPL* L *with dependencies* $\overline{Z}$, *denoted as* $Z_{Int} \preceq L$, *iff (i)* $\mathcal{M}_{Z_{Int}} \preceq \mathcal{M}_L$; *and (ii) the generators* $\mathcal{G}_{Z_{Int}}$, $\mathcal{G}_L$ *and* $\mathcal{G}_{\overline{Z}}$ *are total and for each* $p \in \mathcal{P}_L$, $\mathcal{G}_{Z_{Int}}(p \cap \mathcal{F}_{Z_{Int}}) \preceq \bigcup \mathcal{G}^*_Z(p \cap \mathcal{F}_Z) \cup \mathcal{G}_L(p)$, *where* $\mathcal{G}^*_Z(p \cap \mathcal{F}_Z)$ *is equal to* $\mathcal{G}_Z(p \cap \mathcal{F}_Z)$ *with all method declarations extended with the body* {**return null;**}.

The following definition extends the concept of DPL-SPLs composition (Definition 10) by accepting DPLs as arguments and yielding a DPL as result.

Definition 12 (DPL-DPLs composition). *Let* L *be a DPL with dependencies* $\overline{Z} = Z_1, ..., Z_n$ $(n \geq 0)$ *and* $\overline{L} = L_1, ..., L_n$ *be DPLs such that* $Z_i \preceq L_i$ $(1 \leq i \leq n)$.

---

[1] Because of the delta scope assumption, in the definition of $\mathcal{K}_{L_0}$ the union of the application ordering relations (which denotes the relation obtained by union of their graphs) is well defined.

Let $\overline{Z}^{(i)} = Z_{i,1}, ..., Z_{i,n_i}$ $(n_i \geq 0)$ be the dependencies of L_i $(1 \leq i \leq n)$. The composition of L with $\overline{L}$ is the DPL $L_0 = L(\overline{L})$, with dependencies $\overline{Z}^{(1)}, ..., \overline{Z}^{(n)}$, such that $\mathcal{M}_{Main_{L_0}}$, $\mathcal{K}_{L_0}$ and AB_{L_0} are defined as in Definition 10, and $\mathcal{M}_{Glue_{L_0}}$ is defined by $\mathcal{M}_{Glue_{L_0}} = \mathcal{M}_{Glue_{L_1}} \bullet \cdots \bullet \mathcal{M}_{Glue_{L_n}}$.

Note that, if the DPLs L_i $(1 \leq i \leq n)$ have no dependencies (i.e., $\overline{Z}^{(i)} = \emptyset$ and $\mathcal{M}_{Glue_{L_i}} = \mathcal{M}_{Id}$), then $\mathcal{M}_{Glue_{L_0}} = \mathcal{M}_{Id}$ (like in Definition 10). Thus Definition 12 conservatively extends Definition 10. Moreover, Theorem 1 also holds when $\overline{L}$ and $L_0 = L(\overline{L})$ are DPLs, and Theorem 2 can be extended as follows:

Theorem 3 (DPL-DPLs composition preserves interfacing). *Let Z be an SPLS, L be a DPL with dependencies $\overline{Z} = Z_1, ..., Z_n$ $(n \geq 0)$, and $\overline{L} = L_1, ..., L_n$ be DPLs. If $Z \preceq L$ and $Z_i \preceq L_i$ $(1 \leq i \leq n)$, then $Z \preceq L(\overline{L})$.*

4   Compositionality of Existing SPL Analyses

In this section, we give two initial results illustrating the fact that our MPL model is well-suited for compositional analysis. First, we show that the results about the compositionality of existing analyses of feature models (*void feature model, core features, dead features, void partial configuration,* and *atomic sets*) given in [24, Sect. 5] can be used as-is in our model. Second, we show how to extend existing type systems for SPLs to ensure well-typedness in our model.

Compositional Analysis of Feature Models. The following theorem shows that the construction of the feature model of a DPL can be expressed as a sequence of ∘ operations. This, plus the fact that an SPLS Z is an interface of a DPL L only when $\mathcal{M}_Z \preceq \mathcal{M}_L$ ensures that the results presented in [24, Sect. 5] can be used as-is to analyse the feature models constructed in DPL-DPL compositions by analysing each feature model independently.

Theorem 4. *Let $\mathcal{M}_x = (\mathcal{F}_x, \mathcal{P}_x)$, $\mathcal{M}_{y_1} = (\mathcal{F}_{y_1}, \mathcal{P}_{y_1}), ..., \mathcal{M}_{y_n} = (\mathcal{F}_{y_n}, \mathcal{P}_{y_n})$, with $n \geq 1$, be feature models with pairwise feature disjointness (cf. Remark 2) and $\mathcal{M}_{\overline{y}} = \mathcal{R}(\mathcal{M}_{y_1}) \bullet \cdots \bullet \mathcal{R}(\mathcal{M}_{y_n})$. Then (for every permutation $w_1, ..., w_n$ of $y_1, ..., y_n$): $\mathcal{M}_{x/\overline{y}} = \mathcal{M}_x \circ_{\mathcal{M}_{Glue}} \mathcal{M}_{\overline{y}} = ((\mathcal{M}_x \circ_{\mathcal{M}_{Id}} \mathcal{M}_{w_1}) \cdots \circ_{\mathcal{M}_{Id}} \mathcal{M}_{w_{n-1}}) \circ_{\mathcal{M}_{Glue}} \mathcal{M}_{w_n}$.*

Compositional Type System for MPLs. Type checking an SPL means to check that all its variants can be generated and are well-typed programs. Performing this check by generating each variant and type checking it does not scale (a product line with n features can have up to 2^n products). Therefore, several SPL type checking approaches have been proposed in the literature [27]. Three type checking approaches for delta-oriented SPLs have been proposed and formalized [5,8,9] by means of the IFΔJ calculus.

In our MPL model, we add two structures that can be type-checked: DPLs and DPL-DPL compositions. However, due to the fact that the artifact base of a

DPL depends on code defined in other DPLs, it is too restrictive to require that its variants are well-typed programs: they can indeed contain missing dependencies. The following definition extends the notion of well-typedness to DPL to deal with the missing dependency problem:

Definition 13 (Well-typed DPL). *The* stub-completion *of an SPLS* Z*, written* $Z^\star$*, is the SPL obtained by adding the body* {**return null**;} *to all the method declarations in* Z*. The* stub-completion *of a DPL* L *with dependencies* $\overline{Z} = Z_1, ..., Z_n$ *(*$n \geq 0$*) is the SPL* $L^\star = L(Z_1^\star, ..., Z_n^\star)$ *obtained by composing* L *with the stub-completion of its dependencies. We say that a DPL is* well-typed *iff its stub-completion is well-typed.*

Note that this definition generalizes the notion of well-typedness for SPLs: when the set of dependencies of the DPL L is empty $(n = 0)$, L is well-typed iff it is well-typed in the SPL-sense of the term. Moreover, with this definition, extending the exisiting type-checking algorithms for SPL to manage DPL simply requires a pre-processing of the DPL to transform it in an SPL as described in the definition. An additional important property of this definition is that it is enough to type-check in isolation the DPLs in a DPL-DPL composition to ensure that the resulting DPL is well-typed:

Theorem 5 (Compositionality of DPL-DPLs composition type checking). *Let* L *be a DPL with dependencies* $\overline{Z} = Z_1, ..., Z_n$ *(*$n \geq 0$*) and* $\overline{L} = L_1, ..., L_n$ *be DPLs such that* $Z_i \preceq L_i$ *(*$1 \leq i \leq n$*). If each of the DPLs* $L, L_1, ..., L_n$ *type checks, then* $L(L_1, ..., L_n)$ *type checks.*

Note that the SPLs CapitalAccount and FinancialAccount (in Fig. 3), and the DPL DualAccount (in Fig. 6) type check: we can then conclude that the SPL DualAccount(CapAccount,FinAccount) type checks as well.

Checking the Interface Relation. The compositional analysis of feature models and the well-typedness of a DPL-DPL composition $L(\overline{L})$ presented previously heavily rely on the interface relation being satisfied between the dependencies of L and the DPLs $\overline{L}$. It is possible to automatically check this relation between any SPLS Z and any DPL L using a predicate formula written $match(Z, L)$. Due to lack of space, we cannot give the definition of this formula, we simply state the following theorem:

Theorem 6 (DPL interface checking). *If the SPLS* Z *and DPL* L *type check and* $\mathcal{M}_Z \preceq \mathcal{M}_L$ *holds, then* $match(Z, L)$ *is valid if and only if* $Z \preceq L$ *holds.*

5   Related Work and Conclusions

An extension of DOP to implement MPLs has been outlined in [10] by proposing linguistic constructs for defining an MPL as an SPL that imports other SPLs. The feature model and the artifact base of the importing SPL is deeply integrated with the feature models and the artifact bases of the imported SPLs, respectively.

This extension is very flexible, but it does not enforce any boundary between different SPLs—thus providing no support for compositional analyses.

Schröter et al. [25] advocated investigating suitable interfaces in order to support compositional analyses of MPLs for different stages of the development process. In particular, *syntactical interfaces*, which build on feature model interfaces to provide a view of reusable programming artifacts, and *behavioral interfaces*, which in turn build on syntactical interfaces to support formal verification. More recently, Schröter et al. [24] proposed a concept of feature model interface that consists of a subset of features (thus it hides all other features and dependencies) and used it in combination with a concept of feature model composition through aggregation to support compositional analyses of feature models—see Sect. 2.2. In this paper we build on [24] and propose the concepts of SPLS, DPL, and DPL-DPLs composition and show how to use them to support compositional type checking of delta-oriented MPL. An SPL signature is a syntactical interface that provides a variability-aware API, expressed in the flexible and modular DOP approach, specifying which classes and members of the variants of a DPL are intended to be accessible by variants of other DPLs.

Feature-context interfaces [26] are aimed at supporting type checking SPLs developed according to the FOP approach which, as pointed out in Sect. 1, is encompassed by DOP (see [22] for a detailed comparison between FOP and DOP). A feature-context interface supports type checking a feature module in the context of a set of features *FC*. It provides an invariable API specifying classes and members of the feature modules corresponding to the features in *FC* that are intended to be accessible. In contrast, our concept of SPLS represents a variability-aware API that supports compositional type checking of MPLs. Notably, since DOP is an extension of FOP, our results apply also to FOP SPLs.

Kästner et al. [16] proposed a variability-aware module system, where each module represents an SPL, that allows for type checking modules in isolation. Variability inside each module and its interface is expressed by means of #ifdef preprocessor directives and variable linking, respectively. In contrast to our SPLSs, module interfaces do not support hiding features and dependencies. A major difference with respect to our proposal is in the approach used to implement variability (i.e., to build variants): [16] considers an *annotative approach* (#ifdef preprocessor directives), while we consider a *transformational approach* (DOP)—we refer to [23,27] for classification and survey of different approaches for implementing variability.

Schröter et al. [24] defined a slice function for feature models (similar to the operator proposed by Acher et al. [1]) that generates a feature-model interface by removing a given set of features. In future work we would like to generalize the slice function for feature models to DPLs, thus providing an automatic means for generating an interface for a given DPL.

Recently, Thüm et al. [28] proposed a notion of behavioral interface for supporting compositional verification of FOP SPLs via variability encoding [29]. In future work we would like to enrich SPLSs with method contracts (thus promoting them to behavioral interfaces) in order to support compositional verification of delta-oriented DPLs by building on recently proposed proof systems and techniques for the verification of delta-oriented SPLs [6,11,12].

We plan to implement our approach for both DeltaJ 1.5 [17] (a prototypical implementation of DOP that supports full Java 1.5) and the ABSTRACT BEHAVIORAL SPECIFICATION modeling language [15].

Acknowledgments. We thank the anonymous reviewers for comments and suggestions for improving the presentation. We also thank Lorenzo Testa for comments and suggestions during the preparation of the post-proceedings version.

References

1. Acher, M., Collet, P., Lahire, P., France, R.B: Slicing feature models. In: 26th IEEE/ACM International Conference on Automated Software Engineering (ASE) 2011, pp. 424–427 (2011). doi:10.1109/ASE.2011.6100089
2. Apel, S., Batory, D.S., Kästner, C., Saake, G.: Feature-Oriented Software Product: Concepts and Implementation. Springer, Heidelberg (2013). doi:10.1007/978-3-642-37521-7
3. Batory, D.: Feature models, grammars, and propositional formulas. In: Obbink, H., Pohl, K. (eds.) SPLC 2005. LNCS, vol. 3714, pp. 7–20. Springer, Heidelberg (2005). doi:10.1007/11554844_3
4. Batory, D., Sarvela, J.N., Rauschmayer, A.: Scaling step-wise refinement. IEEE Trans. Softw. Eng. **30**, 355–371 (2004)
5. Bettini, L., Damiani, F., Schaefer, I.: Compositional type checking of delta-oriented software product lines. Acta Informatica **50**(2), 77–122 (2013)
6. Bubel, R., Damiani, F., Hähnle, R., Johnsen, E.B., Owe, O., Schaefer, I., Yu, I.C.: Proof repositories for compositional verification of evolving software systems. In: Steffen, B. (ed.) Transactions on Foundations for Mastering Change I. LNCS, vol. 9960, pp. 130–156. Springer, Cham (2016). doi:10.1007/978-3-319-46508-1_8
7. Clements, P., Northrop, L.: Software Product Lines: Practices & Patterns. Addison Wesley Longman, Boston (2001)
8. Damiani, F., Lienhardt, M.: On type checking delta-oriented product lines. In: Ábrahám, E., Huisman, M. (eds.) IFM 2016. LNCS, vol. 9681, pp. 47–62. Springer, Cham (2016). doi:10.1007/978-3-319-33693-0_4
9. Damiani, F., Schaefer, I.: Family-based analysis of type safety for delta-oriented software product lines. In: Margaria, T., Steffen, B. (eds.) ISoLA 2012. LNCS, vol. 7609, pp. 193–207. Springer, Heidelberg (2012). doi:10.1007/978-3-642-34026-0_15
10. Damiani, F., Schaefer, I., Winkelmann, T.: Delta-oriented multi software product lines. In: Proceedings of the 18th International Software Product Line Conference SPLC 2014, Vol. 1, pp. 232–236. ACM (2014). doi:10.1145/2648511.2648536
11. Hähnle, R., Schaefer, I.: A liskov principle for delta-oriented programming. In: Margaria, T., Steffen, B. (eds.) ISoLA 2012. LNCS, vol. 7609, pp. 32–46. Springer, Heidelberg (2012). doi:10.1007/978-3-642-34026-0_4
12. Hähnle, R., Schaefer, I., Bubel, R.: Reuse in software verification by abstract method calls. In: Bonacina, M.P. (ed.) CADE 2013. LNCS (LNAI), vol. 7898, pp. 300–314. Springer, Heidelberg (2013). doi:10.1007/978-3-642-38574-2_21

13. Holl, G., Grünbacher, P., Rabiser, R.: A systematic review and an expert survey on capabilities supporting multi product lines. Inf. Softw. Technol. **54**(8), 828–852 (2012)

14. Igarashi, A., Pierce, B., Wadler, P.: Featherweight java: a minimal core calculus for java and GJ. ACM TOPLAS **23**(3), 396–450 (2001)

15. Johnsen, E.B., Hähnle, R., Schäfer, J., Schlatte, R., Steffen, M.: ABS: a core language for abstract behavioral specification. In: Aichernig, B.K., Boer, F.S., Bonsangue, M.M. (eds.) FMCO 2010. LNCS, vol. 6957, pp. 142–164. Springer, Heidelberg (2011). doi:10.1007/978-3-642-25271-6_8

16. Kästner, C., Ostermann, K., Erdweg, S.: A variability-aware module system. In: Proceedings of the ACM International Conference on Object Oriented Programming Systems Languages and Applications OOPSLA 2012, pp. 773–792. ACM (2012). doi:10.1145/2384616.2384673

17. Koscielny, J., Holthusen, S., Schaefer, I., Schulze, S., Bettini, L., Damiani, F.: DeltaJ 1.5: delta-oriented programming for Java. In: International Conference on Principles and Practices of Programming on the Java Platform Virtual Machines, Languages and Tools PPPJ 2014, pp. 63–74 (2014). doi:10.1145/2647508.2647512

18. Lienhardt, M., Clarke, D.: Conflict detection in delta-oriented programming. In: Margaria, T., Steffen, B. (eds.) ISoLA 2012. LNCS, vol. 7609, pp. 178–192. Springer, Heidelberg (2012). doi:10.1007/978-3-642-34026-0_14

19. Pohl, K., Böckle, G., van der Linden, F.: Software Product Line Engineering - Foundations, Principles, and Techniques. Springer, Heidelberg (2005). doi:10.1007/3-540-28901-1

20. Rosenmüller, M., Siegmund, N., ur Rahman, S.S., Kästner, C.: Modeling dependent software product lines. In: Proceedings of the GPCE Workshop on Modularization, Composition and Generative Techniques for Product Line Engineering (McGPLE), MIP-0802, pp. 13–18. Department of Informatics and Mathematics, University of Passau (2008)

21. Schaefer, I., Bettini, L., Bono, V., Damiani, F., Tanzarella, N.: Delta-oriented programming of software product lines. In: Bosch, J., Lee, J. (eds.) SPLC 2010. LNCS, vol. 6287, pp. 77–91. Springer, Heidelberg (2010). doi:10.1007/978-3-642-15579-6_6

22. Schaefer, I., Damiani, F.: Pure delta-oriented programming. In: Proceedings of the 2nd International Workshop on Feature-Oriented Software Development, FOSD 2010, pp. 49–56. ACM (2010). doi:10.1145/1868688.1868696

23. Schaefer, I., Rabiser, R., Clarke, D., Bettini, L., Benavides, D., Botterweck, G., Pathak, A., Trujillo, S., Villela, K.: Software diversity: state of the art and perspectives. Int. J. Softw. Tools Technol. Transfer **14**(5), 477–495 (2012)

24. Schröter, R., Krieter, S., Thüm, T., Benduhn, F., Saake, G.: Feature-model interfaces: The highway to compositional analyses of highly-configurable systems. In: Proceedings of the 38th International Conference on Software Engineering ICSE 2016, pp. 667–678. ACM (2016). doi:10.1145/2884781.2884823

25. Schröter, R., Siegmund, N., Thüm, T.: Towards modular analysis of multi product lines. In: Proceedings of the 17th International Software Product Line Conference Co-located Workshops SPLC 2013, pp 96–99. ACM (2013). doi:10.1145/2499777.2500719

26. Schröter, R., Siegmund, N., Thüm, T., Saake, G.: Feature-context interfaces: Tailored programming interfaces for spls. In: Proceedings of the 18th International Software Product Line Conference SPLC 2014, Vol. 1, pp. 102–111. ACM (2014). doi:10.1145/2648511.2648522

27. Thüm, T., Apel, S., Kästner, C., Schaefer, I., Saake, G.: A classification and survey of analysis strategies for software product lines. ACM Comput. Surv. **47**(1), 6:1–6:45 (2014)

28. Thüm, T., Winkelmann, T., Schröter, R., Hentschel, M., Krüger, S.: Variability hiding in contracts for dependent spls. In: Proceedings of the Tenth International Workshop on Variability Modelling of Software-intensive Systems VaMoS 2016, pp. 97–104. ACM (2016). doi:10.1145/2866614.2866628

29. von Rhein, A., Thm, T., Schaefer, I., Liebig, J., Apel, S.: Variability encoding: from compile-time to load-time variability. J. Logical and Algebraic Methods Program. **85**(1, Part 2), 125–145 (2016)

Translating Active Objects into Colored Petri Nets for Communication Analysis

Anastasia Gkolfi[(✉)], Crystal Chang Din, Einar Broch Johnsen,
Martin Steffen, and Ingrid Chieh Yu

Department of Informatics, University of Oslo, Oslo, Norway
{natasa,crystald,einarj,msteffen,ingridcy}@ifi.uio.no

Abstract. Actor-based languages attract attention for their ability to
scale to highly parallel architectures. Active objects combine the asynchronous communication of actors with object-oriented programming by
means of asynchronous method calls and synchronization on futures.
However, the combination of asynchronous calls and synchronization
introduces communication cycles which lead to a form of communication deadlock. This paper addresses such communication deadlocks for
ABS, a formally defined active object language which additionally supports cooperative scheduling to express complex distributed control flow,
using first-class futures and explicit process release points. Our approach
is based on a translation of the semantics of ABS into colored Petri nets,
such that a particular program corresponds to a marking of this net.
We prove the soundness of this translation and demonstrate by example
how the implementation of this net can be used to analyze ABS programs
with respect to communication deadlock.

1 Introduction

The Actor model [1,2] of concurrency is attracting increasing attention for their
decoupling of control flow and communication. This decoupling enables both
scalability (as argued with the Erlang programming language [3] and Scala's
actor model [14]) and compositional reasoning [11]. Actors are independent units
of computation which exchange messages and execute local code sequentially.
Instead of pushing the current procedure (or method activation) on the control
stack when sending a message as in thread-based concurrency models, messages
are sent asynchronously, without any transfer of control between the actors.
In the actor model, a message triggers the execution of a method body in the
target actor, but a reply to the message is not directly supported. Extending the
basic actor model, active object languages (e.g., [8,18]), which combine actor-
like communication with object orientation, use so-called futures to reintroduce
synchronization by combining asynchronous message sending with the call and

---

The work was partially supported by the Norwegian Research Council under the
CUMULUS project.

Published by Springer International Publishing AG 2017. All Rights Reserved
M. Dastani and M. Sirjani (Eds.): FSEN 2017, LNCS 10522, pp. 84–99, 2017.
DOI: 10.1007/978-3-319-68972-2_6

reply structure of method calls. A future can be seen as a mailbox from which a reply may be retrieved, such that the synchronization is decoupled from message sending and associated with fetching the reply from a method call. The caller synchronizes with the existence of a reply from a method call by performing a *blocking* get-operation on the future associated with the call. However, this synchronization may lead to complex dependency cycles in the communication chain of a program, and gives rise to a form of deadlock with a set of mutually blocked objects. This situation is often called a *communication deadlock* [9].

This paper addresses the problem of communication deadlock for the active object language ABS [18,19]. ABS is characteristic in that it supports *cooperative concurrency* in the active objects. Cooperative concurrency allows the execution of a method body to be suspended at explicit points in the code, for example by testing whether a future has received a value. Cooperative concurrency leads to a form of local race-free interleaving for concurrently executing active objects, which allows more execution traces than in standard active objects. Our approach to tackle the callback problem for ABS is based on a translation of the formal semantics of ABS into colored Petri nets (CPN) [17]. Petri nets provide a basic model of concurrency, causality, and synchronization [22,25], which has previously been used to analyze communication patterns and deadlock, e.g., [10,15]. CPNs extend the basic Petri net model with support for modeling data. In contrast to previous work, we do not produce a particular Petri net for each program to be analyzed. Instead, we provide an encoding and implementation of the formal semantics of ABS itself as a net, and use colored tokens in this net to encode the program. Consequently, the number of places in the net is independent of the size of a program, and different programs are captured by different markings of the net. For example, this approach allows us to capture dynamic object creation by firing transitions in the net.

The main contributions of this paper are:

- a deep encoding of the formal semantics of ABS in CPNs;
- a translation of concrete ABS programs into markings of this net;
- a soundness proof for the translation from ABS to CPN; and
- an example demonstrating how to analyze communication deadlocks for active objects in ABS using the implementation of this net in CPN Tools [24].

The paper is organized as follows: Sect. 2 introduces the syntax and semantics of the ABS language, focusing on the language features for communication and synchronization. Section 3 briefly introduces colored Petri nets. Section 4 explains the translation from ABS semantics to colored Petri nets and the soundness proof for this translation. Section 5 presents a concrete ABS example and shows how the CPN Tools detects communication deadlock. Section 6 discusses related work and Sect. 7 concludes the paper.

2   The ABS Concurrency Model

The Abstract Behavioral Specification language (ABS) [18,19] is an object-oriented language for modeling concurrent and distributed systems. ABS

Syntactic categories.   *Definitions.*
s in Stmt $P ::= \overline{CL} \{\overline{T}\ \overline{x};\ s\}$
e in Expr $CL ::= \textbf{class}\ C\,(\overline{T}\ \overline{x})\,\{\overline{T}\ \overline{x};\ \overline{M}\}$
g in Guard $Sg ::= T\ m\ (\overline{T}\ \overline{x})$
                    $M ::= Sg\ \{\overline{T}\ \overline{x};\ s\}$
                    $s ::= s; s \mid \textbf{skip} \mid x = rhs \mid \textbf{if}\ e\ \{s\}\ \textbf{else}\ \{s\}$
                    $\mid \textbf{while}\ e\ \textbf{do}\ s \mid \textbf{suspend} \mid \textbf{await}\ g \mid \textbf{return}\ e$
                    $rhs ::= e \mid cm \mid \textbf{new}\ C(\overline{e})$
                    $cm ::= e!m(\overline{e}) \mid x.\,\textbf{get}$
                    $g ::= x? \mid g \wedge g$

Fig. 1. Abstract syntax of ABS, where overline notation such as $\overline{e}$ and $\overline{x}$ denotes (possibly empty) lists over the corresponding syntactic categories.

combines asynchronous communication from the Actor model [1,2] with object orientation, and supports cooperative scheduling such that process release points are explicit in the program code. For the purposes of this paper, we focus on the communication and synchronization aspects of ABS. Also we ignore other aspects such as concurrent object groups, i.e., we consider one object per group, the functional sublanguage, and deployment aspects such as deployment components and resource annotations [19]. ABS is statically typed, based on interfaces as object types [18]. Ignoring the details of the type system, we let primitive types such as Int and Bool and class names constitute the types of a program, and ignore subtyping issues.

2.1   The Syntax

Figure 1 presents the syntax of ABS [18], focusing on communication and synchronization. Programs P consist of class definitions CL and a main block representing the program's initial activity. Statements s include standard control-flow constructs such as sequential composition, assignment statement, conditionals, and while-loops. ABS supports *asynchronous* method calls $f = e!m(\overline{e})$ where the caller and callee proceed concurrently and f is a so-called *future*. A future is a "mailbox" where the return value from the method call may eventually be returned to by the callee. A future that contains return value is resolved. The result of the asynchronous call can then be obtained by $f.\textbf{get}$. Note that we may alternatively write asynchronous method call statement as $e!m(\overline{e})$, if the return value is not required. ABS also supports local synchronous calls which are more standard. For brevity, we elide discussion of synchronous method calls here (the CPN realization in Sect. 4 also covers synchronous, reentrant self-calls).

The (active) objects of ABS act like monitors, allowing at most one method activation, or process, to be executed at a time. The local execution in an object is based on *cooperative* scheduling by introducing a guard statement **await** g: If g evaluates to true, execution may proceed; if the guard g evaluates to false, execution is suspended and another process may execute. For a future f, the guard $f?$ evaluates true if f contains the return value from the associated method

call and otherwise it evaluates to false. The **suspend**-statement always suspends
the executing process. The typical usage of asynchronous calls follow the pattern
$f = e!m(\overline{e}); \ldots;$ **await** $f?; \ldots; x = f.$**get**.

2.2   The Operational Semantics

The operational semantics of ABS specifies transitions between *configurations*. A
run-time configuration contains objects $o(\!|a, p, q|\!)$, messages $\langle o'.m(v) \rangle_f$, resolved
futures $\langle v \rangle_f$, and unresolved futures $\langle \perp \rangle_f$. We use $\|$ to denote the (associative
and commutative) parallel composition of such entities in a run-time configu-
ration. Class definitions, which do not change during execution, are assumed
to be implicitly available in the operational rules. The semantics maintains as
invariant that object identities o and future identities f are unique. Objects
$o(\!|a, p, q|\!)$ are instances of classes with an identifier o, an object state a which
maps instance variables to values, an active process p, and an unordered queue q
of suspended processes. A *process* p is a triple $\langle l \mid s \rangle_f$ with a local state l (mapping method-local variables to values), a statement s, and a future reference f.
We omit the future reference in the rules if it is unnecessary. The special process
idle is used to represent that there is no active process. A message $\langle o'.m(v) \rangle_f$
represents a method call *before* it starts to execute and the resolved future $\langle v \rangle_f$
the corresponding return value after method execution.

Figure 2 gives the rules of the operational semantics, concentrating on the
behavior of a single active object. A skip-statement has no effect (cf. rule SKIP).
In an idle object, the scheduler selects (and removes) a process p from the queue,
and starts executing it (cf. rule ACTIVATE). Executing **suspend** moves the
active process to the queue, resulting in an idle object (cf. rule SUSPEND). Assignments are either to instance variables or local variables (cf. rules ASSIGN$_1$ and
ASSIGN$_2$, where σ is used to abbreviate the pair of local states l and object states
a. We assume that these are disjoint, so the two cases are mutually exclusive.)
We omit the standard rules for conditionals and while-loops. Object creation is
captured by rule NEW-OBJECT, where a' is the initial state of the new object
(determined by an auxiliary function *atts*) and p' is the object's initial activity. An asynchronous method call creates a fresh future reference f and adds
a message and unresolved future corresponding to the call to the configuration
(cf. rule ASYNC-CALL). Binding a method name to the corresponding method
body is done in rule BIND-MTD. The binding operation, locating the code of the
method body and instantiating the formal parameters, works in the standard
way via late-binding, consulting the class hierarchy.

The return statement stores the return value in the corresponding future,
resolving the future (cf. rule RETURN). The get-command allows the result value
to be obtained from the corresponding future reference if the future's value has
been produced, in which case the future has been *resolved* (cf. rule GET). Otherwise, the get-command blocks. An attempt to fetch a future value via a get
statement does not introduce a scheduling point. Should the value never be
produced, e.g., because the corresponding method activation does not return,
the client object of the future, executing the get-command, will be blocked. A

$$\frac{\text{(SKIP)}}{o(\!|a, \langle l \,|\, \textbf{skip}; s\rangle, q|\!) \rightarrow o(\!|a, \langle l \,|\, s\rangle, q|\!)}$$

$$\frac{\text{(ACTIVATE)}}{p = select(q, a)}{o(\!|a, idle, q|\!) \rightarrow o(\!|a, p, q \backslash p|\!)}$$

$$\frac{\text{(SUSPEND)}}{o(\!|a, \langle l \,|\, \textbf{suspend}; s\rangle, q|\!) \rightarrow o(\!|a, idle, \langle l \,|\, s\rangle :: q|\!)}$$

$$\frac{\text{(ASSIGN}_1) \quad x \in dom(l)}{o(\!|a, \langle l \,|\, x = e; s\rangle, q|\!) \rightarrow o(\!|a, \langle l[x \mapsto [\![e]\!]_\sigma] \,|\, s\rangle, q|\!)}$$

$$\frac{\text{(ASSIGN}_2) \quad x \in dom(a)}{o(\!|a, \langle l \,|\, x = e; s\rangle, q|\!) \rightarrow o(\!|a[x \mapsto [\![e]\!]_\sigma], \langle l \,|\, s\rangle, q|\!)}$$

$$\frac{\text{(RETURN)}}{o(\!|a, \langle l \,|\, \textbf{return } (e); s\rangle_f, q|\!) \,\|\, \langle \perp \rangle_f \rightarrow o(\!|a, idle, q|\!) \,\|\, \langle [\![e]\!]_\sigma \rangle_f}$$

$$\frac{\text{(ASYNC-CALL)} \quad [\![e]\!]_\sigma = o' \quad fresh(f)}{o(\!|a, \langle l \,|\, x = e!m(\bar{e}); s\rangle, q|\!) \rightarrow o(\!|a, \langle l \,|\, x = f; s\rangle, q|\!) \,\|\, \langle o'.m([\![\bar{e}]\!]_\sigma) \rangle_f \,\|\, \langle \perp \rangle_f}$$

$$\frac{\text{(BIND-MTD)} \quad p = bind(o, m, \bar{v}, f)}{o(\!|a, \langle l \,|\, s\rangle, q|\!) \,\|\, \langle o.m(\bar{v}) \rangle_f \rightarrow o(\!|a, \langle l \,|\, s\rangle, p :: q|\!)}$$

$$\frac{\text{(NEW-OBJECT)} \quad fresh(o') \quad a' = atts(C, [\![\bar{e}]\!]_\sigma, o')}{o(\!|a, \langle l \,|\, x = \textbf{new } C(\bar{e}); s\rangle, q|\!) \rightarrow o(\!|a, \langle l \,|\, x = o'; s\rangle, q|\!) \,\|\, o'(\!|a', idle, \emptyset|\!)}$$

$$\frac{\text{(READ-FUT)} \quad f = [\![e]\!]_\sigma}{o(\!|a, \langle l \,|\, x = e. \textbf{ get}; s\rangle, q|\!) \,\|\, \langle v \rangle_f \rightarrow o(\!|a, \langle l \,|\, x = v; s\rangle, q|\!) \,\|\, \langle v \rangle_f}$$

$$\frac{\text{(AWAIT}_1) \quad [\![e]\!]_\sigma = f}{o(\!|a, \langle l \,|\, \textbf{await } e; s\rangle, q|\!) \,\|\, \langle v \rangle_f \rightarrow o(\!|a, \langle l \,|\, s\rangle, q|\!) \,\|\, \langle v \rangle_f}$$

$$\frac{\text{(AWAIT}_2) \quad [\![e]\!]_\sigma = f}{o(\!|a, \langle l \,|\, \textbf{await } e; s\rangle, q|\!) \,\|\, \langle \perp \rangle_f \rightarrow o(\!|a, \langle l \,|\, \textbf{suspend}; \textbf{await } e; s\rangle, q|\!) \,\|\, \langle \perp \rangle_f}$$

Fig. 2. Operational semantics

common pattern for obtaining a future value therefore makes use of await: executing **await** x?; x. **get** checks whether or not the future reference for variable x has been produced. If not, the semantics of the await statement introduces a scheduling point. Once x? evaluates to true, the future's value remains available so x. **get** will not block. (see again rule READ-FUT).

Executing an await with a guard expression which evaluates to the identifier of a resolved future, behaves like a skip (cf. rule AWAIT$_1$). An await on a list of futures are equivalent to a list of awaits for individual futures. If the future corresponding to the guard expression has not been resolved, a **suspend**-statement is introduced to enable scheduling another process (cf. rule AWAIT$_2$).

3   Colored Petri Nets

Places and transitions in Petri nets capture true concurrency in terms of causality and synchronization [22,25]. Colored Petri nets (CPNs) extend the basic Petri net formalism to additionally model, e.g., data [16,17]. A CPN has color sets (=types). The set of types determines the data values and the operations that can be used in the net expressions. A type can be arbitrarily complex, defined by many sorted algebra in the same way as abstract data types. Each place in a CPN has an associated color set, restricting the kind of data a place can contain. Tokens in a typed place represent individual values of that type. CPNs in their basic form (ignoring hierarchical definitions) are defined as follows:

Definition 1 (Colored Petri net). *A colored Petri net (CPN) is a tuple* $(P, T, A, \Sigma, V, C, G, E, I)$ *where*

- places P and transitions T are disjoint finite sets;
- arcs A form a bipartite, directed graph over P and T, i.e., $A \subseteq P \times T \dot{\cup} T \times P$;
- types Σ form a finite set (each type seen as a non-empty "color set");
- typed variables V form a finite set, i.e., $type(v) \in \Sigma$ for all $v \in V$;
- a coloring $C : P \to \Sigma$ associates a type to each place.
- labeling functions $G : T \to Expr_V$ (guards) and $E : A \to Expr_V$ associate expressions to transitions and arcs; and the
- initialization function $I : P \to Expr_\emptyset$ associates expressions to places.

in which expressions are appropriately typed; i.e., $type(G(t)) = Bool$, $type(E(a)) = C(p) \to \mathbb{N}$, where p is the place connected to a, and $type(I(p)) = C(p) \to \mathbb{N}$ for all places.

Transitions and their guards express synchronization conditions which, together with the labels on the arcs, express the transition semantics of Petri nets. Since tokens are individual typed values and expressions contain variables, the enabledness of transitions depends on the choice of values for the free variables.

Bindings (or variable assignments) b are mappings from variables to values; we assume bindings to respect the types of the variables. The *variables of a transition* t, written $Var(t) \subseteq V$, consist of the free variables in the guard of t and in the arc expressions of the arcs connected to t. The binding of a transition covers (at least) all variables from $Var(t)$. Let $[E]_b$ denote the value of expression E under variable binding b. Given a CPN, a *marking* M is a function $P \to (\Sigma \to \mathbb{N})$ (the *initial marking* $M_0(p)$ is defined by $I(p)$) and a *step* is a selection of the net's transitions together with appropriate bindings for the variables of each transition such that the selected transitions are enabled, defined as follows:

Definition 2 (Enabledness). *A transition t is* enabled *in a marking M for binding b, if,*

1. $[G(t)]_b = true$, *and*
2. $M(p) \geq_m [E(p,t)]_b$, *for all places $p \in P$,*

where $\geq_m$ is the usual ordering between multisets.

A step Y is enabled *in a marking M, if for all places p, (t,b) from Y, t is enabled for b in M, $M(p) \geq_m [E(p,t)]_Y$. The semantics $[E(p,t)]_Y$ represents the multi-set $\sum_{(t,b) \in Y} [E(p,t)]_b$.*

When t is enabled for b, in M, it may *occur* or "fire", leading to the marking M' where $M'(p) = (M(p) - [E(p,t)]_b) + [E(t,p)]_b$, for all places p. Similarly for enabled steps Y, $M_1 \overset{Y}{\twoheadrightarrow} M_2$ denotes that a marking M_1 evolves into M_2 by "firing" step Y. A (finite) *occurrence sequence* is a sequence of markings and steps of the form

$$M_1 \overset{Y_1}{\twoheadrightarrow} M_2 \overset{Y_2}{\twoheadrightarrow} M_3 \ldots M_n \overset{Y_n}{\twoheadrightarrow} M_{n+1}. \tag{1}$$

Note that "true concurrency" semantics, typical for Petri nets, allows the simultaneous firing of transitions in a step. Whereas steps are required to be non-empty, a step which only fires one transition t and binding b, is denoted $\overset{t,b}{\twoheadrightarrow}$. A reduction semantics restricted to such single transition steps is equivalent to the unrestricted semantics, but corresponds to "interleaving concurrency".

4   Translating ABS Semantics to Colored Petri Nets

In this section, we define the translation from ABS to CPNs. After a short introduction covering the core ideas of the translation, in Sect. 4.2 we highlight crucial parts of how the ABS semantics are represented on the Petri net level, focusing on parts of the communication mechanism, in particular dealing with asynchronous method calls and the resolution of futures via **get**. In Sect. 4.3, we define an abstraction function relating program configurations and the corresponding Petri net markings. Afterwards, Sect. 4.4 establishes the soundness of the Petri net semantics, defining a simulation relation between the steps of the operational semantics and the transitions of the resulting Petri net.

4.1   Overview over the Petri Net Semantics for ABS

The starting point of the translation are abstract ABS programs, i.e. programs where *data* values have been abstracted already. Still, there are two remaining sources of *infinity* in the state space: creation of (active) objects and creation of processes and accompanying future references via asynchronous method calls. Note in passing that in absence of synchronous, reentrant method calls, unboundedly growing stacks do not contribute to the potential unboundedness of the state space. In the translation, one can conceptually distinguish between *language-specific* aspects and *program-specific* aspects: the ABS language and its semantics is represented by one CPN, common for all programs. This CPN therefore can be seen as a translation of the ABS-language as such. Roughly, each semantic rule from the operational semantics of Fig. 2 is represented by transitions and places, with appropriate types and guards. Figure 3 shows a birds eye view of the overall Petri net as represented in the CPN Tools.

In contrast, one particular program, respectively, one particular run-time configuration of a program, is represented by a *marking* of the Petri net. The expressive power of *colored* Petri nets is crucial to achieve such a conceptually clear and structural translation: since tokens are distinguishable, the transitions and places operated on type values allow to represent the components of a configuration in a clean manner. For instance, object, process, and future identities are all naturally represented in the tool by integers.

4.2   CPN-ABS Communication Mechanism

Figure 3 shows the implementation of this translation with the CPN Tools. From now on, we will refer to it as CPN-ABS. In CPN-ABS, communication takes place between objects represented as tokens which carry information about their identity, their class, and their process pool, therefore triples of the form $(id, class, q)$. CPN-ABS supports not only object communication, but also the construction

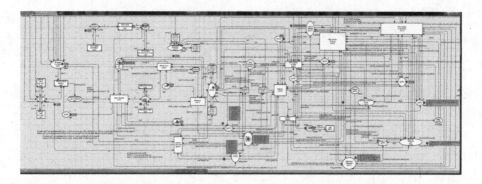

Fig. 3. ABS semantics implemented with the CPN Tools

of the information each object carries. This allows dynamic creation of objects. CPN-ABS can be structurally divided into two parts: the first part, where all this information can be dynamically created through transition firing, and the second part which can simulate the possible communications of the objects. As shown in Fig. 3, CPN-ABS contains a lot of details in order to faithfully simulate ABS. In the following, we concentrate on an extract of the implementation (cf. Fig. 4), which focuses on the asynchronous communication mechanism. The implementation covers all ABS rules from Sect. 2, as well as synchronous reentrant self calls. For simplicity, in Fig. 4, we omit details like places which have an indirect relation with the semantics, and furthermore arcs and inscriptions where obvious.

As we can see in Fig. 4, there are three disjoint places where the object tokens can be located: *"Active Objects"*, *"Idle Objects"*, and *"Blocked Objects"*. When a method of an (active) object returns (here by firing the transition *"Return"*), it resolves a future and it moves the object to the *"Idle Objects"* place, as one can observe from the RETURN rule of the semantics. The inverse can be achieved through the ACTIVATE rule, where a process from the pool is activated. This is simulated by the *"Activate"* transition with the corresponding token moving.

Transition *"Caller"* selects the calling object from the *"Active Objects"* place (here we omit how the object selection is being done). We have two cases of communication through asynchronous method calls: immediately followed by a **get** statement or not. Both are simulated in the yellow region of the picture: It contains one place, *"Is_synchronous"*, which has a token of type *Bool*. Its value corresponds to the presence of a **get** statement in the obvious way. By firing the transition *"Get"*, we alternate the value of the token. So, from this yellow region, transition *"Caller"* takes the information on whether the asynchronous call is followed by a **get** statement or not. In the latter case, the value of b is false and transition *"Caller"* maintains the object in the *"Active Objects"* place (which has the corresponding meaning for the status of the object – see rule ASYNC-CALL of the semantics), otherwise it sends the caller object to the *"Blocked Objects"* place until the waiting future can be retrieved from the *"Future"* place (see rule READ-FUT in the ABS semantics).

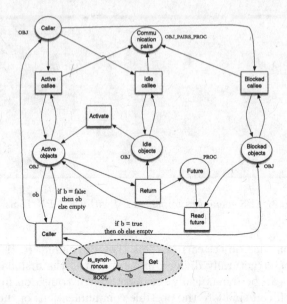

Fig. 4. Extract of the communication mechanism of CPN-ABS

As the places related to the status of an object are disjoint, the callee object can reside only in one among the three corresponding places. Therefore, one among the transitions *"Active callee"*, *"Blocked callee"*, and *"Idle callee"* can fire each time for the selected object (here, again, we omit details about how the object selection is done). In CPN-ABS, the process pool is implemented as a FIFO queue. So, the transitions that refer to the callee update its process queue by adding at the end a new process related to this particular method call. They also create a communication pair token at the *"Communication pairs"* place by matching the token of the *"Caller"* place (created by the *"Caller"* transition) with the callee object and the process created for this method execution.

4.3   The Abstraction Function

In this section, we define a translation from ABS configurations to Petri net markings. The translation is given in the form of an abstraction function α. In it's core, it's a structural translation of ABS-configurations, ignoring the *data* parts of the program, i.e., the value of variables in the instance states and local states. Hence the translation yields an *abstraction* at the same time, and the resulting Petri nets marking over-approximate the original behavior, due to this form of data abstraction. Let *Obj* be the set of objects in an ABS program, *Class* the set of its classes and *Proc* the set of the processes. We define the following injections from those sets to the set of positive integers: $h : Obj \rightarrow \mathbb{Z}^+$, $d : Class \rightarrow \mathbb{Z}^+$, and $g : Proc \rightarrow \mathbb{Z}^+$. Let $\mathcal{C}$ be the set of the configurations of an ABS program and *Msg* the set of the invocation messages. We define the projection functions from the ABS configurations as follows:

- $cl : \mathcal{C} \to Class$ which projects the object class in an ABS configuration,
- $ob : \mathcal{C} \to Obj$ which projects the objects in ABS configurations,
- $pr : \mathcal{C} \to \mathcal{P}(Proc)$ which projects the process pools of the objects of ABS configurations,
- $msg : \mathcal{C} \to Msg$ which projects the messages Msg of ABS configurations and
- $fut : \mathcal{C} \to F$ which projects the set of resolved futures that are related to **get** statements for each configuration.

Then, let $m : Msg \to Proc$ be the injection which maps each invocation message to the process that will be created for the execution of the called method. Let furthermore $fr : F \to Proc$ be the injection from the set of resolved futures F related to **get** statements to the set of processes $Proc$, since they are related to the change of the blocked status of the objects which wait to read those futures. Finally, let $pq : \mathcal{P}(Proc) \to \mathcal{P}(\mathbb{Z}^+)$ be the mapping from the process pools to sets of (unique) positive integers such that for every process pool S, $pq(S) = \{g(s) \in \mathbb{Z}^+ \mid s \in S\}$. In CPN-ABS, we model objects as tokens which carry information about their identity, their class and their process pool. As a consequence, each object is represented as a triple $(id, class, q)$, where id is the object identifier of type Int, $class$ is the corresponding class of the object i.e. the class identifier of type Int and q is the process pool of the object of type list of integers.

Now, we can define the abstraction function α. In the following, P is the set of the places and $M(p)$ the marking of a place p in CPN-ABS. Then, for all configurations $c \in \mathcal{C}$:

$$\alpha(c) = \bigcap \{M \mid \exists p, p', p'' \in P \text{ s.t. } p \neq p' \neq p'' \qquad (2)$$
$$\wedge ((h \circ ob)(c), (d \circ cl)(c), (pq \circ pr)(c)) \in M(p)$$
$$\wedge (m \circ msg)(c) \in M(p')$$
$$\wedge (g \circ fr \circ fut)(c) \in M(p'')\} ,$$

where, $\bigcap$ denotes intersection over sets of multisets. Observe that, for every ABS configuration, the above intersection is nonempty, i.e. there is a marking such that all the objects of the configuration are represented as tokens in specific places of the model.

4.4 Soundness Proof of the Translation

In this section we sketch the soundness proof of the translation, establishing a *simulation* relation between the small step operational semantics of ABS and the transitions of CPN-ABS. In particular, we need to prove that, for any ABS configuration c, if $c \to_r c'$ for some semantic rule r, then there exists a marking M' and a *sequence* of CPN-ABS transitions u, such that $\alpha(c) \xrightarrow{u} M'$ and $\alpha(c') \subseteq_m M'$ (where, with $\subseteq_m$ we denote the subset relation between sets of multisets as an extension of $\leq_m$). To establish the above relation, we need to prove that u has a corresponding CPN-ABS occurrence sequence, i.e. that all the transitions of u can fire in the same order as they appear in u.

Consequently, we try to construct each transitions sequence u in such a way that there exists the corresponding occurrence sequence. We use a finite alphabet $\mathcal{B}$ which consists of the names of the transitions that appear in CPN-ABS and construct words over this alphabet that correspond to occurrence sequences, with ϵ to be the empty word. We should mention here, that, for all $b \in \mathcal{B}$, $b^0 = \epsilon$. We call these words *occurrence words*. The set that contains those occurrence words can be given from the image of a translation function $Tr : Sem \rightarrow \mathcal{B}^*$, where Sem is the set of the ABS semantic rules of Sect. 2. In the following, we provide some definitions and lemmas in order to achieve modularity for the construction of occurrence words. We will denote as $En(M)$ *the set of enabled transitions for a marking* M and $\mathcal{M}_{reach}$ the set of reachable markings of the Petri net.

Definition 3 (Independent transition). *A transition* $t \in T$ *is called* independent *if, for any marking* $M \in \mathcal{M}_{reach}$, $t \in En(M)$ *and* $M \xrightarrow{t} M'$ *implies* $En(M) \subseteq En(M')$.

Definition 4 (Post-transition). *The post-transitions of a transition* $t \in T$ *are given by the function* $PostTrans : T \times \mathcal{M}_{reach} \rightarrow \mathcal{P}(T)$ *where* $PostTrans(t, M) = \{t' \in En(M') \mid M \xrightarrow{t} M'\}$.

Lemma 1 (Composition). *The composition of an occurrence sequence* $M_1 \xrightarrow{t_1} M_2 \xrightarrow{t_2} \ldots \xrightarrow{t_n} M_{n+1}$ *with another occurrence sequence* $M_1' \xrightarrow{t_1'} M_2' \xrightarrow{t_2'} \ldots \xrightarrow{t_m'} M_{m+1}'$ *is the occurrence sequence* $M_1 \xrightarrow{t_1} M_2 \xrightarrow{t_2} \ldots \xrightarrow{t_n} M_{n+1} \xrightarrow{t_1'} M_2'' \xrightarrow{t_2'} \ldots \xrightarrow{t_m'} M_{m+1}''$, *whenever* $M_1' \subseteq_m M_{n+1}$ *and* $[G(t_1')]_{b_{n+1}} = true$ *and furthermore* $\bigwedge_{2 \leq i \leq m}[G(t_i')]_{b_i} = true$ *and* $M_j' \subseteq_m M_j''$, *for all* $1 \leq j \leq m+1$.

Proof. For the prefix of the sequence which is identical to the first composed sequence, the result is trivial. Then, since $M_1' \subseteq_m M_{n+1}$, after t_1', obviously, if $[G(t_2')]_{b_2''} = true$, then $M_2' \subseteq_m M_2''$, and so on. □

In the sequel, we accordingly use the term *composition of occurrence words*.

Lemma 2. *For all ABS semantic rules* r, $Tr(r)$ *is an occurrence word.*

Proof. The idea is to assign to Tr a concrete value for each possible argument (i.e. for each rule of the operational semantics, and then, for each value, to prove that it is an occurrence word). As in Sect. 4.2 we presented just an extract of the real implementation, we will present one representative case, namely rule READ-FUT rule based on the Petri net extract of Fig. 4.

In this case, $Tr(\text{READ-FUT}) = \text{"Get"}^{i-1}\,\text{"Caller"}\,\text{"Read Future"}$, where $i = 1$ if the marking of the place "$Is\_synchronous$" is $true$ before firing "Get", 0 otherwise. We need to prove that it is an occurrence word. Indeed, let c be the configuration before the application of the rule READ-FUT and c' the one after it. Let, ob_1 be the object abstracted from c. Then $ob_1 \in M(\text{"Active Objects"})$. "$Get$" is an independent transition. If $i = 0$, then $M \xrightarrow{\text{Get}} M^{(1)}$ is an occurrence sequence. Otherwise, $M^{(1)} = M$. Obviously, $M^{(1)}(\text{"}Is\_synchronous\text{"}) =$

{*true*}. Transition *"Caller"* $\in$ $En(M^{(1)})$, since *"Caller"* $\in$ $En(M)$ and also *"Caller"* is a post-transition of *"Get"*, so we can take $M^{(1)} \overset{Caller}{\rightarrow} M^{(2)}$ where $ob_1 \in M^{(2)}$ (*"Blocked Objects"*). So, *"Get"* *"Caller"* is an occurrence word. From the hypothesis of READ-Fut we know that there exists a marking $M^{(3)}$ s.t. $f \in M^{(3)}$ (*"Future"*) and from Lemma 1, we obtain that *"Get"*$^{i-1}$ *"Caller"* *"Read Future"* is an occurrence word.   □

Theorem 1 (Simulation). *CPN-ABS is a (weak) simulation of ABS.*

Proof. We need to prove that, for any ABS configuration c, if $c \twoheadrightarrow_r c'$ for some semantic rule $r \in Sem$, then there exists a marking M' and an occurrence word given by $Tr(r)$, such that $\alpha(c) \overset{Tr(r)}{\leadsto} M'$ and $\alpha(c') \subseteq_m M'$. This follows straightforwardly from the definition of the abstraction function α, the image of Tr, and from Lemma 2.   □

5   Deadlock Detection

The translation CPN-ABS and the underlying Petri net tool can be used for the detection of possible communication deadlocks of ABS programs. CPN-ABS contains three disjoint places, where, depending on the status of objects (i.e. active, idle or blocked), objects can be located. The place *"Blocked Objects"* which hosts the blocked objects has a color set of pair (ob, p), where ob is object invoking an asynchronous call with a get-statement, i.e. an asynchronous blocking call, and p is the process that has been added to the process queue of the callee for the execution of the called method. Recall that ob is of color $(id, class, q)$, where id is object identity, $class$ is the class that the object belongs to, and q is the process queue of the object. Given this particular structure of CPN-ABS, *there is a deadlock cycle* [21] *if and only if there exists a marking of the place "Blocked Objects", in which there exists n tokens* (ob_1, p_1) *to* (ob_n, p_n) *that form a cycle, i.e. for* $1 \leq i < n$, $p_i \in q_{i+1}$ *and* $p_n \in q_1$ (where q_i *is the process queue of the* i^{th} *object*). This deadlock situation can be detected by the state space report of the model checker of the CPN Tool used to implement CPN-ABS.

5.1   Example

We now use the publisher-subscriber example of Fig. 5 to illustrate how CPN-ABS detects communication deadlocks. Service objects publish news updates to subscribing clients through a chain of Proxy objects. Each proxy object handles a bounded number of clients. Service objects handle a subscribe request efficiently by delegating its time-consuming parts to Proxy objects, and the proxies publish news to clients using asynchronous calls (without futures) to make the cooperation efficient. As asynchronous method calls without get-statements do not cause deadlocks, we omit them from our analysis and only consider asynchronous blocking calls of the form $f = e!m(\overline{e}); \ldots; x = f.\mathbf{get}$, where there are no suspension

```
1   class Service(Int limit) {
2     Producer prod = new Producer(); Proxy proxy = new Proxy(limit,this,prod);
3     Proxy lastProxy = proxy;
4
5     Void run() { this!produce(); }
6     Void subscribe(Client cl){Fut<Proxyl> f; f = lastProxy!add(cl); lastProxy = f.get;}
7     Void produce(){proxy!start_publish(); }
8   }
9   class Proxy(Int limit, Service server, Producer prod) {
10    List<Client> myClients = Nil; Proxy nextProxy;
11
12    Proxy add(Client cl){ Proxy lastProxy = this; Fut<Proxyl> f';
13     if length(myClients) < limit {myClients = append(myClients, cl);}
14     else {if nextProxy == null {nextProxy = new Proxy(limit,server,prod);}
15       f' = nextProxy!add(cl); lastProxy = f'.get;} return lastProxy; }
16
17    Void start_publish(){ Fut<Proxyl> f''; f'' = prod!detectNews(); await f''?;
18                           News ns = f''.get; this!publish(ns); }
19
20    Void publish(News ns){ myClients!signal(ns);
21     if nextProxy == null {server!produce();} else {nextProxy!publish(ns);} }
22  }
```

Fig. 5. Implementation of the publisher-subscriber example.

points in between. There are two asynchronous blocking calls in lines 6 and 15 in the example, namely $f = lastProxy!add(cl)$; $lastProxy = f.\textbf{get}$ and $f' = nextProxy!add(cl)$; $lastProxy = f'.\textbf{get}$. The former one expresses that a Service object invokes method add on a Proxy object through method subscribe. Similarly, the later one expresses that a Proxy object invokes method add on the next Proxy object through method add. By applying the model checker on an Intel i7 3.4 GHz, in less than 1 s we get the full state space report in which tokens of color $((o_1, Service, q), p)$ and $((o_3, Proxy, q'), p')$ can be found in the place *"Blocked Objects"*, and for all p, p', q, q' we have $p \notin q'$ and $p' \notin q$. This shows that the implementation of the publisher-subscriber protocol is deadlock free.

Now, we slightly modify the protocol, where **get**-statements are added to the method calls in lines 7 and 21 and the **await** statement in line 17 is removed. In this case, CPN-ABS detects a communication deadlock cycle shown in Fig. 6, where $p \in q'$ and $p' \in q$ and both objects are trapped in the place *"Blocked Objects"* and cannot exit from there; in Fig. 6, the third and the fifth argument in the color tuples are outside of the scope of this work, so we ignore them, while, the existence of the two zero value tokens is for initialization reasons and they do not affect the deadlock analysis. Based on the information we obtained from this reachable marking, we can trace back to the program code and determine the deadlock represented by the call chain.

Remark that the translation supports scalability: the size of the net is independent from the program and represents the ABS semantics as such. I.e., by increasing the number of Proxy objects or clients, only the number of tokens is affected and the analysis is highly automated.

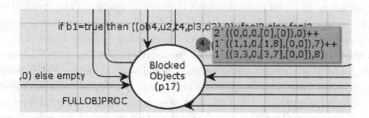

Fig. 6. Deadlock detection by CPN-ABS.

6 Related Work

Deadlock detection is traditionally concerned with the usage of locks for thread-based concurrency. This line of work is surveyed in [23], which develops a type and effect system to capture lock manipulation for such a language. However, in active objects communication deadlocks are caused by call-cycles with synchronization, and the cooperative scheduling of ABS makes the analysis more complex. The problem has been studied using different approaches, including behavioral types [13], cost analysis [12], protocol specifications [21], and Petri nets [10] (discussed below). As the problem is undecidable and the approaches differ substantially, it is difficult to say exactly how they relate to each other in terms of strength of the proposed analyses. Petri nets and its extensions are popular formalisms to model and analyze systems with concurrency, communication and synchronization [22,25]. Petri nets have in particular been applied to protocol and work flow analysis, but have also been used to study process algebra (e.g., [5,7]), more recently including asynchronous communication [4]. Approaches which encode programming language features into Petri nets have been developed for Ada [15] and more recently for, e.g., Java [20], and for choreography languages like Orc [6]. In general, these approaches translate programs into nets such that the size of the program determines the size of the net and dynamic invocations or object creation cause difficulties. Previous work on deadlock analysis for active objects using Petri nets [10] follows a similar approach such that places represent locks on objects, futures, and processes. Transitions are introduced for each possible caller and callee to a method. To obtain a finite net, the approach abstracts from the actual number of futures such that the wrong future may be accessed in the Petri net. But if the net is deadlock free, so is the original active object program. In contrast to these approaches encoding a specific program as a net, our approach directly encodes the language semantics as a CPN and uses markings to define the concrete program; the colors of CPN are used to distinguish different method invocations and to create new objects and the size of the net itself is independent of the specific program.

7   Conclusion

This paper proposes an encoding of the formal semantics of ABS as a net, such that a program is given as a marking for this net. Exploiting the colored tokens, our net can support dynamic program behavior. We provide a soundness proof for our encoding and show how a model checker for colored Petri nets can be used to analyze communication deadlock for active objects in ABS. Whereas this paper has focused on communication and synchronization for ABS programs, ABS supports the specification of real-time behavior, deployment architectures, and resource-aware systems [19]. Our next step is to extend the model to support these features, and explore the usage of colored Petri nets for resource analysis and to compare resource-management strategies for distributed ABS programs.

References

1. Agha, G.: ACTORS: A Model of Concurrent Computations in Distributed Systems. The MIT Press, Cambridge (1986)
2. Agha, G., Hewitt, C.: Concurrent programming using actors. In: Yonezawa, A., Tokoro, M. (eds.) Object-Oriented Concurrent Programming. The MIT Press, Cambridge (1987)
3. Armstrong, J.: Programming Erlang: Software for a Concurrent World. Pragmatic Bookshelf, Dallas (2007)
4. Baldan, P., Bonchi, F., Gadducci, F., Monreale, G.V.: Modular encoding of synchronous and asynchronous interactions using open Petri nets. Sci. Comput. Program. **109**, 96–124 (2015)
5. Best, E., Devillers, R., Koutny, M.: Petri Net Algebra. EATCS. Springer, Heidelberg (2001). doi:10.1007/978-3-662-04457-5
6. Bruni, R., Melgratti, H., Tuosto, E.: Translating orc features into petri nets and the join calculus. In: Bravetti, M., Núñez, M., Zavattaro, G. (eds.) WS-FM 2006. LNCS, vol. 4184, pp. 123–137. Springer, Heidelberg (2006). doi:10.1007/11841197_8
7. Busi, N., Gorrieri, R.: A petri net semantics for pi-calculus. In: Lee, I., Smolka, S.A. (eds.) CONCUR 1995. LNCS, vol. 962, pp. 145–159. Springer, Heidelberg (1995). doi:10.1007/3-540-60218-6_11
8. Caromel, D., Henrio, L.: A Theory of Distributed Object: Asynchrony – Mobility – Groups – Components. Springer, Heidelberg (2005). doi:10.1007/b138812
9. Chandy, K.M., Misra, J., Haas, L.M.: Distributed deadlock detection. ACM Trans. Comput. Syst. **1**(2), 144–156 (1983)
10. de Boer, F.S., Bravetti, M., Grabe, I., Lee, M., Steffen, M., Zavattaro, G.: A petri net based analysis of deadlocks for active objects and futures. In: Păsăreanu, C.S., Salaün, G. (eds.) FACS 2012. LNCS, vol. 7684, pp. 110–127. Springer, Heidelberg (2013). doi:10.1007/978-3-642-35861-6_7
11. de Boer, F.S., Clarke, D., Johnsen, E.B.: A complete guide to the future. In: De Nicola, R. (ed.) ESOP 2007. LNCS, vol. 4421, pp. 316–330. Springer, Heidelberg (2007). doi:10.1007/978-3-540-71316-6_22
12. Flores-Montoya, A.E., Albert, E., Genaim, S.: May-happen-in-parallel based deadlock analysis for concurrent objects. In: Beyer, D., Boreale, M. (eds.) FMOODS/-FORTE -2013. LNCS, vol. 7892, pp. 273–288. Springer, Heidelberg (2013). doi:10.1007/978-3-642-38592-6_19

13. Giachino, E., Laneve, C., Lienhardt, M.: A framework for deadlock detection in core ABS. Softw. Syst. Model. **15**(4), 1013–1048 (2016)
14. Haller, P., Odersky, M.: Scala actors: unifying thread-based and event-based programming. Theor. Comput. Sci. **410**(2–3), 202–220 (2009)
15. Ichbiah, J., Barnes, J.G.P., Heliard, J.C., Krieg-Brückner, B., Roubine, O., Wichmann, B.A.: Modules and visibility in the Ada programming language. In: McKeag, R.M., Macnaghten, A.M. (eds.) On the Construction of Programs. Cambrige University Press, New York (1980)
16. Jensen, K.: Coloured petri nets. In: Brauer, W., Reisig, W., Rozenberg, G. (eds.) ACPN 1986. LNCS, vol. 254, pp. 248–299. Springer, Heidelberg (1987). doi:10. 1007/978-3-540-47919-2_10
17. Jensen, K., Kristensen, L.M.: Coloured Petri Nets - Modelling and Validation of Concurrent Systems. Springer, Heidelberg (2009). doi:10.1007/b95112
18. Johnsen, E.B., Hähnle, R., Schäfer, J., Schlatte, R., Steffen, M.: ABS: a core language for abstract behavioral specification. In: Aichernig, B.K., de Boer, F.S., Bonsangue, M.M. (eds.) FMCO 2010. LNCS, vol. 6957, pp. 142–164. Springer, Heidelberg (2011). doi:10.1007/978-3-642-25271-6_8
19. Johnsen, E.B., Schlatte, R., Tarifa, S.L.T.: Integrating deployment architectures and resource consumption in timed object-oriented models. J. Logic. Algebr. Methods Program. **84**(1), 67–91 (2015)
20. Long, B., Strooper, P.A., Wildman, L.: A method for verifying concurrent Java components based on an analysis of concurrency failures. Concurr. Comput. Pract. Exp. **19**(3), 281–294 (2007)
21. Owe, O., Yu, I.C.: Deadlock detection of active objects with synchronous and asynchronous method calls. In: Proceedings of NIK 2014 (2014)
22. Petri, C.: Kommunikation mit Automaten. Ph.D. thesis, Universität Bonn (1962)
23. Pun, K.I.: Behavioural static analysis for deadlock detection. Ph.D. thesis, Department of informatics, University of Oslo, Norway (2014)
24. Ratzer, A.V., Wells, L., Lassen, H.M., Laursen, M., Qvortrup, J.F., Stissing, M.S., Westergaard, M., Christensen, S., Jensen, K.: CPN tools for editing, simulating, and analysing coloured petri nets. In: van der Aalst, W.M.P., Best, E. (eds.) ICATPN 2003. LNCS, vol. 2679, pp. 450–462. Springer, Heidelberg (2003). doi:10. 1007/3-540-44919-1_28
25. Reisig, W.: Petri Nets. Monographs in Theoretical Computer Science. An EATCS Series, vol. 4. Springer, Heidelberg (1985). doi:10.1007/978-3-642-69968-9

Synthesizing Parameterized Self-stabilizing Rings with Constant-Space Processes

Alex P. Klinkhamer[1] and Ali Ebnenasir[2(✉)]

[1] Google, Mountain View, CA 94043, USA
apklinkh@mtu.edu
[2] Department of Computer Science, Michigan Technological University,
Houghton, MI 49931, USA
aebnenas@mtu.edu

Abstract. This paper investigates the problem of synthesizing parameterized rings that are "self-stabilizing by construction". While it is known that the verification of self-stabilization for parameterized unidirectional rings is undecidable, we present a counterintuitive result that synthesizing such systems is decidable! This is surprising because it is known that, in general, the synthesis of distributed systems is harder than their verification. We also show that synthesizing self-stabilizing bidirectional rings is an undecidable problem. To prove the decidability of synthesis for unidirectional rings, we propose a sound and complete algorithm that performs the synthesis in the local state space of processes. We also generate strongly stabilizing rings where no fairness assumption is made. This is particularly noteworthy because most existing verification and synthesis methods for parameterized systems assume a fair scheduler.

1 Introduction

Developing parameterized Self-Stabilizing (SS) distributed systems is an important and challenging problem since a parameterized SS system must be self-stabilizing regardless of the number of processes. An SS system (i) recovers from *any* configuration/state to a set of legitimate states – that captures the normal behaviors of a system, and (ii) guarantees global recovery to legitimate states solely based on the local actions of its processes (without any central point of coordination). Designing self-stabilization becomes even more challenging for *parameterized* systems that include families of *symmetric* processes, where the code of each process is obtained from a *template* process in a symmetric network. Since the general case synthesis problem is undecidable, several researchers have recently proposed methods where they generate specific parameterized systems from their temporal logic specifications, mainly by exploiting verification techniques (e.g., cutoff theorems [13]) and boundedness assumptions [16]. As the verification of SS parameterized unidirectional rings is known to be undecidable [22], the common understanding has been that synthesizing such systems should also be undecidable. In this paper, we prove otherwise! We show that

Published by Springer International Publishing AG 2017. All Rights Reserved
M. Dastani and M. Sirjani (Eds.): FSEN 2017, LNCS 10522, pp. 100–115, 2017.
DOI: 10.1007/978-3-319-68972-2_7

synthesizing self-stabilization is actually decidable for parameterized unidirectional rings where all processes follow the same synthesized rules.

Numerous approaches exist for the synthesis of parameterized systems, most of which focus on synthesis from temporal logic specifications while assuming some sort of fairness. For example, Finkbeiner and Schewe [16] present a method where they solve the synthesis problem in a scope-based fashion similar to the scope-based verification methods [19]. They formulate the synthesis problem as a set of constraints that are fed to a Satisfiability Modulo Theory (SMT) solver [9]. Jacobs and Bloem [20] reduce the problem of synthesizing parameterized systems to synthesizing a small network of symmetric processes under the assumption of fair token passing. They exploit bounded synthesis and cutoff theorems to enable a semi-decision procedure that will eventually find a solution if one exists. Additionally, some researchers have investigated the synthesis of parameterized self-stabilizing systems in a problem-specific context. For instance, Bloem *et al.* [6] provide a method for the synthesis of synchronous systems that are SS and tolerate Byzantine failures and their underlying communication topology is a clique. Dolev *et al.* [11] present a verification-based method to generate synchronous and constant-space counting algorithms that are self-stabilizing under Byzantine faults. Lenzen and Rybicki [25] provide an SS and Byzantine-tolerant solution for the counting problem with near-optimal stabilization time and message sizes. What the aforementioned methods have in common is that they synthesize from temporal logic specifications and/or make assumptions about synchrony, fairness and complete knowledge of the network for each process. Moreover, some of them investigate specific problems.

In addition to proving some undecidability results for bidirectional rings, this paper presents an algorithmic method for the synthesis of symmetric unidirectional rings that are self-stabilizing by construction. The proposed algorithm works in a graph-theoretic context rather than synthesis from temporal logic specifications. In our work, we consider processes that are deterministic, self-disabling and constant-space, where a self-disabling process stops executing once it executes an action until it is enabled again by an action of its predecessor.[1] Moreover, we investigate this problem for sets of legitimate states that can be specified as the conjunction of local legitimate states. While our assumptions may seem restrictive, there are important applications for such systems [18,28]. The decidability result of this paper is counterintuitive as in our previous work [22] we have shown that verifying self-stabilization for unidirectional rings is undecidable. This is surprising because it is known [26] that, in general, the synthesis of distributed systems is harder than their verification. We first present a *necessary and sufficient* condition for the existence of a symmetric SS unidirectional ring. Our necessary and sufficient condition states that an SS symmetric unidirectional ring exists if and only if (iff) there is a value in the state space of the template process that can make the locality of each process true. We then use this result and design a sound and complete algorithm. The input to our algorithm includes a set of legitimate states and the size of the state space of the

---

[1] We have shown [23] that these assumptions uphold the completeness of synthesis.

template process. The output of the proposed algorithm is the symmetric code of the template process so that the entire ring becomes self-stabilizing for any arbitrary (but finite) number of processes. Our approach is easier than synthesis from temporal logic specifications in that we perform the synthesis in a bottom-up fashion by intelligently searching the state space of the template process. Subsequently, we investigate the synthesis of bidirectional symmetric rings that are self-stabilizing, and show that this problem is undecidable. Our proof of undecidability is a reduction from the problem of verifying self-stabilization for unidirectional rings [22]. While we have used our algorithm to synthesize a few example systems in this paper, we are currently investigating the generalization of our algorithm for other topologies and more interesting case studies.

Contributions. This paper makes the following contributions. We

- present a surprising result that synthesizing parameterized SS unidirectional rings under the interleaving semantics and no fairness assumption is decidable;
- provide an algorithm that takes a set of legitimate states and the size of the state space of the template process, and automatically generates the code of the template process, and
- prove that synthesizing SS bidirectional rings is undecidable.

Organization. Section 2 presents some basic concepts. Section 3 shows that synthesizing SS unidirectional rings is decidable. Section 4 investigates the synthesis of SS bidirectional rings and proves that this problem is undecidable. Section 5 examines related work. Finally, Sect. 6 makes concluding remarks and discusses future extensions of this work.

2   Basic Concepts

This section presents the definition of parameterized rings, their representation as action graphs, and self-stabilization. Wlog, we use the term *protocol* to refer to parameterized rings as we conduct our investigation in the context of network protocols. A protocol p for a computer network includes $N > 1$ processes (finite-state machines), where each process P_i has a finite set of readable and writeable variables. Any *local state* of a process (a.k.a. *locality/neighborhood*) is determined by a unique valuation of its readable variables. We assume that any writeable variable is also readable. The *global state* of the protocol is defined by a snapshot of the local states of all processes. The *state space* of a protocol, denoted by Σ, is the universal set of all global states. A *state predicate* is a subset of Σ. A process *acts* (i.e., *transitions*) when it atomically updates its state based on its locality. The locality of a process is defined by the network topology. In this paper, our focus is on the ring topology. For example, in a unidirectional ring consisting of N processes, each process P_i (where $i \in \mathbb{Z}_N$, i.e., $0 \leq i \leq N - 1$) has a neighbor P_{i-1}, where subtraction and addition are in modulo N. We assume that processes act one at a time (i.e., interleaving semantics).

Thus, each *global transition* corresponds to the action of a single process from some global state. An *execution/computation* of a protocol is a sequence of states $C_0, C_1, \ldots, C_k$ where there is a transition from C_i to C_{i+1} for every $i \in \mathbb{Z}_k$. We consider *symmetric* protocols, where processes have identical rules for changing their state and the rules are *parameterized*. That is, the code of each process can be instantiated from a *template* process. We use triples of the form (a, b, c) to denote actions $(x_{i-1} = a \wedge x_i = b \longrightarrow x_i := c;)$ of the template process P_i in a unidirectional ring protocol. An action has two components; a *guard*, which is a Boolean expression in terms of readable variables and a *statement* that atomically updates the state of the process once the guard evaluates to *true*; i.e., the action is *enabled*.

Definition 1 (Transition Function). *Let P_i be any process with a state variable x_i in a unidirectional ring protocol p. We define its transition function $\xi : \Sigma \times \Sigma \to \Sigma$ as a partial function such that $\xi(a, b) = c$ if and only if P_i has an action $(x_{i-1} = a \wedge x_i = b \longrightarrow x_i := c;)$. In other words, ξ can be used to define all actions of P_i in the form of a single parametric action:*

$$((x_{i-1}, x_i) \in \mathsf{Pre}(\xi)) \longrightarrow x_i := \xi(x_{i-1}, x_i);$$

where $(x_{i-1}, x_i) \in \mathsf{Pre}(\xi)$ checks to see if the current x_{i-1} and x_i values are in the preimage of ξ.

Visually, we depict the actions of a process (hence a protocol) by a labeled directed multigraph, called the *action graph*, where each action (a, b, c) in the protocol appears as an arc from node a to node c labeled b in the graph. For example, consider the self-stabilizing Sum-Not-2 protocol given in [15]. Each process P_i has a variable $x_i \in \mathbb{Z}_3$ and actions $(x_{i-1} = 0 \wedge x_i = 2 \longrightarrow x_i := 1)$, $(x_{i-1} = 1 \wedge x_i = 1 \longrightarrow x_i := 2)$, and $(x_{i-1} = 2 \wedge x_i = 0 \longrightarrow x_i := 1)$. This protocol converges to a state where the sum of each two consecutive x values does not equal 2. The set of such states is formally specified as the state predicate $\forall i : (x_{i-1} + x_i \neq 2)$. We represent this protocol with a graph containing arcs $(0, 2, 1)$, $(1, 1, 2)$, and $(2, 0, 1)$ as shown in Fig. 1.

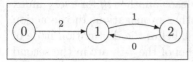

Fig. 1. Graph representing Sum-Not-2 protocol.

Since protocols consist of *self-disabling* processes, an action (a, b, c) cannot coexist with action (a, c, d) for any d. Moreover, when the protocol is deterministic, a process cannot have two actions enabled at the same time; i.e., an action (a, b, c) cannot coexist with an action (a, b, d) where $d \neq c$.

Livelock, deadlock, and closure. A *legitimate* state captures a state to which a protocol is required to recover. Let I be a predicate representing the legitimate states for some protocol p. A *livelock* of p is an infinite execution that never reaches I. When legitimate states are not specified, we assume a livelock is any infinite execution. A *deadlock* of p is a state in $\neg I$ that has no outgoing transition; i.e., no process is enabled to act. The state predicate I is *closed* under p when no transition exists that brings the protocol from a state in I to a state in $\neg I$.

Definition 2 (Self-stabilization). *A protocol p is self-stabilizing [10] with respect to its legitimate state predicate I iff from each illegitimate state in $\neg I$, all executions reach a state in I (i.e., convergence) and remain in I (i.e., closure). That is, p is livelock-free and deadlock-free in $\neg I$, and I is closed under p.*

Definition 3 (Weak Stabilization). *A weakly stabilizing protocol ensures that from each illegitimate state in $\neg I$, there is some execution that reaches a state in I (i.e., reachability) and remains in I.*

Next, we represent some of our previous result that we shall use in this paper.

Propagations and Collisions. When a process acts and enables its successor in a unidirectional ring, it propagates its ability to act. The successor may enable its own successor by acting, and the pattern may continue indefinitely. Such behaviors can be represented as sequences of actions that are propagated in a ring, called *propagations*. A propagation is a walk through the action graph. For example, the Sum-Not-2 protocol has a propagation $\langle (0,2,1),(1,1,2),(2,0,1),(1,1,2)\rangle$ whose actions can be executed in order by processes P_i, P_{i+1}, P_{i+2}, and P_{i+3} from a state $(x_{i-1}, x_i, x_{i+1}, x_{i+2}, x_{i+3}) = (0,2,1,0,1)$. A propagation is *periodic* with period n *iff* its j-th action and $(j+n)$-th action are the same for every index j. A periodic propagation corresponds to a *closed walk* of length n in the graph. The Sum-Not-2 protocol has such a propagation of period 2: $\langle (1,1,2),(2,0,1)\rangle$. A *collision* occurs when two consecutive processes, say P_i and P_{i+1}, have enabled actions; e.g., (a,b,c) and (b,e,f), where $b \neq c$. In such a scenario, $x_{i-1} = a, x_i = b, x_{i+1} = e$. A collision occurs when P_i executes and assigns c to x_i. If that occurs, P_i will be disabled (because processes are self-disabling), and P_{i+1} becomes disabled too because x_i is no longer equal to b. As a result, two enabled processes become disabled by one action.

"Leads" Relation. Consider two actions A_1 and A_2 in a process P_i. We say the action A_1 leads A_2 *iff* the value of the variable x_i after executing A_1 is the same as the value required for P_i to execute A_2. Formally, this means an action (a,b,c) leads (d,e,f) *iff* $e = c$. Similarly, a propagation leads another *iff* for every index j, its j-th action leads the j-th action of the other propagation. In the action graph, this corresponds to two walks where the label of the destination node of the j-th arc in the first walk matches the arc label of the j-th arc in the second walk (for each index j). In [22], we prove the following theorem:

Theorem 1. *A unidirectional ring protocol of symmetric, self-disabling processes has a livelock for some ring size iff there exist some m propagations with some period n, where the $(i-1)$-th propagation leads the i-th propagation for each index i modulo m; i.e., the propagations successively lead each other modulo m.*

Undecidability of Verification. We have shown [15] that verifying deadlock-freedom in unidirectional rings is decidable. However, checking livelock-freedom is an undecidable problem (specifically Π_1^0-complete) for unidirectional ring protocols (with self-disabling and deterministic processes) [22]. The following results hold for cases where the set of legitimate states I is a conjunctive predicate; i.e., $I = \forall i : L(x_{i-1}, x_i)$, where $L(x_{i-1}, x_i)$ captures the locality of process P_i, which depends on its own state and that of its predecessor. Varghese [28,29] presents methods for specifying some global state predicates as conjunctive predicates.

Theorem 2. *Verifying livelock-freedom in a parameterized unidirectional ring protocol (with self-disabling and deterministic processes) is undecidable [22].*

We have also shown that verifying livelock-freedom remains undecidable even for a special type of livelocks, where exactly one process is enabled to execute in every state of the livelocked computation; i.e., *deterministic livelocks* [22].

Theorem 3. *Verifying livelock-freedom in a parameterized unidirectional ring protocol (with self-disabling and deterministic processes) remains undecidable even for deterministic livelocks [22].*

The above results imply the undecidability of verifying self-stabilization for parameterized unidirectional rings.

Theorem 4. *Verifying self-stabilization for a parameterized unidirectional ring protocol (with self-disabling and deterministic processes) is undecidable [22].*

3 Decidability of Synthesizing Unidirectional Rings

In this section, we show that synthesizing SS unidirectional rings is decidable.

Theorem 5. *Given a predicate $I \stackrel{\text{def}}{=} (\forall i : L(x_{i-1}, x_i))$ and variable domain M for a unidirectional ring, $L(\gamma, \gamma)$ is true for some γ if and only if there exists a protocol that stabilizes to I.*

Proof. $\Rightarrow$: Assume that no γ exists such that $L(\gamma, \gamma)$ is true. This implies that $\forall i : x_{i-1} \neq x_i$ in I. In this case, a stabilizing protocol would be a coloring protocol, which Bernard *et al.* [5] have shown is impossible for a unidirectional ring of size greater than M. (If the ring has at most M processes, then assigning unique values modulo M will provide a coloring.) This means if we check the entire domain $\mathbb{Z}_M$ and find no value that makes L true, then using Bernard *et al.*'s result we can *decide* that no solution exists. That is, the problem is decidable when $L(\gamma, \gamma)$ is false for all $\gamma \in \mathbb{Z}_M$. We are left to show how to construct a stabilizing protocol p when some γ can make $L(\gamma, \gamma)$ true. One could argue that a stabilizing protocol could contain just an action $\neg L(x_{i-1}, x_i) \rightarrow x_i := \gamma$, but this protocol is just *weakly* stabilizing.

Find a γ such that $L(\gamma, \gamma)$ is true. Assuming such a γ exists, it is trivial to find it by trying each value in $\mathbb{Z}_M$. Intuitively, we will make the stabilizing protocol p converge to $(\forall i : x_i = \gamma)$ unless it reaches some other state that satisfies I.

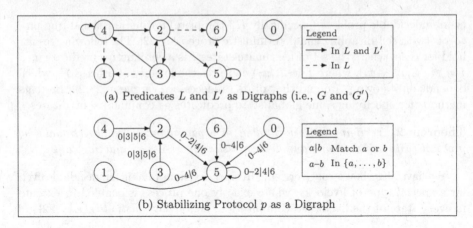

Fig. 2. Synthesis of stabilization to $\forall i : L(x_{i-1}, x_i)$, where $L(x_{i-1}, x_i) \stackrel{\text{def}}{=} ((x_{i-1}^2 + x_i^3)$ mod $7 = 3)$ and $x_i \in \mathbb{Z}_7$.

Figure 2 provides a running example where $L(x_{i-1}, x_i) \stackrel{\text{def}}{=} ((x_{i-1}^2 + x_i^3) \bmod 7 = 3)$ and variables have domain size $M = 7$. We arbitrarily choose $\gamma = 5$ (instead of $\gamma = 4$) to satisfy $L(\gamma, \gamma)$; i.e., the solution is not unique.

Construct relation L' from arcs that form cycles in the digraph of L. The relation L can be represented as a digraph such that each arc (a, b) is in the graph *iff* $L(a, b)$ is true. Let G be this digraph (e.g., formed by both solid and dashed lines in Fig. 2a). Closed walks in G characterize all states in $(\forall i : L(x_{i-1}, x_i))$ [15]. Derive a digraph G' (and corresponding relation L') from G by removing all arcs that are not part of a cycle (e.g., arcs $(4, 1)$, $(3, 1)$, $(2, 6)$, and $(5, 6)$ in Fig. 2a). Since closed walks of G characterize states in I, we know that for every arc (a, b) in G that is not part of a cycle, no legitimate state contains $x_{i-1} = a \wedge x_i = b$ at any index i. All closed walks of G are retained by G', which means $I \stackrel{\text{def}}{=} (\forall i : L'(x_{i-1}, x_i))$.

Construct a bottom-up spanning tree τ with γ at the root. Let τ be a function that returns the parent of a node in a tree; i.e., $\tau(a) = c$ means that c is the parent of a. First, let $\tau(\gamma) \stackrel{\text{def}}{=} \gamma$ represent the root of the tree. Next, create a tree by backward reachability from γ in G', and assign $\tau(a) \stackrel{\text{def}}{=} c$ for each a that has a path $a, c, \ldots, \gamma$ in G'. Finally, let $\tau(a) \stackrel{\text{def}}{=} \gamma$ for each node a that has no path to γ in G'. These extra arcs of τ create no cycles. Since all arcs of G' are involved in cycles, any walk in G' can find its way back to a previously visited node. Therefore, if a node cannot reach γ in G', then γ cannot reach that node. Since the extra arcs of τ would not introduce cycles in G', we know that $(\forall i : (L'(x_{i-1}, x_i) \vee \tau(x_{i-1}) = x_i))$ is yet another equivalent way to write I.

Construct each action (a, b, c) of p by labeling each arc (a, c) of τ with all b values such that $(\neg L'(a, b) \wedge \tau(a) \neq b)$. In this way, τ defines how a process P_i in p will assign x_i when it detects an illegitimate state. Figure 2b illustrates the solution protocol for our example, as well as τ if we ignore the arc labels. The protocol p is written succinctly by the following action for each process P_i.

$$\neg L'(x_{i-1}, x_i) \wedge \tau(x_{i-1}) \neq x_i \longrightarrow x_i := \tau(x_{i-1});$$

This protocol p stabilizes to I. Deadlock-freedom in $\neg I$ and closure of I hold because each process P_i is enabled to act *iff* $(\neg L'(x_{i-1}, x_i) \wedge \tau(x_{i-1}) \neq x_i)$ holds. Livelock-freedom holds because all periodic propagations of p consist of actions of the form (γ, b, γ) where $L(\gamma, b)$ is false (e.g., the self-loops of Node 5 in Fig. 2b). Obviously none of these (γ, b, γ) actions lead each other since $b \neq \gamma$; i.e., no periodic propagations exist. Thus, based on Theorem 1, no livelocks exist in $\neg I$ for any ring size greater than M. Therefore, the protocol p stabilizes to I for any number of processes.

Proof $\Leftarrow$: Let p be a protocol p that stabilizes to I for all ring sizes. Thus, closure of I in p, deadlock-freedom and livelock-freedom of p in $\neg I$ must hold. Since processes are deterministic and self-disabling, each process P_i contains some actions that are enabled in $\neg L(x_{i-1}, x_i)$. After the execution of such actions $L(x_{i-1}, x_i)$ holds by setting x_i to some value $\lambda \in M$, and P_i becomes disabled. Due to livelock-freedom of p and Theorem 1, no periodic propagations should exists in p. That is, there are no closed walks in the action graph of p other than self-loops over λ. The existence of such self-loops means $L(\lambda, \lambda)$ holds. $\square$

Using the proof of Theorem 5, we present Algorithm 1. Since this algorithm is self-explanatory, we just prove its soundness and completeness.

Theorem 6 (Soundness). *Algorithm 1 is sound.*

Proof. The proof of soundness includes two parts, namely proof of closure of I and convergence to I, where $I = \forall i : L(x_{i-1}, x_i)$. Step 7 of the algorithm guarantees closure. Steps 4 to 7 ensure that starting from any state where $L(x_{i-1}, x_i)$ does not hold, process P_i will eventually set the value of x_i to γ, hence evaluating $L(x_{i-1}, x_i)$ to true. Likewise, every process would perform local recovery, thereby eventually ensuring that $\forall i : L(x_{i-1}, x_i)$ holds. $\square$

Theorem 7 (Completeness). *Algorithm 1 is complete.*

Proof. This algorithm declares failure only in Step 2, where no value γ exists that can satisfy $L(x_{i-1}, x_i)$. The non-existence of some value that can make $L(x_{i-1}, x_i)$ true implies that no process can recover to its local invariant; hence self-stabilization to I is impossible. $\square$

We now present some case studies for the synthesis of parameterized unidirectional symmetric rings using Algorithm 1.

Sum-Not-2 protocol. The Sum-Not-2 protocol is a simple but interesting protocol that illustrates the complexities of designing self-stabilizing systems. This is again a protocol on unidirectional parameterized rings with a domain of $M = 3$ values; i.e., $\{0, 1, 2\}$. The invariant of the protocol specifies the legitimate

---

Algorithm 1. Synthesizing parameterized self-stabilizing unidirectional rings.

SynUniRing($L(x_{i-1}, x_i)$: state predicate, M: domain size)

1: Check if a value $\gamma \in \mathbb{Z}_M$ exists such that $L(\gamma, \gamma) = \textbf{true}$.
2: If no such γ exists, then **return** $\emptyset$ since no solution exists for systems with more than M processes due to [5].
3: Construct relation L as a graph $G = (V, E)$, where each vertex $v \in V$ represents a value in $\mathbb{Z}_M$ and each $e \in E$ captures an arc (v, v') from value v to v' if and only if $L(v, v') = \textbf{true}$.
4: Induce a subgraph $G' = (V', E')$ that contains all nodes of G that participate in cycles involving γ.
5: Compute a spanning tree of G' rooted at γ.
6: For each node $v \in G$ that is absent from G', include an arc from v to the root of the spanning tree of G'. The resulting graph would still be a tree, denoted T.
7: Include a self-loop (γ, γ) at the root of T.
8: Transform T into an action graph of a protocol by the following step:

> For each arc (a, c) in T, where $a, c \in \mathbb{Z}_M$, label (a, c) with every value b for which $L(a, b) = \textbf{false}$ and $b \neq c$.

9: Return the actions represented by the arcs of T.

---

states where $\forall i : (x_{i-1} + x_i) \neq 2$ holds, where addition and subtraction are in modulo 3. As such, for each process P_i, we have $L(x_{i-1}, x_i) \overset{\text{def}}{=} (x_{i-1} + x_i) \neq 2$. Figure 3a illustrates the directed graph representing L in the locality of a process. (Notice that processes are symmetric.) In this case, there are two candidate values for γ, where $L(\gamma, \gamma)$ holds; i.e., values of 0 and 2. Wlog, we choose $\gamma = 0$ and form the spanning tree of the graph G with the root of 0. Stripping the graph in Fig. 3b from the labels on its arcs would give us the spanning tree of G, and the graph with the labels is the action graph of the synthesized self-stabilizing protocol (in Fig. 3c).

Even Difference. The Even Difference protocol specifies the local invariant of each process P_i as $L(x_{i-1}, x_i) \overset{\text{def}}{=} ((x_{i-1} - x_i) \bmod 2) = 0$, where $M = 4$. Thus, the set of legitimate states is $\forall i : ((x_{i-1} - x_i) \bmod 2) = 0$. Notice that if there is an even (respectively, odd) value in the ring, then all values will be even (respectively, odd) in a legitimate state. As such, from any state, Even Difference will converge to either an all-odd or an all-even state. This protocol has applications in choosing a common parity policy in a distributed system, where from an arbitrary state all nodes will agree on a common parity policy. Figure 4a represents the graph corresponding to the predicate L. All four values in the domain M are candidate values for γ. We choose $\gamma = 1$, and generate the action graph of Fig. 4b. Figure 4c illustrates the actions of the self-stabilizing protocol. Please notice that this protocol would recover to global states where all values are odd. Symmetrically, one could generate a protocol that would stabilize to states where all values are even. This could be achieved by strengthening $L(x_{i-1}, x_i)$ by an additional constraint $(x_i \bmod 2 = 0)$ (respectively, $(x_i \bmod 2 \neq 0)$).

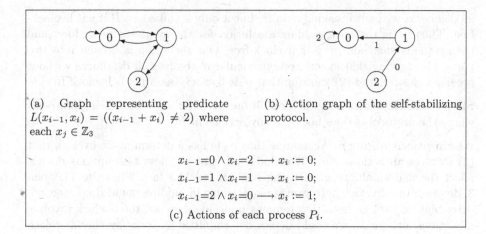

(a) Graph representing predicate $L(x_{i-1}, x_i) = ((x_{i-1} + x_i) \neq 2)$ where each $x_j \in \mathbb{Z}_3$

(b) Action graph of the self-stabilizing protocol.

$$x_{i-1}{=}0 \land x_i{=}2 \longrightarrow x_i := 0;$$
$$x_{i-1}{=}1 \land x_i{=}1 \longrightarrow x_i := 0;$$
$$x_{i-1}{=}2 \land x_i{=}0 \longrightarrow x_i := 1;$$

(c) Actions of each process P_i.

Fig. 3. Synthesis of parameterized Sum-Not-2.

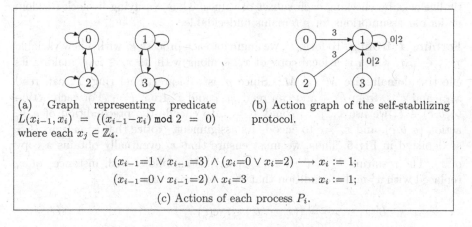

(a) Graph representing predicate $L(x_{i-1}, x_i) = ((x_{i-1}{-}x_i) \bmod 2 = 0)$ where each $x_j \in \mathbb{Z}_4$.

(b) Action graph of the self-stabilizing protocol.

$$(x_{i-1}{=}1 \lor x_{i-1}{=}3) \land (x_i{=}0 \lor x_i{=}2) \longrightarrow x_i := 1;$$
$$(x_{i-1}{=}0 \lor x_{i-1}{=}2) \land x_i{=}3 \qquad\longrightarrow x_i := 1;$$

(c) Actions of each process P_i.

Fig. 4. Synthesis of parameterized Even Difference.

4   Undecidability of Synthesizing Bidirectional Rings

While synthesizing parameterized self-stabilizing protocols is decidable for unidirectional rings, we show that synthesis is undecidable for bidirectional rings.

Theorem 8. *Given a predicate $I \stackrel{\text{def}}{=} (\forall i : L(x_{i-1}, x_i, x_{i+1}))$ and variable domain M (such that each $x_i \in \mathbb{Z}_M$) for a bidirectional ring, it is undecidable (Π_1^0-complete) whether a protocol can stabilize to I for all ring sizes.*

Proof. To show undecidability, we reduce the problem of verifying livelock freedom of a unidirectional ring protocol p to the problem of synthesizing a bidirectional ring protocol p' that stabilizes to I', where I' has some form determined by p. We construct I' such that exactly one bidirectional ring protocol p' resolves all deadlocks without breaking closure, but it only stabilizes to I' if p is livelock-free. Thus, p' is the only candidate solution for the synthesis procedure, and the synthesis succeeds *iff* p is livelock-free. Our reduction is broken into two parts: (1) showing that exactly one particular p' resolves all deadlocks without breaking closure, and (2) showing that p' is livelock-free *iff* p is livelock-free.

Silent stabilization. Wlog, we present our proof for *silent* stabilizing protocols where the protocol p' does not take any actions in I'.

Assumptions about p. We assume that p (1) has a deterministic livelock that (2) involves all actions and (3) includes all values. These assumptions do not affect the undecidability of verifying livelock freedom in p. First, by Theorem 3, deterministic livelock detection is undecidable in unidirectional rings. Second, deterministic livelock detection remains undecidable when the livelock involves all actions; otherwise, we could detect deterministic livelocks by checking each subset of actions. Third, deterministic livelock detection is undecidable even when the livelock involves all values; otherwise, we could detect deterministic livelocks by checking each subset of values. Thus, verifying livelock-freedom under our assumptions for p remains undecidable.

Forming I' from p. To form I', we augment each process P_i with a new variable $x'_{i-1} \in \mathbb{Z}_M$, which is a local copy of x_{i-1}, along with its $x_i \in \mathbb{Z}_M$, making its effective domain size $M' \stackrel{\text{def}}{=} M^2$. Since p' is a bidirectional ring, P_i can read x_{i-1} and x'_{i-2} from P_{i-1} and can read x_{i+1} and x'_i from P_{i+1}. For each action $(a, b, c) \in \xi$, we use $x_{i-1} = a$ and $x'_i = b$ to encode the precondition of a P_i action (a, b, c), and $x_i = c$ to encode its assignment. Notice that x'_i is from P_{i+1} as depicted in Fig. 5. Thus, we must ensure that x'_i eventually obtains a copy of x_i. The resulting $I' \stackrel{\text{def}}{=} (\forall i : L'(x_{i-1}, x_i))$ is as follows with instances of x_i replaced with x'_i and a condition that x'_{i-1} is a copy of x_{i-1}.

$$L'(x_{i-1}, x_i) \stackrel{\text{def}}{=} \big((x_{i-1}, x'_i) \in \mathsf{Pre}(\xi)$$
$$\implies x'_{i-1} = x_{i-1} \wedge x_i = \xi(x_{i-1}, x'_i) \big)$$

Forming p' from I'. We want to show that a particular p' stabilizes to I' when p is livelock-free, and it is the only bidirectional ring protocol that resolves deadlocks without breaking closure. This p' has the following action for each P_i.

$$(x_{i-1}, x'_i) \in \mathsf{Pre}(\xi) \wedge \big(x'_{i-1} \neq x_{i-1} \vee x_i \neq \xi(x_{i-1}, x'_i) \big)$$
$$\longrightarrow \quad x'_{i-1} := x_{i-1}; \ x_i := \xi(x_{i-1}, x'_i);$$

Notice that p' is deadlock-free and preserves closure since a process P_i can act *iff* its $L'(x_{i-1}, x_i)$ is unsatisfied. We now show that this p' is the only such protocol. Consider a ring of 5 processes executing p' where a process P_2 and its readable variables from P_1 and P_3 have arbitrary values. By our earlier assumptions about p, it has an action (a, b, c) for any given a or c (not both), and

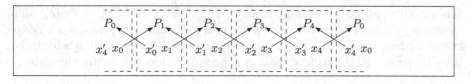

Fig. 5. Topology for bidirectional ring protocol p' in Theorem 8. Each process P_i owns x'_{i-1} and x_i.

$(a, c) \notin \mathsf{Pre}(\xi)$ because processes of p are self-disabling. Thus, we can choose x_0 of P_0 to make $(x_0, x'_1) \notin \mathsf{Pre}(\xi)$ for P_1, and we can choose x'_3 of P_4 to make $(x_2, x'_3) \notin \mathsf{Pre}(\xi)$ for P_3. We have satisfied L'_1 and L'_3, and we can likewise satisfy L'_0 and L'_4 by choosing values of x_4 and x'_4 respectively. Thus, p' is in a legitimate state *iff* L'_2 is satisfied. Therefore, if L'_2 is satisfied, then P_2 cannot act without adding a transition within I' (i.e., breaking closure). As a consequence, no other process but P_2 can act if L'_2 is not satisfied. Since processes are symmetric, each P_i of p' must have the above action to ensure $x'_{i-1} = x_{i-1}$ and $x_i = \xi(x_{i-1}, x'_i)$ when $(x_{i-1}, x'_i) \notin \mathsf{Pre}(\xi)$.

If p has a livelock, then p' has a livelock. Assume p has a livelock. We show that p' has a livelock too. We prove this by showing that p' can simulate the livelock of p. By assumption, p has a deterministic livelock from some state $C = (c_0, \ldots, c_{N-1})$ on a ring of size N where only the first process is enabled; i.e., $(c_{i-1}, c_i) \in \mathsf{Pre}(\xi)$ only for $i = 0$. Let $C' = (c'_0, \ldots, c'_{N-1})$ be the state of this system after all processes act once. That is, $c'_0 = \xi(c_{N-1}, c_0)$ and $c'_i = \xi(c'_{i-1}, c_i)$ for all other $i > 0$. We can construct a livelock state of p' from the same $x_i = c_i$ values for all i and $x'_i = c_i$ for all $i < N - 1$. The value of x'_{N-1} can be c_{N-1}, but can be anything else such that $(x_{N-2}, x'_{N-1}) \notin \mathsf{Pre}(\xi)$. In this state of p', only P_0 is enabled since we assumed that $(c_{i-1}, c_i) \in \mathsf{Pre}(\xi)$ only holds for $i = 0$. P_0 then performs $x_0 := c'_0$ and $x'_{N-1} := c_{N-1}$. This does not enable P_{N-1}, but does enable P_1 to perform $x_1 := c'_1$ and $x'_0 := c'_0$. The execution continues for $P_2, \ldots, P_{N-1}$ to assign $x_i := c'_i$ and $x'_{i-1} := c'_{i-1}$ for all $i > 1$. At this point the system is in a state where $x_i = c'_i$ for all i and $x'_i = c'_i$ for all $i < N - 1$. The value of x'_{N-1} is c_{N-1}, which leaves it disabled. This state of p' matches the state C' of p using the same constraints as we used to match the initial state C. Therefore, p' can continue to simulate p, showing that it has a livelock.

If p is livelock-free, then p' is livelock-free. Assume p is livelock-free. We show that p' is livelock-free too. First, notice that if P_{i+1} acts immediately after P_i in p', then P_i will not become enabled because $x_i = x'_i$ and self-disabling processes of p ensure that $(a, c) \notin \mathsf{Pre}(\xi)$ for every action (a, b, c). This means that in a livelock, if an action of P_{i+1} enables P_i, then P_{i-1} must have acted since the last action of P_i. As such, an action of P_{i-1} must occur between every two actions of P_i in a livelock of p'. The number of such propagations clearly cannot increase, and thus must remain constant in a livelock. In order to avoid collisions, an action of P_{i+1} must occur between every two actions of P_i. Since P_{i+1} always acts before P_i in a livelock of p', it ensures that $x'_i = x_i$ when P_i acts. By making this substitution, we see that P_i is only enabled when $(x_{i-1}, x_i) \in \mathsf{Pre}(\xi)$, and assigns $x_i := \xi(x_{i-1}, x_i)$, which is equivalent to the behavior of protocol p. Since p is livelock-free, p' must also be livelock-free, hence self-stabilizing iff p is livelock-free. Therefore, synthesizing stabilization on bidirectional rings is undecidable.

5   Related Work

This section discusses existing work related to verification and synthesis of parameterized systems.

Verification. The literature for the verification of parameterized systems can broadly be classified into undecidability results and verification methods for decidable cases. In their seminal work, Apt and Kozen [2] prove that verifying an Linear Temporal Logic (LTL) formula for a parameterized system is in general undecidable. Suzuki [27] extends their results by showing that the verification problem remains undecidable for unidirectional ring protocols of symmetric processes. While Farahat and Ebnenasir [15] show that verifying deadlock-freedom of parameterized rings is decidable, Fabret and Petit [14] prove that if the underlying communication graph is a planar grid, then deadlock-freedom becomes undecidable. In our previous work [22], we show that verifying livelock-freedom is undecidable even on a symmetric ring of self-disabling and deterministic processes. Our results imply the undecidability of verifying self-stabilization on unidirectional rings. Several researchers present cutoff theorems that reduce the verification of parameterized systems to the verification of a small-scale instantiation (i.e., cutoff) thereof such that the parameterized system meets a specific property iff its cutoff instantiation satisfies the desired property. For example, Emerson and Namjoshi [13] provide a cutoff theorem for the verification of LTL without the next-state operator in token passing rings. Several other researchers [3, 12, 17, 24] extend Emerson and Namjoshi's results for other topologies and for different properties/systems. Methods based on regular model checking [1, 7] represent states of parameterized rings as strings of arbitrary length, and a protocol is represented by a finite state transducer. The properties such as deadlock and livelock-freedom are formulated in an automata-theoretic context. The aforementioned approaches are mostly used to verify local properties that are specified in terms of the locality of a process or a proper subset of processes, whereas self-stabilization includes a global liveness property that must be met by local actions of all processes.

Synthesis. Existing synthesis methods can be classified into problem-specific and general approaches. The problem-specific methods focus on generating a parameterized solution for a specific problem (e.g., counting [11, 25], consensus [4], sorting [8], etc.). General methods [16, 20] for the synthesis of parameterized systems are mainly *specification-based* in that they provide a decision procedure for extracting the skeleton of symmetric processes from their temporal logic specifications. Some existing methods [6] exploit cutoff theorems to generate the template code of parameterized systems. Moreover, several researchers [6, 11, 21] utilize SMT/SAT solvers for synthesis where they either directly encode the synthesis problem as a set of constraints fed into the solver, or exploit counterexample guided search [11] to find solutions in a bounded scope.

While existing methods are effective in their stated objectives, they often make restrictive assumptions (e.g., synchrony, fairness) to mitigate the complexity of synthesis. We believe that part of this complexity is because of the way synthesis is conceived; that is, generate code skeleton from temporal logic specifications. By contrast, we think that synthesis of parameterized systems must be done on a *property-based* fashion where we devise methods for the synthesis of systems that meet a specific property (e.g., self-stabilization). Such an investigation can be extended to different network topologies (e.g., tree, mesh).

6 Conclusions and Future Work

In this paper, we investigated the problem of synthesizing parameterized rings that have the property of self-stabilization. The ring processes are deterministic and have constant state space. Moreover, we consider self-disabling processes, where a process disables itself after executing an action until it is enabled again by the actions of other processes. While it is known that verifying self-stabilization of unidirectional rings is undecidable [22], in this paper, we present a surprising result that synthesizing self-stabilizing unidirectional rings is actually decidable. We present a sound and complete algorithm for the synthesis of self-stabilizing unidirectional rings, and apply our algorithms to a few case studies. We also show that the synthesis problem becomes undecidable if we assume bidirectional rings. As an extension to this work, we are investigating the application of our approach to other topologies such as trees and meshes. Furthermore, we are integrating our algorithms in Protocon (http://asd.cs.mtu.edu/projects/protocon/), which is a framework for the synthesis of self-stabilizing systems.

References

1. Abdulla, P.A., Jonsson, B., Nilsson, M., Saksena, M.: A survey of regular model checking. In: Gardner, P., Yoshida, N. (eds.) CONCUR 2004. LNCS, vol. 3170, pp. 35–48. Springer, Heidelberg (2004). doi:10.1007/978-3-540-28644-8_3
2. Apt, K.R., Kozen, D.: Limits for automatic verification of finite-state concurrent systems. Inf. Process. Lett. **22**(6), 307–309 (1986)
3. Außerlechner, S., Jacobs, S., Khalimov, A.: Tight cutoffs for guarded protocols with fairness. In: Jobstmann, B., Leino, K.R.M. (eds.) VMCAI 2016. LNCS, vol. 9583, pp. 476–494. Springer, Heidelberg (2016). doi:10.1007/978-3-662-49122-5_23
4. Berman, P., Garay, J.A., Perry, K.J.: Towards optimal distributed consensus. In: 30th Annual Symposium on Foundations of Computer Science, pp. 410–415. IEEE (1989)
5. Bernard, S., Devismes, S., Potop-Butucaru, M.G., Tixeuil, S.: Optimal deterministic self-stabilizing vertex coloring in unidirectional anonymous networks. In: 23rd IEEE International Symposium on Parallel and Distributed Processing, IPDPS 2009, Rome, Italy, 23–29 May 2009, pp. 1–8. IEEE (2009)

6. Bloem, R., Braud-Santoni, N., Jacobs, S.: Synthesis of self-stabilising and byzantine-resilient distributed systems. In: Chaudhuri, S., Farzan, A. (eds.) CAV 2016. LNCS, vol. 9779, pp. 157–176. Springer, Cham (2016). doi:10.1007/978-3-319-41528-4_9

7. Bouajjani, A., Jonsson, B., Nilsson, M., Touili, T.: Regular model checking. In: Emerson, E.A., Sistla, A.P. (eds.) CAV 2000. LNCS, vol. 1855, pp. 403–418. Springer, Heidelberg (2000). doi:10.1007/10722167_31

8. Bundala, D., Závodný, J.: Optimal sorting networks. In: Dediu, A.-H., Martín-Vide, C., Sierra-Rodríguez, J.-L., Truthe, B. (eds.) LATA 2014. LNCS, vol. 8370, pp. 236–247. Springer, Cham (2014). doi:10.1007/978-3-319-04921-2_19

9. De Moura, L., Bjørner, N.: Satisfiability modulo theories: introduction and applications. Commun. ACM 54(9), 69–77 (2011)

10. Dijkstra, E.W.: Self-stabilizing systems in spite of distributed control. Commun. ACM 17(11), 643–644 (1974)

11. Dolev, D., Korhonen, J.H., Lenzen, C., Rybicki, J., Suomela, J.: Synchronous counting and computational algorithm design. In: Higashino, T., Katayama, Y., Masuzawa, T., Potop-Butucaru, M., Yamashita, M. (eds.) SSS 2013. LNCS, vol. 8255, pp. 237–250. Springer, Cham (2013). doi:10.1007/978-3-319-03089-0_17

12. Emerson, E.A., Kahlon, V.: Reducing model checking of the many to the few. In: McAllester, D. (ed.) CADE 2000. LNCS (LNAI), vol. 1831, pp. 236–254. Springer, Heidelberg (2000). doi:10.1007/10721959_19

13. Emerson, E.A., Namjoshi, K.S.: On reasoning about rings. Int. J. Found. Comput. Sci. 14(4), 527–550 (2003)

14. Fabret, A.-C., Petit, A.: On the undecidability of deadlock detection in families of nets. In: Mayr, E.W., Puech, C. (eds.) STACS 1995. LNCS, vol. 900, pp. 479–490. Springer, Heidelberg (1995). doi:10.1007/3-540-59042-0_98

15. Farahat, A., Ebnenasir, A.: Local reasoning for global convergence of parameterized rings. In: IEEE International Conference on Distributed Computing Systems (ICDCS), pp. 496–505 (2012)

16. Finkbeiner, B., Schewe, S.: Bounded synthesis. Int. J. Softw. Tools Technol. Transfer 15(5–6), 519–539 (2013)

17. German, S.M., Sistla, A.P.: Reasoning about systems with many processes. J. ACM 39, 675–735 (1992)

18. Gouda, M.G., Haddix, F.F.: The stabilizing token ring in three bits. J. Parallel Distrib. Comput. 35(1), 43–48 (1996)

19. Jackson, D.: Alloy: a lightweight object modelling notation. ACM Trans. Softw. Eng. Methodol. 11(2), 256–290 (2002)

20. Jacobs, S., Bloem, R.: Parameterized synthesis. In: Flanagan, C., König, B. (eds.) TACAS 2012. LNCS, vol. 7214, pp. 362–376. Springer, Heidelberg (2012). doi:10.1007/978-3-642-28756-5_25

21. Khalimov, A., Jacobs, S., Bloem, R.: Towards efficient parameterized synthesis. In: Giacobazzi, R., Berdine, J., Mastroeni, I. (eds.) VMCAI 2013. LNCS, vol. 7737, pp. 108–127. Springer, Heidelberg (2013). doi:10.1007/978-3-642-35873-9_9

22. Klinkhamer, A., Ebnenasir, A.: Verifying livelock freedom on parameterized rings and chains. In: International Symposium on Stabilization, Safety, and Security of Distributed Systems, pp. 163–177 (2013)

23. Klinkhamer, A., Ebnenasir, A.: Shadow/puppet synthesis: a stepwise method for the design of self-stabilization. IEEE Trans. Parallel Distrib. Syst. 27(11), 3338–3350 (2016)

24. Kurshan, R.P., McMillan, K.L.: A structural induction theorem for processes. Inf. Comput. 117(1), 1–11 (1995)

25. Lenzen, C., Rybicki, J.: Near-optimal self-stabilising counting and firing squads. arXiv preprint arXiv:1608.00214 (2016)
26. Pnueli, A., Rosner, R.: Distributed reactive systems are hard to synthesis. In: Proceedings of 31st IEEE Symposium on Foundation of Computer Science, Computer Society, pp. 746–757. IEEE, Washington, DC (1990)
27. Suzuki, I.: Proving properties of a ring of finite-state machines. Inf. Process. Lett. **28**(4), 213–214 (1988)
28. Varghese, G.: Self-stabilization by local checking and correction. PhD thesis. MIT (1993)
29. Varghese, G.: Self-stabilization by counter flushing. In: The 13th Annual ACM Symposium on Principles of Distributed Computing, pp. 244–253 (1994)

Flexible Transactional Coordination in the Peer Model

Eva Kühn[✉]

Institute of Computer Languages, TU Wien, Vienna, Austria
eva.kuehn@tuwien.ac.at
http://www.complang.tuwien.ac.at/eva

Abstract. The Peer Model is a model for the specification of coordination aspects found in concurrent and distributed systems. It provides modeling constructs for flows, time, remoting and exception handling. The main concepts of the ground model are peers, wirings, containers, entries and services. Its intent is to introduce specific modeling abstractions of concurrency and distribution to make designs more readable and suitable for larger problems. However, there still exist coordination aspects that are not straight forward to model with it. In this paper, therefore the Peer Model is extended by modeling constructs for nested, distributed transactions based on the Flex transaction model. This approach eases the advanced control of structured and distributed coordination scenarios that have to cope with complex, dependent and concurrent flows. The evaluation introduces a coordination challenge that requires adaptive and transactional distribution of resources, dependencies between concurrent activities, error handling and compensation. It demonstrates the improvements that can be achieved with the new modeling concepts.

Keywords: Coordination model · Flexible transactions · Concurrent and distributed systems

1 Introduction

Cooperative information systems involve demanding coordination aspects. Separating coordination from application logic and providing precise models of the coordination is crucial in order to gain robust, distributed software systems [1]. The coordination pattern approach [2] suggests generalizing the aspects of how the participating and distributed processes interact. This enables coordination generics to become reusable among different applications and domains. A major benefit is that these complex parts of a distributed application need not be re-invented for each new application, thus contributing to more reliable systems.

Coordination requirements [3] extend far beyond routing information between processes: They comprise management of complex dependencies among many concurrent and distributed processes in real-time. Therefore, traditional

M. Dastani and M. Sirjani (Eds.): FSEN 2017, LNCS 10522, pp. 116–131, 2017.
DOI: 10.1007/978-3-319-68972-2_8

coordination models quite often reach their limitations with regard to expressive power and usability of resulting models. Well known examples are Petri Nets [4], Actor Model [5] and Reo [6]. All are general and powerful and have mathematical foundations. The Actor Model abstracts asynchronous communication, but the behavior of an actor intertwines application logic with communication and synchronization logic. In contrast to Petri Nets and Actor Model, Reo provides clear separation of coordination from application logic; however, the abstraction level is similar to Petri Nets, where larger models tend to become unreadable [7,8]. An advantage of Petri Nets is that with the concept of transitions they provide a powerful modeling construct for atomic transactions.

The Peer Model is a coordination model that introduces specific assumptions for distributed and concurrent systems in order to make models less complex and easier to understand. The main abstractions comprise modeling concepts for local transactions, remoting, flow correlation, exceptions and timing. It separates coordination from application data and logic. Application data is represented as a "black box" and application logic is encapsulated into services that manipulate the application data and are called by the coordination layer.

All mentioned coordination models are able to model any scenario. However, if the complexity of a use case increases, the strict separation of application and coordination layer might not be maintained (as coordination logic slips into the application logic) or the model requires a lot of cumbersome work to specify details that are not directly related with the problem at hand.

A challenging coordination scenario is defined in Sect. 3 that lets also the original Peer Model reach its limitations with regard to modeling expressiveness. It comprises a factory, distributed and concurrent workers, and shops where resources can be ordered. The workers continuously execute tasks and compete for shared resources. Possible concurrency shall be exploited. A further complicating aspect is the distribution of processes. The specific challenges comprise: complex dependencies between activities, automatic compensation, error and timeout handling, and distributed transaction management.

This paper presents an extension of the Peer Model by a flexible, distributed, nested transaction approach termed flexible wiring transactions (FWTX) in order to ease the design of such advanced coordination scenarios. Also other coordination models can benefit from this concept. As proof-of-concept for the new modeling constructs the mentioned factory example is used.

The structure of the paper is as follows: Sect. 2 explains the original Peer Model. Section 3 introduces a coordination challenge and discusses a solution for it with the original Peer Model. Section 4 presents the new flexible wiring transaction concept (FWTX), inspired by Flex transactions [9]. Section 5 evaluates it with the coordination challenge, demonstrates that designs become leaner, and gives a comparison with related coordination models. Section 6 concludes the paper and gives an outlook for future work.

2   Peer Model

The Peer Model [2,8] is a coordination model with high-level modeling abstractions for concurrent and distributed systems: A *peer* relates to an actor in the

Actor Model [5]. It is an autonomous worker with ingoing and outgoing mail-boxes, termed input and output *containers* (PIC and POC). The foundation of containers is tuple-space-based communication [10,11]. A container relates to a sub-space that maintains tuples (called *entries*) and supports transactional *queries* on them. The coordination behavior of the peer is explicitly modeled by *wirings* that are similar to Petri Net transitions [4]. It is triggered by events represented as *entries* written into containers. A wiring possesses *links* for the transport of entries between containers. Incoming links are termed *guards* and outgoing ones *actions*. A wiring stands for concurrent instances that actively and repeatedly execute the wiring specification. A wiring instance is one atomic local space transaction, termed wiring transaction (WTX) on the peer's space containers. As transaction mechanism we assume pessimistic locking and repeatable read isolation level. The operational behavior of a WTX is to execute in the specified sequential order first guard, then *service*, and finally action links. The WTX collects all entries retrieved by guards in an internal and non-transactional container that serves as a temporary, local entry collection for this wiring instance. Service links transport entries between the internal wiring container and the service and call the application method. Note that guard and action links set locks within the WTX on the space containers. All artifacts have *properties*. System properties have a pre-defined semantics, e.g. if a time-to-live (`ttl`) property on a WTX or on a link expires, this causes the current WTX to rollback and start a new instance.

2.1   Artifacts of the Ground Model

Property $prop = (label, val)$. *label* is a name, and *val* denotes a value. A label that defines a system property is written in typewriter style, otherwise it is an application property. The property is named after its label.

Entry $e = \mathbb{E}prop$. $\mathbb{E}prop$ is a set of properties $\{prop_1, prop_2, \ldots, prop_n\}$. Entry system properties are e.g., `type` (obligatory coordination type of the entry), `ttl` (time-to-live: if it expires the entry is wrapped into an exception entry[1]; default is infinite), `fid` (flow identifier), and `data` (application-specific data).

Container $c = (cid, \mathbb{E}, \mathbb{C}oord, \mathbb{C}prop)$. A container stores entries. *cid* is a unique name, $\mathbb{E}$ a set of entries, $\mathbb{C}oord$ a set of coordinators (see Query below), and $\mathbb{C}prop$ a set of system properties. A container relates to an XVSM container [11]. We differentiate between space containers and internal containers. The former ones support transactions and blocking behavior. Entries are retrieved by a query that necessarily requires the coordination type of the entry.

Query $q = (type, cnt, \mathbb{S}el)$. *type* is an entry coordination type. *cnt* is a number, a range, or the keyword `ALL` or `NONE`, determining the amount of entries to be selected; default is 1. $\mathbb{S}el$ is a sequence of AND/OR connected selectors. A selector is lent from the XVSM query mechanism [12]. It refers to a container

---

[1] In the assumed configuration exception entries are written into the peer's POC.

coordinator (e.g. `fifo`, `key`, `label`, `any`) or is a selection expression involving entry properties, variables and system functions.

Link $l = (c_1, c_2, op, q, \mathbb{E}xpr, \mathbb{L}prop)$. c_1 refers to a source and c_2 to a target container. $op \in \{\texttt{create}, \texttt{copy}, \texttt{move}, \texttt{delete}, \texttt{test}, \texttt{noop}, \texttt{call}\}$. `create` creates new entries and writes them to c_2. `copy` reads entries from c_1 and writes them to c_2. `move` reads and deletes entries from c_1 and writes them to c_2. `delete` reads and deletes entries from c_1. `test` checks entries in c_1. `noop` only executes q which must not refer to entries. `call` calls a service. All operations must fulfill the query q, if it is not empty, on c_1. $\mathbb{E}xpr$ is a sequence of expressions that set or get properties of selected entries and/or of variables [2]. $\mathbb{L}prop$ is a set of system properties, e.g.: `tts` (time-to-start: how long the link execution must wait to start; default is 0), `ttl` (time-to-live: how long the link execution may be retried until it succeeds; if it expires, a system entry of type exception is created that wraps the original entry and provides the type of the original entry in a property termed `ettl`; default is infinite), `dest` (specifies the id of a destination peer to which all selected entries on an action link are automatically transported via intermediary I/O peers [2]), `flow` (if `true` (default), the link transports only "flow-compatible" [2] entries – this means that the `fid` of all entries transported by links of this WTX must be the same or not set), and `mandatory` (if `true` (default), the fulfillment of the link is obligatory).

Wiring $w = (wid, \mathbb{G}, \mathbb{S}, \mathbb{A}, wic, \mathbb{W}prop)$. wid is a unique name, $\mathbb{G}$ is a sequence of guard links, $\mathbb{S}$ is a sequence of service links, $\mathbb{A}$ is a sequence of action links, wic is the id of an internal container, and $\mathbb{W}prop$ is a set of system properties, e.g., `tts` (time-to-start; time that the next instance of this wiring waits until its start; default is 0), and `ttl` (time-to-live; maximal execution time of one instance of this wiring; default is infinite). All links are numbered, specifying an execution order which has impact on concurrency and performance. Entries selected by guards are written into wic. Then w calls the service links in the specified sequence. Finally, the wiring executes the action links. c_2 of a guard and c_1 of an action link is wic. There is one dedicated wiring in a peer termed init wiring with its first guard having the identifier "*"; it is fulfilled exactly once, namely when the peer is activated.

Service $s = (sid, app)$. sid is the name of the service and app a reference to the implementation of its application logic (method). A service gets entries from its wiring's wic as input and emits result entries there (via service links). It has access to all entry properties including `data`.

Peer $p = (pid, pic, poc, \mathbb{W}id, \mathbb{S}pid, \mathbb{P}prop)$. pid is a unique name, pic and poc are the ids of incoming and outgoing space containers where p receives and delivers

---

[2] Application variables have the scope of the current wiring instance and start with a "$". They are set by $\mathbb{E}xpr$. $\mathbb{E}xpr$ may involve system functions like "fid()" which generates a new unique flow identifier, as well as system variables (starting with "$$") that are set by the system, e.g., \$\$PID (name of the current peer), \$\$FID (actual flow id within the current wiring instance), and \$\$CNT (number of entries selected by the current link).

entries, $\mathbb{W}id$ is a set of wiring ids, $\mathbb{S}pid$ is a set of ids of sub-peers, and $\mathbb{P}prop$ is a set of system properties.

Peer Model $PM = (\mathbb{P}, \mathbb{W}, \mathbb{C})$. $\mathbb{P}$ is the set of all peers including sub-peers, $\mathbb{W}$ is the set of all wirings, and $\mathbb{C}$ is the set of all containers in the system.

2.2   Graphical Notation

The graphical representation of the Peer Model is shown in Fig. 1, outlining one peer with one wiring that has two links and calls one service (the depiction of service links is skipped). The guard link connects the peer's *pic* with the wirings's *wic*, and the action link connects the wiring's *wic* with the peer's *poc*. Note that the source space container of a guard can also be the peer's *poc* or the *poc* of a sub-peer. Analogously the target space container of an action link can also be the peer's *pic* or the *pic* of a sub-peer. A wiring can have many links that are numbered with $G_1, \ldots, G_k, S_1, \ldots, S_m, A_1, \ldots, A_n$ (the link ids are not depicted in Fig. 1). A peer can have many wirings.

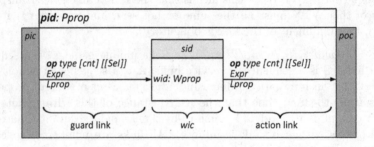

Fig. 1. Example peer.

3   Coordination Challenge

The contrived coordination example is a bakery with autonomous bakers who are specialized in producing certain products like bread, pizza, cake etc. Each product requires a defined amount of ingredients (eggs, flour, sugar etc.). The bakery operator provides the ingredients for the bakers which compete for them. If an ingredient runs short, the concerned bakers cannot proceed. The bakery tries to procure all missing ingredients at respective shops.

A baker's job is to produce doughs for the respective product as fast as possible and to send each dough immediately to the bakery. For this, he/she must first get hold of the needed ingredients. Another critical time is the stirring of the dough. If 5 pieces of dough are ready they form a "charge" that is baked in the oven. The baker informs the bakery when a charge must be sent to the oven. Only doughs of the same charge of a baker are baked together. However, the baker has a timeout for producing one dough. If it exceeds, the current charge – although incomplete – shall nevertheless be baked to avoid the risk of already produced dough to go off, provided the charge contains at least one dough.

The example is complicated to model, because of challenging **dependencies between the concurrent coordination steps**: The occurrence of failures (the lack of an ingredient) and timeouts (the obtaining of the ingredients or the dough stirring service takes too long) influence the completion of a charge. The baker must recognize in real-time whether a charge is complete or whether the production is stuck (due to **errors or timeouts**) and inform the bakery to start the delivery of the current charge to the oven at the right moment. The bakery is responsible to fill up its stock if resources run low. Let us assume a simple policy whereby in a defined time interval the bakery checks its stock to be below a certain boundary and tries to completely fill it up. It orders each kind of ingredient at a different shop. The **distributed procurement transaction** shall succeed only if all ingredients can be purchased; otherwise nothing is bought and the bakery retries the procurement process later on. Shops are autonomous and not willing to hold locks on items: They immediately remove the ordered ingredients from their stock and put them in a temporary container for the client. If the global transaction succeeds, they deliver the ingredients to the client; otherwise a **compensation** must take place that moves the reserved ingredients back to the shop's stock. This means that other clients might think that the shop has no items any more, albeit later on they are put back to the stock because the client has aborted the global transaction.

3.1   Bakery Without FWTX

Figures 2 and 3 model the use case with the original Peer Model, i.e. without FWTX. The three main peers types are shown: Baker, Bakery and Shop. Their behavior is represented by wirings as detailed below for each peer. The dough production must be split into two wirings to model the acquisition of ingredients before the dough stirring can start. All phases of the distributed procurement transaction between bakery and shops and the cleaning up of outdated entries used by the distributed transaction management must be modeled explicitly.

Baker Peer:

- *Init:* Create an entry for the next charge with a new `fid`, a `ttl`, and 0 doughs (property k), and set current phase to 1 (A1).
- *ProduceDough1:* If there is a charge with less than 5 doughs in phase 1 (G1), then set its phase to 2 (A1) and create a request in the current flow with a `ttl` and the baker's pid, and send it to the bakery, asking to send ingredients for the next dough (A2).
- *ProduceDough2:* If there is a charge with less than 5 doughs in phase 2 (G1), and if the needed ingredients are there (G2–G3), then call the dough stirring service, increment the dough count of the charge, and set its phase to 1 (A1), and send the dough, that was produced by the service, within the current

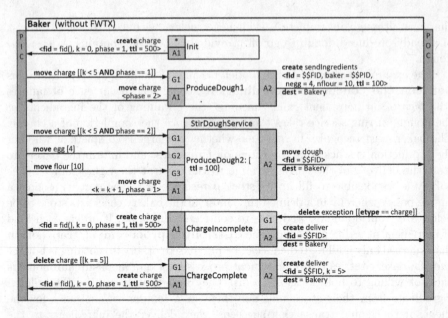

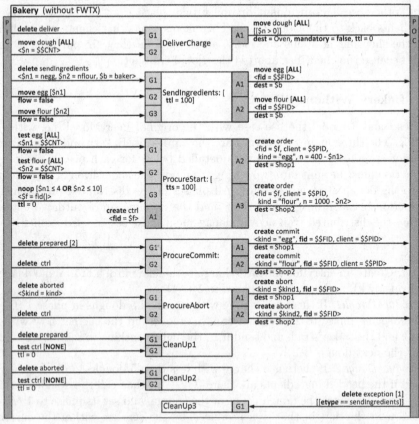

Fig. 2. Baker and Bakery (without FWTX).

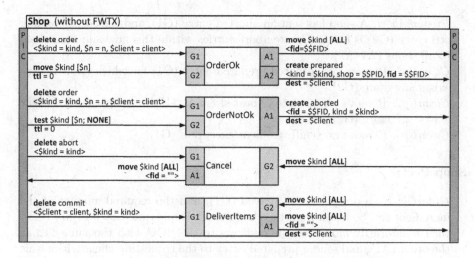

Fig. 3. Shop (without FWTX).

charge's flow to the bakery (A2). The WTX is bounded by a timeout (`ttl`). If it expires, it performs a rollback, releases all locks on entries, and retries.

- *ChargeIncomplete:* If the charge has expired and turned into an exception (G1), then create a new charge with a new flow id (A1), and tell the bakery to deliver the incomplete charge, referred to by its flow id, to the oven (A2).
- *ChargeComplete:* If the current charge is complete with 5 doughs (G1), then start a new charge within a new flow id (A1), and tell the bakery to deliver the complete charge, referred to by its flow id, to the oven (A2).

Bakery Peer:

- *DeliverCharge:* Upon receipt of a deliver request (G1), take all doughs of the same charge (correlated by their flow id) and remember in the local variable $n how many were taken (G2), and send them to the oven (A1) if there exists at least one dough.
- *SendIngredients:* If a sendIngredients request is received (G1) and if the requested ingredients (G2–G3) are there, then send them to the requesting baker (A1–A2).
- *ProcureStart:* In a defined interval (modeled as `tts` of the wiring) check how many ingredients are still there (G1–G2). If one of them has fallen below a defined threshold create a new `fid` (G3). If ingredients are missing, then create a ctrl entry within this flow and store it in the PIC in order to control the distributed procurement transaction (A1), and send an order request for each ingredient to the corresponding shops (A2–A3).
- *ProcureCommit:* The information that all shops are in prepared state has received (G1), and the corresponding ctrl entry (G2) for this flow exists: Create commit entries within this flow carrying the id of this peer and send them to all shops with information about the confirmed order (A1–A2).

- *ProcureAbort:* A shop has sent an aborted entry (G1), and the corresponding ctrl entry (G2) is found: Create abort entries within this flow and send them to all shops (A1–A2).
- *CleanUp1:* Remove an outdated prepared entry (G1) for which no ctrl entry exists any more (G2).
- *CleanUp2:* Remove an outdated aborted entry (G1) for which no ctrl entry exists any more (G2).
- *CleanUp3:* Remove an sendIngredient exception (G1).

Shop Peer:

- *OrderOk:* If an order request arrived (G1), and the required amount of the ingredient can be taken from the shop's stock (represented by its PIC) (G2), then temporarily move these ingredients to the POC with the same `fid` as the order (A1), and send a prepared entry to the requesting client within this flow indicating what has been reserved for it and by which shop (A2).
- *OrderNotOk:* If an order request is received (G1), but the required amount of this ingredient is not in stock (G2), then send aborted to the client in this flow (A1). Note the counter expression "[$n; NONE]" on G2: It models a range with the meaning "not at least $n entries".
- *Cancel:* A client has aborted the distributed transaction (G1), and the reserved amount of ingredients is therefore withdrawn from the intermediate storage (G2): Write these ingredients back to the shop's stock (A1).
- *DeliverItems:* The client has issued a commit for the distributed transaction (G1), and the ingredients are therefore removed from the intermediate storage (G2): Send them to the respective client (A1).

4 Flexible Wiring Transactions (FWTX)

The Flex transaction model [9,13,14] defines nested transactions that allow the early commit of sub-transactions, thus relaxing the isolation property of transactions. The tradeoff is that so-called compensate actions must be supported. Compensate actions are motivated by Sagas [15]. They are application defined logic that carries out a compensation of the effects of committed sub-transactions, however they cannot really "undo" in the strict sense an effect that was already seen by others, but only perform a "semantic" compensation. They are activated by the transaction manager if a sub-transaction has committed and then one of its parent transactions fails. No cascading compensation is done, i.e. if a sub-transaction commits, it is responsible for the compensation of its sub-transactions. The Flex transaction model supports compensatable as well as non-compensatable sub-transactions. The former perform an early commit, the latter delegate their commit to the caller (cf. nested transactions [16]).

The idea to use a flexible transaction model to coordinate distributed processes in heterogeneous systems was firstly used by the coordination kernel [14], implementing a distributed virtually shared object space. The coordination kernel extends the Flex transaction model by on-commit and on-abort actions that are called if a transaction commits respectively aborts. It was the basis for the later CORSO (coordinated shared objects) coordination system [17] that demonstrates that the Flex transaction model can be implemented efficiently.

We adapt here this concept for the Peer Model. The local transaction of a wiring (WTX) is extended towards flexible wiring transactions (FWTX). A WTX locally executes all links in one atomic step (see Sect. 2.1). A FWTX in addition supports nested flexible transactions, as well as compensate actions (optionally cascading or not), on-commit actions, on-top-commit actions, and on-abort actions. The definition of a wiring is enhanced by introducing passive wirings which are not actively executing instances, but must be activated by other FWTXs. Passive wirings therefore may take input parameters so that the calling FTWX can pass local variables values (by value). Note: the communication between peers must be carried out by exchanging entries.

An instance of a passive wiring is activated by a parent FWTX either (i) via a guard link, or (ii) as a compensate, on-commit, on-top-commit or on-abort action (which in turn are FWTXs). For (i) the link definition (see Sect. 2.1) is extended in that op can also be **wiring**, denoting the sub-wiring to be called in a new sub-FWTX. For (ii) new wiring system properties ($\mathbb{W}prop$) are introduced: on-top-commit, on-commit, on-abort, and compensate to specify a passive local or remote wiring; and a boolean property termed cascading to define whether a compensation action is cascading or not. Parameters to be passed to the sub-wiring activation are modeled as part of $\mathbb{E}xpr$ as variables, where the i-th parameter is referred to by $i. A sub-FWTX is activated exactly once. It inherits the flow id of the parent-FWTX, and vice versa, if at the time of its activation the flow id of the parent-FWTX is not yet determined, it can set it.

A parent FWTX is only dependent on synchronous sub-FWTXs that are called via guard links, provided that the property mandatory of this link is not turned off. The link execution must wait until the sub-FWTX – which can be a remote one – has finished. This concept extends the expressiveness of guards in that it becomes possible to send a request to a remote peer and wait in a subsequent guard for entries that the peer sends back. Otherwise this would require two or more wirings – implying that the flow of control becomes more complicated – as well as the explicit treatment of possible errors.

Let a FWTX X have an on-commit (OC), an on-top-commit (OTC), an on-abort (OA), and a compensate (COMP) action. OC is called immediately after X has committed. OTC is called immediately after the top-level-FWTX of X has committed. If X is the top-level-FWTX then OTC is called immediately after OC. OA is called immediately after X has aborted. COMP is called if X has committed and later on a parent-FWTX of it aborts. It runs asynchronously to X. If cascading is true, then the compensation is recursively propagated to all sub-FWTXs of X that were called via guard links. X waits with the execution of its next wiring instance (X') until all OC, OTC or OA executions have completed. The time how long it waits can optionally be configured by respective ttl wiring system properties for on-(top-)commit and on-abort actions. X is neither dependent on OC, OTC, COMP nor OA. On-commit, on-top-commit, on-abort and compensate actions are automatically committed.

The distributed transaction managers jointly control the execution of FWTXs: A FWTX must persist the information about each called sub-FWTX. If FWTX itself is nested, it must store its parent-FWTX and top-level-FWTX. It passes the id of its own FWTX and the top-level FWTX to each called sub-FWTX. If a sub-FWTX commits or aborts, it reliably sends this decision to its parent-FWTX, i.e. it repeats the sending until an acknowledgment is received. If it commits, it stores its compensate action until it receives the final decision of the top-level-FWTX. The necessary assumptions are that a crashed site eventually will recover and that eventually each pair of sub-FWTX and its direct parent-FWTX is available at the same time.

The model avoids that resources are locked for a long period of time or forever. The interesting error cases are caused by dependent sub-FWTX activations via guards. Breaking it down to the pair of a parent-FWTX and its sub-FWTX these situations comprise: *) A committed sub-FWTX must wait for its parent-FWTX's decision whether to compensate or not. During this time, because the relaxation of the isolation property allowed the early commitment of the sub-FWTX, no data need to be locked. The compensation is a semantic one; it is standalone and may run even a long time after the commitment of the sub-FWTX. *) A parent-FWTX cannot commit because its sub-FWTX did not answer yet. In this case it is recommended that the parent-FWTX uses a `ttl`. If the `ttl` fires then eventually the sub-FWTX will be aborted, too or needs to compensate. *) A sub-FWTX has committed, but the commit did not reach its parent-FWTX. Either the parent-FWTX waits until it can communicate again with sub-FWTX, or it aborts meanwhile. In the former case parent-FWTX can proceed, in the latter case eventually sub-FWTX learns about parent-FWTX's abort and will compensate.

In the graphical notation, the declaration of a passive wiring has a box with a dotted line and a parameter list enclosed by "()" brackets. The activation of a sub-FWTX via a guard uses the `wiring` operation.

5   Proof-of-Concept

As a proof-of-concept for the new FWTX concepts of the Peer Model, we present a solution with it for the bakery example. The number of wirings could be reduced from 17 to 10 (i.e. by ca. 41%) and the total number of links from 66 to 28 (i.e. by ca. 58%).

5.1   Bakery with FWTX

The baker uses a sub-FWTX to get ingredients from the bakery. If it fails, an on-abort action sends the incomplete charge immediately to the oven and starts a new charge. The distributed procurement transaction of the bakery uses sub-FWTXs with compensation to order ingredients at shops. If one shop fails, the other one is automatically aborted or compensated. If both succeed, their commit is implicitly triggered by the commit of the Procure FWTX; on-top-commit-actions at the shops start the goods delivery to the client.

The improvements of the version with FWTX (see Sect. 3.1) over the one without FWTX are summarized in the following.

Baker Peer (with FWTX):

- *Init:* No difference.
- *ProduceDough:* Consolidates ProduceDough1 and ProduceDough2 in one wiring where G2 calls a sub-wiring at the bakery termed SendIngredients. The definition of an on-abort action is added to the wiring to call a local sub-wiring termed StartNewCharge.
- *ChargeComplete:* Has only one guard (G1) that tests if the charge is complete and if so, calls the sub-wiring StartNewCharge as on-commit action.
- *StartNewCharge:* Is a new passive wiring. It takes the current charge entry (G1), resets both its fid and k and writes it back to the PIC (A1). It calls the DeliverCharge sub-wiring of the bakery as on-commit action and passes it the number of doughs in this charge as parameter.

Bakery Peer (with FWTX):

- *DeliverCharge:* Is a passive wiring called by the baker every time it starts a new charge via StartNewCharge. Therefore the original G1 is not needed.
- *SendIngredients:* Is a passive wiring called by the baker's wiring Produce-Dough in G2. On start it calls Procur. The original G1 is not needed.
- *Procure:* Consolidates ProcureStart, ProcureCommit, ProcureAbort, Clean-Up1, CleanUp2 and CleanUp3 in one wiring. G1–G3 correspond to G1–G3 of the original ProcureStart wiring. Instead of sending order entries to the shops it calls the passive Order wiring of each shop as a sub-FWTX (G4–G5). This models the distributed transaction with compensation.

Shop Peer (with FWTX):

- *Order:* Consolidates OrderOk and OrderNotOk. It is a passive wiring that is called by the Procure wiring of the bakery (G4–G5). It has a compensate action that cancels the reservation and an on-top-commit action that delivers the reserved ingredients if the top-level-FWTX commits.
- *Cancel:* Passive wiring called as compensate action of the Order wiring.
- *DeliverItems:* Passive wiring called by Order upon top-level commit.

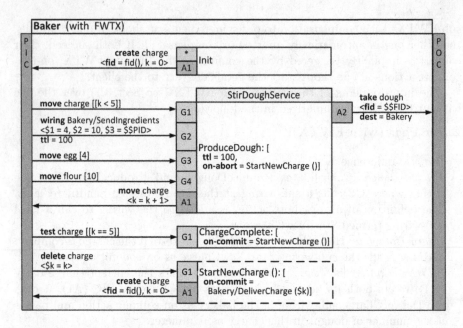

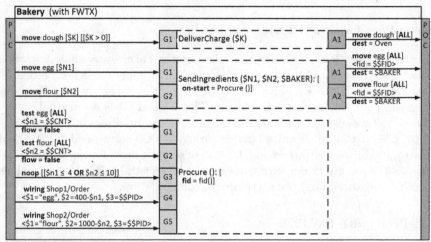

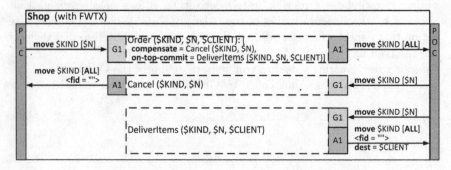

Fig. 4. Baker, Bakery and Shop (with FWTX).

5.2   Related Coordination Models

A realization of the bakery example with the Actor Model is quite straight forward, but mixes application and coordination logic. On the other side, models like Petri Nets and Reo [18] are very general and therefore powerful enough to also model complex coordination scenarios, however, such designs will become complex and exhibit deficiencies and/or become verbose and unreadable (compare with [7,8] who demonstrated this fact with even less demanding coordination and collaboration problems like split/join and leader election without the assumption of failures etc.). The problem is that "lack of appropriate modeling primitives has often resulted in descriptions with either reduced concurrency or increased complexity of the net structure and/or the net inscriptions" [19].

The Transactor Model [20] follows a similar goal like our approach, i.e. to provide language constructs that ease the management of distributed states. It introduces the following concepts: stabilize, checkpoint, dependent test, and rollback. With stabilize an actor guarantees that its state will not change any more (it refers to the prepared phase in a two-phase-commit protocol). A checkpoint is successful if the transactor is not dependent on any other actor that is in a volatile state. Otherwise it will either perform a rollback or is equivalent to a noop (if there have not yet been enough messages received to determine the dependency). A successful checkpoint stores the state of the actor so that a rollback to this state is possible. The dependent test checks whether the actor is dependent on another one. As the entire protocol is asynchronous, this test does not block and therefore the user must take care of this situation explicitly.

A major difference of FWTX is that they support multiple concurrently running flows and automatic execution of user defined actions at certain points in time, namely on-top-commit, on-commit and on-abort of transactions. In addition, the isolation property is relaxed and sub-transactions may early commit. Semantic compensation is used in contrast to the Transactor Model that carries out a rollback. The advantage of compensation is that distributed processes stay autonomous and need not hold locked states over a long period of time.

6   Conclusion

Coordination requirements are challenging and lack of adequate modeling primitives leads to unusable models. We presented an extension of the Peer Model by distributed "flexible wiring transactions (FWTX)" to make wirings more powerful. FWTX enable the control of complex distributed interactions in a very flexible way. The new modeling concepts are on-commit, on-top-commit, on-abort and compensation actions that are designed as passive wirings. With help of FWTX also coordination situations where complex dependencies between concurrent distributed interactions take place or where multi-direction interactions are demanded, can be modeled straight ahead. The treatment of failure situations is easy because the distributed transaction management automatically coordinates the activation of the on-commit, on-top-commit, on-abort and compensation actions. As evaluation, a proof-of-concept is given that shows the design of the selected coordination scenario whereby the separation of application and coordination data and logic could be preserved. The model with FWTX is significantly leaner: the total number of wirings could be reduced by 41% and the number of links by 58%. We believe that also other coordination models can benefit from the introduction of a Flex transaction based coordination mechanism. In future work we will use FWTX to bootstrap other distributed transaction models and implement a simulation tool for automatic analysis.

Acknowledgment. Many thanks to Stefan Craß, Geri Joskowicz, Martin Planer, Matthias Schwayer, Jörg Schoba, Peter Tilian, and the anonymous reviewers for their comments on this paper.

References

1. Astley, M., Sturman, D.C., Agha, G.A.: Customizable middleware for modular distributed software. Commun. ACM **44**(5), 99–107 (2001)
2. Kühn, E.: Reusable coordination components: reliable development of cooperative information systems. Int. J. Coop. Inf. Syst. **25**(4), 1740001 (2016). World Scientific Publishing Company
3. Malone, T.W., Crowston, K.: The interdisciplinary study of coordination. ACM Comput. Surv. (CSUR) **26**(1), 87–119 (1994)
4. Petri, C.A.: Kommunikation mit Automaten. Ph.D. thesis, Technische Hochschule Darmstadt (1962)
5. Agha, G.A.: ACTORS: A Model of Concurrent Computation in Distributed Systems. MIT Press, Cambridge (1990)
6. Arbab, F.: Reo: a channel-based coordination model for component composition. Math. Struct. Comput. Sci. **14**(3), 329–366 (2004). Cambridge University Press
7. Börger, E.: Modeling distributed algorithms by abstract state machines compared to petri nets. In: Butler, M., Schewe, K.-D., Mashkoor, A., Biro, M. (eds.) ABZ 2016. LNCS, vol. 9675, pp. 3–34. Springer, Cham (2016). doi:10.1007/978-3-319-33600-8_1
8. Kühn, E., Craß, S., Joskowicz, G., Marek, A., Scheller, T.: Peer-based programming model for coordination patterns. In: De Nicola, R., Julien, C. (eds.) COORDINATION 2013. LNCS, vol. 7890, pp. 121–135. Springer, Heidelberg (2013). doi:10.1007/978-3-642-38493-6_9
9. Bukhres, O., Elmagarmid, A.K., Kühn, E.: Implementation of the flex transaction model. IEEE Data Eng. Bull. **16**(2), 28–32 (1993)
10. Gelernter, D.: Generative communication in Linda. ACM Trans. Program. Lang. Syst. (TOPLAS) **7**(1), 80–112 (1985)
11. Kühn, E., Mordinyi, R., Keszthelyi, L., Schreiber, C.: Introducing the concept of customizable structured spaces for agent coordination in the production automation domain. In: 8th International Conference on Autonomous Agents and Multiagent Systems (AAMAS), IFAAMAS, pp. 625–632 (2009)
12. Craß, S., Kühn, E., Salzer, G.: Algebraic foundation of a data model for an extensible space-based collaboration crotocol. In: International Database Engineering and Applications Symposium (IDEAS), pp. 301–306. ACM (2009)
13. Elmagarmid, A.K.: Database Transaction Models for Advanced Applications. Morgan Kaufmann, San Francisco (1992)

14. Kühn, E.: Fault-tolerance for communicating multidatabase transactions. In: 27th Annual Hawaii International Conference on System Sciences (HICSS), pp. 323–332. IEEE (1994)
15. Garcia-Molina, H., Salem, K.: Sagas. SIGMOD Record **16**(3), December 1987
16. Moss, E.B.: Nested Transactions: An Approach to Reliable Distributed Computing. Technical report, Cambridge, MA, USA (1981)
17. Kühn, E.: Virtual Shared Memory for Distributed Architecture. Nova Science Publishers, New York (2001)
18. Meng, S., Arbab, F.: A model for web service coordination in long-running transactions. In: Fifth IEEE International Symposium on Service Oriented System Engineering (SOSE), pp. 121–128 (2010)
19. Christensen, S., Hansen, N.D.: Coloured Petri nets extended with place capacities, test arcs and inhibitor arcs. In: Ajmone Marsan, M. (ed.) ICATPN 1993. LNCS, vol. 691, pp. 186–205. Springer, Heidelberg (1993). doi:10.1007/3-540-56863-8_47
20. Field, J., Varela, C.A.: Transactors: A programming model for maintaining globally consistent distributed state in unreliable environments. In: 32nd ACM SIGPLAN-SIGACT Symposium on Principles of Programming Languages (POPL), pp. 195–208 (2005)

Using Swarm Intelligence to Generate Test Data for Covering Prime Paths

Atieh Monemi Bidgoli, Hassan Haghighi[✉], Tahere Zohdi Nasab,
and Hamideh Sabouri

Department of Computer Science and Engineering,
Shahid Beheshti University G.C., Tehran, Iran
h_haghighi@sbu.ac.ir

Abstract. Search-based test data generation methods mostly consider the branch coverage criterion. To the best of our knowledge, only two works exist which propose a fitness function that can support the prime path coverage criterion, while this criterion subsumes the branch coverage criterion. These works are based on the Genetic Algorithm (GA) while scalability of the evolutionary algorithms like GA is questionable. Since there is a general agreement that evolutionary algorithms are inferior to swarm intelligence algorithms, we propose a new approach based on swarm intelligence for covering prime paths. We utilize two prominent swarm intelligence algorithms, i.e., ACO and PSO, along with a new normalized fitness function to provide a better approach for covering prime paths. To make ACO applicable for the test data generation problem, we provide a customization of this algorithm. The experimental results show that PSO and the proposed customization of ACO are both more efficient and more effective than GA when generating test data to cover prime paths. Also, the customized ACO, in comparison to PSO, has better effectiveness while has a worse efficiency.

Keywords: Search based test data generation · Prime paths · Swarm intelligence algorithms · Ant colony optimization · Particle swarm optimization

1 Introduction

Software testing is an important activity of the software development life cycle that aims at revealing failures in a Software Under Test (SUT). Among many activities that help improving software quality, testing is still the most popular method, even though being expensive. Although testing is usually done manually in industrial applications, its automation has been a burgeoning interest of many researchers [1, 2]. Automation reduces cost and time and improves the quality degree of the testing activity.

Test data generation is the activity of finding a set of input values with the aim of detecting more failures of software systems. In the graph-based, structural approach to test data generation, the given software artifact (e.g., the source code concerned in this paper) is modeled as a graph. Control Flow Graph (CFG) is a graph that is obtained from source code for this purpose. According to the graph based criteria, some parts of the resulting graph should be covered by the test data. The simplest criteria are node

© IFIP International Federation for Information Processing 2017
Published by Springer International Publishing AG 2017. All Rights Reserved
M. Dastani and M. Sirjani (Eds.): FSEN 2017, LNCS 10522, pp. 132–147, 2017.
DOI: 10.1007/978-3-319-68972-2_9

coverage, edge coverage, and edge-pair coverage. The edge-pair criterion can be logically extended to the Complete Path Coverage (CPC) criterion. Because of the possibility of infinite number of test requirements, CPC is not practical for programs with loops. To resolve this issue, some solutions have been proposed by researchers, including a coverage criterion based on the prime path notion [4]. Unlike CPC, which is not practical, Prime Path Coverage (PPC) is a practical criterion that subsumes all other graph-based, structural coverage criteria. Thus, in this paper, we consider PPC as the coverage criterion.

The emphasis on the prime path coverage is due to the fact that covering prime paths may reveal failures that cannot be detected using other criteria. For instance, Fig. 1 shows a sample program along with its CFG. It contains a fault in line 11 (i.e., $c = 0$) which causes an exception (division by zero) in the second iteration of the existing loop. Based on the test requirements represented in Table 1, we can reveal the failure if we traverse path 7 which results when using the prime path coverage as the test criterion. Other coverage criteria may never find this fault.

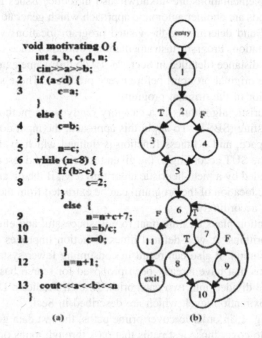

Fig. 1. (a) The sample program (b) The corresponding CFG

Test data generation is an expensive and time consuming activity. Therefore, development of methods to automate this activity is necessary. One approach for automatic test data generation is symbolic execution [6] that assigns symbolic values to program parameters in order to formulate program paths in terms of logical constraints. These constraints should be solved to find values which cause the program to follow specific paths. The main issue with this approach is that it is dependent on the

Table 1. Test paths according to node, edge and prime path coverage for the given example

	Node coverage	Edge coverage	Prime path
1	[1,2,3,5,6,11]	[1,2,3,5,6,11]	[1,2,3,5,6,7,9,10,6,11]
2	[1,2,4,5,6,7,9,10,6,11]	[1,2,4,5,6,7,9,10,6,11]	[1,2,3,5,6,7,8,10,6,11]
3	[1,2,4,5,6,7,8,10,6,11]	[1,2,3,5,6,7,8,10,6,11]	[1,2,4,5,6,11]
4			[1,2,3,5,6,11]
5			[1,2,4,5,6,7,9,10,6,7,8,10,6,11]
6			[1,2,4,5,6,7,8,10,6,7,9,10,6,11]
7			[1,2,4,5,6,7,9,10,6,7,9,10,6,11]
8			[1,2,4,5,6,7,8,10,6,7,8,10,6,11]

capabilities of constraint solvers. Constraint solvers either are unable to resolve complex constraints or resolve such constraints in a computationally expensive way. Loop-dependent or array-dependent variables, pointer references and calls to external libraries whose implementations are unknown also introduce issues for this approach.

Dynamic methods are another automatic approach which generate test data through executing the SUT and determining the visited program locations via some form of program instrumentation. Program instrumentation is done to trace run-time information such as branch distance (detailed in Sect. 2). To do this, some extra statements will be added inside the original program before every predicate. These statements should not alter the behavior of the original program.

Using meta-heuristic algorithms is a category of dynamic methods called Search Based Software Testing (SBST). To apply this approach, the input domain of the SUT forms the search space, and a fitness function is defined which evaluates and scores different inputs to the SUT according to the given test criteria and test requirements. All the information needed by a meta-heuristic algorithm (e.g., if the given test data lead to traversing a specific location of the program) can be extracted from the execution of the instrumented SUT, accordingly.

The fitness function plays an important role in successful and efficient searches in meta-heuristic algorithms. A well-defined fitness function improves the likelihood of finding a proper solution. It also can result in consuming fewer system resources [7]. The fitness functions that have already been proposed for search based test data generation methods are divided into two categories: Branch Predicate Distance Function (BPDF) and Approximation level, which are described in Sect. 2.

As shown in Fig. 1, in order to cover prime paths, the test data generation method should be capable to cover those test paths that pass through loops one or more times. Therefore, a search-based test data generation method which regards the prime path coverage criterion needs an appropriate fitness function. To the best of our knowledge, only two works [8, 21] exist proposing fitness functions that can support the prime path coverage criterion. We refer to these fitness functions as NEHD [8] and BP1 [21]. However, the mentioned works are based on GA, while swarm intelligence algorithms have shown considerable results in the optimization problems [19].

NEHD has been designed to measure the Hamming distance from the first order to the nth order between two paths to consider the notion of sequences of branches. It results in time intensive calculations for long paths because the fitness function must continuously search for the number of combinations of branches from 1 to n order at each stage. Therefore, according to [20] the method of [8] has a poor efficiency.

BP1 is the linear combination of two measures, BPDF and Approximation level. BDPF is normalized in the range [0,1] but the Approximation level is not normalized despite the importance of normalization [18]. In this situation, normalization is essential to consider equal weights for the two measures of the fitness function (BPDF and Approximation level) for guiding individuals in the search process (Sect. 4).

We propose a new search-based approach for test data generation which aims at covering prime paths more effectively and more efficiently through two contributions: (1) we apply Ant Colony Optimization (ACO) and Particle Swarm Optimization (PSO) as two prominent swarm intelligence algorithms for test data generation, and (2) we propose a new normalized fitness function. ACO is a powerful method for finding shortest paths in dynamic networks. But, it is not always straightforward to apply it to other problems such as function optimization or searching n-dimensional spaces [10]. Thus, we should adapt ACO for the test generation problem in this paper.

The results of our experiments show that the customized ACO and PSO have better average coverage and better average time in comparison to GA. Also, ACO leads to a better average coverage comparing with PSO while, it has a worse average time.

The rest of the paper is structured as follows. In the next section, we review the basic ACO, PSO, and the current fitness functions for test data generation. The third section provides a brief overview of some related works. In Sect. 4, the customized ACO algorithm and the new fitness function are addressed. Then, the experimental analysis and results are presented and discussed in Sect. 5, followed by the conclusion and outline of the future works in Sect. 6.

2 Background

2.1 Basic ACO

ACO is one of the swarm intelligence algorithms [19, 28] whose application in various problems is known. Like many other meta-heuristic algorithms, the main idea of ACO is inspired by observing the natural behavior of living organisms. In ACO, different behaviors of ants in their community have been the source of inspiration.

ACO algorithms were originally conceived to find the shortest route in traveling salesman problems. In ACO, several ants travel across the edges that connect the nodes of a graph while depositing virtual pheromones. Ants that travel the shortest path will be able to make more return trips and deposit more pheromones in a given amount of time. Consequently, that path will attract more ants in a positive feedback loop. However, in nature, if more ants choose a longer path during the initial search, that path will become reinforced even if it is not the shortest. To overcome this problem, ACO assumes that virtual pheromones evaporate, thus reducing the proba-bility that long paths are selected.

Several types of ACO algorithms have been developed with variations to address the specificities of the problems to be solved. Here, we briefly describe the basic ACO algorithm, known as the ant system [9]. Initially, ants are randomly distributed on the nodes of the graph. Each artificial ant chooses an edge from its location with a probabilistic rule that takes into account the length of the edge and the value of pheromones on that edge, as shown in Fig. 2 a virtual ant arriving from node A considers which edge to choose next on the basis of pheromone levels τ_{ij} and visibilities η_{ij} (inverse of distance). The edge to node A is not considered because that node has already been visited. Once all ants have completed a full tour of the graph, each of them retraces its own route while depositing on the traveled edges a value of pheromones inversely proportional to the length of the route. Before restarting the ants from random locations for another search, the pheromones on all edges evaporate by a small quantity. The pheromone evaporation, combined with the probable choice of the edge, ensures that ants eventually converge on one of the shortest paths, but some ants continue to travel also on slightly longer paths.

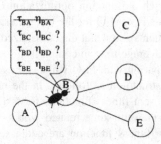

Fig. 2. Choosing an edge with a probabilistic rule

Because the basic ACO is suitable for search space with graph structure, a customization of the ACO is required to make this algorithm applicable for the test data generation problem with an n-dimensional search space.

2.2 PSO

In PSO [3], each particle keeps track of a position which is the best solution it has achieved so far as *pbx*; and the globally optimal solution is stored as *gbest*. The basic steps of PSO are as follow.

1. Initialize N particles with random positions px_i and velocities vi on the search space. Evaluate every particle's current fitness $f(px_i)$. Initialize $pbxi = px_i$ and $gbest = i$, $f(px_i) = min(f(pbx_0), f(pbx_2), \ldots, f(pbx_n))$;
2. Check whether the criterion (i.e. desired fitness function) is met. If the criterion is met, loop ends; else continue;
3. Change velocities according to formula (1):

$$v_i = v_i + c1(pbx_i - px_i) + c2(pbx_{gbest} - px_i) \tag{1}$$

where ω is an intra weight c_1, c_2 are learning factors.

4. Change positions according to formula (2):

$$px_i = px_i + vi \tag{2}$$

5. Evaluate every particle's fitness $f(px_i)$; if $f(px_i) < f(pbx_i)$ then $pbx_i = px_i$;
6. Update *gbest* and loop to step 2.

2.3   Fitness Functions for Test Data Generation

In this section, an overview of the two general categories of fitness functions [5], BPDF and Approximation level, is given. After that, BP1 and NEHD which support the coverage of prime paths are explained.

In a CFG, each decision node is associated with a branch predicate. The outgoing edges from decision nodes are labeled with true or false values of the corresponding predicate. To traverse a path during execution, it is necessary to find appropriate values for the input variables such that they satisfy all of the related branch predicates. One way to define a proper fitness function to guide such a search is using BPDF [5] that examines the branching node at which the actual path deviated from the intended path. Its objective is to measure how close this test data is to fulfill the branch predicate condition that would have sent it down the intended path. For instance, suppose that branch predicate C is $(a = b)$ and f is the BPDF-based fitness function. When $|a - b| = 0$, then f = 0; otherwise, f = $|a - b| + k$ where factor k is a positive constant which is always added if the predicate is not true. In this way, the fitness function returns a non-negative value if the predicate is false, and zero when it is true. A complete list of branch distance formulas for different relational predicate types is presented in [1].

The other way to define fitness functions is using Approximation level [5]. The Approximation level indicates how close the actual path taken was to reaching the partial aim (for example, the number of correct nodes the test data encountered or how often that path was generated). In the case of correct nodes, test data with higher Approximation levels are judged to be more fit than those with low values.

The Normalized Extended Hamming Distance (NEHD) is designed to measure the Hamming distance from the first order to the nth order between two paths. But, according to [20] the method proposed in [8] has a poor efficiency.

The fitness function BP1 is a linear combination of BDPF and Approximation level that has the form shown in formula 3.

$$BP1 = NC - \frac{EP}{MEP} \tag{3}$$

- NC is the value of the path similarity metric computed based on the number of coincident nodes between the executed path and the target one, starting from the entry node up to the node where the executed path is different from the target one. This value can vary from 1 to the number of nodes in the target path. In the case similarity = 1, only the entry node is common to both paths.

- EP is the absolute value of the BDPF associated with the branch which is deviated from the target path.
- MEP is the BDPF maximum value among the candidate solutions that executed the same nodes of the intended path.

$\frac{EP}{MEP}$ is a measure of the candidate solution error with respect to all the solutions that executed the right path up to the same deviation predicate. This value is used as a solution penalty. Thus, the search dynamics is characterized by the co-existence of two objectives: maximize the number of nodes correctly executed with respect to the intended path and minimize the predicate function of the reached predicates. It should be noted that the range of BP1 is between 0 and the length of the target path (because of NC) so when the target path is long, the significance of the BPDF parameter is deceased. The reason is that BPDF is in the range [0,1] and it is linearly combined with the Approximation level part.

Experimental results [5] show that BP1 has a better performance than NEHD [5, 20]. BP1 has two parts where the first part is normalized between [0,1] but the second part is not normalized. The importance of normalization is shown in [7, 18]. In this paper, we use a normalized fitness function based on BP1.

3 Related Work

In this section, we review the related work for test data generation based on various meta-heuristic algorithms. In the literature, there are many works addressing search based test data generation [1, 2]. In this section, we review the prominent methods that center around different meta-heuristic algorithms.

Jones [22] and Pargas [16] investigated the usage of GA for automated test data generation regarding branch coverage. Their experiments on several small programs showed that in general, GA significantly outperforms the random method. Harman and McMinn [24] performed an empirical study on GA-based test data generation for large-scale programs and validated its effectiveness over other search algorithms such as hill climbing. Fraser et al. [25] have implemented a tool named EvoSuite to generate a whole test suite for satisfying the given coverage goals. The default coverage criterion used by EvoSuite is branch coverage, but there is also rudimentary support for some coverage criteria in the context of mutation and data flow testing. In their tool, GA and Memetic are used to generate JUnit test suites for classes in Java.

Simulated Annealing (SA) is a well-known search algorithm which solves complex optimization problems using the idea of neighborhood search. Tracey et al. proposed a framework to generate test data based on SA [26] with the aim of overcoming some of the problems associated with the application of local search. In this method, test data can be generated for specific paths without loops, or for specific statements or branches. Also, Cohen et al. adopted SA to generate test data for combinatorial testing [27].

Windisch et al. applied PSO to generate test data [29]. They compared their method with a GA-based technique in terms of the convergence characteristic. Mao et al. have built a new method, called TDGen-PSO [17] which has exhibited better performance comparing with GA and SA.

ACO has shown a comparable effect on solving optimization problems in comparison to other meta-heuristic search algorithms like GA [32–34]. Applying ACO for solving the problems in software testing have been investigated in [35]. ACO was adopted in [36, 37] to produce test sequences (not test data) for state-based software testing.

Li et al. [31] used ACO to generate test data in accordance with the branch coverage criterion. Unlike our approach, this work transforms the search space (to a graph form) instead of adapting the ACO algorithm. In addition, [31] has not provided any implementation and evaluation for its idea. Mao et al. [30] used ACO to generate test data for the branch coverage criterion. They set the pheromone to each ant in the colony; thus, pheromone is not distributed in the search space. By defining pheromone in each ant, a memory is dedicated to each ant so ACO has in fact converted to a memory-based algorithm [10] like PSO. Their findings show that ACO is better than GA and SA in this regard. Ayari et al. proposed an ACO-based method for mutation testing [23]. Their measure for test data adequacy is the mutation score. Meanwhile, their experimental analysis is based on just two benchmark programs. Bauersfeld et al. used ACO to find input sequences for testing applications with Graphical User Interface (GUI) [19].

As two approaches capable of covering prime paths, Lin et al. [8] and Bueno et al. [21] introduced methods for test data generation based on the GA algorithm. They proposed NEHD and BP1 as their fitness function, respectively. These works are based on GA while scalability and performance of evolutionary algorithms are questionable [13, 14]. In addition, as reported in [19], swarm intelligence algorithms have shown considerable results in the optimization problems.

In this paper, we propose a new search based approach for test data generation which aims at covering prime paths more effectively and more efficiently through a new normalized fitness function and using ACO and PSO as two prominent swarm intelligence algorithms. A customization of the ACO is required to make this algorithm applicable for the test data generation problem.

4   Test Data Generation

The aim of this work is to produce a set of test data to satisfy the given test paths. There is no restriction on test paths and they can involve prime paths as well. For this purpose, our method considers every test path as a target, separately, and repeats the data generation process until the target path is covered or the maximum number of iterations is exceeded. For PSO, we use its basic algorithm, explained in Sect. 2, so in this section, we only explain our customization on ACO. A top-level view of the algorithm is shown in Fig. 3. For each test path of the program, ants are randomly scattered in the search space. The instrumented program is executed by a test data td which is determined by the location of a specific ant in the search space. According to the covered path, the fitness value is computed. Then, for each ant of the population, local search, global search, and pheromone updating are performed iteratively.

4.1   The Customized ACO

The basic ACO algorithm is mainly used in discrete optimization problems which are formulated on the graph structure. We customize the basic ACO to generate test data in an n-dimensional space. The test data generation can be formally described as follows: Given a program under test P, suppose it has d input variables represented by vector $X_k = (x_k, x_k, \ldots, x_k)$ can be treated as the position vector of an ant in ACO. For each input variable $x_i (1 \leq i \leq d)$, assume it takes its values from domain D_i. Thus, the corresponding input domain of the whole program is $D = D_1 \times D_2 \times \ldots \times D_d$.

```
Loop for every test path of the program as the target path
Initialize location of ants from the input domain of the program to be tested at random
Do
          Feed the program with the test data (which is the location of ant);
          If any of ants has reached to the target path
                    Output the successful message and the location of this ant as test data;
                    Exit;
          End if
          Do local and global search in n-dimensional space for each ant;
          Update pheromone
While (iteration limit exceeds)
End of loop
```

Fig. 3. Algorithm for test data generation

In the basic ACO, the search space has a graph structure. Thus, the neighbor area of an ant is the set of the adjacent nodes of its corresponding position in the graph. Since the structure of the test data generation problem does not form a graph, the basic ACO algorithm must be modified such that it can be applied on the non-graph structure of the problem. For the test data generation problem, each ant's position can be viewed as a test data and represented as a vector in input domain D. For any ant k $(1 \leq k \leq n)$, its position can be denoted as $X_k = (x_k, x_k, \ldots, x_k)$ is the number of input variables and therefore the number of dimensions).

A major challenge for applying ACO to test data generation is the form of pheromone because the search space is continuing and it does not have either node or edge for defining pheromone on it. To tackle this problem, we partition the search space by partitioning every domain of each input variable to b equivalent parts that can be any number dividable by the range of input domain. The best value for b is obtained from sensitivity analysis which is explained more in Sect. 5.

The number of partitions for each input variable is determined separately. To illustrate partitioning, consider a program with two inputs x and y. If we partition the input domain of x to b1 parts and the input domain of y to b2 parts, there are totally $\varphi = b1 \times b2$ partitions on the 2-dimensional space (Fig. 4). Each partition has a special pheromone value. Therefore, the number of pheromones in the search space is equal to the number of partitions in this space.

		The number of dimensions	The number of neighbors	
		1	3-1	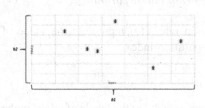
		2	3*3-1	
		3	3*3*3-1	
		d	3^d-1	

Fig. 4. A sample partitioned search space   **Fig. 5.** The number of neighbors in local search based on the number of domains

Local Search. During the local search, each ant looks for a better solution in its own neighborhood area. To compute the neighbors of ant k, we must consider it in the n-dimensional space D. The neighbors of ant with position vector $X_k = (x_{k1}, x_{k2}, \ldots, x_{kd})$ have the position vector $Xk' = (x'_{k1}, x'_{k2}, \ldots x'_{kd})$ where $x'_{ki} = x_{ki} + s$, $-1 \leq s \leq 1$ and $X'_k \neq X$. If an input has integer domain, s is 0 or 1 or -1. For a continues variable, three random numbers are selected for s. In a 2-dimensional search space, the location of an ant can be (1, 1). Thus, the positions of the neighbors are: (0, 1), (1, 0), (0, 0), (2, 1), (1, 2), (2, 2), (2, 0), (0, 2). The number of neighbors for an ant in a d-dimensional space is $3^d - 1$ as it is shown in Fig. 5.

The rule for local search or local transfer of ant's position can be represented as follows: ant k transfers from Xk to a new position Xk' if the fitness of Xk' is better than that of Xk (*i.e.*, *Fitness*(Xk') < *Fitness*(Xk)), and Xk' has the best fitness value among Xk' neighbors. Otherwise, the ant must stay at its current position (i.e., Xk). It should be mentioned that according to our implementation, the best fitness value is 0. Thus, a lower value is considered as a better fitness.

Global Search. The previous step is an activity of local optimization for each ant in the colony. But, this is not sufficient to find a high-quality solution because, at the local transfer stage, there might be an ant with no movement since it could not find a neighboring position with better fitness value. This situation is known as local optima trap [10] which could be resolved by an action called global transfer.

For any ant k in the colony ($1 \leq k \leq n$), if its fitness is lower than the average level, i.e., Fitness(X_k) > Fitness$_{avg}$, a random number q is selected. Fitness$_{avg}$ is the average fitness of whole ant colony and q is a random number from 0 to 1. When Fitness(X_k) > Fitness$_{avg}$ and $q < q0$, the position of ant k is randomly set in the whole search space ($q0$ is a preset parameter). When Fitness(X_k) > Fitness$_{avg}$ and $q \geq q0$, the position of ant k is randomly set to a position in a partition which has a maximum value of pheromone. With doing global search any ant that has in the local optima situation is transferred with probability $q0$ to a random position in the whole search space and with a probability $1 - q0$ to a position which has a maximum value of pheromone.

Update Pheromone. After doing global and local search for all ants in each run, the pheromone is updated (Fig. 3). To update pheromone value in every partition, the following rule is used:

$$\tau(j) \leftarrow (1 - \alpha) \times \tau(j) + \alpha \times number\ of\ ants\ in\ partition\ j. \qquad (4)$$

Where $\alpha \in (0, 1)$ is a pheromone evaporation rate, $\tau(j)$ represents the value of pheromone in the jth partition; j stands for the partition index.

4.2 Fitness Function

We represent a test path by sequences of characters which are the labels of edges in the CFG of the SUT. Therefore, for test data generation, the fitness function is calculated for the target path and the path traversed by any test data. To formulate the fitness function considering the order of the branches, both branch distance and Approximation level are used. The fitness function FT that is used to evaluate each candidate solution has the form shown in formula 5 and has two separately normalized parts. One part relates to the branch distance and the other relates to the Approximation level. Each part has the value between 0 and 1. Thus, FT is ranged from 0 to 2.

$$FT = \left(1 - \frac{NC}{TP}\right) + \frac{EP}{EP + \beta} \qquad (5)$$

- NC is the value of the path similarity metric. (described in Sect. 2.3)
- TP is the length of the target path, thus $(1 - NC/TP)$ has a normalized value between 0 and 1. The value zero is the optimal value for this part of FT.
- EP is the value of branch distance. (described in Subsect. 2.3)
- β is a parameter for the normalization proposed in [18]; based on the experiment done in [18], we set it to 1.

It should be mentioned that the normalization function that we used (i.e. $\frac{EP}{Ep + \beta}$) is the same as what proposed in [18]. By using this function instead of $\frac{EP}{MEP}$ (in BP1), there is no need to calculate MEP which leads to more efficiency.

In contrast to BP1, the values of fitness are normalized between 0 and 2, and fitness = 0 means the target path is fully met. Normalization is separately done for two parts of FT because the two parts of the fitness function would have the same share to conduct the individuals.

5   Experiments

In this section, we assess our proposed approach, which uses two prominent swarm intelligence algorithms PSO and ACO, against the GA-based method proposed in [21]. As mentioned before, it is shown by experiment in [20] that the method proposed in [8] has low efficiency. Thus, we do not compare our approach with [8]. To perform the experiment, all the three algorithms have been implemented with the same fitness function, proposed in Subsect. 4.2. We define the following two criteria as evaluation metrics:

- Average Coverage (AC), i.e., the average percentage of covered test paths in repeated runs.
- Average Time (AT), i.e., the average execution time (in milliseconds) of realizing test path coverage.

5.1 Experimental Setup

We selected a set of benchmark programs from the literature. Most of these programs, including "Triangle Type" (1), "Power x^y" (2), "Remainder" (3), "GCD" (4), "LCM" (5) and "ComputeTax" (6), are commonly used in software testing research. Table 2 shows the number of lines of code (LoC) and the number of prime paths (No. PP) of each program.

Table 2. Programs selected for the experiment

#P	Program name	LoC	No. PP	Description
1	Triangle Type	43	4	Find the type of triangle [17, 23]
2	Power x^y	27	3	Determine the value of x^y
3	Remainder	30	3	Determine remainder of x/y [17, 23]
4	GCD	24	2	Find greatest common divisor
5	LCM	38	7	Find least common multiplier
6	Compute Tax	164	24	Compute tax amount [17, 23]
7	Synthetic	45	8	Synthetic of while, for and if [15]

Table 3. Parameter setup

Algorithm	Parameter	Value
GA	Selection method	Roulette wheel
	Crossover method	Single point
	Crossover probability	80%
	Mutation probability	0.05%
	Chromosome-type	Binary string
PSO	ω	1
	c_1	2.05
	c_2	2.05
ACO	α	0.3
	q_0	0.5
	b	Varies based on program
All Algorithms	Population size	50
	No of iteration	100

We manually instrumented each original program without changing its semantics. Then, we constructed the corresponding CFG by using Control flow graph factory tool [12] and extracted a list of prime paths using the tool available in [11].

Before using GA, ACO, and PSO, their parameters must be initialized. The chosen values are shown in Table 3.

5.2   Experimental Results

The experimental results are presented in Table 4. The results show that our customized ACO is better than GA in terms of both criteria. Furthermore, our customized ACO has equal or better average coverage comparing with the PSO algorithm. However, PSO reaches the solution in less time in comparison to ACO because this algorithm is basically less complex.

Table 4. Comparison between the customized ACO, PSO, and GA

#P	Average coverage (%)			Average time (milliseconds)		
	GA	PSO	Customized ACO	GA	PSO	Customized ACO
1	74.5	96.5	100	103.7241	18.18289	31.2224
2	95.66667	100	100	223.9718	22.72688	138.9988
3	94.33332	100	100	209.9785	1.981523	27.81944
4	100	100	100	49.63726	1.92135	20.21426
5	51.4285	71.4285	71.4285	475.3366	32.66283	236.5719
6	98.29	100	100	440.2108	10.53734	286.0023
7	58	80.75	87.5	209.352	155.7802	182.85854

In the customized ACO, selecting the best value for parameter "b" (i.e. the number of parts) is important, therefore, the sensitivity analysis is done for this parameter. To do this, we calculate the values of the two evaluation criteria with different number of parts. As can be seen in Figs. 6 and 7, the average coverage and average time are increased with increasing the number of parts, but when we reach to the maximum coverage, we do not have any change in the average coverage with increasing the number of the parts. Also, the best value of parameter b for programs "Triangle Type" and "Synthetic" is 5000, for "compute tax" is 50000, for "Remainder" and "LCM" is 1000 and for "Pow x^y" and "GCD" is 500. In each program, when parameter b is set to this value, the least average time and the most average coverage are gained.

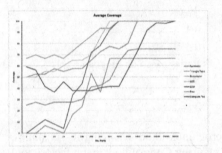

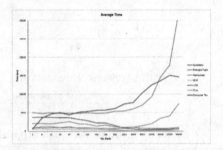

Fig. 6. Average coverage against the number of partitions

Fig. 7. Average time against the number of partitions

6 Conclusions and Future Works

In this paper, we have presented a search-based test data generation approach to cover prime paths of the program under test. The proposed approach uses ACO and PSO as two prominent swarm intelligence algorithms and a new normalized fitness function. We customized the ACO algorithm by combining it with the idea of input space partitioning. Also, the proposed fitness function is a normalization of the fitness function BP1 proposed in the [2]. We compared the customized ACO, PSO, and GA when all of these three algorithms are applied with the proposed fitness function. The results have shown that our method is stronger than GA in terms of both evaluation criteria. In addition, the results manifest that in comparing with PSO, the customized ACO results in a better coverage, but has worse efficiency. As future work, we will consider the following research areas:

- The main reason that causes the swarm intelligence algorithms do not widely apply in the test data generation problem is the search space of the string type. Most swarm intelligence based algorithms work on the structural search space, while the input domain of the string variables does not have a defined neighborhood concept.
- Using the static structure of the program in the partitioning of the search space (i.e. defining parameter "b" in the customized ACO).
- Multiple path test data generation (i.e. in each run, we consider multiple paths as target instead of one path) by swarm intelligence algorithms is another issue that could be considered in the future. There are approaches for multiple test path generation by evolutionary algorithms, but they cannot be applied directly using the swarm intelligence (i.e., population-based) algorithms.

References

1. McMinn, P.: Search-based software test data generation: a survey. Softw. Testing Verification Reliab. **14**(2), 105–156 (2004)
2. Ali, Sh, Briand, L.C., Hemmati, H., Panesar-Walawege, R.K.: A systematic review of the application and empirical investigation of search-based test case generation. IEEE Trans. Softw. Eng. **36**(6), 742–762 (2010)
3. Kennedy, J., Eberhart, R.: Particle swarm optimization. In: Proceeding of IEEE International Conference Neural Networks, vol. 4, pp. 1942–1948 (1995)
4. Ammann, P., Offutt, J.: Introduction to Software Testing. Cambridge University Press, New York (2008)
5. Watkins, A., Hufnagel, E.M.: Evolutionary test data generation: a comparison of fitness functions. Softw. Pract. Exp. **36**(1), 95–116 (2006)
6. King, J.C.: A new approach to program testing. ACM SIGPLAN Not. **10**(6), 228–233 (1975)
7. Baresel, A., Harmen, S., Michael, S.: Fitness function design to improve evolutionary structural testing. In: GECCO 2002, vol. 2, pp. 1329–1336 (2002)
8. Lin, J.C., Yeh, P.L.: Automatic test data generation for path testing using GAs. Inf. Sci. **131**(1), 47–64 (2001)

9. Dorigo, M., Maniezzo, V., Colorni, A.: Ant system: optimization by a colony of cooperating agents. IEEE Trans. Syst. Man Cybern. Part B (Cybern.) **26**(1), 29–41 (1996)
10. Floreano, D., Mattiussi, C.: Bio-Inspired Artificial Intelligence: Theories, Methods, and Technologies. MIT press, Cambridge (2008)
11. Graph Coverage Web Application. https://cs.gmu.edu:8443/offutt/coverage/GraphCoverage
12. Control Flow Graph Factory. http://www.drgarbage.com/control-flow-graph-factory
13. Thierens, D.: Scalability problems of simple genetic algorithms. Evol. Comput. **7**(4), 331–352 (1999)
14. Feldt, R., Poulding, S.: Broadening the search in search-based software testing: It need not be evolutionary. In: Proceedings of the Eighth International Workshop on Search-Based Software Testing, pp. 1–7. IEEE Press, May 2015
15. Ghiduk, A.S.: Automatic generation of basis test paths using variable length genetic algorithm. Inform. Process. Lett. **114**(6), 304–316 (2014)
16. Pargas, R.P., Harrold, M.J., Peck, R.R.: Test-data generation using genetic algorithms. Softw. Testing Verification Reliab. **9**(4), 263–282 (1999)
17. Mao, C.: Generating test data for software structural testing based on particle swarm optimization. Arab. J. Sci. Eng. **39**(6), 4593–4607 (2014)
18. Arcuri, A.: It really does matter how you normalize the branch distance in search-based software testing. Softw. Testing Verification Reliab. **23**(2), 119–147 (2013)
19. Blum, C., Li, X.: Swarm Intelligence in Optimization. In: Blum, C., Merkle, D. (eds.) Swarm Intelligence. Natural Computing Series, pp. 43–85. Springer, Heidelberg (2008)
20. Chen, Y., Zhong, Y., Shi, T., Liu, J.: Comparison of two fitness functions for GA-based path-oriented test data generation. In: 2009 Fifth International Conference on Natural Computation, pp. 177–181. IEEE (2009)
21. Bueno, P., Jino, M.: Automatic test data generation for program paths using genetic algorithms. Int. J. Softw. Eng. Knowl. Eng. **12**(6), 691–709 (2002)
22. Jones, B.F., Sthamer, H.H., Eyres, D.E.: Automatic structural testing using genetic algorithms. Softw. Eng. J. **11**(5), 299–306 (1996)
23. Ayari, K., Bouktif, S., Antoniol, G.: Automatic mutation test input data generation via ant colony. In: Proceedings of the 9th Annual Conference on Genetic and Evolutionary Computation, pp. 1074–1081. ACM (2007)
24. Harman, M., et al.: A theoretical and empirical study of search-based testing: Local, global, and hybrid search. IEEE Trans. Softw. Eng. **36**(2), 226–247 (2010)
25. Fraser, G., Arcuri, A.: Whole test suite generation. IEEE Trans. Softw. Eng. **39**(2), 276–291 (2013)
26. Tracey, N., Clark, J., Mander, K., McDermid, J.: An automated framework for structural test-data generation. In: 13th IEEE International Conference on Automated Software Engineering, Proceedings, pp. 285–288. IEEE (1998)
27. Cohen, M.B., Colbourn, C.J., Ling, A.C.: Augmenting simulated annealing to build interaction test suites. In: 14th International Symposium on Software Reliability Engineering, ISSRE 2003, 17 November 2003, pp. 394–405. IEEE (2003)
28. Kennedy, J.F., Eberhart, R.C., Shi, Y.: Swarm Intelligence. Morgan Kaufman, San Francisco (2001)
29. Windisch, A., Wappler, S., Wegener, J.: Applying particle swarm optimization to software testing. In: Proceedings of the 9th Annual Conference on Genetic and Evolutionary Computation, 7 July 2007, pp. 1121–1128. ACM (2007)
30. Mao, C., et al.: Adapting ant colony optimization to generate test data for software structural testing. Swarm Evol. Comput. **20**, 23–36 (2015)

31. Li, K., Zhang, Z., Liu, W.: Automatic test data generation based on ant colony optimization. In: Fifth International Conference on Natural Computation, 14 August 2009, pp. 216–220 (2009)
32. Elbeltagi, E., Hegazy, T., Grierson, D.: Comparison among five evolutionary-based optimization algorithms. Adv. Eng. Inform. **19**(1), 43–53 (2005)
33. Dorigo, M., Birattari, M., Stützle, T.: Ant colony optimization. IEEE Comput. Intell. Mag. **1**(4), 28–39 (2006)
34. Simons, C., Smith, J.: A comparison of evolutionary algorithms and ant colony optimization for interactive software design. In: Proceedings of the 4th Symposium on Search Based-Software Engineering 28 September 2012, p. 37 (2012)
35. Suri, B., Singhal, S.: Literature survey of ant colony optimization in software testing. In: CSI Sixth International Conference on (CONSEG), pp. 1–7. IEEE (2012)
36. Li, H., Lam, C.P.: An ant colony optimization approach to test sequence generation for state based software testing. In: Quality Software, (QSIC 2005), pp. 255–262. IEEE (2005)
37. Srivastava, P.R., Baby, K.: Automated software testing using metahurestic technique based on an ant colony optimization. In: Proceedings of 2010 (ISED 2010), pp. 235–240 (2010)

LittleDarwin: A Feature-Rich and Extensible Mutation Testing Framework for Large and Complex Java Systems

Ali Parsai$^{(\boxtimes)}$, Alessandro Murgia, and Serge Demeyer

Antwerp Systems and Software Modelling Lab, University of Antwerp,
Antwerpen, Belgium
{ali.parsai,alessandro.murgia,serge.demeyer}@uantwerpen.be

Abstract. Mutation testing is a well-studied method for increasing the quality of a test suite. We designed LittleDarwin as a mutation testing framework able to cope with large and complex Java software systems, while still being easily extensible with new experimental components. LittleDarwin addresses two existing problems in the domain of mutation testing: having a tool able to work within an industrial setting, and yet, be open to extension for cutting edge techniques provided by academia. LittleDarwin already offers higher-order mutation, null type mutants, mutant sampling, manual mutation, and mutant subsumption analysis. There is no tool today available with all these features that is able to work with typical industrial software systems.

Keywords: Software testing · Mutation testing · Mutation testing tool · Complex Java systems

1 Introduction

Along with the popularity of agile methods in recent times came an emphasis on test-driven development and continuous integration [5,10]. This implies that developers are interested in testing their software components early and often [28]. Therefore, the quality of the test suite is an important factor during the evolution of the software. One of the extensively studied methods to improve the quality of a test suite is mutation testing [8].

Mutation testing was first proposed by DeMillo, Lipton, and Sayward to measure the quality of a test suite by assessing its fault detection capabilities [8]. Mutation testing has been shown to simulate faults realistically [4,17]. This is because the faults introduced by each mutant are modeled after common mistakes developers make [16]. Mutation testing is demonstrated to be a more powerful coverage criteria in comparison with data-flow, statement, and branch coverage [11,43].

Recent trends in scientific literature indicate a surge in popularity of this technique, along with an increased usage of real projects as the subjects of scientific experiments [16]. In literature, topics such as creating more robust mutants

© IFIP International Federation for Information Processing 2017
Published by Springer International Publishing AG 2017. All Rights Reserved
M. Dastani and M. Sirjani (Eds.): FSEN 2017, LNCS 10522, pp. 148–163, 2017.
DOI: 10.1007/978-3-319-68972-2_10

using higher-order mutation [15,20,32,35], reducing redundancy among mutants using mutant subsumption [3,24,34], and reducing the number of mutants using mutant selection [12,13,44] are gaining popularity. Despite its benefits, the idea of mutation testing is not widely used in industry. Consequently, mutation testing research stays behind since it lacks fundamental experiments on industrial software systems. We believe that, beyond the computationally expensive nature of mutation testing [31], the reluctance of industry can stem from the shortage of mutation testing tools that can both (i) work on large and complex systems, and (ii) incorporate new and upcoming techniques as an experimental framework.

In this paper, we try to fill this gap by introducing LittleDarwin. LittleDarwin is designed as a mutation testing framework aiming to target large and complex systems. The design decisions are geared towards a simple architecture that allows the addition of new experimental components, and fast prototyping. In its current version, LittleDarwin facilitates experimentation on higher-order mutation, null type mutants, mutant sampling, manual mutation, and mutant subsumption analysis. LittleDarwin has been used for experimentation on several large and complex open source and industrial projects [36–38].

The rest of the paper is structured as follows. We provide background information about mutation testing in Sect. 2. We explain the design and the implementation of our tool in Sect. 3, and summarize the experiments that have been performed using our tool in Sect. 4. We conclude the paper in Sect. 5.

2 Mutation Testing

Mutation testing[1] is the process of injecting faults into a software system to verify whether the test suite detects the injected fault. Mutation testing starts with a *green* test suite — a test suite in which all the tests pass. First, a faulty version of the software is created by introducing faults into the system *(Mutation)*. This is done by applying a known transformation *(Mutation Operator)* on a certain part of the code. After generating the faulty version of the software *(Mutant)*, it is passed onto the test suite. If there is an error or failure during the execution of the test suite, the mutant is marked as killed *(Killed Mutant)*. If all tests pass, it means that the test suite could not catch the fault, and the mutant has survived *(Survived Mutant)* [16].

Mutation Operators. A mutation operator is a transformation which introduces a single syntactic change into its input. The first set of mutation operators were reported in King et al. [19]. These mutation operators work on essential syntactic entities of the programming language such as arithmetic, logical, and relational operators. They were introduced in the tool Mothra which was designed to mutate the programming language FORTRAN77. In 1996, Offutt et al. determined that a selection of few mutation operators is enough to produce similarly

---

[1] The idea of mutation testing was first mentioned by Lipton, and later developed by DeMillo, Lipton and Sayward [8]. The first implementation of a mutation testing tool was done by Timothy Budd in 1980 [6].

capable test suites with a four-fold reduction of the number of mutants [29]. This reduced-set of operators remained more or less intact in all subsequent research papers. With the advent of object-oriented programming languages, new mutation operators were proposed to cope with the specifics of this programming paradigm [18,25].

Equivalent Mutants. If the output of a mutant for all possible input values is the same as the original program, it is called an *equivalent mutant*. It is not possible to create a test case that passes for the original program and fails for an equivalent mutant, because the equivalent mutant is indistinguishable from the original program. This makes the creation of equivalent mutants undesirable, and leads to false positives during mutation testing. In general, detection of equivalent mutants is undecidable due to the halting problem [30]. Manual inspection of all mutants is the only way of filtering all equivalent mutants, which is impractical in real projects due to the amount of work it requires. Therefore, the common practice within today's state-of-the-art is to take precautions to generate as few equivalent mutants as possible, and accept equivalent mutants as a threat to validity (accepting a false positive is less costly than removing a true positive by mistake [9]).

Mutation Coverage. Mutation testing allows software engineers to monitor the fault detection capability of a test suite by means of mutation coverage (see Eq. 1) [16]. A test suite is said to achieve *full mutation test adequacy* whenever it can kill all the non-equivalent mutants, thus reaching a mutation coverage of 100%. Such test suite is called a *mutation-adequate test suite*.

$$Mutation\,Coverage = \frac{Number\,of\,killed\,mutants}{Number\,of\,all\,non\text{-}equivalent\,mutants} \quad (1)$$

Higher-Order Mutants. First-order mutants are the mutants generated by applying a mutation operator on the source code only once. By applying mutation operators more than once we obtain higher-order mutants. Higher-order mutants can also be described as a combination of several first-order mutants. Jia et al. introduced the concept of higher-order mutation testing and discussed the relation between higher-order mutants and first-order mutants [14].

Mutant Subsumption. Mutant subsumption is defined as the relationship between two mutants A and B in which A subsumes B if and only if the set of inputs that kill A is guaranteed to kill B [23]. The subsumption relationship for faults has been defined by Kuhn in 1999 [21], but its use for mutation testing has been popularized by Jia et al. for creating hard to kill higher-order mutants [14]. Later on, Ammann et al. tackled the theoretical side of mutant subsumption [3]. In their paper, Ammann et al. define *dynamic* mutant subsumption, which redefines the relationship using test cases. Mutant A dynamically subsumes Mutant B if and only if (i) A is killed, and (ii) every test that kills A also kills B. The main purpose behind the use of mutant subsumption is to reliably detect redundant mutants, which create multiple threats to the validity of mutation testing [34]. This is often done by determining the dynamic subsumption relationship among a set of mutants, and keeping only those that are not subsumed by any other mutant.

Mutant Sampling. To make mutation testing practical, it is important to reduce its execution time. One way to achieve this is to reduce the number of mutants. A simple approach to mutant reduction is to randomly select a set of mutants. This idea was first proposed by Acree [2] and Budd [6] in their PhD theses. To perform random mutant sampling, no extra information regarding the context of the mutants is needed. This makes the implementation of this technique in mutation testing tools easier. Because of this, and the simplicity of random mutant sampling, its performance overhead is negligible. Random mutant sampling can be performed uniformly, meaning that each mutant has the same chance of being selected. Otherwise, random mutant sampling can be enhanced by using heuristics based on the source code. The percentage of mutants that are selected determines the *sampling rate* for random mutant sampling.

3   Design and Implementation

In this section, we discuss the implementation details of LittleDarwin, and provide information on our design decisions.

3.1   Algorithm

LittleDarwin is designed with simplicity in mind, in order to increase the flexibility of the tool. To this effect, it mutates the Java source code rather than the byte code in order to defer the responsibility of compiling and executing the code to the build system. This allows LittleDarwin to remain as flexible as possible regarding the complexities stemming from the build and test structures of the target software. The procedure is divided into two phases: *Mutation Phase* (Algorithm 1), and *Test Execution Phase* (Algorithm 2).

Mutation Phase. In this phase, the tool creates the mutants for each source file. LittleDarwin first searches for all source files contained in the path given as input, and adds them to the processing queue. Then, it selects an unprocessed source file from the queue, parses it, applies all the mutation operators, and saves all the generated mutants.

Input : Java source files
Output: Mutated Java source files

queue ← all Java source files;
while queue ≠ ∅ **do**
　　srcFile ← queue.pop();
　　mutants[srcFile] ← mutate(srcFile);
end
return mutants ;

Algorithm 1. Mutation Phase

Test Execution Phase. In this phase, the tool executes the test suite for each mutant. First the build system is executed without any change to ensure that the test suite runs "green". Then, a source file along with its mutants are read from the database, and the output of the build system is recorded for each mutant. If the build system fails (exits with non-zero status) or times out, the mutant is categorized as killed. If the build system is successful (exits with zero status), the mutant is categorized as survived. Finally, a report is generated for each source file, and an overall report is generated for the project (see Fig. 3 for an example of this).

Input : Mutated Java source files
Output: Mutation Testing Report

if executeTestSuite() *is successful* then
    foreach srcFile do
        queue ← mutants[srcFile];
        backup(srcFile);
        while queue ≠ ∅ do
            mutantFile ← queue.pop();
            replace(srcFile,mutantFile);
            result[mutantFile] ← executeTestSuite();
        end
        restore(srcFile);
        Generate report for srcFile ;
    end
    Generate overall report;
end
return reports;

Algorithm 2. Test Execution Phase

3.2 Components

The data flow diagram of the main internal components of LittleDarwin is shown in Fig. 1. The following is an explanation of each main component:

JavaRead. This component provides methods to perform input/output operations on Java files. LittleDarwin uses this component to read the source files, and write the mutants back to disk.

JavaParse. This component parses Java files into an abstract syntax tree. This is necessary to produce valid and compilable mutants. To implement this functionality, an Antlr4[2] Java 8 grammar is used along with a customized version of Antlr4 runtime. Beside providing the parser, this component also provides the functionality to pretty print the modified tree back to a Java file.

---

[2] http://www.antlr.org/.

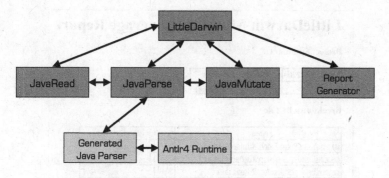

Fig. 1. Data flow diagram for LittleDarwin components

JavaMutate. This component manipulates the abstract syntax tree (AST) created by the parser. Subsection 3.3 explains the mutation operators of LittleDarwin in detail. The currently implemented mutation operators search the provided AST for mutable nodes matching the predefined patterns (for example, *AOR-B* looks for all binary arithmetic operator nodes that do not contain a string as an operand), and they perform the mutation on the tree itself. This gives the developer flexibility in creating new complicated mutation operators. Even if a mutation operator introduces a fault that needs to change several statements at once, and depends on the context of the statements, it can be implemented using a complicated search pattern on the AST. The mutation operators are designed to exclude mutations that would lead to compilation errors. However, not all of these cases can be detected using an AST (e.g. AOR-B on two variables that contain strings). Handling of such cases are therefore left for the post-processing unit that filters such mutants based on the output of the Java compiler. In order to preserve the maximum amount of information for post-processing purposes, for each mutant a commented header is created. This header contains the following information: (i) the mutation operator that created the mutant, (ii) the mutated statement before and after the mutation, (iii) the line number of the mutated statement in the original source file, and (iv) the id number of the mutated node(s). An example is shown in Fig. 2.

```
/* LittleDarwin generated mutant
 mutant type: relationalOperatorReplacement
 ----> before: daysRented    <= 0
 ----> after: daysRented    >0
 ----> line number in original file: 35
 ----> mutated nodes: 66
*/
```

Fig. 2. The header of a LittleDarwin mutant

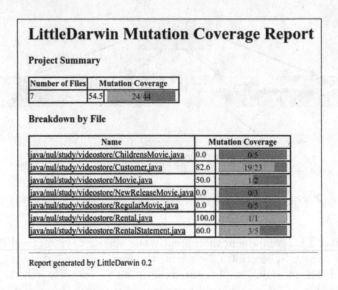

Fig. 3. LittleDarwin project report (Color figure online)

Report Generator. This component generates HTML reports for each file. These reports contain all the generated mutants and the output of the build system after the execution of each mutant. In the end, an overall report is generated for the whole project (Fig. 3).

3.3 Mutation Operators of LittleDarwin

There are 9 default mutation operators implemented in LittleDarwin listed in Table 1. These operators are based on the reduced-set of mutation operators that

Table 1. LittleDarwin mutation operators

Operator	Description	Example	
		Before	After
AOR-B	Replaces a binary arithmetic operator	$a + b$	$a - b$
AOR-S	Replaces a shortcut arithmetic operator	$++a$	$--a$
AOR-U	Replaces a unary arithmetic operator	$-a$	$+a$
LOR	Replaces a logical operator	$a \& b$	$a \mid b$
SOR	Replaces a shift operator	$a >> b$	$a << b$
ROR	Replaces a relational operator	$a >= b$	$a < b$
COR	Replaces a binary conditional operator	$a \&\& b$	$a \parallel b$
COD	Removes a unary conditional operator	$!a$	a
SAOR	Replaces a shortcut assignment operator	$a * = b$	$a / = b$

were demonstrated by Offutt et al. to be capable of creating similar-strength test suites as the full set of mutation operators [29]. Since the number of mutation operators of LittleDarwin is limited, it is possible that no mutants are generated for a class that lacks mutable statements. In practice, we observed that usually only very small compilation units (e.g. interfaces, and abstract classes) are subject to this condition.

In addition to these mutation operators, there are four experimental mutation operators in LittleDarwin that are designed to simulate null type faults. These mutation operators along with the faults they simulate are provided in Table 2. We included these mutation operators based on the conclusions offered by Osman et al. [33]. In their study, they discover that the null object is a major source of software faults. The null type mutation operators are able to simulate such faults, and consequently assess the quality of the test suite with respect to them. These mutation operators cover fault-prone aspects of a method: *NullifyInputVariable* mutates the method input, *NullifyReturnValue* mutates the method output, and *NullifyObjectInitialization* and *RemoveNullCheck* mutate the statements in method body.

Table 2. Null type faults and their corresponding mutation operators

Fault	Mutation operator	Description
Null is returned by a method	NullifyReturnValue	If a method returns an object, it is replaced by null
Null is provided as input to a method	NullifyInputVariable	If a method receives an object reference, it is replaced by null
Null is used to initialize a variable	NullifyObjectInitialization	Wherever there is a new statement, it is replaced with null
A null check is missing	RemoveNullCheck	Any binary relational statement containing null at one side is negated

3.4 Design Characteristics

To foster mutation testing in industrial setting it is important to have a tool able to work on large and complex systems. Moreover, to allow researchers to use real-life projects as the subjects of their studies, it is also important to provide a framework that is easy to extend. In this section, we show to what extent LittleDarwin, and its main alternatives, can satisfy these requirements. As alternatives, we use PITest [7], Javalanche [41], and MuJava [27], since they are popular tools used in literature. In Table 3, we summarize the design highlights.

Compatibility with Major Build Systems. To make the initial setup of a mutation testing tool easier, it needs to work with popular build systems for Java programs. LittleDarwin executes the build system rather than integrate into it, and therefore, can readily support various build systems. In fact, the only restrictions imposed by LittleDarwin are: (i) the build system must be able

Table 3. Comparison of features in mutation testing tools

Features		LittleDarwin	PITest [1]	Javalanche [41]	MuJava [26]
Compatibility with	Maven	✓	✓	×	×
	Ant	✓	✓	×	×
	Gradle	✓	✓	×	×
	Others	✓	×	×	×
Support for complex test structures		✓	×	×	×
Optimized for performance		×	✓	✓	✓
Optimized for experimentation		✓	×	×	×
Tested on large systems		✓	✓	✓	×
Ability to retain detailed results		✓	×	×	✓
Open source		✓	✓	✓	✓

to run the test suite, and (ii) the build system must return non-zero if any tests fail, and zero if it succeeds. PITest address the challenge via integration into the popular build systems by means of plugins. At the time of writing it supports Maven[3], Ant[4], and Gradle[5]. Javalanche and MuJava do not integrate in the build system.

Support for Complex Test Structures. One of the difficulties of performing mutation testing on complex Java systems is to find and execute the test suite correctly. The great variety of testing strategies and unit test designs generally causes problems in executing the test suite correctly. LittleDarwin overcomes this problem thanks to a loose coupling with the test infrastructure, instead relying on the build system to execute the test suite. Other mutation testing tools reported in Table 3 have problems in this regard.

Optimized for Performance. LittleDarwin mutates the source code and performs the execution of the test suite using the build system. This introduces a performance overhead for the analysis. For each mutant injected, LittleDarwin demands a rebuild and test cycle on the build system. The rest of the mutation tools use byte code mutation, which leads to better performance.

Optimized for Experimentation. LittleDarwin is written in Python to allow fast prototyping [40]. To parse the Java language, LittleDarwin uses an Antlr4 parser. This allows us to rapidly adapt to the syntactical changes in newer versions of Java (such as Java 8). This parser produces a complete abstract syntax tree that makes the implementation of experimental features easier. In addition, the modular and multi-phase design of the tool allows reuse of each module independently. Therefore, it becomes easier to customize the tool according to the requirements of a new experiment. The other mutation tools work on byte code, and therefore do not offer such facilities.

---

[3] https://maven.apache.org/.
[4] https://ant.apache.org/.
[5] https://gradle.org/.

Tested on Large Systems. LittleDarwin has been used in the past on software systems with more than 82 KLOC [37,38]. PITest and Javalanche have been used in experiments with softwares of comparable size [39,41]. We did not find evidence that MuJava has been tested on large systems.

Ability to Retain Detailed Results. PITest and Javalanche only output a report on the killed and survived mutants. However, in many cases this is not enough. For example, subsumption analysis requires the name of all the tests that kill a certain mutant. To address this problem, LittleDarwin retains all the output provided by the build system for each mutant, and allows for post-processing of the results. This also allows the researchers to manually verify the correctness of the results. MuJava provides an analysis framework as well, allowing for further experimentation [27].

Open Source. LittleDarwin is a free and open source software system. The code of LittleDarwin and its components are provided[6] for public use under the terms of GNU General Public License version 2. PITest and MuJava are released under Apache License version 2. Javalanche is released into public domain without an accompanying license.

3.5   Experimental Features

In order to facilitate the means for research in mutation testing, LittleDarwin supports several features up to date with the state of the art. A summary of these features and their availability in the alternative tools is provided in Table 4. An explanation of each feature follows.

Table 4. Comparison of experimental features in mutation testing tools

Experimental features	LittleDarwin	PITest	Javalanche	MuJava
Higher-order mutation	✓	×	×	×
Mutant sampling	✓	×	×	✓
Subsumption analysis	✓	×	×	×
Manual mutation	✓	×	×	×

Higher-Order Mutation. This feature is designed to combine two first-order mutants into a higher-order mutant. It is possible to link the higher-order mutants to their first-order counterparts after acquiring the results.

Mutant Sampling. This feature is designed to use the results for sampling experiments. LittleDarwin by default implements two sampling strategies: uniform, and weighted. The uniform approach selects the mutants randomly with the same chance of selection for all mutants. In the weighted approach, a weight is assigned to each mutant that is proportional to the size of the class containing the mutant. The given infrastructure also allows for the development of other techniques.

---

[6] https://github.com/aliparsai/LittleDarwin.

Subsumption Analysis. This feature is designed to determine the subsumption relationship between mutants. For each mutant, this feature can determine whether the mutant is subsuming or not, which tests kill the mutant, which mutants are subsuming the mutant, and which mutants are subsumed by the mutant. It is also capable of exporting the mutant subsumption graph proposed by Kurtz et al. for each project [22,23].

Manual Mutation. This feature allows the researcher to use their manually created mutants with LittleDarwin. LittleDarwin is capable of automatically matching the mutants with the corresponding source files, and creating the required structure to perform the analysis. For example, this is useful in case the mutants are created with a separate tool.

4   Experiments

In this section, we provide a brief summary of the experiments we already performed using the experimental features of LittleDarwin on large and complex systems.

Mutation Testing of a Large and Complex Software System. We used LittleDarwin to analyze a large and complex safety critical system for Agfa HealthCare. Our attempts to use other mutation testing tools failed due to the complex testing structure of the target system. Due to this complexity, these tools were not able to detect the test suite. This is because (i) the project used OSGI[7] headers to dynamically load modules, and (ii) the test suite was located in a different component, and required several frameworks to work. The loose coupling of LittleDarwin with the testing structure allowed us to use the build system to execute the test suite, and thus, successfully perform mutation testing on the project. For more details on this experiment, including the specification of the target system, and the run time of the experiment, please refer to Parsai's master's thesis [36].

Experimenting Up to Date Techniques on Real-Life Projects. LittleDarwin was used to perform three separate studies using the up to date techniques reported in Table 4. We were able to perform these studies on real-life projects.

In our study on random mutant sampling, we noticed that related literature have two shortcomings [37]. They focus their analysis at project level and they are mainly based on toy projects with adequate test suites. Therefore, we evaluated random mutant sampling at class level, and on real-life projects with non-adequate test suites. We used LittleDarwin to study two sampling strategies: uniform, and weighted. We highlighted that the weighted approach increases the chance of inclusion of mutants from classes with a small set of mutants in the sampled set, and reduces the viable sampling rate from 65% to 47% on average. This analysis was performed on 12 real-life open source projects.

---

[7] https://www.osgi.org/developer/specifications/.

In our study on higher-order mutation testing, we used LittleDarwin to perform our experiments [38]. We proposed a model to estimate the first-order mutation coverage from higher-order mutation coverage. Based on this, we proposed a way to halve the computational cost of acquiring mutation coverage. In doing so, we achieved a strong correlation between the estimated and actual values. Since LittleDarwin retains the information necessary for post-processing the results, we were able to analyze the relationship between each higher-order mutant and its corresponding first-order mutants.

We performed a study on simulating the null type faults which is currently under peer-review. In this study, we show that mutation testing tools are not adequate to strengthen the test suite against null type faults in practice. This is mainly because the traditional mutation operators of current mutation testing tools do not model null type faults. We implemented four new mutation operators in LittleDarwin to model null type faults explicitly, and we show how these mutation operators can be operatively used to extend the test suite in order to prevent null type faults. Using LittleDarwin, we were able to analyze the test suites of 15 real-life open source projects, and describe the trade offs related to the adoption of these operators to strengthen the test suite. We also used the mutant subsumption feature of LittleDarwin to perform redundancy analysis on all 15 projects.

Pilot Experiment. We performed a pilot experiment on a real life project in order to compare LittleDarwin with two of its alternatives: PITest and Javalanche. In this experiment, we used Jaxen[8] as the subject, since it has been used before to evaluate Javalanche by its authors [42]. Jaxen has 12,438 lines of production code, and 7,539 lines of test code. Table 5 shows the results of our pilot experiment. As we can see, even though LittleDarwin creates the least number of mutants, it is still slowest per-mutant. This is mainly because PITest and Javalanche both filter the mutants prior to analysis based on statement coverage. In addition, LittleDarwin relies on the build system to run the test suite, which introduces per-mutant overhead.

Table 5. Pilot experiment results

Tool	Generated mutants	Killed mutants	Mutation coverage	Analysis time	Per-mutant time
LittleDarwin	1,390	805	57.9%	2 h 23 min 45 s	6.21 s
PITest	4,315	2,145	49.8%	1 h 13 min 13 s	1.02 s
Javalanche	9,285	4,442	47.8%	1 h 35 min 23 s	0.62 s

5   Conclusion

We presented LittleDarwin, a mutation testing framework for Java. On the one hand, it can cope with large and complex software systems. This lets

---

[8] http://jaxen.org/.

LittleDarwin foster the adoption of mutation testing in industry. On the other hand, the tool is written in Python and released as an open source framework, namely it enables fast prototyping, and the addition of new experimental components. From this point of view, LittleDarwin shows its keen interest in representing an easy to extend framework for researchers on mutation testing. Combining these aspects allows researchers to use real-life projects as the subjects of their studies.

In the current version, LittleDarwin is compatible with major build systems, supports complex test structures, can work with large systems, and retains lots of useful information for further analysis of the results. Moreover, it already includes the following experimental features: higher-order mutation, mutant sampling, mutant subsumption analysis, and manual mutation. Using these features, we have already performed four studies on real-life projects that would otherwise not have been feasible.

Acknowledgments. This work is sponsored by the Institute for the Promotion of Innovation through Science and Technology in Flanders through a project entitled Change-centric Quality Assurance (CHAQ) with number 120028.

References

1. Pitest. http://pitest.org/
2. Acree Jr., A.T.: On mutation. Ph.D. thesis, Georgia Institute of Technology, Atlanta (1980)
3. Ammann, P., Delamaro, M.E., Offutt, J.: Establishing theoretical minimal sets of mutants. In: 2014 IEEE Seventh International Conference on Software Testing, Verification and Validation, pp. 21–30, March 2014
4. Andrews, J.H., Briand, L.C., Labiche, Y.: Is mutation an appropriate tool for testing experiments? In: Proceedings of the 27th International Conference on Software Engineering (ICSE 2005), pp. 402–411. ACM, New York (2005)
5. Beck, K.: Test-Driven Development: By Example. Addison-Wesley, Boston (2003). Kent Beck Signature Book
6. Budd, T.A.: Mutation analysis of program test data. Ph.D. thesis, Yale University, New Haven (1980). aAI8025191
7. Coles, H., Laurent, T., Henard, C., Papadakis, M., Ventresque, A.: Pit: a practical mutation testing tool for Java (demo). In: Proceedings of the 25th International Symposium on Software Testing and Analysis (ISSTA 2016), pp. 449–452. ACM, New York (2016)
8. DeMillo, R.A., Lipton, R.J., Sayward, F.G.: Hints on test data selection: help for the practicing programmer. Computer **11**(4), 34–41 (1978)
9. Fawcett, T.: An introduction to ROC analysis. Pattern Recognit. Lett. **27**(8), 861–874 (2006). rOC Analysis in Pattern Recognition
10. Fowler, M., Foemmel, M.: Continuous integration. Technical report, Thoughtworks (2006)
11. Frankl, P.G., Weiss, S.N., Hu, C.: All-uses vs mutation testing: an experimental comparison of effectiveness. J. Syst. Softw. **38**(3), 235–253 (1997)

12. Gligoric, M., Zhang, L., Pereira, C., Pokam, G.: Selective mutation testing for concurrent code. In: Proceedings of the 2013 International Symposium on Software Testing and Analysis (ISSTA 2013), pp. 224–234. ACM, New York (2013)

13. Gopinath, R., Alipour, A., Ahmed, I., Jensen, C., Groce, A., et al.: An empirical comparison of mutant selection approaches. Oregon State University, Technical report (2015)

14. Jia, Y., Harman, M.: Constructing subtle faults using higher order mutation testing. In: Proceedings of the Eighth IEEE International Working Conference on Source Code Analysis and Manipulation (SCAM 2008), pp. 249–258. Institute of Electrical & Electronics Engineers (IEEE), September 2008

15. Jia, Y., Harman, M.: Higher order mutation testing. Inf. Softw. Technol. **51**(10), 1379–1393 (2009). Source Code Analysis and Manipulation (SCAM 2008)

16. Jia, Y., Harman, M.: An analysis and survey of the development of mutation testing. IEEE Trans. Softw. Eng. **37**(5), 649–678 (2011)

17. Just, R., Jalali, D., Inozemtseva, L., Ernst, M.D., Holmes, R., Fraser, G.: Are mutants a valid substitute for real faults in software testing? In: Proceedings of the 22nd ACM SIGSOFT International Symposium on Foundations of Software Engineering (FSE 2014), pp. 654–665. ACM, New York (2014)

18. Kim, S., Clark, J.A., McDermid, J.A.: Class mutation: mutation testing for object-oriented programs. In: Proceedings of Net Object Days, pp. 9–12 (2000)

19. King, K.N., Offutt, A.J.: A Fortran language system for mutation-based software testing. Softw. Prac. Exp. **21**(7), 685–718 (1991)

20. Kintis, M., Papadakis, M., Malevris, N.: Isolating first order equivalent mutants via second order mutation. In: Proceedings of the 2012 IEEE Fifth International Conference on Software Testing, Verification and Validation (ICST 2012), pp. 701–710. Institute of Electrical & Electronics Engineers (IEEE), April 2012

21. Kuhn, D.R.: Fault classes and error detection capability of specification-based testing. ACM Trans. Softw. Eng. Methodol. **8**(4), 411–424 (1999)

22. Kurtz, B., Ammann, P., Delamaro, M.E., Offutt, J., Deng, L.: Mutant subsumption graphs. In: 2014 IEEE Seventh International Conference on Software Testing, Verification and Validation Workshops (ICSTW), pp. 176–185, March 2014

23. Kurtz, B., Ammann, P., Offutt, J.: Static analysis of mutant subsumption. In: 2015 IEEE Eighth International Conference on Software Testing, Verification and Validation Workshops (ICSTW), pp. 1–10, April 2015

24. Kurtz, B.: On the utility of dominator mutants for mutation testing. In: Proceedings of the 24th ACM SIGSOFT International Symposium on Foundations of Software Engineering (FSE 2016), pp. 1088–1090. Association for Computing Machinery (ACM), New York (2016)

25. Ma, Y.S., Kwon, Y.R., Offutt, J.: Inter-class mutation operators for java. In: Proceedings of the 13th International Symposium on Software Reliability Engineering (ISSRE 2002), pp. 352–363. Institute of Electrical & Electronics Engineers (IEEE) (2002)

26. Ma, Y.S., Offutt, J., Kwon, Y.R.: MuJava: an automated class mutation system. Softw. Test. Verif. Reliab. **15**(2), 97–133 (2005)

27. Ma, Y.S., Offutt, J., Kwon, Y.R.: MuJava: a mutation system for Java. In: Proceedings of the 28th International Conference on Software Engineering (ICSE 2006), pp. 827–830. ACM, New York (2006)

28. McGregor, J.D.: Test early, test often. J. Object Technol. **6**(4), 7–14 (2007). (column)

29. Offutt, A.J., Lee, A., Rothermel, G., Untch, R.H., Zapf, C.: An experimental determination of sufficient mutant operators. ACM Trans. Softw. Eng. Methodol. 5(2), 99–118 (1996)
30. Offutt, A.J., Pan, J.: Automatically detecting equivalent mutants and infeasible paths. Softw. Test. Verif. Reliab. 7(3), 165–192 (1997)
31. Offutt, A.J., Untch, R.H.: Mutation 2000: uniting the orthogonal. In: Wong, W. (ed.) Mutation Testing for the New Century, The Springer International Series on Advances in Database Systems, vol. 24, pp. 34–44. Springer, Boston (2001). doi:10.1007/978-1-4757-5939-6_7
32. Omar, E., Ghosh, S., Whitley, D.: HOMAJ: a tool for higher order mutation testing in AspectJ and Java. In: Proceedings of the IEEE Eighth International Conference on Software Testing, Verification and Validation Workshops (ICSTW 2014), pp. 165–170. IEEE Computer Society, Washington, DC (2014)
33. Osman, H., Lungu, M., Nierstrasz, O.: Mining frequent bug-fix code changes. In: Proceedings of the Software Evolution Week - IEEE Conference on Software Maintenance, Reengineering, and Reverse Engineering (CSMR-WCRE 2014), pp. 343–347. Institute of Electrical and Electronics Engineers (IEEE), February 2014
34. Papadakis, M., Henard, C., Harman, M., Jia, Y., Le Traon, Y.: Threats to the validity of mutation-based test assessment. In: Proceedings of the 25th International Symposium on Software Testing and Analysis (ISSTA 2016), pp. 354–365. ACM, New York (2016)
35. Papadakis, M., Malevris, N.: An empirical evaluation of the first and second order mutation testing strategies. In: Proceedings of the 2010 Third International Conference on Software Testing, Verification, and Validation Workshops (ICSTW 2010), pp. 90–99. IEEE Computer Society, Washington, DC, April 2010
36. Parsai, A.: Mutation analysis: an industrial experiment. Master's thesis, University of Antwerp (2015)
37. Parsai, A., Murgia, A., Demeyer, S.: Evaluating random mutant selection at class-level in projects with non-adequate test suites. In: Proceedings of the 20th International Conference on Evaluation and Assessment in Software Engineering (EASE 2016), pp. 11:1–11:10. ACM, New York (2016)
38. Parsai, A., Murgia, A., Demeyer, S.: A model to estimate first-order mutation coverage from higher-order mutation coverage. In: Proceedings of the IEEE International Conference on Software Quality, Reliability and Security (QRS 2016), pp. 365–373. Institute of Electrical and Electronics Engineers (IEEE), August 2016
39. Parsai, A., Soetens, Q.D., Murgia, A., Demeyer, S.: Considering polymorphism in change-based test suite reduction. In: Dingsøyr, T., Moe, N.B., Tonelli, R., Counsell, S., Gencel, C., Petersen, K. (eds.) XP 2014. LNBIP, vol. 199, pp. 166–181. Springer, Cham (2014). doi:10.1007/978-3-319-14358-3_14
40. Prechelt, L.: An empirical comparison of seven programming languages. Computer 33(10), 23–29 (2000)
41. Schuler, D., Zeller, A.: Javalanche: efficient mutation testing for Java. In: Proceedings of the 7th Joint Meeting of the European Software Engineering Conference and the ACM SIGSOFT Symposium on the Foundations of Software Engineering (ESEC/FSE 2009), pp. 297–298. ACM, New York (2009)
42. Schuler, D., Zeller, A.: (Un-)covering equivalent mutants. In: Proceedings of the Third International Conference on Software Testing, Verification and Validation (ICST 2010), pp. 45–54. Saarland University, Saarbrucken, IEEE Computer Society, Washington, DC (2010)
43. Walsh, P.J.: A measure of test case completeness. Ph.D. thesis, State University of New York at Binghamton, Binghamton (1985)

44. Zhang, L., Gligoric, M., Marinov, D., Khurshid, S.: Operator-based and random mutant selection: better together. In: Proceedings of the 28th IEEE/ACM International Conference on Automated Software Engineering (ASE 2013), pp. 92–102. Institute of Electrical & Electronics Engineers (IEEE), November 2013

TCE+: An Extension of the TCE Method for Detecting Equivalent Mutants in Java Programs

Mahdi Houshmand and Samad Paydar[(⊠)]

Dependable Distributed Embedded Systems (DDEmS) Laboratory, Computer
Engineering Department, Ferdowsi University of Mashhad, Mashhad, Iran
mahdi.houshmand@mail.um.ac.ir, s-paydar@um.ac.ir

Abstract. While mutation testing is considered to be an effective technique in
software testing, there are some impediments to its widespread use in industrial
projects. One of these challenges is the equivalent mutant problem, and a line of
research is dedicated to proposing new methods for addressing this problem.
Trivial Compiler Equivalence (TCE) method is recently introduced as a simple
technique that actually relies only on the optimizations made by the compiler. It
is shown by empirical studies that employing TCE with the *gcc* compiler results
in a fast and effective technique for detecting equivalent mutants in *C* programs.
However, considering the fact that the Java compilers generally do not perform
noticeable optimizations, the question is how effectively does TCE perform on
Java programs? In this paper, experimental evaluations are discussed which
demonstrate that using TCE technique with *javac* compiler results in very poor
performance. As a result, this paper proposes to use the Java obfuscators as the
complementary component, because of the optimizations they make. The
experimental evaluations confirm that using TCE with the *ProGuard* obfuscation tool provides an effective and efficient method for detecting equivalent
mutants in Java programs.

Keywords: Mutation testing · Equivalent mutant · Trivial compiler
equivalence · Java

1 Introduction

Mutation testing is considered to be an effective approach to evaluate and also to
improve an existing test set [1]. It works based on the notion of mutants, where each
mutant is created by making a simple modification on the program under test. The set
of possible modifications are defined by the mutation operators that are defined for the
programming language of the target program. If there is a test set that the program has
successfully executed on, then mutation testing can be applied to provide a measure of
the quality of that test set. This is performed by running each mutant M on the test
cases to investigate whether the test cases are powerful enough to detect the injected
fault, i.e. the mutation. If the result of running the mutant on a test cases is different
from the result of running the original program on that test case, then the test case has
been able to distinguish, or kill, that mutant. The greater ratio of the mutants of the

M. Dastani and M. Sirjani (Eds.): FSEN 2017, LNCS 10522, pp. 164–179, 2017.
DOI: 10.1007/978-3-319-68972-2_11

program are killed by the test set, the higher is the score of that test set. Finally, if there remains any live mutant, i.e. mutants that are not killed by any test case, then there are two possible cases for each live mutant: (1) whether this is a sign of the weakness of the test set, or (2) the mutant is an equivalent mutant, i.e. the corresponding mutation has made a syntax change without changing the semantic, and hence, the mutant cannot be killed by any test case.

When applying mutation testing, a method is necessary to distinguish which of the above cases holds for a live mutant. Without differentiating these two cases, it is possible that the test case designer wastes his time and effort in trying to find a test case for killing an equivalent mutant, which is actually not killable. Further, an equivalent mutant may cause the quality of the test set to be underestimated.

While mutation testing has been empirically proven to be able to simulate real-world programming errors [24], and hence to be an effective method for evaluating and improving test sets, there some non-negligible impediments towards its application in industrial software. The first problem is that mutation testing is a costly method, since the number of possible mutants, even for a relatively small program is usually high. Creating the mutants, compiling and executing them over the test cases and comparing the execution result usually requires noticeable time and computation resources.

Another problem is the equivalent mutants introduced before. Consequently, different approaches have been introduced during the last two decades for addressing this problem by employing different techniques like machine learning [14], logical constraint solving [15], data flow pattern analysis [8], gamification [17], program slicing [10] and code similarity measures [13]. One of the approaches introduced recently, is the Trivial Compiler Equivalence (TCE) approach [12] which is a simple, fast and effective technique for detecting equivalent mutants.

The TCE technique actually relies on the optimizations performed by the compiler, and it tries to determine equivalence of a mutant by comparing it with the original program, in their binary, i.e. compiled, format. TCE has been evaluated in [12] on C programs using the *gcc* compiler that is capable of performing different levels of optimizations when compiling the program. The evaluations have shown that TCE is an effective method for equivalent mutant detection in C programs. Considering Java programs, however, TCE is not expected to perform noticeably, since the Java compiler performs almost no specific optimization, and it leaves the optimizations to be performed by Java Virtual Machine at runtime (JVM) [26]. We believe there is room for evaluating the TCE technique on Java programs. Hence, in this paper, we experimentally evaluate performance of TCE on Java programs, and further, we introduce TCE+ as an extension of TCE which utilizes the ProGuard[1] Java obfuscator in addition to the compiler to address the lack of compiler optimizations.

The rest of the paper is organized as follows. Section 2 briefly reviews the related works. In Sect. 3, the experimental evaluation of the TCE and TCE+ techniques on Java programs is discussed. Finally, Sect. 4 concludes the paper.

---

[1] http://proguard.sourceforge.net/.

2 Related Work

In order to address the equivalent mutant problem in the mutation testing domain, different approaches have been proposed during the last two decades. This problem, in its general form is an undecidable problem [2, 3] and therefore it is not expected to be able to find an automated method that can solve every instance of this problem correctly and completely. As a result, some of the proposed approaches employ heuristics or limit the characteristics of the program under study, for instance restricting the number of iterations of the loops [25]. A literature review on the approaches for tackling with the equivalent mutant problem is provided in [4], where it is concluded that the equivalent mutant detection techniques are still *"far from perfect"*.

Some works attempt to deterministically determine whether a specific mutant is equivalent or not. For instance, in [8, 18] a set of 9 data flow patterns is introduced that result in equivalent mutants. In addition, a framework is proposed which uses static analysis of data flow to check each mutant of a program against these patterns. If a mutant follows one of the predefined patterns, then it is equivalent, otherwise it is considered to be non-equivalent. As another example, [15] introduces a technique that extracts a set of logical constraints from a mutant such that solving those constraints proves that the mutant is equivalent to the original program. Then, the constraints are given to a constraint solver tool for the purpose of detecting equivalent mutants. The method assumes certain characteristics on the mutants which limits applicability of the method (e.g. recursive functions are not supported). A similar approach based on constraint solving techniques is also introduced in [16].

Some works implicitly use the idea that for an undecidable problem, it is not possible to provide a complete automated solution and hence human intervention is unavoidable. Therefore, they try to help the human experts in analyzing the mutants and in making decision about their equivalence. This help can be provided in form of identifying the mutants that are more likely to be equivalent. Therefore, these methods follow a inexact approach and generate a recommended list of mutants, ordered by their equivalence probability, that need to be manually analyzed by the human expert to make the final decision. For instance, in [11], the idea is that the probability that a mutant is not equivalent is related to how its coverage on a specific test set differs from the coverage of the original program. In other words, the greater the coverage is affected, the lower is the probability of the mutant being equivalent. A similar approach for determining equivalent mutants based on the coverage impact is also proposed in [5, 6]. Machine learning techniques are also used in some works like [14] to provide a probabilistic approach to detection of equivalent mutants.

Another example of the works that count on human involvement for detection of equivalent mutants is [17] that uses gamification technique. It introduces a two-player game in which one player tries to create mutants that are hard to kill, and the other one tries to introduce test cases that kill the mutants. The game indirectly can contribute to detecting mutants that are more likely to be equivalent.

Another group of works try to avoid creation of equivalent mutants by more advanced mutation generation techniques. For instance, [19] proposes to consider the fact that different mutation operators perform differently from the point of view of the difficulty of killing their resulting mutants. This can be employed to selectively use mutation operators that less frequently create equivalent mutants. Another group of works have shown that using higher order mutants instead of first-order mutants can reduce the number of equivalent mutants generated for a program [9, 20–22].

Other techniques that have been used for exact equivalent mutant detection include code similarity measures and clone detection techniques [13], program slicing techniques [10], co-evolution algorithms [7].

An interesting approach that is recently proposed for detection of the equivalent mutants is the TCE approach [12], which uses a very simple and straightforward technique. TCE works based on the idea that the advanced optimizations performed by a compiler can remove some type of the mutations that have not affected the semantic of the program, and hence if the equivalent mutant is compiled, the result of compiling can be the same as the result of compiling the original program. It is demonstrated through experimental evaluations that the TCE technique is successful in effectively detecting equivalent mutants of a C program using the *gcc* compiler optimizations. However, since the Java compilers generally do not perform noticeable optimizations, the performance of TCE on Java programs needs to be investigated. As a result, current paper proposes TCE+ technique as an extension of TCE that utilizes ProGuard for the purpose of optimizing Java code. In addition to performing different optimizations, e.g. dead code removal, unused variable removal and peephole optimizations, ProGuard is also able to obfuscate, shrink and pre-verify Java byte codes. However, TCE+ uses ProGuard only for the purpose of optimizations and it does not use obfuscation or shrinking capabilities of ProGuard. It is beyond the scope of this paper to describe the optimization techniques employed by ProGuard or *gcc*, however, Table 1 briefly mentions some of the main optimizations performed by each of these tools.

In [12], TCE has been shown to be able to find, in addition to equivalent mutants, the duplicated mutants, i.e. mutants that are equivalent to each other, but not necessarily equivalent to the original program. Since there is no advantage in using two duplicated mutants, it is interesting to be able to detect duplicated mutants. In this paper, we evaluate the TCE and TCE+ methods for the purpose of detecting equivalent and duplicated mutants of Java programs.

Table 1. Some of the optmization techniques employed by the subject tools

Tool	Optimization techniques
gcc Compiler	Dead Code Elimination, Transforming Conditional Jumps, Constant Folding, De-Virtualization, Function Inlining, Predictive Commoning, Elimination of Useless Null Pointer Checks, Peephole Optimization, Global Common Subexpression Elimination
ProGuard	Dead Code Elimination, Peephole Optimization, Marking Classes as Final, Variable Allocation Optimization, Method Inlining, Return Value Propagation, Removing Write-only Fields

3 Experimental Study

In this section, the experimental evaluation of the TCE and TCE+ approaches over Java programs is discussed. First, the research questions are introduced and then, different elements of the experiments are described. Finally, the results of the experiments are discussed.

3.1 Research Questions

Since the TCE approach has been shown to be both effective and efficient in detecting equivalent and duplicated mutants in C programs, the main research question this paper seeks to answer is:

RQ.   How do the TCE and TCE+ approaches perform on Java programs?
            To answer this question, two more specific research questions are introduced.
RQ1.   How effective are the TCE and TCE+ approaches at detecting equivalent and duplicated mutants in Java programs?
            To answer this question, the number of equivalent and duplicated mutants detected by the TCE and TCE+ techniques, and also the ratio of the detected equivalent mutants to the existing equivalent mutants is reported.
RQ2.   How efficient is TCE+ for the purpose of equivalent mutant detection?
            This question is answered by computing the execution time of the TCE+ approach to see if it is efficient enough to be used in practice. While we have not evaluated TCE+ on large programs, we believe that the efficiency of the technique for the large programs can be estimated based on the results obtained for the small programs.

3.2 Dataset and Golden Standard

For the purpose of the experimental evaluations, first, a dataset is prepared including 5 java programs, and then, for each program, its mutants are created by the MuJava mutation testing tool [23]. Table 2 shows the name of each program, its size in terms of physical Source Line of Code (SLOC) and the number of its mutants. The mutation operators that MuJava has applied on the subject programs are mentioned in Table 3.

In addition, a golden standard is created by manually checking each mutant of the subject programs to determine whether it is equivalent to the original program. This manual analysis is performed separately by three experts who have had more than 10 years of experience in object oriented programming in Java. After each expert has

Table 2. Dataset used in the experiments

Program	Subject program	Physical SLOC	Number of mutants
P1	BubbleSort	15	111
P2	Bisect	25	189
P3	Triangle	46	456
P4	QuickSort	50	341
P5	java.util.StringTokenizer	174	772

Table 3. Mutation operators applied by MuJava on the subject programs

Operator	Operator definition
AODS: Short-cut Arithmetic Operator Deletion	$\{(x, \text{remove}(x)) \mid x \in \{++, --\}\}$
AODU: Unary Arithmetic Operator Deletion	$\{(-v, v)\}$
AOIS: Short-cut Arithmetic Operator Insertion	$\{(v, --v), (v, v-), (v, ++v), (v, v++)\}$
AOIU: Unary Arithmetic Operator Insertion	$\{(v, -v)\}$
AORB: Binary Arithmetic Operator Replacement	$\{(x,y) \mid x,y \in \{+, -, *, /, \%\} \wedge x \neq y\}$
AORS: Shortcut Arithmetic Operator Replacement	$\{(x,y) \mid x,y \in \{++, --\} \wedge x \neq y\}$
ASRS: Shortcut Assignment Operator Replacement	$\{(x,y) \mid x,y \in \{+=, -=, *=, /=, \%=\} \wedge x \neq y\}$
CDL: Constant DeLetion	$\{(\text{op } c, \text{remove}(\text{op } c)) \mid \text{op} \in \{+, -, *, /, \%, >, >=, <, <=\}\}$
COD: Conditional Operator Deletion	$\{(!(e), e) \mid e \in \{\text{if}(e), \text{while}(e), \text{for}(s; e; s)\}\}$
COI: Conditional Operator Insertion	$\{(e, !(e)) \mid e \in \{\text{if}(e), \text{while}(e), \text{for}(s; e; s)\}\}$
COR: Conditional Operator Replacement	$\{(x,y) \mid x,y \in \{\&\&, \|, \wedge\} \wedge x \neq y\}$
LOI: Logical Operator Insertion	$\{(v, \sim v)\}$
ODL: Operator DeLetion	$\{(v \text{ op}, \text{remove}(v \text{ op})), (\text{op } v, \text{remove}(\text{op } v)) \mid \text{op} \in \{+, -, *, /, \%, <, <=, >, >=\}\}, \{(v++, v), (v--, v), (--v, v), (++v, v) \mid \text{op} \in \{++, -\}\}$
ROR: Relational Operator Replacement	$\{(x,y) \mid x,y \in \{>, >=, <, <=, ==, !=\} \wedge x \neq y\}$
SDL: Statement DeLetion	$\{(s, \text{remove}(s))\}$
VDL: Variable DeLetion	$\{(v \text{ [op]}, \text{remove}(v \text{ [op]})) \mid \text{op} \in \{+, --, *, /, \%, ++, -, <, <=, >, >=\}\}$

finished his job, the results have been compared so that any possible conflict is resolved. Actually, there were 7 such cases that needed the experts to discuss with each other to agree on the result.

3.3 Experimental Environment

All the experiments are performed on a PC with Microsoft Windows 7 operating system, Intel Core i5-4400 processor and 8 GB RAM. Further, we have used the Oracle's Java compiler javac version 1.8.0_60 to compile the programs and the mutants, and also ProGuard 5.3 to optimize the compilation results. Finally, for the purpose of comparing the binary files, the Windows utility program FC is used with the parameters /B and /LB1.

3.4 Experiments

To answer the research questions, four experiments are designed. The first two experiments evaluate the TCE and TCE+ techniques for the purpose of equivalent mutant detection and the second two experiments evaluate them for detecting duplicated mutants. The processes used in these experiments are shown in Figs. 1, 2, 3 and 4.

```
Input: P (original program)
Output: EM (list of the equivalent mutants of P)

//compile step
compile P to P_class
for each mutant M of P
  compile M to M_class
//comparison step
for each mutant M of P
  result = compare M_class to P_class
  if (result == 'no difference')
    add M to EM
return EM
```

Fig. 1. Process of experiment 1: TCE for equivalent mutant detection

```
Input: P (original program)
Output: EM (list of the equivalent mutants of P)

//compile step
compile P to P_class
for each mutant M of P
  compile M to M_class
//optimization step
convert P_class to P_jar
optimize P_jar to P_jar,op
extract P_class,op from P_jar,op
P_class = P_class,op
for each mutant M of P
  convert M_class to M_jar
  optimize M_jar to M_jar,op
  extract M_class,op from M_jar,op
  M_class = M_class,op
//comparison step
for each mutant M of P
  result = compare M_class to P_class
  if (result == 'no difference')
    add M to EM
return EM
```

Fig. 2. Process of experiment 2: TCE+ for equivalent mutant detection

```
Input: P (original program)
Output: DM (list of the removable duplicated mutants of
P)

//compile step
for each mutant M of P
   compile M to M_class
//comparison step
Pairs: empty list
for each mutant M1 of P
   for each mutant M2 of P
      if (M1 != M2 and filesize(M1_class)==filesize(M2_class))
         result = compare M1_class to M2_class
         if (result == 'no difference')
            add pair(M1, M2) to Pairs
//removal step
sort Pairs based on the first element of the pairs
for each Pair in Pairs
    M1 = first element of Pair
   M2 = second element of Pair
   if not (DM contains M1)
      add M2 to DM
return DM
```

Fig. 3. Process of experiment 3: TCE for duplicated mutant detection

In the first experiment, for each subject program P, P is compiled to P_{class} and each mutant M of P is compiled to M_{class}. Then each compiled mutant M_{class} is compared to the P_{class}. If no difference is identified in this comparison, it is considered that TCE has determined the corresponding mutant as an equivalent mutant.

The second experiment evaluates the TCE+ approach by including an optimization phase before the comparison step. In order to perform the optimization, first a jar file is created from the compiled file, i.e. P_{class} or M_{class}. The jar file is then given to ProGuard to do the optimizations. The resulting jar file is then decompressed to extract the optimized compiled file which then goes through the binary comparison.

In the third experiment, each compiled mutant of the program is compared to all other compiled mutants of that program that have the same file size. If there is no difference between the corresponding binary files, those two mutants are added as a pair to the list of duplicated mutants. After processing all the mutants, a simple algorithm shown in Fig. 3 is used to determine the list of mutants that can be removed.

The fourth experiment is very similar to the third experiment and the only difference is that it compares the optimized version of the compiled mutants which are created by the process described for the second experiment.

```
Input: P (original program)
Output: DM (list of the removable duplicated mutants of
P)

//compile step
for each mutant M of P
  compile M to M_class
//optimization step
for each mutant M of P
  convert M_class to M_jar
  optimize M_jar to M_jar,op
  extract M_class,op from M_jar,op
  M_class = M_class,op
//comparison step
Sort mutations based on their file size
for each mutant M1 of P
  if (M1 in DM)
    continue;
  for each mutant M2 of P
    if (M2 in DM)
      continue;
    if (M1 != M2
      and filesize(M1_class) == filesize(M2_class))
      result = compare M1_class to M2_class
      if (result == 'no difference')
        add M2 to DM
    else
        break;
return DM
```

Fig. 4. Process of experiment 4: TCE+ for duplicated mutant detection

3.5 Result Analysis

The results of the first two experiments are shown in Table 4. As it is shown in this table, TCE approach has not detected any equivalent mutant in the subject programs. Therefore, it can be concluded that since the Java compiler does not perform noticeable optimizations [26], applying TCE on Java programs is not effective for detecting equivalent mutants. However, the TCE+ technique, which compensates the limitation of the Java compiler by utilizing ProGuard's optimizations, has identified some equivalent mutants for each of the subject programs. Therefore, TCE+ has been able to address the shortcomings of the TCE method. However, the number of detected equivalent mutants is small and at the best case, i.e. the Bisect program, it accounts for only 7% of all the mutants. The worst case is also the BubbleSort program that the detected equivalent mutants are only 2% of all the mutants.

In order to judge the effectiveness of the TCE+ approach, it is required to know the ratio of the detected equivalent mutants to all the existing equivalent mutants. Therefore, the results of the first two experiments have been compared with the golden standard. As shown in the last column of Table 4, TCE+ has been able to detect from 18% to 100% of all the existing equivalent mutants. It has missed 9, 2 and 7 equivalent mutants respectively for the BubbleSort, QuickSort and StringTokenizer programs. For the other two programs, i.e. Bisect and Triangle, all the existing equivalent mutants have been found by TCE+ .

Based on these results, we conclude that TCE+ is generally effective and it is successful in detecting a good ratio of the existing equivalent mutants. However, it is interesting to analyze the detected and undetected equivalent mutants based on their mutation operators.

The distribution of the mutation operators over all the generated mutants is shown in Table 5. The top-3 mutation operators that have created the greatest proportion of the mutants are AOIS, ROR and SDL, which have created respectively 33%, 20% and 10% of all the mutants. There are some operators like AOSE and AODU that have negligible contribution to the number of mutants created.

Table 4. Results of experiments 1 and 2: Detecting equivalent mutants

Program	Number of detected equivalent mutants		Percentage of detected equivalent mutants to all mutants		Percentage of detected equivalent mutants to all existing equivalent mutants	
	TCE	TCE+	TCE	TCE+	TCE	TCE+
P1	0	2	0	2	0	18
P2	0	14	0	7	0	100
P3	0	23	0	5	0	100
P4	0	10	0	3	0	83
P5	0	34	0	4	0	83

In Table 6, the distribution of the mutation operators over all the existing equivalent mutants is shown. An interesting point is that the AOIS operator which has created about 33% of all the mutants is also responsible for creating about 77% of all the equivalent mutants in the golden standard. Further, the ROR operator has created about 14% of all the equivalent mutants. From another point of view, about 13% of the mutants created by the AOIS operator have been equivalent. This value for the ROR operator has been about 4%. This means that the performance of the TCE+ technique over these two mutation operators is of greater importance, compared to other mutation operators.

Table 5. Distribution of the mutation operators over all the mutants

Program	Mutation operator															
	AODS	AODU	AOIS	AOIU	AORB	AORS	ASRS	CDL	COD	COI	COR	LOI	ODL	ROR	SDL	VDL
P1			30	3	16	2		4		3		11	8	19	10	5
P2			80	13	32			2		3			16	19	14	10
P3			128	11	36			3		24	14	43	32	119	31	15
P4	2		108	18	36	6		8		9		40	20	55	28	11
P5		2	262	33		7	20		6	39	20	80	33	163	100	7
Total	2	2	608	78	120	15	20	17	6	78	34	174	109	375	183	48
Ratio (%)[a]	<1	<1	33	4	6	1	1	1	<1	4	2	9	6	20	10	3

[a] Percentage to all the mutants

The distribution of the mutation operators over all the equivalent mutants that are found by TCE+ is shown in Table 7. Comparing this table with Table 6 shows that TCE+ has successfully detected all the equivalent mutants created by the AOIS operator, which account for about 77% of all the equivalent mutants. Hence, considering the ratio of AOIS-generated equivalent mutants, it can be concluded that the TCE + approach is an effective method for detection of equivalent mutants in Java programs. However, it is also important to note that TCE+ has not detected any of the 14 equivalent mutants created by the ROR operator (5 for BubbleSort, 2 for QuickSort and 7 for StringTokenizer). It also has missed 4 other equivalent mutants of BubbleSort, 2 created by the AORB operator, 1 by ODL and 1 by the CDL operator.

Regarding detection of the duplicated mutants, the results of the third and the fourth experiments are presented in Table 8. This table shows that TCE and TCE+ have identified respectively from 8% to 14% and from 13% to 23% of the mutants of the subject programs as being duplicated. Since the duplicated mutants do not contribute to the mutation testing results, they can be removed from the mutants. Considering all the five subject programs, TCE and TCE+ have identified respectively 9% and 16% of all the mutants as being duplicated. As a result, we conclude that while TCE+ noticeably outperforms TCE, both approaches are effective in detecting duplicated mutants.

An interesting point is that while TCE has not detected any equivalent mutant, but it has detected non-negligible number of duplicated mutants. Further analysis of the

Table 6. Distribution of the mutation operators over the existing equivalent mutants

Program	Mutation operator															
	AODS	AODU	AOIS	AOIU	AORB	AORS	ASRS	CDL	COD	COI	COR	LOI	ODL	ROR	SDL	VDL
P1			2		2			1					1	5		
P2			12	2												
P3			20	1									1			1
P4			10											2		
P5			34											7		
Total	0	0	78	3	2	0	0	1	0	0	0	0	2	14	0	1
Ratio (%)[a]	0	0	77	3	2	0	0	1	0	0	0	0	2	14	0	1

[a] Percentage to Existing Equivalent Mutants

Table 7. Distribution of the operators over the equivalent mutants detected by TCE+

Program	Mutation operator															
	AODS	AODU	AOIS	AOIU	AORB	AORS	ASRS	CDL	COD	COI	COR	LOI	ODL	ROR	SDL	VDL
P1			2													
P2			12	2												
P3			20	1									1			1
P4			10													
P5			34													
Total	0	0	78	3	0	0	0	0	0	0	0	0	1	0	0	1
Ratio (%)[a]	0	0	94	4	0	0	0	0	0	0	0	0	1	0	0	1

[a] Percentage to all equivalent mutants detected by TCE+

Table 8. Results of experiments 3 and 4: Detecting duplicated mutants

Program	Number of detected duplicated mutants		Percentage of detected duplicated mutants to all mutants	
	TCE	TCE+	TCE	TCE+
P1	15	25	14	23
P2	16	31	8	16
P3	52	89	11	20
P4	34	59	10	17
P5	60	99	8	13

results reveals that the detected duplicated mutants are not a result of the optimizations made by TCE, but they are resulted from the fact that applying some MuJava mutation operators on some program statements may create exactly the same syntactic changes. In other words, for each pair of duplicated mutants detected by TCE, both mutants are syntactically-equal. An example pair is shown in Table 9. While TCE+ has detected all the duplicated mutants found by TCE, it has also detected other results which are syntactically different but semantically duplicated. An example is shown in Table 10.

Another interesting point is that, as shown in Table 11, 44% of all the duplicated mutants detected by TCE are created by the ROR operator. The other 23% are associated with the VDL operator. Only about 1% of the detected duplicated mutants are results of the AOIS operator. The results for the TCE+ technique are also presented in Table 12. This table shows that, compared to TCE, the TCE+ technique is able to detect the duplicated mutants that are created by a wider set of mutation operators. Actually, TCE+ has detected duplicated mutants of type AOI, AORB, CDL and LOI operators, of which none is detected by the TCE method.

Finally, to answer RQ1, we conclude that TCE is not effective for detecting equivalent mutants of Java programs, but it can effectively detect the duplicated mutants. Further, TCE+ is effective for detecting both equivalent and duplicated mutants.

Table 9. An example duplicated mutant detected by TCE

Original statement	Mutant by ODL operator	Mutant by CDL operator
x = (M + x)/2;	x = M + x;	x = M + x;

Table 10. An example duplicated mutant detected by TCE+ but missed by TCE

Original Statement	Mutant by AOIS Operator	Mutant by AOIS Operator
public void setEpsilon (double epsilon) {this. mEpsilon = epsilon;}	public void setEpsilon (double epsilon) {this. mEpsilon = epsilon−−;}	public void setEpsilon (double epsilon) {this. mEpsilon = epsilon++;}

Table 11. Distribution of the operators over the duplicated mutants detected by TCE

Program	Mutation Operator															
	AODS	AODU	AOIS	AOIU	AORB	AORS	ASRS	CDL	COD	COI	COR	LOI	ODL	ROR	SDL	VDL
P1													4	3	3	5
P2													4		2	10
P3													3	27	7	15
P4			2										10	9	5	8
P5													8	39	11	2
Total	0	0	2	0	0	0	0	0	0	0	0	0	29	78	28	40
Ratio (%)[a]	0	0	1	0	0	0	0	0	0	0	0	0	16	44	16	23

[a] Percentage to all duplicated mutants detected by TCE

Table 12. Distribution of the operators over the duplicated mutants detected by TCE+

Program	Mutation Operator															
	AODS	AODU	AOIS	AOIU	AORB	AORS	ASRS	CDL	COD	COI	COR	LOI	ODL	ROR	SDL	VDL
P1			1		4			4					4	4	3	5
P2			13	2									4		2	10
P3			19	1	3			1				1	4	38	7	15
P4			14		6			6					10	10	5	8
P5			34										8	43	12	2
Total	0	0	81	3	13	0	0	11	0	0	0	1	30	95	29	40
Ratio (%)[a]	0	0	27	1	4	0	0	4	0	0	0	0	10	31	10	13

[a] Percentage to all duplicated mutants detected by TCE+

In order to evaluate efficiency of TCE+ for detecting equivalent mutants, its execution time for different steps, i.e. (1) compiling the mutants, (2) optimization of the compiled mutants, and (3) comparison of the optimization results, is separately measured for each subject program. The process of detecting duplicated mutants also includes the first two steps, but in the third step, it compares the optimization results differently. Therefore, the execution time of this step is also measured to evaluate efficiency of TCE+ for detecting duplicated mutants. The results are presented in Table 13.

Table 13. Execution time of TCE+ for detecting equivalent and duplicated mutants

Program	Execution time (s)					
	Compile	Optimization	Comparison for detecting equivalent mutants	Comparison for detecting duplicated mutants	Total for detecting equivalent mutants	Total for detecting duplicated mutants
P1	36	68	1	1	105	105
P2	57	124	3	1	184	182
P3	137	289	6	3	432	429
P4	101	188	5	2	294	291
P5	235	617	12	5	864	857

As shown in Table 13, the execution times of detecting equivalent mutants and duplicated mutants do not differ noticeably, and they are about 1s per mutant. Therefore, to answer RQ2, we conclude that TCE+ can be considered as an efficient method. Further, the comparison times, both for equivalent and duplicated mutants, are negligible. However, the optimization time is about 2–3 times the compile time. It is worth noting that the compile time is an inherent overhead of mutation testing, since in mutation testing, each mutant should be compiled and executed against the test cases. Therefore, the overhead imposed by TCE+ is the optimization time. Considering the fact that TCE+ can effectively detect equivalent and duplicate mutants, and these mutants do not need to be executed over the test cases, it means that TCE+ reduces the cost of mutation testing by reducing the number of mutants that need to be run and specially by removing the mutants that due to their equivalence, can waste the time of the test case designers. Hence, we believe the overhead of optimization time which involves CPU cycles can be considered as acceptable by the reduction it provides in required human effort. Consequently, we conclude that TCE+ is cost effective.

4 Conclusion

In this paper, the performance of TCE technique for detecting equivalent mutants in Java programs is evaluated. As the experimental evaluations have demonstrated, TCE has not detected any equivalent mutant in the subject programs and hence it cannot be considered to effective. To address this problem, current paper has proposed the TCE+ technique which extends TCE by utilizing an obfuscator like ProGuard, capable of performing some optimizations on Java programs.

The experimental evaluations show that while there are mutation operators like ROR for which TCE+ performance is weak, there are also operators like AOIS that TCE+ is able to find all of its equivalent mutants. Considering the contribution of each operator to the number of equivalent mutants of a typical program, TCE+ can be considered to be an effective and efficient method for detecting both equivalent and duplicated mutants for Java programs.

Current paper has investigated performance of TCE+ on small programs. Hence, it is required to perform similar experiments on larger Java programs to see how the performance of TCE+ changes as the program size increases. A challenge in this regard is preparation of the golden standard, since for large programs, the number of mutants is noticeable and it needs considerable effort to build a reliable golden standard. This is a main direction of our future work. Further, more precise analysis of the behavior of TCE+ on different mutation operators is an important job that we have scheduled for our future works. The results of such analysis will provide insights on possible improvements on ProGuard from the specific point of view of equivalent mutant detection.

References

1. Jia, Y., Harman, M.: An analysis and survey of the development of mutation testing. IEEE Trans. Softw. Eng. **37**(5), 649–678 (2011)
2. Budd, T.A., Angluin, D.: Two notions of correctness and their relation to testing. Acta Informatica **18**(1), 31–45 (1982)
3. Offutt, A.J., Pan, J.: Automatically detecting equivalent mutants and infeasible paths. Softw. Testing Verification Reliab. **7**(3), 165–192 (1997)
4. Madeyski, L., et al.: Overcoming the equivalent mutant problem: a systematic literature review and a comparative experiment of second order mutation. IEEE Trans. Softw. Eng. **40**(1), 23–42 (2014)
5. Schuler, D., Zeller, A.: Covering and uncovering equivalent mutants. Softw. Testing Verification Reliab. **23**(5), 353–374 (2013)
6. Papadakis, M., Le Traon, Y.: Mutation testing strategies using mutant classification. In: Proceedings of the 28th Annual ACM Symposium on Applied Computing. ACM (2013)
7. Adamopoulos, K., Harman, M., Hierons, R.M.: How to overcome the equivalent mutant problem and achieve tailored selective mutation using co-evolution. In: Deb, K. (ed.) GECCO 2004. LNCS, vol. 3103, pp. 1338–1349. Springer, Heidelberg (2004). doi:10.1007/978-3-540-24855-2_155
8. Kintis, M., Malevris, N.: Using data flow patterns for equivalent mutant detection. In: 2014 IEEE Seventh International Conference on Software Testing, Verification and Validation Workshops (ICSTW). IEEE (2014)
9. Jia, Y., Harman, M.: Higher order mutation testing. Inf. Softw. Technol. **51**(10), 1379–1393 (2009)
10. Hierons, R., Harman, M., Danicic, S.: Using program slicing to assist in the detection of equivalent mutants. Softw. Testing Verification Reliab. **9**(4), 233–262 (1999)
11. Schuler, D., Andreas Z.: (Un-) Covering equivalent mutants. In: 2010 Third International Conference on Software Testing, Verification and Validation. IEEE (2010)
12. Papadakis, M., et al.: Trivial compiler equivalence: a large scale empirical study of a simple, fast and effective equivalent mutant detection technique. In: 2015 IEEE/ACM 37th IEEE International Conference on Software Engineering, vol. 1. IEEE (2015)
13. Kintis, M., Malevris, N.: Identifying more equivalent mutants via code similarity. In: 2013 20th Asia-Pacific Software Engineering Conference, vol. 1. IEEE (2013)
14. Vincenzi, A.M.R., et al.: Bayesian-learning based guidelines to determine equivalent mutants. Int. J. Softw. Eng. Knowl. Eng. **12**(06), 675–689 (2002)
15. Nica, S., Wotawa, F.: Using constraints for equivalent mutant detection. arXiv preprint arXiv:1207.2234 (2012)
16. Just, R., Ernst, M.D., Fraser, G.: Using state infection conditions to detect equivalent mutants and speed up mutation analysis. arXiv preprint arXiv:1303.2784 (2013)

17. Rojas, J.M., Fraser, G.: Code defenders: a mutation testing game. In: The 11th International Workshop on Mutation Analysis. IEEE (2015)
18. Kintis, M., Malevris, N.: MEDIC: A static analysis framework for equivalent mutant identification. Inf. Softw. Technol. **68**, 1–17 (2015)
19. Yao, X., Harman, M., Jia, Y.: A study of equivalent and stubborn mutation operators using human analysis of equivalence. In: Proceedings of the 36th International Conference on Software Engineering. ACM (2014)
20. Harman, M., Jia, Y., Langdon, W.B.: A manifesto for higher order mutation testing. In: 2010 Third International Conference on Software Testing, Verification, and Validation Workshops (ICSTW). IEEE (2010)
21. Nguyen, Q.V., Madeyski, L.: Searching for strongly subsuming higher order mutants by applying multi-objective optimization algorithm. In: Le Thi, H.A., Nguyen, N.T., Do, T.V. (eds.) Advanced Computational Methods for Knowledge Engineering. AISC, vol. 358, pp. 391–402. Springer, Cham (2015). doi:10.1007/978-3-319-17996-4_35
22. Omar, E., Ghosh, S., Whitley, D.: Constructing subtle higher order mutants for Java and AspectJ programs. In: 2013 IEEE 24th International Symposium on Software Reliability Engineering (ISSRE). IEEE (2013)
23. Ma, Y.-S., Offutt, J., Kwon, Y.-R.: MuJava: a mutation system for Java. In: Proceedings of the 28th International Conference on Software Engineering. ACM (2006)
24. Just, R., et al.: Are mutants a valid substitute for real faults in software testing? In: Proceedings of the 22nd ACM SIGSOFT International Symposium on Foundations of Software Engineering. ACM (2014)
25. Weitao, W., Hirohide, H.: Improvement of equivalent mutant detection using loop count restriction. In: The International Conference on Software Engineering, Mobile Computing and Media Informatics (SEMCMI 2015) (2015)
26. Diehl, S.: A formal introduction to the compilation of Java. Softw.-Pract. Experience **28**(3), 297–327 (1998)

Quality-Aware Reactive Programming
for the Internet of Things

José Proença$^{(\boxtimes)}$ and Carlos Baquero

HASLab, INESC TEC and University of Minho, Braga, Portugal
{jose.proenca,cbm}@di.uminho.pt

Abstract. The reactive paradigm recently became very popular in user-interface development: updates — such as the ones from the mouse, keyboard, or from the network — can trigger a chain of computations organised in a dependency graph, letting the underlying engine control the scheduling of these computations. In the context of the Internet of Things (IoT), typical applications deploy components in distributed nodes and link their interfaces, employing a publish-subscribe architecture. The paradigm for *Distributed Reactive Programming* marries these two concepts, treating each distributed component as a reactive computation. However, existing approaches either require expensive synchronisation mechanisms or they do not support *pipelining*, i.e., allowing multiple "waves" of updates to be executed in parallel.

We propose *Quarp* (Quality-Aware Reactive Programming), a scalable and light-weight mechanism aimed at the IoT to orchestrate components triggered by updates of data-producing components or of aggregating components. This mechanism appends meta-information to messages between components capturing the context of the data, used to dynamically monitor and guarantee useful properties of the dynamic applications. These include the so-called glitch freedom, time synchronisation, and geographical proximity. We formalise Quarp using a simple operational semantics, provide concrete examples of useful instances of contexts, and situate our approach in the realm of distributed reactive programming.

Keywords: Reactive programming · Component-based systems · Pervasive systems · Distributed systems · Failure

1 Introduction

Reactive programming is a paradigm that uses functions defined over streams of data, rather than the more traditional functions over values. Data sources are

J. Proenca—FCT grant SFRH/BPD/91908/2012 and H2020 project 732505 LightKone (2017-19).

C. Baquero—Project "TEC4Growth - Pervasive Intelligence, Enhancers and Proofs of Concept with Industrial Impact/NORTE-01-0145-FEDER-000020" is financed by the NORTE 2020 and through the European Regional Development Fund (ERDF).

© IFIP International Federation for Information Processing 2017
Published by Springer International Publishing AG 2017. All Rights Reserved
M. Dastani and M. Sirjani (Eds.): FSEN 2017, LNCS 10522, pp. 180–195, 2017.
DOI: 10.1007/978-3-319-68972-2_12

producers of data streams, and functions produce new streams based on their input streams. Producing a new value triggers a wave of functions that process the new values. This paradigm became especially popular among developers of user-interfaces and reactive web pages [1–4], helping to manage the dependencies between updates (from the mouse, keyboard, network, etc.) and the display.

Recent attempts bring this paradigm to a distributed setting [5–7], carrying new challenges. Consider, for example, a twitter message (a *tweet*) being posted, consequently activating two independent services: one to make the tweet available, and one to notify all subscribers. Currently it is possible for a twitter client to be notified without the tweet being made available, leading to a *glitch* – a temporarily inconsistent state. In (non-distributed) reactive programming this is typically solved by scheduling the client execution after the executions of both the twitter data feeds and the notification engine. However, in a distributed setting some different, and leaner, coordination approach is required.

Distributed reactive programming [8] can attempt to fix this problem by adding extra constraints to ensure that all processing occurs on globally coordinated rounds. While this is simple and accurate, strong coordination does not scale well as more and more components need to agree on an order of execution, and faster components may have to wait for slower ones to catchup. Distributed systems are prone to regular failures on message transmission and transient partitions [9], calling for weaker coordination among components. In networks of low-resource devices such as the ones used by the LooCI middleware [10], common in the IoT, computation and communication is kept to a minimum to preserve energy, and it is often unrealistic to assume reliable communication.

This paper proposes Quarp — quality aware reactive programming — a more flexible approach to source coordination that rethinks on the amount of *out-of-synchrony* that qualifies as a genuine *glitch*, i.e. one that induces incorrect results. For instance, when combining slow varying data sources, such as environmental temperature, sensible outputs can still be derived when measurements are a few seconds apart. Reducing the synchronization requirements makes the overall system more resilient and fault tolerant. The key to this is to associate metadata to data emitted by a source, and to assume a realistic network infrastructure where messages are eventually delivered, but can transiently be lost or received out of order. A tradeoff is to allow data loss, and still be able to progress when data goes through with sufficient synchronization quality. The alternative, of trying to act on all data, can easily stall all activity in complex deployments.

The key contributions of this paper are the formalisation of a core reactive language tailored for the IoT, that: (1) measures the quality of incoming messages; (2) can guarantee properties such as glitch-freedom; (3) supports more relaxed notions such as *"data sources are located nearby"* and *"glitch-freedom with an error margin"*; and (4) can be used in lightweight nodes since it does not rely on heavy computations or complex coordination protocols.

Organisation of the paper. Section 2 introduces the key challenges addressed by Quarp via a motivating example. Section 3 formalises the semantics of a simple pseudo-language for reactive programs: first without quality awareness, and later extended with quality attributes. Section 4 illustrates the generality of Quarp by exploring different notions of quality useful in reactive programs. Section 5 discusses the key advantages and disadvantages of our approach with respect to existing approaches to distributed reactive programming. Finally, Sects. 6 and 7 present related work and main conclusions, respectively.

2   Motivation: Composition of Reactive IoT Components

We use as a running example a simple distributed reactive application in the context of the Internet of Things (IoT), where different sensors produce values that are aggregated and displayed by different services. This example motivates our approach and helps explaining the design choices that influenced our framework.

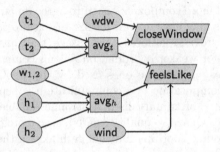

Fig. 1. Application that reacts to sensor values to either notify to close the window or to produce a feels-like value.

The reactive application in Fig. 1 is composed of: *data sources* (⬭), *observers* (▱), and mixed components (▢). The data sources t_1, t_2 represent temperature sensors, h_1, h_2 represent humidity sensors, wind represents a wind sensor, wdw the open/closed status of a window, and w $_{1,2}$ produces weights that capture the relevance of each sensor for averaging. The avg_t and avg_h services calculate the weighted averages of temperatures and humidity values, respectively. Finally, the observers closeWindow and feelsLike are capable of producing side effects, namely to send a warning to close a window and to display a *feels-like* temperature value, respectively.

This IoT example illustrates some possible challenges that can occur when managing dataflows triggered by new values being produced by data sources.

Glitches. A glitch can occur, for example, if $w_{1,2}$ produces a value, triggering avg_t and avg_h to recalculate the averages, and later feelsLike updates its value after receiving a new value from avg_t but *before* receiving from avg_h.

Timestamps. Alternatively, the `feelsLike` observer may chose to inspect the timestamps for when the original data sources produced the readings, and decide on whether these are within an acceptable time window.

Geo-location. The physical proximity of the sensors could also be considered when deciding on whether the input values of `feelsLike` should be taken together.

Context and Quality. The concept of *how good* are the input parameters of a given service call, with respect to the original source of the data, is captured in Quarp by what we call the *context* of a message, and the *quality* of a context. Furthermore, we do not fix upfront what a context and a quality measurement are. Instead, we specify simple properties of contexts and operations, and properties of operations that must be defined over contexts and qualities. We also provide concrete examples of contexts and qualities that we found useful for reactive programs.

As a running example we will focus on glitch-freedom. We will use a simple context that labels every message with pairs of values, each containing a globally unique ID of a data source and the value of a local grow-only counter of the same data source. Every data source component starts by labelling its published values with a pair with its ID and counter value; every service that aggregates data, such as avg_q, labels its published values with the joint labels of its input arguments. These labels are used to provide glitch-freedom guarantees, which is a typical concern in reactive programming. More complex labels, described later in this paper, can also include location information and wall-clock time sources.

More generally, contexts are expected to form a *commutative monoid*, i.e., to be able to be composed via an associative and commutative operator, and their associated qualities are expected to form a *bounded semi-lattice*, i.e., to have a partial order over possible qualities and to have a minimal quality.

Observe that, since every context is expected to have an associated quality, one could merge the concepts of context and quality, and require this merged qualified context to form both a commutative monoid and a bounded semi-lattice. We decided to keep this split for readability. Our notion of context and quality is inspired in constraint semirings [11], which possess two binary operators. One is similar to our composition of contexts, and the other is an idempotent operator that induces a partial order similar to our bounded semi-lattice.

3   Quarp: Quality-Aware Reactive Programming

We formalise the Quarp framework, generalising the notions of *context* and *quality*, and providing different examples of concrete instantiations for contexts and qualities. Components in a reactive system receive data by their *source ends* and publish data on their *sink ends*. A component is called a *data source* if it has no source ends, *observer* if it has no sink ends, and *mixed component* otherwise.

This section starts by formalising reactive programs, followed by an extension with quality-aware semantics and examples of useful quality metrics.

3.1 Basic Reactive Programs

A reactive program p is formally a set of component definitions, each written as $c \leftarrow func(\overline{arg})$, where $func$ is a function with a list of arguments arg, and each argument $a \in \overline{arg}$ can be either a constant or a component. Our example in Fig. 1 can be written as in Fig. 2, where the interpretation of the functions is expected to be defined elsewhere. In practice, this abstraction of a reactive program could be derived from the source code of the individual components.

```
t1 ← getTemp("North")
t2 ← getTemp("South")
w12← getWeights()
h1 ← getHum("North")
h2 ← getHum("South")
wdw← getWindowStatus()
```

```
wind ← getWind()
avgt ← calc-avg(t1, t2, w12)
avgh ← calc-avg(h1, h2, w12)
closeWindow ← notifyWindow(wdw, avgt)
feelsLike ← publishFL(avgt, avgh, wind)
```

Fig. 2. Encoding of the program in Fig. 1.

Given a program p we say c_2 *subscribes to* c_1, written $c_1 \prec_p c_2$, if p contains $c_2 \leftarrow func(...,c_1,...)$. We omit p in $\prec$ when clear from context. In our example program we say that the avgt component subscribes to the components t1, t2, and w12, written $t1 \prec avgt$, $t2 \prec avgt$, and $w12 \prec avgt$. Hence $\prec$ defines a *dependency graph* between components, starting from the source components.

Informal runtime semantics. Components communicate via a publish-subscribe mechanism, as in our IoT example. A program starts when a source component produces a value to be published. For example, when t1 decides to publish the value 17. It places the value in an *output buffer* linked to avgt, representing the (non order-preserving) network communication. In turn, components like avgt have *input buffers*, one for each input, storing their last received value.

The program proceeds when the network atomically transfers one of its values to an input buffer. In our example, the networks transfers the output value 17 to the input buffer of avgt. Previously stored data in this buffer is overwritten, even if it was not processed yet by avgt, simulating failure in the communication.

Once the avgt service receives a new value, it checks if all its input values are ready, i.e., if all their associated input buffers are non-empty. This will only be the case after both t1 and w12 publish values that arrive to avgt. Upon receiving an update for one of its buffers, avgt calculates an average value based on its three parameters and places the result in its output buffer, which buffers data going to two components: closeWindow and feelsLike.

Note that, even though mixed components and observers can only process parameters when these are updated, these components can decide to ignore incoming messages, even if all the buffers are non-empty. This effectively mimics data being lost, since newer messages override previously received ones.

Formal runtime semantics. Let $\mathcal{C}$ be the set of all components, $\mathcal{D}$ the domain of data produced by components, $\mathbb{P}\, X$ the set of all sets over X, and $\mathbb{M}\, X$ the set of all multisets over X. The runtime semantics of a reactive program is modelled by the evolution of so-called *input and output buffers*.

- Every source and mixed component $c \in \mathcal{C}$ has exactly one *output buffer*, written $\mathsf{out}_c : \mathcal{C} \to \mathbb{M}\mathcal{D}$, responsible for storing event data values published by c until they are consumed by its subscribers.
- Every observer and mixed component $c \in \mathcal{C}$ has exactly one *input buffer*, written $\mathsf{in}_c : \mathcal{C} \to (\mathcal{D} \cup \{-\})$, used to store the last value used by each input of c, whereas "$-$" represents the absence of a value used by a given input.

For example, $\mathsf{out}_{w12} = \{\mathsf{avgt} \mapsto \{17, 19\}, \mathsf{avgh} \mapsto \{19\}\}$ means that the component avgt has pending values 17 and 19 from w12, and avgh has only a pending value 19 from w12. Regarding input buffers, $\mathsf{in}_{\mathsf{closeWindow}} = \{\mathsf{avgt} \mapsto 18, \mathsf{wdw} \mapsto \mathsf{open}\}$ means that the component closeWindow has previously used the values 18 and open as input from avgt and wdw, respectively, and $\mathsf{in}_{\mathsf{closeWindow}} = \{\mathsf{avgt} \mapsto 18, \mathsf{wdw} \mapsto -\}$ means that closeWindow never received a value from wdw before.

The use of multisets in input buffers instead of sequences captures the lack of order guarantees in the sending of messages. The state of a reactive program p is therefore captured by the set of all input and output buffers I_p and O_p in p, written $\langle I_p, O_p \rangle$. We write $\mathcal{I}$ and $\mathcal{O}$ to represent the set of all possible input and output buffers, respectively, and drop the program p in subscript when clear.

Finally the semantics of a reactive program is given by the rules in Fig. 3, labelled by pairs $?c$ denoting that c is ready to be executed, and $!c, d$ denoting that c published the value d. The rule (src) represents a source component becoming ready to publish a value, the rule (rcv) represents a data value being delivered to a given component, and the rule (pub) represents a connector publishing a given data value. These rules use the auxiliary functions active_I, eval_I, $O + (c, d)$, $O - (c, d, c')$, and $I + (c, d, c')$, defined as follows.

$$\frac{\mathsf{in}_c = \emptyset}{\langle I, O \rangle \xrightarrow{?c} \langle I, O \rangle} \ (\mathrm{src}) \qquad \frac{\mathsf{out}_c \in O \quad d \in \mathsf{out}_c(c')}{\langle I, O \rangle \xrightarrow{?c'} \langle I + (c, d, c'), O - (c, d, c') \rangle} \ (\mathrm{rcv})$$

$$\frac{\langle I, O \rangle \xrightarrow{?c} \langle I', O' \rangle \quad \mathsf{active}_{I'}(c) \quad \mathsf{eval}_{I'}(c) = d}{\langle I, O \rangle \xrightarrow{!c, d} \langle I', O' + (c, d) \rangle} \ (\mathrm{pub})$$

Fig. 3. Operational semantics of basic reactive components.

- $\mathsf{active}_I : \mathbb{P}\mathcal{C}$. Predicate that says whether a given component c is *active* by checking if all its input buffers contain a value. Formally, $c \in \mathsf{active}_I$, also written as $\mathsf{active}_I(c)$, holds if for all $c' \prec c$, $\mathsf{in}_c(c') \neq -$, where $\mathsf{in}_c \in I$.
  Example: $\mathsf{active}_I(\mathsf{avgt})$ means that avgt is ready to be executed, i.e., $\mathsf{in}_{\mathsf{avgt}}(t1) \neq -$, $\mathsf{in}_{\mathsf{avgt}}(t2) \neq -$, and $\mathsf{in}_{\mathsf{avgt}}(w12) \neq -$, where $\mathsf{in}_{\mathsf{avgt}} \in I$.
- $\mathsf{eval}_I : \mathcal{C} \to \mathcal{D}$. Function that, given the current buffers I and a connector c where $c \leftarrow func(\overline{args})$, (1) calculates $\overline{args}'$ by replacing in $\overline{args}$ all occurrences of input components c' by their last received value $\mathsf{in}_c(c')$ (where $\mathsf{in}_c \in I$), and returns the result of evaluating $func(\overline{args}')$.

Example: $\text{eval}_I(\texttt{avgt})$ $=$ 17.6 *means that the result of evaluating* `calc-avg(t1,t2,w12)`, *after replacing* `t1`, `t2`, *and* `w12` *by the values in* I, *is 17.6.*

- $O + (c,d)$: $\mathcal{O}$ and $O - (c,d,c')$: $\mathcal{O}$. Functions that add and remove data to output buffers in O, respectively. Formally, when $\text{out}_c \in O$ then: (1) $O + (c,d) = \{\text{out}_c + d\} \cup (O \backslash \{\text{out}_c\})$, where $\text{out}_c + d = \{c_{out} \mapsto (M \cup d) \mid (c_{out} \mapsto M) \in \text{out}_c\}$; and (2) $O - (c,d,c') = \{\text{out}_c - (d,c')\} \cup (O \backslash \{\text{out}_c\})$, where $(\text{out}_c - (d,c'))(e) =$ if $(e = c')$ then $\text{out}_c(e) - \{d\}$ else $\text{out}_c(e)$.

- $I + (c,d,c')$: $\mathcal{I}$. Function that updates the buffers I by replacing the previous value of $\text{in}_{c'}(c)$ with d. Formally, when $\text{in}_{c'} \in I$ then $I + (c,d,c') = \{\text{in}_{c'} + (c,d)\} \cup (I \backslash \{\text{in}_{c'}\})$, where $(\text{in}_{c'} + (c,d))(e) =$ if $(e = c)$ then d else $\text{in}_{c'}(e)$.

Example. Consider our running example from Fig. 1. Initially the input and output buffers I and O are empty, defined as follows:

$$I = \{\text{in}_c \mid c \in \{\texttt{avgt}, \texttt{avgh}, \texttt{closeWindow}, \texttt{feelsLike}\}\}$$
$$\text{in}_c = \{c' \mapsto - \mid c' \prec c\}$$
$$O = \{\text{out}_c \mid c \in \{\texttt{t1}, \texttt{t2}, \texttt{w12}, \texttt{h1}, \texttt{h2}, \texttt{wdw}, \texttt{wind}, \texttt{avgt}, \texttt{avgh}\}\}$$
$$\text{out}_c = \{c' \mapsto \emptyset \mid c \prec c'\}$$

A possible trace that triggers the execution of `closeWindow` without data losses or re-orderings is, for some I^k and O^k with $k \in \{1, \ldots, 6\}$:

$$\langle I, O \rangle \xrightarrow{!\texttt{t1},17} \langle I^1, O^1 \rangle \xrightarrow{!\texttt{w12},\langle 0.6,0.4 \rangle} \langle I^2, O^2 \rangle \xrightarrow{!\texttt{wdw},\texttt{open}} \langle I^3, O^3 \rangle$$
$$\xrightarrow{!\texttt{t2},19} \langle I^4, O^4 \rangle \xrightarrow{!\texttt{avgt},17.8} \langle I^5, O^5 \rangle \xrightarrow{!\texttt{closeWindow},-} \langle I^6, O^6 \rangle$$

If a label starting with ? appears in a trace, it represents a trigger that was never used by a publish rule, i.e., data that was received but not used. After this trace, the input and output buffers in the state $\langle I^6, O^6 \rangle$ should have updated into the following ones:

$$\text{in}_{\texttt{avgt}} = \{\texttt{t1} \mapsto 17, \texttt{t2} \mapsto 19, \texttt{w12} \mapsto \langle 0.6, 0.4 \rangle\}$$
$$\text{in}_{\texttt{closeWindow}} = \{\texttt{wdw} \mapsto \texttt{open}, \texttt{avgt} \mapsto 17.8\}$$
$$\text{out}_{\texttt{w12}} = \{\texttt{avgt} \mapsto \emptyset, \texttt{avgh} \mapsto \langle 0.6, 0.4 \rangle\}$$
$$\text{out}_{\texttt{avgt}} = \{\texttt{closeWindow} \mapsto \emptyset, \texttt{feelsLike} \mapsto 17.8\}$$

In this final state `w12` and `avgt` published values that were not delivered yet, and `avgt` and `closeWindow` updated their input buffers with their last received values.

3.2 Adding Quality Awareness

We extend sources and mixed components to produce not only streams of data $d_1, \ldots, d_n$, but also to: (1) mark each produced data with a *context* Γ attribute, written $\Gamma \vdash d$, and (2) to compute a *quality* value $Q = (\![\Gamma]\!)$ of contexts used to filter low-quality messages.

Context. We write $\mathcal{G}$ to denote the set of all contexts, and $\mathcal{QD}$ to denote the set of data extended with a context. A data value $\Gamma \vdash d \in \mathcal{QD}$ represents a value $d \in \mathcal{D}$ that was calculated based on sources with context that were combined into $\Gamma \in \mathcal{G}$ via an associative and commutative operator $\otimes$. Hence, choosing a monoid $(\mathcal{G}, \otimes)$ defines what is a context and how are contexts composed.

Quality. We write $\mathcal{Q}$ to denote the set of all quality values, and the function $(\![\cdot]\!)$ assigns quality values to contexts. Quality values form a bounded join semi-lattice $(\mathcal{Q}, \oplus)$, where the partial order is defined in the usual way: $(Q_1 \leq Q_2) \Leftrightarrow (Q_1 \oplus Q_2 = Q_2)$. We write $Q \in \mathcal{Q}$ to range over quality values, and $\emptyset_{\mathcal{Q}}$ to denote the minimal quality. Hence, choosing the semi-lattice $(\mathcal{Q}, \oplus)$ defines what is a quality value and their order, and $(\![\cdot]\!)$ defines how to qualify contexts.

Summarising, different reactive behaviours can be attained by using different definitions of the context monoid $(\mathcal{G}, \otimes)$, the semi-lattice $(\mathcal{Q}, \oplus)$, and the qualification function $(\![\cdot]\!)$.

Example: Glitch-freedom. We instantiate the structures $\mathcal{G}$ and $\mathcal{Q}$, and the operator $(\![\cdot]\!)$ as follows.

- $\mathcal{G} = \mathbb{P}(\mathcal{C} \times K)$ are sets of pairs that associate the (globally unique) ID of source components to the value of a local grow-only counter. Contexts are combined via set union, i.e., $\otimes = \cup$ with identity $\emptyset$.
- $\mathcal{Q} = \{\bot, \top\}$ are booleans indicating whether data is has glitches ($\bot$) or not ($\top$), and $\oplus = \vee$ and $\emptyset_{\mathcal{Q}} = \bot$. Observe that $\oplus$ induces the order $\bot \leq \top$.
- $(\![\Gamma]\!) = \forall (s_1, k_1), (s_2, k_2) \in \Gamma \cdot s_1 = s_2 \Rightarrow k_1 = k_2$ returns true if the context is glitch-free, i.e., if the same source is always mapped to the same identifier.

The order of the quality lattice is used by the runtime semantics (below), by allowing only values with a certain minimal quality $Q^{\min}$ to be published, and discarding the data value otherwise. In this glitch-freedom example, a sensible $Q^{\min}$ would be $\top$, meaning that only glitch-free values can be published.

Using the IoT running example with this glitch-freedom context, assume this program starts by t1, t2, and w12 publishing the values 17, 19, and $\langle 0.6, 0.4 \rangle$, respectively. Using quality-awareness, each of these values are marked with a context value, e.g., $\{(\mathtt{t1}, 0)\} \vdash 17$, $\{(\mathtt{t2}, 0)\} \vdash 19$, and $\{(\mathtt{w12}, 0)\} \vdash \langle 0.6, 0.4 \rangle$. The service avgt, upon receiving these three values, combines their contexts calculating $\{(\mathtt{t1}, 0)\} \otimes \{(\mathtt{t2}, 0)\} \otimes \{(\mathtt{w12}, 0)\}$, obtaining $\Gamma = \{(\mathtt{t1}, 0), (\mathtt{t2}, 0), (\mathtt{w12}, 0)\}$. It then calculates the quality of this context $(\![\Gamma]\!) = \top$, indicating that the combined context is glitch-free ($Q^{\min} \leq (\![\Gamma]\!)$). This gives green light to proceed, i.e., avgt will calculate `calc-avg(17,19,(0.6,0.4))` $= 17.8$ and publish $\Gamma \vdash 17.8$ to its buffer linked to closeWindow and feelsLike.

If, at some point in the execution, feelsLike receives $\Gamma \vdash 17.8$ from avgt and some value $\Gamma' \vdash v$ from avgh, it will combine $\Gamma \otimes \Gamma'$ and calculate its quality. This quality will yield $\top$ if and only if $\Gamma'(\mathtt{w12}) = 0$, i.e., if the only shared data source of avgt and avgh (w12) has the same associated counter value (0). Otherwise $([\Gamma \otimes \Gamma']) = \bot$ and feelsLike does not publish a new value.

Formal runtime semantics. This subsection extends the previous runtime semantics from Sect. 3, extending the domain from $\mathcal{D}$ to $\mathcal{QD}$. The minimum quality for publishing a value is a globally defined constant $Q^{\min}$, such that $Q^{\min} \leq Q$ means that the quality Q is good enough for publishing.

In this extended semantics the output buffer of each component c is now over $\mathcal{QD}$, i.e., $c : \mathcal{C} \to \mathbb{P}\,\mathcal{QD}$. The functions active_I, eval_I, $O + x$, $O - x$, and $I + x$ are trivially adapted to data values in $\mathcal{QD}$ where necessary, and we replace the rule (pub) by two new rules that publish only when the minimal quality is met. For example, $d \in \mathrm{out}_c(c')$ is now written as $\Gamma \vdash d \in \mathrm{out}_c(c')$.

The new quality-aware semantics uses the same rules (src) and (rcv) as before (replacing d by $\Gamma \vdash d$), and the rule (pub) is replaced by the two new rules in Fig. 4, which describe how (and when) components publish data values with context information. As before, the auxiliary functions used by these rules cxt_B and $Q^{\min}$ are presented below.

$$\frac{\langle I, O \rangle \xrightarrow{?c} \langle I', O' \rangle \quad \mathrm{active}_{I'}(c) \quad \mathrm{eval}_{I'}(c) = d}{\langle I, O \rangle \xrightarrow{!c,(\Gamma \vdash d)} \langle I', O' + (c, (\Gamma \vdash d)) \rangle} \ \mathrm{cxt}_{I'}(c) = \Gamma \quad Q^{\min} \leq ([\Gamma]) \qquad (\text{pub}\,\checkmark)$$

$$\frac{\langle I, O \rangle \xrightarrow{?c} \langle I', O' \rangle \quad \mathrm{active}_{I'}(c)}{\langle I, O \rangle \xrightarrow{!c,-} \langle I', O' \rangle} \ \mathrm{cxt}_{I'}(c) = \Gamma \quad Q^{\min} \nleq ([\Gamma]) \qquad (\text{pub}\,\textbf{✗})$$

Fig. 4. Publishing rules for the quality-aware extension.

- $\mathrm{cxt}_I : \mathcal{C} \to \mathcal{G}$. Function that, given an active component c, collects all contexts from its inputs and returns their combination with $\otimes$. Formally, when $\mathrm{in}_c \in I$ then $\mathrm{cxt}_I(c) = \bigotimes_c \{\Gamma \mid c' \prec c, \exists d \in \mathcal{D} \cdot \mathrm{in}_c(c') = (\Gamma \vdash d)\}$, where $\bigotimes_c \emptyset = \Gamma_c$ (with Γ_c being the context of the source component c), and $\bigotimes_c \{\Gamma_1, \ldots, \Gamma_n\} = \Gamma_1 \otimes \ldots \otimes \Gamma_n$ (with $n > 0$).
  Example: $\mathrm{cxt}_I(t1) = \{(t1, 1)\}$ *means that the current context of* $t1$ *is* $\{(t1, 1)\}$, *and* $\mathrm{cxt}_I(avgt)$ *returns the combined context* $\Gamma_1 \otimes \Gamma_2 \otimes \Gamma_3$, *where* $\mathrm{in}_{avgt}(t1) = \Gamma_1 \vdash d_1$, $\mathrm{in}_{avgt}(t2) = \Gamma_2 \vdash d_2$, *and* $\mathrm{in}_{avgt}(w12) = \Gamma_3 \vdash d_3$, *for some* $d_1, d_2, d_3 \in \mathcal{D}$.
- $Q^{\min} : \mathcal{Q}$. Globally defined minimum quality required to publish a value.
  Example: Following our glitch-freedom example, let $Q \in \{\bot, \top\}$ *and* $\oplus = \vee$, *inducing* $\bot \leq \top$. *Hence,* $Q^{\min} = \top$ *means that, if* $Q^{\min} \leq x$, *then* x *must be* $\top$.

4   Beyond Glitch-Freedom: Modelling Different Contexts.

Glitch-freedom is one possible distributed property that can be guaranteed dynamically using contexts in reactive programs. This mechanism to discard messages that violate a minimal quality standard can be applied to a variety of quality notions. This section presents three of these.

Geographical location. The context of a value produced by a data source is now either (1) a pair of values with the geographical location where the data value was produced, or (2) the identity context if the notion of location does not apply. Combining contexts means collecting all possible locations, and they are ordered by size of the smallest bounding square, i.e., better quality means closer by locations. More precisely:

- $\mathcal{G} = \mathbb{P}(\mathcal{R} \times \mathcal{R})$ – a context is a set of coordinates that influenced the published value. Here $\otimes = \cup$ and $\emptyset$ is the identity.
- $\mathcal{Q} = \mathcal{R}_{\geq 0} \cup \{\infty\}$ – a quality value is a non-negative number measuring the size of the smallest bounding square that contains all coordinates, $\oplus = \min$, and $\emptyset_{\mathcal{Q}} = \infty$. Observe that smaller square means better quality, hence $\oplus$ induces a reversed order $\sqsubseteq$, i.e., $v_1 \sqsubseteq v_2$ iff $v_2 \leq v_1$.
- $([\Gamma]) = (\max(\pi_1(\Gamma)) - \min(\pi_1(\Gamma)))^2 + (\max(\pi_2(\Gamma)) - \min(\pi_2(\Gamma)))^2$, where π_1 and π_2 return the first and second values of the pairs in a given list, respectively, returns the (square of) the diagonal of the smallest square that can contain all coordinates.
- $([\emptyset]) = 0$, which captures the ideal quality.

Using these definitions of $\mathcal{G}$ and $\mathcal{Q}$ one needs only to specify a minimal quality $Q^{\min}$ defining the maximal accepted distance between input sources so a value can be published. Furthermore, data sources without an associated location (such as w12) can simply produce the empty context $\emptyset$.

In our example, assume we define $Q^{\min} = 10$ (for some distance unit) and t1, t2, w12, h1, h2 publish the values, respectively, $\{(2,3)\} \vdash 17$, $\{(4,2)\} \vdash 19$, $\emptyset \vdash \langle 0.6, 0.4 \rangle$, $\{(16,18)\} \vdash 56$, and $\{(18,20)\} \vdash 58$. In this case, both services avgt and avgh are able to publish a value with an acceptable quality. For example, avgt will publish a value with context $\Gamma = \{(2,3),(4,2)\}$, which has the associated quality $([\Gamma]) = 2^2 + 1^2 = 5$ (and $10 \sqsubseteq 5$, i.e., $5 \leq 10$). However, the service feelsLike is not able to publish a value with the data from these sensors: the combined context would be $\{(2,3),(4,2),(16,18),(18,20)\}$, which has a quality of $16^2 + 18^2 = 580$, wich is worse than the minimal quality 10.

Relaxed glitch-freedom. This example relaxes the notion of glitch freedom, by introducing tolerance with respect to the counters used for glitch freedom. I.e., *small* glitches are ignored and allowed, whereas a small glitch is found whenever counters from the same source data are close enough. $\mathcal{G}$ and $\mathcal{Q}$ are defined as before, and a fix tolerance value is used to assign a quality to contexts.

- $\mathcal{G} = \mathbb{P}(\mathcal{C} \times K)$ are the same as before: pairs that associate the globally unique ID of source components to the value of a local grow-only counter, and $\otimes = \cup$. Unlike with strict glitch-freedom, the values in K must have a total order and there must be a distance $\text{dist}(k_1, k_2)$ defined between counters.
- $\mathcal{Q} = \{\bot, \top\}$ are also the same: booleans indicating whether data is (relaxed) glitch-free ($\top$) or not ($\bot$).

- $([\varGamma]) = \forall(s_1, k_1), (s_2, k_2) \in \varGamma \cdot s_1 = s_2 \Rightarrow \mathsf{dist}(k_1, k_2) \leq \mathsf{tolerance}$ – returns true if the distance between counters from the same data source do not differ more than the pre-defined value tolerance.

In our example, start by defining K to be the natural numbers, $\mathsf{dist}(k_1, k_2) = \mathsf{abs}(k_1 - k_2)$, and $\mathsf{tolerance} = 1$. This choice means that counters for the same counter in different arguments can differ up to 1. For example, if feelsLike receives an argument from avgt whose context maps w12 to a counter value ahead by 1 from the counter of the previously received argument from avgh, the service will still react to this input.

Wall-clock difference. In some scenarios the hardware platform provides a highly accurate wall-clock among distributed data sources, guaranteeing that their internal clock is consistent up to a small error.[1] Here one may use a context with a pair of bounds with the smallest and the largest timestamps, and require their difference to be smaller than a fixed threshold. More precisely:

- $\mathcal{G} = \mathbb{P}\,TS$ sets of relevant timestamps. Unlike in the other cases, there is no reference to the associated data source. As before, $\otimes = \cup$.
- $\mathcal{Q} = \mathcal{R}_{\geq 0} \cup \{\infty\}$ is a positive number denoting the largest time difference between timestamps. Similarly to geo-location, smaller values represent higher qualities: $\oplus = \min$ and $\emptyset_{\mathcal{Q}} = \infty$.
- $([\varGamma]) = \max(\varGamma) - \min(\varGamma)$, where $\max(\emptyset) = \infty$ and $\min(\emptyset) = 0$, returns the largest difference between timestamps.

In our example, assume that our tolerance is $5\,\mathrm{s}$, i.e., $Q^{\min} = 5\,s$, and that t1, t2, w12, h1, h2 publish the values, respectively, $\{13{:}10{:}20\} \vdash 17$, $\{13{:}10{:}21\} \vdash 19$, $\emptyset \vdash \langle 0.6, 0.4\rangle$, $\{13{:}15{:}00\} \vdash 56$, and $\{13{:}15{:}03\} \vdash 58$. This means that temperatures and humidities are published around $5\,\mathrm{min}$ apart, the update time of the stamps is neglectable, and pairs of the same kind of sensors are less than $5\,\mathrm{s}$ apart. Hence, both services avgt and avgh are able to publish a value with an acceptable quality, but the service feelslike will fail to publish a value because the combine context will be $\{13{:}10{:}20, 13{:}10{:}21, 13{:}15{:}00, 13{:}15{:}03\}$, which has an associated quality of more than $5\,\mathrm{s}$.

Combining dimensions. Given any two different choices for context $\mathcal{G}_1$, $\mathcal{G}_2$ and for quality $\mathcal{Q}_1$, $\mathcal{Q}_2$, these can be merged into a new context monoid $\mathcal{G}_{12}$ and quality metric $\mathcal{Q}_{12}$ as follows.

- $\mathcal{G}_{12} = \mathcal{G}_1 \times \mathcal{G}_2$ are pairs with an element from the first context and an element from the second one.
- $\mathcal{Q}_{12} = \mathcal{Q}_1 \times \mathcal{Q}_2$ are again pairs from both qualities, where $(q_1, q_2) \oplus_{12} (q_1', q_2') = (q_1 \oplus_1 q_1', q_2 \oplus_2 q_2')$ and $\emptyset_{\mathcal{Q}} = (\emptyset_{\mathcal{Q}_1}, \emptyset_{\mathcal{Q}_2})$. Observe that $(q_1, q_2) \leq (q_1', q_2')$ when $q_1 \leq q_1'$ and $q_2 \leq q_2'$.
- $([(\varGamma_1, \varGamma_2)])_{12} = (([\varGamma_1])_1, ([\varGamma_2])_2)$ simply applies the encodings of each context.

---

[1] This is true, for example, for modules using SmartMesh IP™ (http://www.linear.com/products/smartmesh_ip).

One can easily prove that $\mathcal{G}_{12}$ is indeed a commutative monoid and that $\mathcal{Q}$ is a bounded semi-lattice. This allows the combination of any set of desired contexts; for example, one may want to have both glitch-freedom and geographical bounds.

5   Discussion

The Quarp approach for distributed reactive programming takes inspiration in algorithms for distributed systems that manage eventually consistent structures, such as CRDTs [12]. It does so by appending extra meta-information to messages that is used to help local nodes to react appropriately to inputs.

Unlike other approaches to distributed reactive programming (DRP) [5,6,13], we claim to be more *scalable*, more *dynamic*, and better suited for *non-reliable communication*. The cost for these desired properties is the possible loss of some values, as explained below. To support these claims we start by introducing some existing DRP approaches, and discuss each claim individually.

REScala. [5,13] Drechsler et al. present an algorithm to implement distributed glitch-freedom in reactive programs, called SID-UP, and include a careful comparison with other approaches with respect to: (1) the number of steps, each consisting of a round of messages from a set of components to another set of components, and (2) the number of messages sent. Their algorithm makes the strong assumption that rounds are synchronised, i.e., the algorithm does not support *pipelining*: a round starts when a set of data sources publish some value, and it ends when no more messages are pending – a new round can only start after the previous round finished. The comparison approaches are Scala.React [14], Scala.Rx,[2] and a variation of ELM [2] that supports dynamic updates of the topology of the reactive program (but does not support pipelining). Their approach and evaluation focuses exclusively on the performance of a single round, while Quarp focuses on the performance of multiple (concurrent) rounds, where pipelining is a must. Dynamic updates to the topology are not problematic in Quarp because of the lack of a clear notion of round, and because the eventual loss of messages during reconfiguration is already tolerated by Quarp, effectively allowing for more unrestricted forms of reconfiguration than SID-UP.

DREAM. [6] Is a Java distributed implementation with an acyclic overlay network of brokers that support publish-subscribe communication. The communication sub-system provides reliable message transmission by buffering and retransmission of messages, and in this case the sub-system uses point-to-point TCP connections to provide basic FIFO properties. Several consistency guaranties are provided, ranging from causal consistency to a globally unique order of delivery by way of a central coordinator. Comparatively to Quarp, the DREAM approach is more rigid when it comes to dynamic reconfiguration. Reliable message delivery can require considerable buffering in the communication subsystem and can stale system availability when the network is dropping messages. In contrast Quarp has much weaker requirements on the communication middleware.

---

[2] https://github.com/lihaoyi/scala.rx.

It allows message loss and re-ordering while still enabling the system to progress when messages get received and the required quality criteria is met.

Scalability in Quarp. Our proposed approach can scale up to a large number of components under the assumption that the size of the contexts does not grow too much. For example, our glitch-freedom implementation combines the local counters of all involved data sources, which behaves well with large chains of dependent components, but may require some attention when the number of dependent data sources is large. Observe that the generality of our approach allows customisation, e.g., defining the combination of contexts to create abstractions that hide information regarded as unnecessary. When compared with the above approaches, Quarp brings a large improvement with respect to the size of supported applications, since there is no need to either lock every round of data propagation (as in REScala), nor to require certain nodes to have full knowledge of the dependency graphs (as in DREAM). This advantage derives from the relaxation made that locally found inconsistencies (regarded as low quality inputs) do not need to be fully solved, but can simply be blocked and ignored. I.e., when an issue such as a glitch is found, the input is ignored without guarantees that future messages will solve this glitch.

Dynamicity in Quarp. Support for dynamic updates of the dependency among components was regarded as a key requirement from REScala. So much that the evaluation used a modified version of ELM's propagation algorithm that adds support for dynamic updates at the cost of losing support for pipelining, i.e., of allowing multiple rounds to be executing in parallel. In Quarp dynamic updates are trivially supported, again due to the fact that it accepts the possible loss of messages as part of the intended semantics.

Failure handling in Quarp. Unlike other approaches for distributed reactive programming, Quarp uses the basic assumption that messages can be lost (and re-ordered). Lost messages are not resent – instead Quarp assumes newer messages will be more relevant, and does not try to recover from failures. This approach targets systems such as the Internet of Things, where the cost of maintaining a reliable communication is often too high or infeasible (due to mobility). Furthermore, orthogonal approaches to support reliable communication, such as TCP/IP, can be safely used with Quarp.

6   Related Work

Reactive programming is a form of event-driven programming that deals with propagating change through a program by representing events as time-varying values. Its most popular versions are not concurrent, focusing on local reactive programming on a single network node and dealing with functional transformations of time-varying values [8]. Several approaches exist on top of object-oriented languages [15,16], functional languages [2,16], and in the context of web-based applications [1–3]. Most approaches enforce glitch freedom, ensuring that a node in a dependency graph is updated only after all its antecedents are.

Distributed Reactive Programming (DRP) deals with time-varying inputs, distributed over multiple network nodes, and with the management of dependencies between concurrent components. In a distributed setting, the problem of glitch freedom is of crucial importance, since inconsistencies may endure due to network partitioning. Carreton et al. [17] integrate DRP with the actor model, but do not support glitch freedom. Drechsler et al. [5] propose an efficient algorithm that enables glitch free DRP for distributed programs with strong network guarantees, but not considering highly dynamic networks, network failures and partitioning. Margara and Salvaneschi [6] propose a Java-based framework that offers multiple layers of consistency each having their impact on performance. It supports glitch-freedom, but under a significant performance penalty.

Another body of related work on DRP are reactive frameworks or languages for web programming, such as Meteor,[3] Play,[4] Flapjax [1], Elm [2], and React.JS [3]. These are usually two-tier, client-server applications where change either originates from user interaction with the DOM (e.g., clicking buttons) or by server acknowledgements. The server and DOM elements are considered the time-varying values. Even though events may originate on a remote node (the server), the reactive program actually resides on the client and the distribution of logic is therefore much simpler than in truly distributed reactive programs.

Quarp proposes a new approach to distributed reactive programming that allows individual nodes to locally identify glitches. Glitches are not only identified but also measured, based on meta-information aggregated to events. By selecting relevant properties over measurements and over such meta-information, tradeoffs can be made between performance and quality of the produced values. This approach suits well cyber-physical systems because it avoids global synchronisers or schedulers, and supports aspects such as dynamic reconfiguration.

Observe that, in the context of the IoT, other formalisations have been proposed, many as calculus of concurrent nodes [18,19]. These focus on how to accurately describe existing IoT systems and on how to reason about notions such as behaviour equivalences. Quarp does not explore properties of the presented formal semantics; instead it experiments with a new approach to think and design distributed applications for networks of resource-constrained devices: by separating the concerns of reactive components with dependencies on other components, from when to decide when data is good enough to be used.

7   Conclusion and Future Work

This paper proposes Quarp — a quality aware approach for distributed reactive programming. This approach investigates how reactive languages could be used to program distributed applications for the Internet of Things (IoT), taking into account the presence of resource-constrained devices, high mobility, and unreliable communication. Furthermore, data from sensors have often some redundancy (older values are less important than new ones), making current reactive

---

[3] www.meteor.com.

[4] www.playframework.com.

paradigm too synchronization heavy, possibly leading to never-ending waits for a message that has been lost. Our solution is to locally find unwanted inconsistencies, discarding data when they are found. Quarp is general enough to capture a range of possible inconsistencies, using attributes that must be "good enough" to be considered consistent. Hence Quarp, by not requiring messages to be always delivered, provides better performance (no need to agree with neighbours), scalability (large number of components can be executing in parallel), and availability (the system does not deadlock upon lost messages), while still guaranteeing that the messages are consistent, for some relaxed notion of consistency.

Our future work is two fold. On one hand we plan to apply Quarp to a concrete domain, exploring instances of quality attributes and performing a comprehensive evaluation. On the other hand we expect to use our formalisation to reason about reactive programs, e.g., defining notions of bisimulation to compare or minimize programs, to prove properties over reactive programs in Quarp.

References

1. Meyerovich, L.A., Guha, A., Baskin, J.P., Cooper, G.H., Greenberg, M., Bromfield, A., Krishnamurthi, S.: Flapjax: a programming language for Ajax applications. In: OOPSLA, , pp. 1–20. ACM (2009)
2. Czaplicki, E.: Elm: Concurrent FRP for functional GUIs, Master's thesis. Harvard (2012)
3. Gackenheimer, C.: What is react? Introduction to React, pp. 1–20. Apress, Berkeley (2015). doi:10.1007/978-1-4842-1245-5_1
4. Reynders, B., Devriese, D., Piessens, F.: Multi-tier functional reactive programming for the web. In: Onward!, pp. 55–68. ACM (2014)
5. Drechsler, J., Salvaneschi, G., Mogk, R., Mezini, M.: Distributed rescala: an update algorithm for distributed reactive programming. In: OOPSLA, pp. 361–376. ACM (2014)
6. Margara, A., Salvaneschi, G.: We have a DREAM: distributed reactive programming with consistency guarantees. In: DEBS, pp. 142–153. ACM (2014)
7. Salvaneschi, G., Margara, A., Tamburrelli, G.: Reactive programming: a walkthrough. In: ICSE, vol. 2, pp. 953–954. IEEE Computer Society (2015)
8. Bainomugisha, E., Carreton, A.L., Cutsem, T.V., Mostinckx, S., Meuter, W.D.: A survey on reactive programming. ACM Comput. Surv. **45**(4), 52:1–52:34 (2013)
9. Bailis, P., Kingsbury, K.: The network is reliable. Commun. ACM **57**(9), 48–55 (2014)
10. Hughes, D., Thoelen, K., Maerien, J., Matthys, N., Del Cid, J., Horre, W., Huygens, C., Michiels, S., Joosen, W.: LooCI: the loosely-coupled component infrastructure. In: Proceeding of NCA, pp. 236–243 (2012)
11. Bistarelli, S., Montanari, U., Rossi, F.: Semiring-based constraint satisfaction and optimization. J. ACM **44**(2), 201–236 (1997)
12. Shapiro, M., Preguiça, N., Baquero, C., Zawirski, M.: Conflict-free replicated data types. In: Défago, X., Petit, F., Villain, V. (eds.) SSS 2011. LNCS, vol. 6976, pp. 386–400. Springer, Heidelberg (2011). doi:10.1007/978-3-642-24550-3_29
13. Drechsler, J., Salvaneschi, G.: Optimizing distributed REScala. In: Workshop on Reactive and Event-based Languages & Systems (REBLS) (2014)

14. Maier, I., Odersky, M.: Deprecating the observer pattern with scala. React, École Polytechnique Fédérale de Lausanne, Technical report EPFL-REPORT-176887, May 2012
15. Salvaneschi, G., Hintz, G., Mezini, M.: REScala: bridging between object-oriented and functional style in reactive applications. In: Proceedings of the 13th International Conference on Modularity, pp. 25–36. ACM (2014)
16. Courtney, A.: Frappé: functional reactive programming in java. In: Ramakrishnan, I.V. (ed.) PADL 2001. LNCS, vol. 1990, pp. 29–44. Springer, Heidelberg (2001). doi:10.1007/3-540-45241-9_3
17. Lombide Carreton, A., Mostinckx, S., Van Cutsem, T., De Meuter, W.: Loosely-coupled distributed reactive programming in mobile ad hoc networks. In: Vitek, J. (ed.) TOOLS 2010. LNCS, vol. 6141, pp. 41–60. Springer, Heidelberg (2010). doi:10.1007/978-3-642-13953-6_3
18. Lanese, I., Bedogni, L., Felice, M.D.: Internet of Things: a process calculus approach. In: SAC, pp. 1339–1346. ACM (2013)
19. Lanotte, R., Merro, M.: A semantic theory of the Internet of Things. In: Lluch Lafuente, A., Proença, J. (eds.) COORDINATION 2016. LNCS, vol. 9686, pp. 157–174. Springer, Cham (2016). doi:10.1007/978-3-319-39519-7_10

Purpose-Based Policy Enforcement in Actor-Based Systems

Shahrzad Riahi$^{(\boxtimes)}$, Ramtin Khosravi$^{(\boxtimes)}$, and Fatemeh Ghassemi$^{(\boxtimes)}$

School of Electrical and Computer Engineering, College of Engineering,
University of Tehran, Tehran, Iran
{sh.riahi,r.khosravi,fghassemi}@ut.ac.ir

Abstract. Preserving data privacy is a challenging issue in distributed systems as private data may be propagated as part of the messages transmitted among system components. We study the problem of preserving data privacy on actor model as a well known reference model for distributed asynchronous systems. Our approach to prevent private data disclosure is to enforce purpose-based privacy policies which control the access and usage of private data. We propose a method to specify purposes based on workflows modeled by Petri nets in which transitions correspond to message communications. We first use model checking to verify whether the actor model behaves conforming to the purpose model. Then, the satisfaction of the policies are checked using data dependence analysis. We also provide a method to evaluate the effectiveness of policies through checking of private data disclosure in the presence of privacy policies. Since these checks are performed statically at design time, no runtime overhead is imposed on the system.

Keywords: Actor-based systems · Privacy · Purpose · Data disclosure · Formal verification · Rebeca

1 Introduction

Actor [1] is a well known model for concurrent and distributed systems, in which objects (called actors) encapsulate data and communicate via asynchronous message passing. In such systems, data of an actor can flow among other actors through message passing. Since the actors can send private data to each other as part of the transmitted messages, in systems where privacy is a concern, it is essential to protect private data from disclosure. Actor model can be used for modeling real world distributed systems, so disclosure of private data in the model indicates the privacy violation in the real world. Solove [2] classifies different types of privacy violations in four classes: information collection, information processing, information dissemination, and invasions.

Our concern in this paper, is the third case which is affected by actor communication model. A special form of information dissemination is disclosure, which, according to [3], means "making private information known outside the group

© IFIP International Federation for Information Processing 2017
Published by Springer International Publishing AG 2017. All Rights Reserved
M. Dastani and M. Sirjani (Eds.): FSEN 2017, LNCS 10522, pp. 196–211, 2017.
DOI: 10.1007/978-3-319-68972-2_13

of individuals expected to know it". In actor-based systems, if there is no sufficient control on the transmitted messages and their included data, disclosure of private data may happen.

A useful method to prevent private data disclosure would be to enforce system-wide privacy policies which control the access and usage of these data in the system. In this way, private data are used only as intended. The purpose of using a private data is an important aspect of privacy protection. Purpose refers to the intention behind accessing or using data items. In other words, as stated in [4], "purposes often refer to an or a set of abstract actions". For example, patient's health record can be accessed for the purpose of treatment, research, insurance, and so on. To incorporate purpose in privacy policies, privacy constraints can be explained as access or usage control policies which contain purpose. This type of privacy policies is called purpose-based policies. Based on [5,6,12], purpose-based policies can be categorized in two groups: data-centric and rule-centric policies. Data-centric policies focus on data and specify the purposes for which a data item can be used. A Rule-centric policy specifies that a subject can perform an action on a private data item with a certain purpose.

How the purpose of using a data item or performing an action is identified, is an important part of data-centric and rule-centric policy enforcement. Most existing work on specification and enforcement of purpose, do not consider semantics for purposes. Some work like [6,11,12] consider that "an action is for a purpose if and only if the action is part of a plan for achieving that purpose", and define the purpose semantics using formalisms based on planning. Nevertheless, to the best of our knowledge, there is no work that specifies and enforces purposes for actor-based systems. We consider the idea of planning for specification and enforcement of purpose for actor-based systems and model plans using workflows (Sect. 4).

In this paper, we focus on avoiding disclosure of private data in the actor-based systems by enforcing purpose-based policies at system design time. We assume that the actor-based system is modeled by Rebeca modeling language. Rebeca [13] (Reactive Objects language) is an actor-based modeling language, with a formal foundation, that is used to model concurrent and distributed systems. It is important to note that our method does not depend on the choice of the language and can be tailored to any kind of actor-based modeling or programming language with the assumption that the messages are delivered in the order they are sent.

Having the system model, a set of data-centric policies, a set of rule-centric policies, and the description of the purposes, we first model the purposes in a manner suitable for actor systems and then check whether the system satisfies the given policies. We use a two-step mechanism for purpose-based policy enforcement. In the first step (called purpose enforcement), we verify whether the system works exactly based on the defined purposes (Sect. 5) and in the second step (called policy enforcement), data-centric and rule-centric policies are checked (Sect. 6). We use model checking for purpose enforcement and data dependence analysis for policy enforcement. In addition to purpose and policy enforcement, we introduce another method, called data disclosure analysis, which determines each actor in the system can access which private data of other actors (Sect. 7). So it can be used as an evaluation of the effect of purpose-based policies on avoiding data disclosure.

If the purpose enforcement or policy enforcement step determines that the model does not behave according to the intended purpose model or policies, we guide the modeler to correct the model by providing counterexamples. But if data disclosure happens, despite the system satisfies the purpose-based policies, the purposes and policies must be reviewed.

2   Related Work

The existing methods for specifying and enforcing purpose can be categorized in three groups: self-declaration, role-based approach, and action-based approach.

In the self-declaration approach (e.g. [8,14]), the subject (i.e. initiator of an access request) explicitly expresses the purpose of its action. This approach is based on trusting the requester to honestly declare its purpose of action. But this approach is unable to detect if a malicious user claims a false purpose. In role-based approach (e.g. [7,9,10]), the purpose is identified based on the subject's role in the system. This approach cannot exactly identify the purpose of an action, because members of the same role may practice different purposes in their actions.

The main problem of these two approaches is that they do not consider that the purpose of an action may be determined by "its relationships with other interrelated actions" [6]. Action-based approaches consider that "an action is for a purpose if and only if the action is part of a plan for achieving that purpose" [6]. Tschants et al. [11] define the purpose semantics using a formalism based on planning and using a modified version of Markov Decision Processes to model this planning. With this formal semantics, they automate auditing for purpose restrictions. Jafari et al. [12] use a modal logic language to define purpose semantics. They present a model-checking algorithm for evaluating purpose constraints in a workflow-based information system (which is modeled by a workflow formalism based on Petri nets) and use this model checker for enforcing purpose-based policies using a workflow reference monitor. Masellis et al. [6] define semantics of purpose-aware policies based on a first-order temporal logic and design a runtime monitor for enforcing purpose-aware policies. They consider that the semantics of a purpose is its associated workflow and specify workflows using Linear-Time Temporal Logic (LTL).

We use the same idea that the semantics of a purpose is its associated workflow. [11] uses Markov Decision Processes, [12] a modal logic language, and [6] Linear-Time Temporal Logic, as the formalism for purpose semantics, but we formalize purposes using an interpretation of Petri nets tailored for actor systems (why we have chosen Petri nets is explained in Sect. 4). Another difference with previous work is that [6] uses run-time monitoring for enforcing purpose-aware policies, [11] tries to audit purpose restrictions, and [12] uses a workflow reference monitor to enforce purpose-based polices. We use model checking and data dependence analysis for purpose-based policy enforcement. This is performed statically at design time, so no runtime overhead is imposed on the system. This way, we can make sure that all the actors do nothing that violates the purpose-based policies and there is no disclosure of private data in this system.

3 Preliminaries

3.1 Running Example

In this section we describe an educational institute as the running example which will be used throughout this paper. We consider students request this institute for two purposes: educational consulting (called Consulting purpose) and class registration (called Registration purpose). This system includes five actors: student which requests the system for one of the two purposes, and four employees (Em1, Em2, Em3 and Em4) with different responsibilities. We consider Contact-Info (including student's name and phone number), EduRec (including student's educational record), and CPersonal (including student's complete personal information) as private data of student. We assume that if an employee knows a student's private data item without permission, then she can abuse it.

3.2 System Model in Rebeca

A Rebeca [13] model consists of a set of reactive classes (called rebec) which are concurrently executed and communicate via asynchronous message passing. Each rebec has three main parts: known rebecs (rebecs which can be receivers of this actor sending messages), state variables, and message servers. Each rebec has a FIFO queue to automatically receive messages. When a message is taken from the queue, the corresponding message server is executed atomically. We define a new type of state variables, called *private data*, and assume that each actor has its own private data (e.g. postal code, medical records, telephone number, and so on). Figure 1 shows an incomplete portion of our running example modeled in Rebeca[1].

3.3 Purpose-Based Privacy Policy

The purpose-based policies, including data-centric and rule-centric policies, are specified in an actor system as below:

1. A data-centric policy is defined as a pair of a data item, which is an actor's private data item, and the purpose for which it can be used. For example, (Student's ContactInfo, Registration) specifies that the ContactInfo of a student can be used for the purpose of Registration.

---

[1] The complete Rebeca code for our running example is accessible from http:// ramtung.ir/privacymodel.zip.

```
reactiveclass Student {                    reactiveclass Employee1 {
   knownrebecs {                              knownrebecs {
      Employee1 Em1;                             Student St;
      Employee3 Em3;                             Employee2 Em2;
   }                                             Employee3 Em3;
   statevars {                                }
      @Private string ContactInfo;           msgsrv ConsultingReq(string contact
      @Private string EduRec;                                    ,string cv){
   }                                             //forward consulting request to Em2
   msgsrv StartConsulting() {                    Em2.NewConsulting(cv);
      // prepare consulting request          }
      Em1.ConsultingReq(ContactInfo, EduRec); msgsrv provideresult(string result){
   }                                             // forward the consulting result,
   msgsrv ConsultingResult(string result) {              received from Em2, to St
      // process consulting result              St.ConsultingResult(result);
   }                                          }
   // other message servers                  // other message servers
}                                          }
```

Fig. 1. An incomplete portion of our running example modeled in Rebeca

Table 1. Data-centric policies for the running example

Actor's private data	Purpose
(Student, EduRec)	Consulting
(Student, ContactInfo)	Consulting
(Student, ContactInfo)	Registration
(Student, CPersonal)	Registration

Table 2. Rule-centric policies for the running example

Sender	Actor's private data	Purpose
Em1	(Student, EduRec)	Consulting
Em1	(Student, ContactInfo)	Registration
Student	(Student, EduRec)	Consulting
Student	(Student, ContactInfo)	Consulting
Student	(Student, ContactInfo)	Registration
Student	(Student, CPersonal)	Registration

2. A rule-centric policy is defined as a tuple of a subject (one of the actors in the system), a data item (an actor's private data item), an action, and the purpose. For example, (Em1, Student's EduRec, Send, Consulting) specifies that Em1 can send the student's EduRec for the purpose of Consulting.

As we will explain in Sect. 4, it is sufficient for our analysis to only consider message sending as actions in an actor-based system, since we do not explicitly express the action in a rule-centric policy and assume that all the actions appeared in the rule-centric policies correspond to sending of messages in the system. The given data-centric and rule-centric policies for the running example are presented in Tables 1 and 2 respectively.

As mentioned before, we use workflows to describe purposes in the actor model. Actions in these workflows are messages communicated among actors in the system. The workflow of Consulting purpose is defined as follow:

1. Student gets her request for educational consulting to Em1. This request includes ContactInfo and EduRec of student.
2. Em1 forwards this request to Em2. This request includes student's EduRec.

3. Em2 queries Em3 for current state of the classes, if needed, and provides the consulting result.
4. Em1 delivers the consulting result to student.

The workflow of Registration purpose is defined as follow:

1. Student gets her request for registration to Em1. This request includes ContactInfo of student.
2. Em1 forwards this request to Em3 (including student's ContactInfo).
3. Em3 requests student for complete personal information and queries Em4 for payment information.
4. When Em3 receives both of the student and Em4 responses, the registration is done.

4   Purpose Model

As mentioned in Sect. 2, the self-declaration and role-based approaches for specifying and enforcing purpose, do not assume a semantics for the purpose, so a major problem is the ambiguity in the interpretation of purposes. Hence, we use action-based approach and address the mentioned problem by relating the actions using the workflow-based plan.

Masellis et al. [6] refer to workflow as "collections of activities (called tasks) together with their causal relationships, so that the successful termination of a workflow corresponds to achieving the purpose which it is associated to". There are various types of workflow definition languages, that can be categorized in two groups. The first group includes models such as Petri nets [17] and process algebra [18], which have a proper formal semantics. The second group includes approaches like Web Services Business Process Execution Language (BPEL) [19] and the Business Process Modeling Notation (BPMN) [20]. These languages often have no proper formal semantics [16].

Our goal is to formalize the notion of purpose in a manner suitable for actor models. According to [15], it is possible to formalize most aspects of privacy policies by abstracting all activities as communications between actors. Workflows are normally expressed at the requirements (or business level), which comprise the tasks and the control flow among the activities in the system. During the design process, these tasks must be mapped into elements of the system model. In our case, since the actor model is based on the object-oriented paradigm, tasks are mapped into methods (message processors) of the actors based on the principles of data encapsulation. Furthermore, a behavioral model of the purpose is constructed based on the control flow specified in the workflow, to describe the order of interactions among the actors. We call this workflow "message flow".

In the case of sequential models, the behavioral model may be expressed as UML sequence diagrams. However, since actors communicate asynchronously, the underlying behavioral model must be able to clearly express concurrent computation. Hence, we choose Petri nets to describe the global control flow of the system. Aalst [22] presents several good reasons for using Petri nets to specify workflows: "formal semantics despite the graphical nature, state-based instead of event-based, abundance of analysis techniques".

In addition to the above reasons, there are transformations from workflows described in modeling languages like BPMN and BPEL to Petri net models ([16] surveys these transformations). We consider the standard definition of Petri net [17] that consists of two finite disjoint sets of places and transitions together with a flow relation. In a Petri net, the places, transitions and flow relations are graphically represented by circles, squares and directed arcs respectively. We borrow Definitions 1 and 2 from [21]:

Definition 1 (Petri net). *A Petri net is a triple (P, T, F) where:*

1. *P is a finite set of places.*
2. *T is a finite set of transitions (P and T are disjoint sets).*
3. *F ⊆ (P × T) ∪ (T × P) is a set of arcs (or flow relations)*

In a Petri net, places model intermediate states and transitions model tasks. In [16], the mapping of some workflow patterns to Petri nets are presented. A Petri net that models a workflow definition is called a workflow net (WF-net).

Definition 2 (WF-net). *A Petri net PN = (P, T, F) is a WF-net (workflow net) if and only if:*

1. *PN has two special places source and sink. The source place has no input arc and the sink place has no output arc (a token in the source place corresponds to a new instance of workflow, and a token in the sink place corresponds to a completed instance of workflow).*
2. *If we add a new transition to PN which connects sink place with source place, then the resulting Petri net is strongly connected.*

We specify purposes using message flows, and model the message flows using a modified version of WF-net, referred to as message flow net (MF-net), in which transitions are messages.

Definition 3 (Message flow net (MF-net)). *A message flow net MFN = (P, T, F) is a WF-net in which:*

1. *Each transition corresponds to a specific message in actor system.*
2. *Flow relations specify the order in which the actors are allowed to take their messages.*

Each message is modeled as a triple (s, m, r) in which s is the name of the sender actor, m is the message name, and r is the name of the receiver actor. A transition (s, m, r) in a MF-net means actor r takes message m from its message queue (and starts the execution of the corresponding message server) which is sent by actor s. The MF-net models of Consulting and Registration purposes specified in running example, are shown in Figs. 2 and 3 respectively.

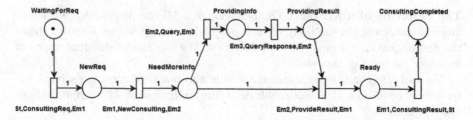

Fig. 2. Consulting purpose in educational institute modeled in MF-net

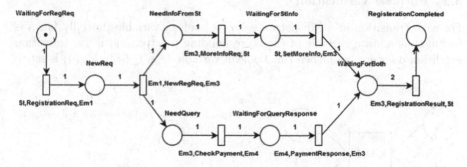

Fig. 3. Registration purpose in educational institute modeled in MF-net

5   Purpose Enforcement

As discussed in the previous section, each purpose is modeled by a MF-net. We add a new actor to the system for each MF-net, called *purpose actor* or *p-actor*, aiming to verify whether the actor system behaves according to the corresponding purpose. Each p-actor checks the state of the MF-net and decides whether an execution of a message server conforms to the corresponding purpose.

5.1   Constructing Purpose Actor

Since p-actors are defined to check the conformance of the transmitted messages to the purposes of the system, when an actor takes a message from its message queue, a copy of this message, parameterized with its sender and receiver, is sent to the corresponding p-actor. Therefore, we define one message server in the p-actor for each message in the MF-net. For simplicity, we assume that a message can only be part of one purpose.

The state of a MF-net: A state in a MF-net (as in Petri net) is represented by the distribution of tokens over the places (also referred to as marking). For keeping the state of the MF-net in the corresponding p-actor, we define an integer variable for each place that represents the number of tokens in that place. So, the state of the MF-net is modeled by the values of this set of integer variables which are the state variables of the p-actor. The variables $p_1, ..., p_n$ in Fig. 4, are the variables corresponding to the places of a Petri net.

The behavior of a MF-net: The behavior of a MF-net is modeled with conditional statements in the body of each p-actor's message server. Figure 4 shows the description of a simple MF-net behavior. We can model different types of workflow patterns in this way.

We call the conditional statement inside the p-actors' message servers the *transition condition*. It is noticeable that the execution of M in right side of Fig. 4 is atomic.

5.2 Purpose Verification

For each transition in a MF-net model, one boolean variable (initially false) is included as a state variable of the corresponding p-actor, and if the transition condition does not hold, then this boolean variable (e.g. t_M in Fig. 4) is set to

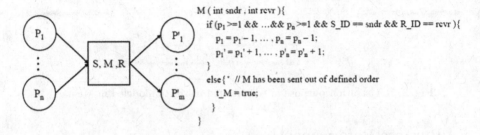

Fig. 4. Modeling a transition in the purpose actor

```
reactiveclass RegistrationPurpose        msgsrv RegistrationReq (int sndr, int rcvr){
{                                             if (WaitingForRegReq > 0 && sndr == StID &&
    knownrebecs{                                                    rcvr == Em1ID){
        Student St; Member1 Em1;                  WaitingForRegReq = WaitingForRegReq - 1;
        Member3 Em3; Member4 Em4;                 NewReq = NewReq + 1;
    }                                         }
    statevars{                                else
          ┌ int WaitingForRegReq;                 t_RegistrationReq = true;
Place     │ int NewReq;                       }
variables │ ...                             msgsrv NewRegReq(int sndr, int rcvr){
          └ int ConsultingCompleted;            if (NewReq > 0 && sndr == Em1ID &&
                                                                rcvr == Em3ID){
          ┌ boolean t_RegistrationReq;             NewReq = NewReq - 1;
Transition │ boolean t_NewRegReq;                  NeedInfoFromSt = NeedInfoFromSt + 1;
variables  │ ...                                   NeedQuery = NeedQuery + 1;
          └ boolean t_RegistrationResult;       }
    }                                         else
    msgsrv initial(){                             t_NewRegReq = true;
          ┌ WaitingForRegReq = 1;            }
Initial   │ NewReq = 0;                          ...
marking   │ ...
          └ ConsultingCompleted = 0;      msgsrv RegistrationResult (int sndr, int rcvr){
                                              if (WaitingForBoth > 1 && sndr == Em3ID &&
        t_RegistrationReq = false;                              rcvr == StID){
        t_NewRegReq = false;                      WaitingForBoth = WaitingForBoth - 2;
        ...                                       ConsultingCompleted = ConsultingCompleted + 1;
        t_RegistrationResult = false;             WaitingForRegReq = WaitingForRegReq + 1;
    }                                         }
}                                             else
                                                  t_RegistrationResult = true;
                                          }}
```

Fig. 5. Purpose actor for Consulting purpose

true, representing an error has occurred. So, the property that must be checked is the invariant property $(\neg t_1) \wedge ... \wedge (\neg t_n)$ $(t_1, ..., t_n$ are the mentioned boolean variables for the transitions).

We use model checking to verify whether the system satisfies the above invariant property. If it is not satisfied, counterexamples are reported for the correction of the model. We use RMC (Rebeca Model Checker) [24] to model check our running example. The p-actor for Consulting purpose, is presented in Fig. 5.

We can define multiple instances of one MF-net in its corresponding p-actor for different instances of its execution, and distinguish them by a workflow ID.

6   Policy Enforcement

Now that we have a system that works exactly according to the defined purposes, we aim to check whether the data-centric and rule-centric policies hold in the system. As data is an important aspect of these policies, we need a mechanism which can trace the flow of data in both actors' message servers as well as sending messages to other actors. To achieve this, we use data dependence graph analysis.

6.1   Data Dependence Graph

In [23], a special dependence graph based on Rebeca [13] semantics is introduced and used as an intermediate graph representation for slicing a Rebeca model. We modify this dependence graph and use it for verifying data-centric and rule-centric policies and analyzing the disclosure of private data in the actor systems.

Rebeca Dependence Graph

Rebeca Dependence Graph (RDG) introduced in [23], has three types of nodes, including reactive class entry, message server, and statement (for Rebeca state variables and statements) nodes, and four types of edges, including data dependence, control dependence, member dependence, and parameter-in edge/activation edges. Table 3 presents how [23] models Rebeca features by RDG. Activation, formal-in and actual-in nodes are of statement nodes which are defined to model message passing.

In addition to the above dependencies, there is one more dependency called intra-rebec data dependency. According to [23], "this dependency exists between the last statement of a message server which is assigning value to a variable and the first use of that variable in another message server". In RDG, intra-rebec data dependency is modeled using data dependence edges.

Modified Rebeca Dependence Graph

We introduce a modified version of Rebeca dependence graph which is suitable for our policy enforcement. The modified Rebeca dependence graph differs from the original version [23] in the following ways:

Table 3. Mapping Rebeca features to RDG according to [23]

Rebeca features	RDG nodes	RDG edges
Reactive class	A reactive class entry node	The reactive class entry node is connected to each of its state variables and message servers by the member dependence edges
Message server	An entry node and a set of nodes representing its statements	The existing dependencies within the body of the message server modeled by data dependence edges and control dependence edges
Message passing	An activation node	The activation node is connected to the entry node of the related message server by an activation edge
Parameters of the messages	Formal-in and actual-in nodes	Parameter-in edges connect the formal-in and actual-in nodes

Table 4. DDG nodes

Name	Description
V-RC	Set of reactive class nodes
V-PD	Set of private data nodes
V-MS	Set of message server nodes
V-ST	Set of statement nodes
V-AC	Set of activation nodes

Table 5. DDG edges

Name	Description
E-CD	Set of control dependence edges
E-DD	Set of data dependence edges
E-MD	Set of member dependence edges
E-PI	Set of parameter-in edges

1. For modeling the actors' private data, we add a new type of node, called private data node.
2. According to [23], a data dependence edge exists "between two statement nodes if assigning value to a variable at one statement might reach the usage of the same variable at another statement". We categorize assignment of value to a variable in two cases: reversible and irreversible. In reversible assignment the operands can be extracted from the result. For example in $a = b \times 10$ we can extract value of b from the value of a. In irreversible assignment, the operands cannot be conducted from the result. For example in $a = b \mod 3$, the exact value of b cannot be conducted from the value of a. We only use data dependence edges for reversible assignments.
3. We consider the activation nodes, which correspond to send statements, as a separate type of nodes.

So, in a modified Rebeca dependence graph $DDG = \{V, E\}$, $V(DDG) =$ V-RC $\cup$ V-MS $\cup$ V-PD $\cup$ V-ST $\cup$ V-AC, and $E(DDG) =$ E-CD $\cup$ E-DD $\cup$ E-MD $\cup$ E-PI. The description of these sets are given in Tables 4 and 5.

An incomplete portion of the data dependence graph for our running example is shown in Fig. 6 (due to space restriction, we eliminate some parts of this graph).

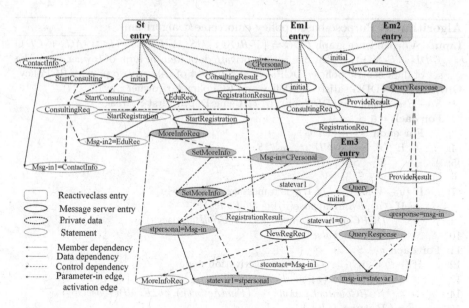

Fig. 6. Applying Algorithm 1 to DDG of running example for the sets of policies shown in Tables 1 and 2, and student's CPersonal private data item. The gray nodes are nodes which have access to CPersonal private data item.

6.2 Data-Centric and Rule-Centric Policy Enforcement

For policy enforcement, we first construct the data dependence graph (DDG) for Rebeca model, and then apply Algorithm 1 to determine whether the system satisfies the data-centric and rule-centric policies. This algorithm, gets a data dependence graph, an actor's private data item (pv), the sets of data-centric and rule-centric policies as the inputs. First, the set of all nodes which can affect the given private data is computed (lines 1–5). To check data-centric policies, all message servers that have access to pv (possibly passed through a series of messages or assignments) are selected (lines 6–7). Then, the corresponding purpose of each such message server (determined by FindPurpose(v)), is checked against the data-centric policies (lines 8–10). To check rule-centric policies, all send statements that potentially send pv as a parameter (again, possibly indirectly) are selected (lines 11–12). Then, the permission of such communication is checked against the rule-centric policies (lines 13–15). For complete data-centric and rule-centric policy enforcement, this algorithm must be run for all private data in the system.

Figure 6 shows an example execution of Algorithm 1. The inputs of this example are the data dependence graph of our running example, the sets of policies shown in Tables 1 and 2, and student's CPersonal private data item. As shown in Fig. 6, CPersonal can be used in *Query* message server with the purpose of Consulting. As the pair (student's CPersonal, Consulting) is not a member of Table 1, the algorithm indicates a violation of the data-centric policy. This

---

Algorithm 1. Purpose-based policy enforcement algorithm

Input: A dependence graph $DDG = \{V\text{-}RC \cup V\text{-}MS \cup V\text{-}PD \cup V\text{-}ST \cup V\text{-}AC,\ E\text{-}CD \cup$
$E\text{-}DD \cup E\text{-}MD \cup E\text{-}PI\}$, one actor's private data item in form of (owner , pv), the
set of data-centric policies DCPolicy and the set of rule-centric policies RCPolicy
Output: Does DDG satisfy DCPolicy and RCPolicy for (owner , pv)?

1: $S \leftarrow ReachableFrom(DDG, pv)$ // Using Depth First Search
2: **For each** $v \in S$
3:     **For each** $u \in V(DDG)$
4:         **If** $((u, v) \in E\text{-}CD \ \wedge \ u \notin S)$
5:             $S \leftarrow S \cup \{u\}$
6: **For each** $v \in S$
7:     **If** $(v \in V\text{-}MS)$ // If v is a message server node
8:         **If** $((pv, FindPurpose(v)) \notin DCPolicy)\{$
9:             $DCPCounterExample \leftarrow (pv, FindPurpose(v))$
10:            **Return** *False* $\}$
11: **For each** $v \in S$
12:     **If** $(v \in V\text{-}AC)$ // If v is an activation node
13:         **If** $((FindActor(v), pv, FindPurpose(v)) \notin RCPolicy)\{$
14:             $RCPCounterExample \leftarrow (FindActor(v), pv, FindPurpose(v))$
15:            **Return** *False* $\}$
16: **Return** *True*

---

violation occurs because *SetMoreInfo* message server (with Registration purpose) assigns CPersonal to a state variable while *Query* message server (with Consulting purpose) uses this state variable and sends its value to another actor. Although the actor is eligible to access its own state variable, its access should be controlled when it contains private data.

7   Data Disclosure Analysis

In addition to policy enforcement, we can analyze the disclosure of private data in an actor system. This analysis needs to determine each actor in the system can access which private data of other actors. This access can be done in one of the following forms:

1. Direct receive: the owner of private data directly sends its private data to another actor.
2. Indirect receive: an actor sends private data of another actor to a third actor.
3. Receive by inferring: the actors can infer other actors' private data based on some inference rules (these rules are defined based on data model or message model of the system).

In this paper we only consider the first two forms, and receive by inferring is remained as our future work.

For data disclosure analysis, we introduce Algorithm 2 based on data dependence graph analysis. In this algorithm, first the set of all nodes which can affect the given private data item, is computed (lines 2–6), and then the parent of each message server node in this set, is added to the output set (lines 7–9). The function $Parent(v)$ returns an actor node which v is a member of it. The output of this algorithm is the set of actors which can know the input private data item.

Algorithm 2. Data disclosure analysis algorithm

Input: A dependence graph $DDG = \{V\text{-}RC \cup V\text{-}MS \cup V\text{-}PD \cup V\text{-}ST \cup V\text{-}AC,\ E\text{-}CD \cup$
$E\text{-}DD \cup E\text{-}MD \cup E\text{-}PI\}$, one actor's private data item in form of (owner , pv)

Output: $ActorsKnownpv$ (the set of actors which can know pv)

1: $ActorsKnownpv \leftarrow \emptyset$
2: $S \leftarrow ReachableFrom(DDG, pv)$ // Using Depth First Search
3: **For each** $v \in S$
4:     **For each** $u \in V(DDG)$
5:         **If** $((u, v) \in E\text{-}CD\ \wedge\ u \notin S)$
6:             $S \leftarrow S \cup \{u\}$
7: **For each** $v \in S$
8:     **If** $(v \in V\text{-}MS)$ // If v is a message server node
9:         $ActorsKnownpv \leftarrow ActorsKnownpv \cup \{Parent(v)\}$
10: **Return** $ActorsKnownpv$

If the result of this algorithm indicates the existence of data disclosure, despite the system satisfies the purpose-based policies, the purposes and policies must be reviewed.

8   Conclusion and Future Work

In this paper, we provided a way for purpose-based policies enforcement in actor-based systems with the aim of avoiding disclosure of private data in such systems. We modeled purposes using Petri nets, and make sure that the system works exactly according to them by model checking and if needed, correction of the system model. Then the data-centric and rule-centric policies are checked by analysis of the data dependence graph of the system. Data disclosure analysis algorithm has also been introduced, which can be used for evaluating of the effect of purpose-based policies on disclosure of data. However, this analysis can be used for each actor model to specify the distribution of data among actors.

Using our method, we can statically check that in a distributed asynchronous system there is no privacy violation. Since we model purposes using workflows, our method is usable for practitioners. All of our analysis are performed statically at system design time so, no runtime overhead is imposed on the system.

In future work, we intend to consider receive by inferring, as well as direct and indirect receive, for data disclosure analysis, which needs to apply required inference rules in our analysis. We also interest to provide a runtime monitoring mechanism for purpose-based policy enforcement in actor systems. This extends the scope of our method to the systems in which policies may change during time.

References

1. Agha, G.A.: ACTORS - a model of concurrent computation in distributed systems. MIT Press series in artificial intelligence. MIT Press, Cambridge (1985)
2. Solove, D.J.: A taxonomy of privacy. Univ. PA Law Rev. **154**(3), 477–560 (2006)
3. Tschantz, M.C., Wing, J.M.: Formal methods for privacy. In: Cavalcanti, A., Dams, D.R. (eds.) FM 2009. LNCS, vol. 5850, pp. 1–15. Springer, Heidelberg (2009). doi:10.1007/978-3-642-05089-3_1
4. Rath, A.T., Colin, J.N.: Modeling and expressing purpose validation policy for privacy-aware usage control in distributed environment. In: Proceedings of the 8th International Conference on Ubiquitous Information Management and Communication, ACM, New York (2014)
5. Jafari, M., Safavi-Naini, R., Sheppard, N.P.: Enforcing purpose of use via workflows. In: Proceedings of the 8th ACM Workshop on Privacy in the Electronic Society (WPES 2009), pp. 113–116. ACM, New York (2009)
6. Di Masellis, R., Ghidini, C., Ranise, S.: A declarative framework for specifying and enforcing purpose-aware policies. In: Foresti, S. (ed.) STM 2015. LNCS, vol. 9331, pp. 55–71. Springer, Cham (2015). doi:10.1007/978-3-319-24858-5_4
7. Masoumzadeh, A., Joshi, J.B.D.: PuRBAC: purpose-aware role-based access control. In: Meersman, R., Tari, Z. (eds.) OTM 2008. LNCS, vol. 5332, pp. 1104–1121. Springer, Heidelberg (2008). doi:10.1007/978-3-540-88873-4_12
8. Jawad, M., Alvarado, P.S., Valduriez, P.: Design of PriServ, a privacy service for DHTs. In: Proceedings of the 2008 International Workshop on Privacy and Anonymity in Information Society. PAIS 2008, pp. 21–25. ACM, New York (2008)
9. Byun, J., Bertino, E., Li, N.: Purpose based access control of complex data for privacy protection. In: Proceedings of the Tenth ACM Symposium on Access Control Models and Technologies, New York, USA, pp. 102–110 (2005)
10. Ni, Q., Bertino, E., Lobo, J., Brodie, C., Karat, C., Karat, J., Trombeta, A.: Privacy-aware role-based access control. ACM Trans. Inf. Syst. Secur. (TISSEC) **13**(3), 24:1–24:31 (2010)
11. Tschantz, M.C., Datta, A., Wing, J.M.: Formalizing and enforcing purpose restrictions in privacy policies. In: IEEE Symposium on Security and Privacy (SP), pp. 176–190. IEEE (2012)
12. Jafari, M., Safavi-Naini, R., Fong, P.W.L., Barker, K.: A framework for expressing and enforcing purpose-based privacy policies. ACM Trans. Inf. Syst. Secur. (TISSEC) **17**(1), 3:1–3:31 (2014)
13. Sirjani, M., Movaghar, A., Shali, A., de Boer, F.: Modeling and verification of reactive systems using Rebeca. Fundam. Informaticae **63**, 385–410 (2004)
14. Kabir, M.E., Wang, H.: Conditional purpose based access control model for privacy protection. In: Proceedings of the Twentieth Australasian Conference on Australasian Database, Australia, vol. 92, pp. 135–142 (2009)
15. Ronne, J.: Leveraging actors for privacy compliance. In: Proceedings of the 2nd edn. on Programming Systems, Languages and Applications Based on Actors, Agents, and Decentralized Control Abstractions (AGERE! 2012), pp. 133–136. ACM, New York (2012)
16. Lohmann, N., Verbeek, E., Dijkman, R.: Petri net transformations for business processes – a survey. In: Jensen, K., van der Aalst, W.M.P. (eds.) Transactions on Petri Nets and Other Models of Concurrency II. LNCS, vol. 5460, pp. 46–63. Springer, Heidelberg (2009). doi:10.1007/978-3-642-00899-3_3

17. Reisig, W.: Petri Nets, An Introduction. EATCS Monographs on Theoretical Computer Science. Springer-Verlag, Berlin Heidelberg (1985). doi:10.1007/978-3-642-69968-9

18. Best, E., Koutny, M.: Process algebra. In: Desel, J., Reisig, W., Rozenberg, G. (eds.) ACPN 2003. LNCS, vol. 3098, pp. 180–209. Springer, Heidelberg (2004). doi:10.1007/978-3-540-27755-2_5

19. Web Services Business Process Execution Language Version 2.0, OASIS Standard, 11 April 2007, OASIS (2007). http://docs.oasis-open.org/wsbpel/2.0/OS/wsbpel-v2.0-OS.pdf

20. OMG: Business Process Modeling Notation (BPMN) Version 2.0., Object Management Group (2011). http://www.omg.org/spec/BPMN/2.0/

21. Aalst, W.M.P.: The application of petri nets to workow management. J. Circ. Syst. Comput. 8(1), 21–66 (1998)

22. Aalst, W.M.P.: Three good reasons for using a petri-net-based workflow management system. In: Wakayama, T., Kannapan, S., Khoong, C.M., Navathe, S., Yates, J. (eds.) Information and Process Integration in Enterprises. The Springer International Series in Engineering and Computer Science, vol. 428, pp. 161–182. Springer, Boston (1998). doi:10.1007/978-1-4615-5499-8_10

23. Sabouri, H., Sirjani, M.: Slicing-based reductions for Rebeca. In: Proceedings of FACS08, pp. 209–224. Elsevier ENTCS Post-proceedings (2008)

24. RMC (Rebeca Model Checker) tool (2016). http://www.rebeca-lang.org/wiki/pmwiki.php/Tools/RMC

Automatic Transition System Model Identification for Network Applications from Packet Traces

Zeynab Sabahi-Kaviani[✉], Fatemeh Ghassemi, and Fateme Bajelan

School of Electrical and Computer Engineering, University of Tehran, Tehran, Iran
{z.sabahi,fghassemi,bajelan.fateme}@ut.ac.ir

Abstract. A wide range of network management tasks such as balancing bandwidth usage, firewalling, anomaly detection and differentiating traffic pricing, depend on accurate traffic classification. Due to the diversity and variability of network applications, port-based and statistical signature detection approaches become inefficient and hence, behavioral classification approaches have been considered recently. However, so far, there is no automated general method to obtain the behavioral models of applications. In this research, we propose an automatic procedure to infer a transition system model from generated traffic of an application. Our approach is based on passive automata learning theory and evidence driven state merging technique using the rules of the network domain. We consider the behavior of well-known network protocols to generate the model which includes unobserved behaviors and excludes invalid ones as much as possible. To this aim, we present a new equivalence relation regarding the given protocol behaviors to induce proper state merging conditions. This idea has led the time complexity order of the algorithm to be linear rather than exponential. Finally, we apply the model of some real applications to evaluate the precision and execution time of our approach.

1 Introduction

The importance of traffic classification for network administration tasks such as ensuring the security and quality of service of applications in computer networks has long been acknowledged. The growing number of network applications and protocols has limited the efficiency of classical methods. In the past, packets were easily classified by their transport layer ports. As the use of random or non-standard ports is dramatically increasing, payload inspection [1,2] and statistical methods [3,4] are proposed. However, drawbacks of these techniques such as insufficiency in encrypted traffic and their high computation cost lead to the emergence of behavioral classifiers. The merit of the behavioral classification is to use the behavioral pattern of an application instead of the content of packets or flow statistics. This point makes these classifiers useful for encrypted traffic or unknown protocols. But, so far, no automated method to obtain the behavioral model of applications is provided which currently requires human inspection.

© IFIP International Federation for Information Processing 2017
Published by Springer International Publishing AG 2017. All Rights Reserved
M. Dastani and M. Sirjani (Eds.): FSEN 2017, LNCS 10522, pp. 212–227, 2017.
DOI: 10.1007/978-3-319-68972-2_14

There are a few studies for automating inference of the behavioral patterns which are application specific and cannot be widely used, for instance [5] has been presented for P2P-TV traffic.

To overcome the challenges of traffic classification and behavioral pattern detection approaches, we aim at providing an automatic approach to derive formal behavioral models, i.e., transition systems, for applications in the domain of the network. Our focus is mainly on programs at the application layer of the TCP/IP model [6]. We reduce our problem to the automata learning problem [7] which aims at inferring an automaton which accepts the set of given words. If the input traffic is considered as the given words of the language, then the desired model will be the identified automaton. However, the classical approaches in the literature of automata learning are not efficient to derive the most general model such that not only it subsumes valid unobserved traces as much as possible, but also disallows invalid traces. This is not achievable unless concepts of the domain are utilized to tailor the basic algorithm.

Intuitively, we assume that the behavior of an application can be identified in terms of how it executes well-known network protocols (below the application layer) Therefore, given the formal specification of well-known network protocols and execution traces of a program, we automatically generate a transition system. Hence, we customize the automata learning algorithm of [8] using rules in the network context to derive the most general model. Noting to the fact that each trace of a program is an interleaving of network protocol execution traces, the inferred model must preserve the behavior of each network protocol. In other words, the model of various applications differ in how they interleave the traces of well-known network protocols. Therefore, we take advantage of a behavioral pre-order relation in the theory of transition systems to conduct the process of model generation such that invalid traces are prohibited. Due to our abstraction (of application variables), the states of the inferred model which identify the same state with the same number of the flows for each network protocol, can be aggregated together using the counter abstraction technique [9] to include not observed behaviors.

To illustrate the applicability of our approach, we have implemented our algorithm in a tool and applied it on two version control system applications and two remote desktop sharing programs. Our results indicate that the techniques that are used to generalize the model, are sufficiently conservative. and unobserved behaviors are covered with a high precision. Furthermore, the worst case time complexity order of our algorithm is linear rather than exponential in contrast to the related automata learning techniques.

2   Preliminaries

In this section, we describe the necessary network background, an overview of automata learning, the definitions of the main concepts related to transition systems and the counter abstraction technique used to find the equivalent states.

2.1 Network Background

Each packet transferred across a network is composed of two parts: the header and the content. The header includes the control information needed by the corresponded protocol and is appended to the beginning of the content. Protocols defined over the Internet follow the *TCP/IP* layered architecture [6]. This model consists of four layers: *Application*, *Transport*, *Internet*, and *Link*. The layered architecture means that the packet content of each layer is the built packet of its upper layer.

To send a message over the network, at first, the Application layer receives the user message from the software which is running (e.g., email client, web browser, instant messaging software, etc.), and passes it to the lower layer. The Transport layer segments data from the upper levels, then establishes a connection between the packet's point of origin and where it has to be received, and ensures that the packets are reassembled in the correct order [10]. The Network layer is responsible for the packet's addressing and routing. Finally, the Link layer manages the formats of packets based on the mediums being used in transmitting the packets. For each layer, a number of different protocols is standardized. Protocols are divided into connection-less and connection-oriented categories. Connection-oriented are those that need to establish a connection before data transmission. Thus there are handshake (initialization) and finalization phases in these protocols. These phases are not required in connection-less protocols. They just send a request packet for each desired data. A sequence of packets which have the same value for the parameters source IP, source port, destination IP, destination port, and the protocol name is called *flow*. An execution of an application gives rise to initiating a number of flows. These flows are the connections which are established between the initiator system and the other end systems.

2.2 Automata Learning

There are equivalent keywords in the literature to automata learning such as grammar inference or regular inference, language or automata identification. The goal of automata learning is to find a (non-unique) smallest automaton which is consistent with the set of given examples [11]. Gold has proved that this problem when the alphabet is finite, the two input sets of positive and negative samples are given, and the number of the states of the output automaton is determined, is a NP-complete problem [7]. If all of the words with the size equal and less than n are given, then it is possible to solve the problem in the polynomial time. The algorithms of this problem can be divided into the two categories: active and passive.

The active techniques are based on Angluin L^* algorithm which solves the problem in polynomial time by asking some membership or equivalence queries [12]. It is assumed that there is an oracle than answer the required queries. Passive techniques tend to build tree-like automata, called prefix tree automata, from input examples and then by merging their states according to some heuristics evidence, achieve the smallest deterministic finite automata (this technique is called *Evidence Driven State Merging (EDSM)*[8]). In this category, there is no oracle and the algorithm should find the solution only from the positive and negative words of the language.

Since we aim to infer the behavioral model only from the input traces when there is no oracle system, our solution in this paper is based on the passive techniques. The most important challenge of these techniques is how to find the candidate states which should be merged to include unobserved traces. KTail algorithm merges states which have K common future (i.e., states that accept the same set of strings of length K) [13]. Several research has been conducted to decrease the $O(n^2)$ search space of the states which should be merged. Red-Blue is one of them and becomes a popular framework which limits the number of pairs of states by determining sufficient conditions on their colors.

2.3   Transition Systems

In this section we define the concepts used in the proposed methodology which are related to transition systems. These definitions have been adapted from [14].

Definition 1 (Transition System). *A transition system is a tuple* $TS = (S, Act, \rightarrow, s_0, \downarrow)$ *where* S *is a set of states,* Act *is a set of actions,* $\rightarrow \subseteq S \times Act \times S$ *is a transition relation,* s_0 *is the initial state, and* $\downarrow \subseteq S$ *is a set of final states. We use* $s \xrightarrow{\alpha} t$ *to denote* $(s, \alpha, t) \in \rightarrow$.

TS is called action-deterministic if for all $s \in S$, *there are not* $(s, \alpha, t) \in \rightarrow$ *and* $(s, \alpha, v) \in \rightarrow$, *where* $\alpha \in Act$ *and* $t, v \in S$, *such that* $t \neq v$.

From this definition, the transition system in the left side of Fig. 1 is action-deterministic. A finite *execution fragment* $\eta = s_0 \alpha_0 s_1 \alpha_1 \ldots \alpha_n s_{n+1}$ of TS is an alternating sequence of states and actions starting with the initial state and ending with a final state such that $(s_i, \alpha_i, s_{i+1}) \in \rightarrow$ where $0 \leq i \leq n$. A finite sequence of actions $\varrho = \alpha_0 \alpha_1 \ldots \alpha_n$ of TS is an *execution trace* if $\exists s_0, \ldots, s_{n+1} \in S$ such that $\eta = s_0 \alpha_0 s_1 \alpha_1 \ldots \alpha_n s_{n+1}$ is an execution fragment. For instance, $s_0 \ x \ s_1 \ a \ s_2 \ x \ s_3 \ a \ s_4 \ y \ s_5 \ b \ s_6 \ y \ s_7$ and $s_0 \ a \ s_8 \ a \ s_9 \ x \ s_{10} \ b \ s_{11} \ y \ s_{12}$ are the execution fragments of the transition system in the left side of Fig. 1. By eliminating states from these sequences, the execution traces are generated ($x \ a \ x \ a \ y \ b \ y$ and $a \ a \ x \ b \ y$ respectively).

There is an abstraction operator which has the responsibility to hide some actions of a transition system to make them internal and thus unobservable to external entities. We formally define the abstraction operator in the following definition:

Definition 2 (Abstraction Operator). *Let* $TS = (S, Act, \rightarrow, s_0, \downarrow)$ *be a transition system. The abstraction of TS via a set of actions* $L \subseteq Act$, *denoted by* $\tau_L(TS)$, *is* $(S, Act \setminus L, \rightarrow', s_0, \downarrow)$ *such that:* $\rightarrow' = \{(s, \alpha, t) \mid (s, \alpha, t) \in \rightarrow, \alpha \notin L\} \cup \{(s, \tau, t) \mid (s, \alpha, t) \in \rightarrow, \alpha \in L\}$

To compare the behavior of transition systems, several behavioral pre-order and equivalence relations have been proposed ranging from strict to liberal ones.

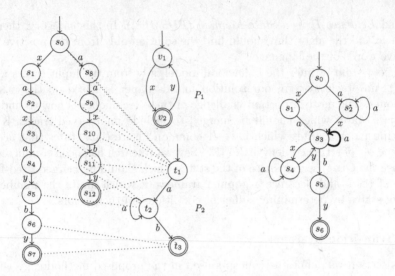

Fig. 1. Left: The initial transition system and the specification of protocols. Right: Applying the steps of proposed method on an example.

The *Simulation* relation is a finest pre-order relation which requires a transition system to precisely mimic transitions of another one [15]. In the case of existing internal actions in the system, the *Weak Simulation* relation is defined to relax the conditions only for the observable actions.

Let $\overset{\tau}{\to}^*$ be reflexive and transitive closure of τ-transitions:

- $t \overset{\tau}{\to}^* t$;
- $t \overset{\tau}{\to}^* s$ and $s \overset{\tau}{\to} r$, then $t \overset{\tau}{\to}^* r$.

Definition 3 (Weak Simulation Relation). *A binary relation R on the set of states S is a weak simulation relation if for any s_1, s_1', and $t_1 \in S$ and $\alpha \in Act$, $s_1 \, R \, t_1$ implies:*

- $s_1 \overset{\alpha}{\to} s_1' \Rightarrow (\alpha = \tau \wedge s_1' \, R \, t_1) \vee (\exists t_1', t_1'', t_1''' \in S : t_1 \overset{\tau}{\to}^* t_1''' \overset{\alpha}{\to} t_1'' \overset{\tau}{\to}^* t_1' \wedge s_1' \, R \, t_1')$;
- $s_1 \in \downarrow \Rightarrow (\exists t_1' \in \downarrow : t \overset{\tau}{\to}^* t')$.

For the given transition systems $TS_i = (S_i, Act_i, \to_i, s_{0i}, \downarrow_i)$, where $i \in \{1, 2\}$, TS_1 is weakly simulated by TS_2 or TS_2 simulates TS_1, denoted by $TS_1 \preceq_w TS_2$, if $s_{01} \, R \, s_{02}$ for some weak simulation relation R.

A weak simulation relation R is minimal, if for all simulation relation R' witnessing $TS_1 \preceq_w TS_2$, $R \subseteq R'$. Hence, a minimal weak simulation relation R is not necessarily unique.

2.4   Counter Abstraction

The *Counter Abstraction* is a technique to abstract states of a system. The idea is to represent each state as a vector of counters one per each value instead of a vector of state variables. For instance, consider there are three integer variables x, y and z. The states $\{x = 1, y = 2, z = 1\}$, $\{x = 2, y = 1, z = 1\}$ and $\{x = 1, y = 1, z = 2\}$ are equivalent because they have the identical counter abstracted state $\{count(1) : 2, count(2) : 1\}$. This technique has been used in various applications. In symmetry reduction which is a technique to avoid state space explosion problem, the counter abstraction has the role of finding identical clusters of states space so as to reduce the symmetry states and decrease the cost of model checking [16]. This concept is also used in [9] in order to abstract a parameterized system of an unbounded size into a finite-state system to be verifiable.

3   Methodology

In this section, our proposed methodology for learning the network behavioral model of an application is discussed.

3.1   Problem Statement

The captured traffic is the sequence of packets sent or received as the result of the execution of an application during a specified time. Each packet contains data and headers of layers as the result of encapsulation. We only consider information of the upper layer instead of the whole headers and data (for instance, we only take into account information of the application layer of HTTP packets while they subsume information of the TCP layer).

To facilitate the processing of each packet content and close up the concept to the automata theory, a function is exploited which corresponds each packet to its equivalent action-like abstract representation. This function is defined as *PMapper* : *Packets* → *Act* where *Packets* is the set of possible packets captured through the pre-processing step. For example, a received TCP packet in the handshake phase is mapped to *TCPInitI* which is a member of the model actions set. In Sect. 4 we explain how the action set is defined in terms of the packet information. Therefore, by applying the *PMapper* function to each captured packet, we obtain a trace of actions. Hence, one input of our problem is N executions of an application which are transformed by the *PMapper* into the N action traces (packet trace) denoted by PT, ranged over by π. Let π_i indicate the ith action of the trace π, and $len(\pi)$ show the length of the trace. We remark that the length of each input execution is arbitrary, and in potentially independent of the length of other traces.

Besides the packet traces, another important input of our problem is the specifications of K network protocols. We assume that the specifications are provided in the form of action-deterministic transition systems $P_i = (S_i, Act_i, \rightarrow_i, s_{0i}, \downarrow_i)$

where $1 \leq i \leq K$, $\tau \notin Act_i$, and $\forall i, j \leq K : (Act_i \cap Act_j = \emptyset)$. We remark that each action trace π is the interleaving of a set of flows f_1, $f_2, \ldots$ where f_i is an execution trace of P_j $(j \leq K)$.

The goal of our problem is to derive a model in the form of transition system, i.e., $M = (S_M, Act_M, \to_M, s_{0M}, \downarrow_M)$ such that $Act_M = \bigcup_{\pi \in PT}\{\pi_i \mid 1 \leq i \leq len(\pi)\}$, and $\pi \in Traces(M)$, where $Traces(M)$ is the set of the execution traces of M. In fact, each of the input traces is an execution trace of the desired transition system.

3.2 Projection Relation

Initially, a tree-like automaton which consists of all action traces is generated. Intuitively, each application needs to establish a number of connections with other systems in order to perform each of its functionality. Each connection follows a protocol specification. For instance, an execution of the *Map* application of *Windows 8* contains four flows where two are for the DNS protocol, one for the TCP and one for the TLS protocols. Hence, each state of the initial transition system can be considered as a vector of states, each of which identifies a state of the corresponding protocol. Note that the size of the vector is equal to the number of flows. To generalize the initial transition system to cover more behavior, some states are selected to merge together. Hence, the new model accepts extra not observed valid behavior. Merged states are those called *project equivalent*. Two states are project equivalent if their vectors (of flow states) are identical with respect to the counter abstraction technique. For the sake of efficiency, the resulting transition system is determined.

Before describing the method, we mention some definitions and theorems. As we explained, each packet from the application execution belongs to a flow. We assume the total number of the flows of the all input traces is denoted by F. Furthermore, the auxiliary function $Flow : S \times Act \times S \to Nat$, defined over the initial transition system, maps each packet, specified by the transition with the corresponding action of the packet, to its flow number such that $Flow(s, \alpha, t) \leq F$, where $s, t \in S$ and $\alpha \in Act$. From the flow definition each flow has a protocol attribute. Let function $Protocol$ identify the protocol name of a flow, denoted by $Protocol : Nat \to Nat$, such that $\forall f \leq F : Protocol(f) \leq K$.

Definition 4 (Projection Relation). *Let $TS_i = (S_i, Act_i, \to_i, s_{0i}, \downarrow_i)$, for $i = 1, 2$, be transition systems such that $TS_1 \preceq_w TS_2$ witnessed by a minimal weak simulation relation $\mathcal{R}$. Two states s_1 and s_2 of S_1 have projection relation under TS_2 if $\exists t \in S_2 : s_1 \mathcal{R} t \wedge s_2 \mathcal{R} t$. Then, we say that s_1 and s_2 are the same projection of t under the transition system TS_2, denoted by $s_1 \sim_{\downarrow TS_2} s_2$.*

To define states that are project equivalent, the following lemma identifies the conditions under which the project relation can act as an equivalence relation, and consequently can partition states. If a transition system has a *tree-like* structure, any of its two states can be connected by a unique simple path.

Lemma 1. *Let $TS_i = (S_i, Act_i, \rightarrow_i, s_{0i}, \downarrow_i)$, for $i = 1, 2$, be transition systems such that TS_1 is a tree-like transition system and TS_2 is an action-deterministic transition system without any τ-transition (i.e., $\tau \notin Act_2$). If TS_1 is weakly simulated by TS_2, witnessed by a minimal weak simulation $\mathcal{R}$, then each state of S_1 relates to only one state of S_2 under $\mathcal{R}$:*

$$\forall s \in S_1, \forall t_1, t_2 \in S_2 : s \; \mathcal{R} \; t_1 \wedge s \; \mathcal{R} \; t_2 \Rightarrow t_1 = t_2$$

Theorem 1. *Let $TS_i = (S_i, Act_i, \rightarrow_i, s_{0i}, \downarrow_i)$, for $i = 1, 2$, be transition systems such that TS_1 is a tree-like transition system and TS_2 is an action-deterministic transition system without any τ-transition (i.e., $\tau \notin Act_2$). The projection relation under the transition system TS_2 over the states of TS_1 is an equivalence relation.*

See [17] for the proof of Lemma 1 and Theorem 1. As a consequence of Theorem 1, the states of a transition system can be partitioned into equivalance classes by a projection relation. The equivalence class for projection relation is defined in the following definition.

Definition 5 (Projection Relation Partitioning). *Let $TS_i = (S_i, Act_i, \rightarrow_i, s_{0i}, \downarrow_i)$, for $i = 1, 2$, be transition systems such that TS_1 is a tree-like transition system and TS_2 is an action-deterministic transition system without any τ-transition (i.e., $\tau \notin Act_2$). States of TS_1 are partitioned under the projection relation under TS_2 into the equivalence classes each of which is identified by the unique state $t \in S_2$ such that:$[t]_{TS_1 \sim_\downarrow TS_2} = \{s \in S_1 \mid s \; \mathcal{R} \; t\}$ where $\mathcal{R}$ is a minimal weak simulation relation.*

Running Example. Consider the specifications of two sample protocols in the right side of Fig. 1, we assume that two input traces $x\ a\ x\ a\ y\ b\ y$ and $a\ a\ x\ b\ y$ are given. In the first trace, there are three flows, two are of the protocol P_2 and one of the protocol P_1. They are given such that the first x and the last y belongs to a flow and the second x and the first y are related together. In the second trace, there are two flows each of which is instantiated from each protocol. It is assumed that the flows are enumerated by the order of their first packets. We use this example in the rest of this section.

3.3   Step 1: Building the Initial Transition System

From Sect. 2, there is an execution fragment for each execution trace. We generate for each input trace π, its corresponding execution fragment $\eta^\pi = s_0 \pi_1 s_1^\pi \pi_2 \ldots \pi_{len(\pi)} s_{len(\pi)}^\pi$. Note that the initial state in the fragments of the all traces are intentionally identical. In the first step, the tree-like transition system M_0 is built from aggregating the execution fragments of the input traces. Therefore, the initial transition system $M_0 = (S, Act, \rightarrow, s_0, \downarrow)$ is obtained as follows:

$- S = \{s_i^\pi \mid 1 \leq i \leq len(\pi), \pi \in PT\} \cup \{s_0\},$

- $Act = \{\pi_i \mid 1 \leq i \leq len(\pi),\ \pi \in PT\}$,
- $\rightarrow = \bigcup_{\pi \in PT}(\{(s_k^\pi, \pi_{k+1}, s_{k+1}^\pi) \mid 1 \leq k \leq len(\pi)\} \cup \{(s_0, \pi_1, s_1^\pi)\})$,
- $\downarrow = \{s_{len(\pi)}^\pi \mid \pi \in PT\}$.

The transition system in the left side of Fig. 1 is the result of performing this step. This initial transition system does not cover new execution traces of the application which are not given in the input. Therefore, some operations are needed to generalize the initial transition system and cover more execution traces. Next steps (step 2 and 3) are the efforts to reach this goal.

3.4   Step 2: Generalizing by Counter Abstraction

The generalization method in this step is addressed in two sub-steps.

1. Finding Equivalent States. Intuitively, two states are equivalent under the flow f, if they belong to the same equivalence class based on the projection relation under the transition system of the attributed protocol of f, i.e., $Protocol(f)$. To this aim, we introduce the flow-based abstraction operator, which renames actions not included in the flow f to τ. By generalizing this intuition, two states s_1 and s_2 of transition system M_0 are equivalent if and only if they are equivalent under all flows of the initial transition system M_0.

Definition 6 (Flow-based Abstraction Operator). *Let* $TS = (S, Act, \rightarrow, s_0, \downarrow)$ *be a transition system. Then* $\tau_{\bar{f}}(TS) = (S, Act', \rightarrow', s_0, \downarrow)$ *such that:* $\rightarrow' = \{(s, \alpha, t) \in \rightarrow \mid Flow(s, \alpha, t) = f\} \cup \{(s, \tau, t) \mid \exists (s, \alpha, t) \in \rightarrow (Flow(s, \alpha, t) \neq f)\}$ *and* $Act' = Act_i$ *where* $Protocol(f) = i$ *and* $P_i = (S_i, Act_i, \rightarrow_i, s_{0i}, \downarrow_i)$.

We remark that if the abstraction operator is defined under protocol actions instead of a flow, then the resulting abstracted transition system may not preserve the protocol behavior due to interleaving of flows. For instance, the abstraction of the transition system in Fig. 1 under the protocol P_2 contains the sequence of $x\ \tau\ x\ \tau\ y\ \tau\ y$ at its left branch which does not have any weak simulation relation with P_2.

Let $count(s, t)$ denote the number of flows like f_i that the state t of the protocol P_j weakly simulates s in the abstraction of M_0 under f_i:

$$count(s, t) = |\{f_i \leq F \mid s \in [t]_{\tau_{\bar{f_i}}(TS(M_0)) \sim \downarrow P_j}\}|.$$

We remark that each state s is uniquely simulated by a state t as the result of our projection relation. The two states s_1 and s_2 can be aggregated together under the counter abstraction technique if and only if $\forall j \leq K, t \in S_j : count(s_1, t) = count(s_2, t)$.

The results of applying the counter abstraction on the states of the initial transition system of the running example are presented in [17]. For each state of obtained model, a vector of count values for all states of the transition systems of protocols is calculated. To obtain each vector, at first, the projection relation under abstraction of each flow is computed. After that, the number of flows in each state of protocols is counted. For example, for s_0, the vector is $< 5, 0, 0, 5, 0 >$ which is the value of $< c(s, t_1), c(s, t_2), c(s, t_3), c(s, v_1), c(s, v_2) >$ where c is the abbreviation of *count*. It shows that all the flows are related to the initial states of the protocols. Because of the transition (s_0, x, s_1) of flow f_1, the state of s_1 is simulated by the state v_2 of the protocol P_2, and hence, the counter of flows in the state v_1 decreases by one and the counter of flows in the state v_2 increases by one. Hence, the projection relation partitioning for s_1 produces $< 5, 0, 0, 4, 1 >$. After calculating the counters for each state, the set of equivalent states are achieved: $\{(s_2, s_5, s_{10}), (s_3, s_4), (s_6, s_{11}), (s_7, s_{12}), (s_8, s_9)\}$.

2. Merging Equivalent States. After finding the set of equivalent states of M_0, merging process should be done. Let $[s]$ donote the equivalence class of the state s, i.e., $\forall s' \in S : s' \in [s] \Leftrightarrow s' \equiv s$. A merged state inherits the union of the incoming and outgoing transitions of its origin states. By applying all merge candidates, the final transition system $M_1 = (S', Act, \rightarrow', s_0', \downarrow')$ is obtained, where $S' = \{[s] \mid \forall s \in S\}$, $\rightarrow' = \{([s], \alpha, [t]) \mid \exists s, t \in S : (s, \alpha, t) \in \rightarrow\}$, $s_0' = [s_0]$, and $\downarrow' = \{[s] \mid \forall s \in \downarrow\}$. Figure 1 (without the tick transition a on the state s_3) is the final result of performing this step. After this step, the resulting transition system is action-deterministic. We have proved this fact in the [17].

3.5   Step 3: Generalizing by Completing Transitions

The next generalization idea is completing the transitions set according to the transition systems of the network protocols. We add self-loops of each protocol state $t \in P_i$, for some $i \leq K$, to the state $[s]$ if $count(s, t) > 0$. Adding such transitions does not affect the equivalent classes of M_1. Then, after applying this step, the resulting generalized transition system is $M_g = (S', Act, \rightarrow_g, s_0', \downarrow')$ such that:

$$\rightarrow_g = \rightarrow' \cup \{([s], \alpha, [s]) \mid \forall j \leq K, t \in S_j, \forall s \in S : count(s, t) > 0 \land (t, \alpha, t) \in \rightarrow_j\}.$$

After applying this step, the tick transition a on state s_3 is added to the Fig. 1. The time complexity of the algorithm is linear in the size of the input. See [17] for the psuedocode of the algorithm and a discussion of the time complexity.

4   Evaluation

To evaluate the proposed method, we have implemented our algorithm in Java and applied it to some applications. Two categories of applications, *version control system* and *remote desktop sharing*, are selected for testing our methodology. For the first category, two applications TortoiseSVN client of SVN[1] and Source Tree Client of GIT[2] are selected. The traffic of the *update* command of these

---

[1] https://tortoisesvn.net/.
[2] https://www.atlassian.com/software/sourcetree.

applications are gathered as their captured packet traces. Also, we have selected two remote desktop sharing applications, namely *TeamViewer*[3] and *JoinMe*[4] for which their traffic is encrypted. Hence, they cannot be easily identified by signature based approaches on the content of packets. Each one has run for 100 times and their network traces are captured via the Wireshark[5] tool. Packets of the application layer protocols (used by these programs), namely *TCP, SSL, SSLv2, TLSv1, TLSv1.2, HTTP* and *UDP* have been considered and the others are filtered. The more protocols are considered, the more precision will be achieved. Some preprocessing operations have been performed to eliminate the repetitive and truncated packets. Also, we have reassembled segments of fragmented packets. The mapper function which is responsible for translating the packets to their corresponding actions is defined such that it assigns the concatenation of the packet protocol name, the control phase and the direction to each packets. We divide the operation of each protocol into a set of phases to abstractly consider its progress. The control phases are assumed to be *Init, Data,* and *Fin* for connection-oriented protocols and *Init* and *Data* for connection-less ones. Intuitively, *Init* indicates to the establishment of the connection, *Data* to the transmission of data, and *Fin* to the termination of the connection. The direction is a binary tag which can be either I or O to indicate that the packet is sent or received, respectively. The amount of detail about packets embedded in their corresponded actions, shows how much the final generated model is sensitive to packet variations. By this mapper function, different manners of each control phase (initialization/ transferring data/ finalization) are considered to be the same.

We assume that the specifications of protocols are given in the form of transition systems and defined according to the mapper function abstraction level. By applying the mapper function on the packet traces, 100 action traces have been obtained for each application. These traces are divided into the train and test sets. The train traces are the input of our proposed method to infer the behavioral model which should accept the test traces. The overall scheme of an obtained model is shown in [17]. We use the cross validation technique for 100 times to calculate the average value of precision with a reasonable confidence interval. Table 1 shows the final result of our experiments. Regarding to impossibility of measuring the real value of false positive rate (because it is not possible to gather all negative traces), researchers tend to consider the traces of the other applications which have the same functionality. Thus, we use traces of applications in the same category crossly to calculate the false positive rates.

The major point is that by applying our proposed generalization steps, the false positive rate does not grow. This means that our conservative approach prevents over-generalization from occurring. Each generalization step improves the completeness of the model. Note that since the update command of SVN and GIT generates a short packet trace, their captured traffic are similar and

---

[3] https://www.teamviewer.com/en/.
[4] https://www.join.me/.
[5] https://www.wireshark.org/.

Table 1. The average result of applying the proposed approach step by step, run on system with CPU Corei7 and 2G RAM. TPR stands for true positive rate.

Step	App	States Num	FP	TPR (observed)	TPR (unobserved)	Train time	Test time
Initial Transition System	SVN	3982	100%	100%	2%	<5 s	<1 s
	GIT	4115	100%	100%	1%		
	TeamViewer	8637	0	100%	0%		
	JoinMe	34484	0	100%	0%		
Applying Counter Abstraction	SVN	78	100%	100%	55%	<2 min	<1 s
	GIT	45	100%	100%	100%		
	TeamViewer	407	0	100%	36%		
	JoinMe	5458	0	100%	25%		
Completing Self-Loop Transitions	SVN	78	100%	100%	100%	<5 min	<1 s
	GIT	45	100%	100%	100%		
	TeamViewer	407	0	100%	98%		
	JoinMe	5458	0	100%	56%		
Relaxing Unnecessary Orders*	SVN	*	100%	100%	100%	*	*
	GIT	*	100%	100%	100%		
	TeamViewer	*	0	100%	100%		
	JoinMe	*	0	100%	91%		

misclassified. As a future work, we plan to map packets to parametric actions in order to enhance the precision of the classifier. Adding (self-loop) transitions has increased our precision by 31 percent in the worst case. In the next step, we aim to relax unnecessary interleaving which stems from the concurrent development of applications or parallel network connections. Such a step which is our future work increases our precision to 100 or 91 percent. Now, we have applied the step manually, by examining the counter examples of the previous step. Those traces which can be covered by the generated model via modifying the orders of packets, is counted as the successful result for this step. We plan to automate this idea so as to automatically induce strict orders among transitions and relax the unnecessary ones in our future work. Our approach fails to recognize 9 percent of test traces (the last row of the Table 1) which are mainly those that include new unpredictable subsequences based on the train set.

4.1 Comparison with Other Packet Classification Methods

To clarify the applicability of our methods, it should be compared with other packet classification techniques which we have described in Sect. 1. **Port-based** detection method does not have the ability of detecting most of the current applications because that they tend to use random or non-standard ports. Due to growing usage of encrypted traffic **payload inspection** methods become useless and it can not be used in our dataset. Furthermore, the proposed **behavioral classification** methods are application specific (e.x. for P2P applications) and they are not enough general to apply to our selected applications. Finally **statistical classification methods** are the only related work which we can compare

Table 2. The result of statistical classification

Method	FP	TPR	Train Time	Test Time
TeamViewer	0.12%	83%	3 s	<1 s
JoinMe	0.10%	87%	5 s	<1 s

our work with. To this aim, Netmate[6] is used to obtain the feature vectors of flows of captured traffic. Then, using Weka tool-set[7], the average precision of classification and false positive metrics among three algorithms SVM, Native Bayes and C4.5 were measured. The final result of these metrics are reported in Table 2.

5   Related Work

Two research areas are related to our problem. In the following we explore related work in each area.

Automata Learning. Some research has been conducted to extend the expressiveness of inferred models. The KTail algorithm is extended in [18] with the aim to generate models from methods invocation traces. This approach is conducted in four steps. At first, the traces with the identical sequence of methods (those differ in the values of parameters) are merged together. Next, constraints on parameters are obtained via Daikon invariant detector [19]. At the third step, a prefix tree automaton is built. Finally, the states are merged according to a criterion which can be equivalence of method and parameters, weak subsumption or strong subsumption for their next k actions. In [20], the authors extends the Angluin L^* algorithm to infer relationships between input and output parameters in the form of the Mealy machines. In [21], the automate learning problem is extended to infer deterministic timed automata.

Some studies address the application of automata learning problem. Among them, [22] is the most related work to ours which elaborates on inferring mealy machine models of communication protocols. The authors indicate that the parameters in the message format of protocols such as sequence number, configuration parameter and session id, result in infinite-states model. To minimize the state space, the abstract representation of protocol states are derived automatically in terms of operations that a requester and responder may perform. Hence, they have a similar assumption to ours which is the existence of protocol specifications. Their algorithm is based on query evaluation (active automata learning), while, we have extended the passive automata learning. Also, there are other applications of automata learning in different areas, especially in software specification mining [23,24] which are not directly related to our work and we do not elaborate on.

---

[6] https://dan.arndt.ca/projects/netmate-flowcalc/.

[7] http://www.cs.waikato.ac.nz/ml/weka/.

Reverse Engineering of Protocol Specification. In this part we enumerate the works that focus on inferring protocol specifications from traffic. These works are related to ours because of their restriction on inferring a model by observing the behavior of the application in a black-box style. In [25], a probabilistic method was investigated to obtain a finite state machine of a protocol. It was assumed that the format of protocol messages is not determined. At the first step, messages are segmented into l-length bytes and clustered with the aim of recognizing their control parts. Next, the most frequent patterns are selected as message units by statistical analysis. Then, the main messages of the protocols are defined by computing the centers of the clusters. Finally, the finite state machine is constructed whose states are the main messages and probabilistic transitions are the frequencies of each pairs of messages.

In ReverX algorithm [26], a prefix tree automaton is built from traces and then the states which are the destination of identical transitions, are merged. Therefore, transitions with the same source and destination are created. They claim that if these transitions are merged the parameters of message headers are induced. Actually, despite their work is similar to us in using passive automata learning, we differ in the conditions for state merging. If the states are just similar in their 1-future action, they merge them, while we have investigated a domain specific condition based on well-known protocol.

6   Conclusion

The classical methods which identify the traffic based on packet header information or statistical metrics, are not effective anymore. Classification approaches based on the behavioral patterns of applications are of a new trend to this problem. No general and automated method to derive behavioral models has been provided. We proposed a method to reach this goal based on the automata identification problem and evidence driven state merging technique combined by transition system theories. Intuitively, we assumed that the behavior of an application can be identified in terms of how it executes well-known network protocols, abstracting the state variables of the application. Hence, we have introduced our merging conditions to identify the equivalent states based on the specification of a set of well-known network protocols such as TCP, TLS, SSL, etc. To this aim, we have provided the projection relation to identify the states with the same number of the flows for each network protocol which can be counted together using the counter abstraction technique.

We have presented two extra steps to complete the inferred model to cover unobserved behaviors At first, the model is completed by including the self-loop behaviors of the network protocols. After that, the possible valid interleaving of the packets based on the repetition of their orders is predicted. The model is extended to subsume such predicted orders. We also implemented and evaluated our procedure which does not require human inspection. The experiments show very encouraging results that the generalization steps significantly increase the accuracy from 0% to 91% in the worst case. The future work is to mechanize the last step which induces the essential orders with the aim of relaxing the unnecessary ones. We plan to extend our case study and compare the result of our method with the real traffic classification tools.

References

1. Moore, A.W., Papagiannaki, K.: Toward the accurate identification of network applications. In: Dovrolis, C. (ed.) PAM 2005. LNCS, vol. 3431, pp. 41–54. Springer, Heidelberg (2005). doi:10.1007/978-3-540-31966-5_4
2. Sen, S., Spatscheck, O., Wang, D.: Accurate, scalable in-network identification of p2p traffic using application signatures. In: Proceedings of 13th International Conference on World Wide Web, pp. 512–521. ACM (2004)
3. Moore, A., Zuev, D.: Internet traffic classification using bayesian analysis techniques, In: ACM SIGMETRICS Performance Evaluation Review, vol. 33, no. 1, pp. 50–60. ACM (2005)
4. McGregor, A., Hall, M., Lorier, P., Brunskill, J.: Flow clustering using machine learning techniques. In: Barakat, C., Pratt, I. (eds.) PAM 2004. LNCS, vol. 3015, pp. 205–214. Springer, Heidelberg (2004). doi:10.1007/978-3-540-24668-8_21
5. Bermolen, P., Mellia, M., Meo, M., Rossi, D., Valenti, S.: Abacus: accurate behavioral classification of P2P-TV traffic. Comput. Netw. **55**(6), 1394–1411 (2011)
6. Fall, K., Stevens, R.: TCP/IP illustrated, volume 1: The Protocols. Addison-Wesley (2011)
7. Gold, E.: Language identification in the limit. Inf. Control **10**(5), 447–474 (1967)
8. Lang, K.J., Pearlmutter, B.A., Price, R.A.: Results of the abbadingo one DFA learning competition and a new evidence-driven state merging algorithm. In: Honavar, V., Slutzki, G. (eds.) ICGI 1998. LNCS, vol. 1433, pp. 1–12. Springer, Heidelberg (1998). doi:10.1007/BFb0054059
9. Pnueli, A., Xu, J., Zuck, L.: Liveness with (0, 1, infty)-counter abstraction. In: Proceedings of 14th CAV, pp. 107–122. Springer, Heidelberg (2002)
10. Parsons, C.: Deep Packet Inspection in Perspective: Tracing Its Lineage and Surveillance potentials. Citeseer (2008)
11. Heule, M.J.H., Verwer, S.: Exact DFA identification using SAT solvers. In: Sempere, J.M., García, P. (eds.) ICGI 2010. LNCS, vol. 6339, pp. 66–79. Springer, Heidelberg (2010). doi:10.1007/978-3-642-15488-1_7
12. Angluin, D.: Learning regular sets from queries and counterexamples. Inf. Comput. **75**(2), 87–106 (1987)
13. Biermann, A., Feldman, J.: On the synthesis of finite-state machines from samples of their behavior. IEEE Trans. Comput. **100**(6), 592–597 (1972)
14. Baier, C., Katoen, J.-P.: Principles of Model Checking. MIT press, Cambridge (2008). vol. 26202649
15. van Glabbeek, R.: The Linear Time - Branching Time Spectrum, pp. 278–297. Springer, Heidelberg (1990)
16. Emerson, E.A., Trefler, R.J.: From asymmetry to full symmetry: new techniques for symmetry reduction in model checking. In: Pierre, L., Kropf, T. (eds.) CHARME 1999. LNCS, vol. 1703, pp. 142–157. Springer, Heidelberg (1999). doi:10.1007/3-540-48153-2_12
17. Sabahi, Z., Ghassemi, F., Bajelan, F.: Automatic transition system model identifications for network applications from packet traces, January 2017. http://fghassemi.adhoc.ir/shared/TechReport.pdf

18. Lorenzoli, D., Mariani, L., Pezzè, M.: Automatic generation of software behavioral models. In: Proceedings of 30th ICSE, pp. 501–510. ACM (2008)
19. Ernst, M., Cockrell, J., Griswold, W., Notkin, D.: Dynamically discovering likely program invariants to support program evolution. IEEE Trans. Softw. Eng. **27**(2), 99–123 (2001)
20. Khalili, A., Tacchella, A.: Learning nondeterministic mealy machines. In: Proceedings of 12th ICGI, pp. 109–123 (2014)
21. Verwer, S.: "Efficient identification of timed automata: Theory and practice," Ph.D. dissertation, TU Delft, Delft University of Technology (2010)
22. Aarts, F., Jonsson, B., Uijen, J.: Generating models of infinite-state communication protocols using regular inference with abstraction. In: Petrenko, A., Simão, A., Maldonado, J.C. (eds.) ICTSS 2010. LNCS, vol. 6435, pp. 188–204. Springer, Heidelberg (2010). doi:10.1007/978-3-642-16573-3_14
23. Walkinshaw, N., Derrick, J., Guo, Q.: Iterative refinement of reverse-engineered models by model-based testing. In: Cavalcanti, A., Dams, D.R. (eds.) FM 2009. LNCS, vol. 5850, pp. 305–320. Springer, Heidelberg (2009). doi:10.1007/978-3-642-05089-3_20
24. Lo, D., Maoz, S.: Scenario-based and value-based specification mining: better together. Autom. Softw. Eng. **19**(4), 423–458 (2012)
25. Wang, Y., Zhang, Z., Yao, D.D., Qu, B., Guo, L.: Inferring protocol state machine from network traces: a probabilistic approach. In: Lopez, J., Tsudik, G. (eds.) ACNS 2011. LNCS, vol. 6715, pp. 1–18. Springer, Heidelberg (2011). doi:10.1007/978-3-642-21554-4_1
26. Antunes, J., Neves, N., Verissimo, P.: Reverse engineering of protocols from network traces. In: Proceedings of 18th WCRE, pp. 169–178, October 2011

Gray-Box Conformance Testing for Symbolic Reactive State Machines

Masoumeh Taromirad[(✉)] and Mohammad Reza Mousavi

Centre for Research on Embedded Systems (CERES),
Halmstad University, Halmstad, Sweden
{m.taromirad,m.r.mousavi}@hh.se

Abstract. Model-based testing (MBT) is typically a black-box testing technique. Therefore, generated test suites may leave some untested gaps in a given implementation under test (IUT). We propose an approach to use the structural and behavioural information exploited from the implementation domain to generate effective and efficient test suites. Our approach considers both specification models and implementation models, and generates an enriched test model which is used to automatically generate test suites. We show that the proposed approach is sound and exhaustive and cover both the specification and the implementation. We examine the applicability and the effectiveness of our approach by applying it to a well-known example from the railway domain.

1 Introduction

Model-based testing (MBT) has received significant attention in testing complex software systems. The benefit of model-based testing is primarily in automated test case generation and automated analysis of the test results. In an MBT process, test cases are automatically derived from a (preferably formal) model of the specification and are executed on the implementation under test (IUT). MBT is typically a black-box testing technique, in which the implementation is only accessible through its interfaces and thus, test data is generally selected based on the specification. Therefore, generated test suites may leave some untested gaps in a given IUT and/or redundantly cover the same logical path several times.

To address this issue test models and test case generation processes can be enriched with structural or behavioural information extracted from the implementation. This is a promising approach considering the existing techniques for extracting models from implementations, in particular, recent learning-based approaches inferring models from software (e.g., [1,2]). Such models provide an *abstraction* of the implementation based on its observable behaviour. Using these models in testing improves the coverage of the IUT, up to the accuracy of the extracted model.

This paper proposes a gray-box testing strategy in that test suites are generated considering both the specification and an *abstraction* of the IUT. With such a test suite the coverage of the specification model and the implementation would be complementary to each other and hence, more faults could be

Published by Springer International Publishing AG 2017. All Rights Reserved
M. Dastani and M. Sirjani (Eds.): FSEN 2017, LNCS 10522, pp. 228–243, 2017.
DOI: 10.1007/978-3-319-68972-2_15

uncovered. Moreover, such test suites are tailored to a given IUT and thus, a fewer number of test cases are generated –to satisfy a certain testing goal– in comparison to universal test suites that are supposed to detect faults in any possible implementation. The main contribution of this work is considering the partitioning of the input domain which can be obtained from (black-box) implementations (e.g., by model learning techniques) in generating test suites. We show that although such information may be generated for different purposes, it can be used in test generation and does improve the coverage of the generated test cases.

In this work, specifications and implementations are modelled with a specific type of transition systems, called *Symbolic Reactive State Machines (SRSMs)*. Given the SRSMs of the specification and the IUT, a *complete* test suite is generated based on the, so-called, *transition composition* of these models. In generating test cases, the justification of the proposed data selection is demonstrated by a special case of the *uniformity hypothesis* [3] –the theoretical foundation for testing with a finite subset of values.

The rest of the paper is structured as follows: Sect. 2 provides an overview of the related work. Section 3 introduces the formalism used in this paper and Sect. 4 defines our notion of conformance. The proposed testing strategy is outlined in Sect. 5. In Sect. 6, we provide the experimental results of examining the effectiveness of our approach. Section 7 discusses the future work and concludes the paper.

2 Background and Related Work

Several black-box test case generation methods are proposed in the literature for various formalisms (e.g., finite state machines [4,5] and labeled transition systems [6]). The completeness of these methods (i.e., specifying all possible behaviour of a system) is typically explained with respect to a specified subset of possible implementations which is referred to as a *fault model* [7]. This is because in many practical cases, it is not possible to have a complete test suite as such a test suite would be infinitely large.

Gray-box model-based testing strategies provide a combination of black-box model-based testing with white-box testing to tune fault detection with respect to a given implementation. For example, in [8], the structure of the tests is generated using MBT (from the specification model) and then a white-box testing technique is used to find a set of concrete values for parameters that maximise code coverage. The approach presented in this paper, in a similar way, considers the IUT in generating test cases. However, it differs from [8] in that both the structure and the parameters of test cases are influenced by a combination of a test model and information from the implementation.

Our proposed approach has been largely established considering the promising results from existing learning-based techniques for inferring and extracting models from implementations. Some of the techniques have focused on sequential models typically in the form of FSMs (e.g., [9,10]) and some on data-dependant behaviour in the form of pre- and post-conditions (e.g., [11]). More recently, EFSMs are considered to infer more complete models (combining control and data). For example, Cassel et al. [2] introduce an active learning algorithm to infer a class of EFSMs. Walkinshaw et al. [1] provide a model inference technique (called MINT) which infers EFSMs from software executions. We believe that the model inference techniques which, in particular, infer EFSMs can provide the required abstract model of implementations in the context of our work (i.e., an inferred model can be translated into our formalism).

There are also a number of similar models, to our formalism, in the literature of MBT such as action machines (AM) [12], symbolic transition systems (STS) [13], FSMs with symbolic inputs [14], and symbolic input output FSMs (SIOFSM) [15]. SIOFSMs particularly support inputs with infinite domain. We expect that each of these underlying models (and their associated test case generation algorithms) can be adopted in our approach.

Another closely related line of work is equivalence-class-based testing. The theoretical foundation for this approach has been presented in [3] by the *uniformity hypothesis*, which states that it suffices to check the representatives of sub-domains in which the behaviour is the same among all elements. We discuss the justification of our strategy based on this hypothesis. Huang et al. [16] propose a complete model-based equivalence testing strategy applicable to reactive systems with large, possibly infinite input data types but finite internal and output data. Our approach is inspired by [16] and extends it by replacing the heuristics for refinement with the information extracted from the IUT. It also differs from [16] in that it allows for infinite output domains.

2.1   Motivating Example

To motivate this work, we use one of the benchmarks provided in [2], namely the prepaid card, in which the card's balance is limited to 500 SEK, and no more than 300 SEK can be topped up in a single transaction. Figure 1a illustrates the behaviour of this card for the update balance operation. Variable a is the amount to update the balance of the card, and variable b is the current balance of the card. Labels of the form 'C/O' on transitions state that the transition is triggered by inputs satisfying C and the outputs are updated according to O.

Assume that there is an implementation of this card and we have an abstract model of it which is generated by RaLib [2], depicted in Fig. 1b. As it is observed in Fig. 1b, the learned model introduces a different partitioning of the inputs comparing to the specification's. This difference is typically observable between a learned model and the already existing (reference) models. In this work, we suggest to consider such information and we show that it will improve the coverage of the specification and the IUT in a testing experiment. Note that the abstract models extracted from implementations may not contain the exact input-output relation. They largely provide useful information about the partitioning of the input domain. Accordingly, we mainly consider and use the complementary information about the partitioning of inputs in generating tests.

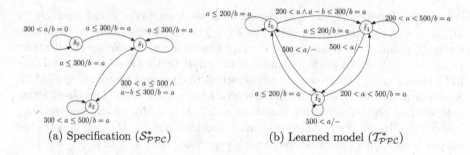

(a) Specification ($\mathcal{S}^*_{\mathcal{PPC}}$)　　　　　(b) Learned model ($\mathcal{T}^*_{\mathcal{PPC}}$)

Fig. 1. The behaviour of the example prepaid card.

3　Preliminaries

For formal reasoning, we need a model of a specification, and also assume that the behaviour of the IUT can be captured by some (unknown) formal model in a given formalism. In the following, we introduce the formalism used in this work to model specifications and abstractions of implementations, and then define conformance in its context.

3.1　Symbolic Reactive State Machines

A Symbolic Reactive State Machine (SRSM) is a symbolic representation of the state-based behaviour of a system, with a set of input/output variables. It is symbolic as it explicitly uses the notion of variables, rather than concrete values, in specifying transitions (e.g., data-dependent transitions) and outputs (e.g., output as a function of input variables).

Definition 1 (Symbolic Reactive State Machine (SRSM)). *An SRSM $\mathcal{S}^*$ is a 6-tuple $(\bar{S}, \bar{s}_0, \bar{\delta}, \bar{\lambda}, V, D)$, where*

- *$\bar{S}$ is the non-empty and finite set of symbolic states,*
- *$\bar{s}_0 \in \bar{S}$ is the initial symbolic state,*
- *V is the set of variables such that $V = I \cup O$, i.e., V is partitioned into disjoint sets I and O of input and output variables, respectively,*
- *D is the range of all variable valuations,*
  - *D_I: domain of input variables*
  - *D_O: domain of output variables*
- *$\bar{\delta}: \bar{S} \times \mathcal{P}(D_I) \to \bar{S}$ is the transition function, and*
- *$\bar{\lambda}: \bar{S} \times \mathcal{P}(D_I) \to \bar{\mathcal{E}}(I)$ is the output function.*
  - *$\mathcal{E}(I)$ is the set of expressions over input variables (I).*
  - *$\bar{\mathcal{E}}(I) \in \underbrace{\mathcal{E}(I) \times \ldots \times \mathcal{E}(I)}_{|O|}$, i.e., each expression gives the value of one output variable.*

Notations. Input variables are enumerated as $I = \{x_1, \ldots, x_k\}$ and $D_I = D_{x_1} \times \ldots \times D_{x_k}$ is the domain of inputs. $\mathcal{P}(D_I)$ is the powerset (the set of all subsets) of D_I, and $\boldsymbol{x} = (x_1, \ldots, x_k)$ is the input variable vector. We use small letters (e.g., c) to represent a single valuation of the input vector ($\boldsymbol{x} = c \in D_I$) and capital letters (e.g., C) to show a set of valuations of the input vector ($C \in \mathcal{P}(D_I)$). Symbolic states are labelled with overscored letters (e.g., $\bar{s}, \bar{S}$). The Greek letter φ is used to represent output functions and it is a vector of expressions (i.e., $\varphi \in \bar{\mathcal{E}}(I)$). Given a vector of expressions φ and an input $c \in D_I$, $\varphi[c]$ denotes the output vector with the valuation of each expression for input c: $\varphi[c] = o \in D_O$.

Example. Figure 1a shows the behaviour of our example prepaid card as SRSM $S^*_{PPC} = (\bar{S}, \bar{s}_0, \bar{\delta}_s, \bar{\lambda}_s, I \cup O, D_I \cup D_O)$, where $\bar{S} = \{\bar{s}_0, \bar{s}_1, \bar{s}_2\}$, $\bar{s}_0$ is the initial state, $I = \{a\}$, $D_I = D_a = \mathcal{N}$, $O = \{b\}$, $D_O = D_b = [0, 500]$, $\bar{\delta}_s$, and $\bar{\lambda}_s$ are defined based on the given transitions. (Note that the machine remains in a same state and the outputs will remain unchanged for any input not satisfying the conditions in the labels.)

3.2   Concrete and Symbolic Paths

The behaviour of an SRSM is described in terms of the outputs produced for given inputs, which is formally represented by a set of paths (i.e., sequences of transitions) in the model. In an SRSM model, there are two types of paths, namely *concrete paths* and *symbolic paths*, which are defined below.

Definition 2 (Concrete Path). *In an SRSM $S^* = (\bar{S}, \bar{s}_0, \bar{\delta}, \bar{\lambda}, V, D)$, a concrete path cp is a finite sequence $\bar{s}_0(c_1, \bar{s}_1)(c_2, \bar{s}_2) \ldots (c_k, \bar{s}_k)$ such that $\exists C \in \mathcal{P}(D_I)$ • $\bar{\delta}(\bar{s}_i, C) = \bar{s}_{i+1} \wedge c_{i+1} \in C$, for $1 \leq i \leq k$. $State(cp) = \bar{s}_0 \ldots \bar{s}_k$, $In(cp) = c_1 c_2 \ldots c_k$, and $Out(cp) = o_1 o_2 \ldots o_k$ where $\exists C \in \mathcal{P}(D_I)$ • $\bar{\lambda}(\bar{s}_i, C) = \varphi_{i+1} \wedge c_{i+1} \in C \wedge o_{i+1} = \varphi_{i+1}[c_{i+1}]$, for $0 \leq i < k$. The set of all concrete paths in S^* is denoted by $Path(S^*)$ and for a set of concrete paths CP, $In(CP) = \{In(cp) \mid cp \in CP\}$.*

Definition 3 (Symbolic Path). *In an SRSM $S^* = (\bar{S}, \bar{s}_0, \bar{\delta}, \bar{\lambda}, V, D)$, a symbolic path sp is a finite sequence $\bar{s}_0(C_1, \bar{s}_1)(C_2, \bar{s}_2) \ldots (C_k, \bar{s}_k)$ such that $\bar{\delta}(\bar{s}_i, C_{i+1}) = \bar{s}_{i+1}$, for $1 \leq i \leq k$. $State(sp) = \bar{s}_0 \ldots \bar{s}_k$, $In(sp) = C_1 C_2 \ldots C_k$, and $Out(sp) = \varphi_1 \varphi_2 \ldots \varphi_k$ is the associated sequence of (output) expressions where $\bar{\lambda}(\bar{s}_i, C_{i+1}) = \varphi_{i+1}$, for $0 \leq i < k$. Also, a subpath of sp is a finite sequence $\bar{s}_0(C'_1, \bar{s}_1)(C'_2, \bar{s}_2) \ldots (C'_k, \bar{s}_k)$ such that $C'_i \subseteq C_i$, for $1 \leq i \leq k$. The set of all symbolic paths in S^* is denoted by $SymPath(S^*)$ and for a set of symbolic paths SP, $In(SP)$ is defined as $\{In(sp) \mid sp \in SP\}$.*

Each transition represents a set of concrete transitions and thus, a symbolic path sp specifies a set of concrete paths, called its interpretation.

Definition 4 (Symbolic Path Interpretation). *In an SRSM S^*, the interpretation of a symbolic path $sp = \bar{s}_0(C_1, \bar{s}_1) \ldots (C_n, \bar{s}_n)$, denoted by $[\![sp]\!]$, is the set of concrete paths defined as $\{cp_1, cp_2, \ldots\}$ such that for each cp_i $(i = 1, 2, \ldots)$*

- $State(cp_i) = State(sp)$,
- $In(cp_i) = c_{i,1}c_{i,2}\ldots c_{i,n}$ such that $c_{i,j} \in C_j$, for $j = 1, 2, \ldots, n$
- $Out(cp_i) = \varphi_1[c_{i,1}]\varphi_2[c_{i,2}]\ldots\varphi_n[c_{i,n}]$, where $Out(sp) = \varphi_1\varphi_2\ldots\varphi_n$

A symbolic path can be partitioned into a set of *subpaths* such that these paths do not have any concrete path in common and altogether, they cover all the concrete paths in the main symbolic path.

Definition 5 (Symbolic Path Partitioning). *In an SRSM S^*, a partitioning of a symbolic path $sp = \bar{s}_0(C_1, \bar{s}_1)\ldots(C_n, \bar{s}_n)$, denoted by $Part(sp)$, is a set of subpaths defined as $Part(sp) = \{sp_1, sp_2, \ldots, sp_k\}$ such that*

1. $\forall sp_i, sp_j \in Part(sp) \bullet i \neq j \implies \exists 0 < m \leq n \bullet C_{i,m} \cap C_{j,m} = \emptyset \; (In(sp_l) = C_{l,1}\ldots C_{l,n})$, and
2. $[\![sp]\!] = \bigcup\limits_{p \in Part(sp)} [\![p]\!]$.

3.3   SRSM Models and Conformance

This section defines our notion of behavioural conformance between two SRSMs.

Definition 6 (Conformance). *Assume that S^* and T^* are two SRSMs defined over the same I/O variables. Then, T^* conforms to S^*, denoted by T^* **conf** S^*, if and only if the following two statements hold.*

1. $\forall seq_{in} \in In(Path(S^*)) \; \exists cp \in Path(T^*) \bullet In(cp) = seq_{in}$, and
2. $\forall cp \in Path(T^*) \; (\exists cp' \in Path(S^*) \bullet In(cp) = In(cp')) \implies \exists cp'' \in Path(S^*) \bullet In(cp) = In(cp'') \wedge Out(cp) = Out(cp'')$.

The first statement indicates that all the input sequences defined in the specification should be defined in the IUT. In particular, for non-deterministic behaviour, it indicates that the IUT should at least have one concrete path with the same inputs. Then, the second statement says that for those concrete paths whose inputs are defined in the specification, the IUT should satisfy the specification. The statement also implies that the IUT may have additional behaviour (i.e., sequences of inputs which are not defined in the specification).

The above definition of conformance implies that we need to examine each and every path in $Path(S^*)$ with all paths in $Path(T^*)$ and vice versa in order to detect a non-conformant IUT. However, this is not feasible in most practical contexts (e.g., infinite input domain or a large number of concrete paths). We address this problem by defining conformance in terms of symbolic paths. To do so, we first define two relationships, namely *compatibility* and *containment*, for comparing two symbolic paths with each other. These relations allow determining conformance by comparing symbolic paths rather than concrete paths. Subsequently, we show how checking conformance at the symbolic level can be reduced to checking conformance of a finite number of concrete paths in their interpretation.

Definition 7 (Symbolic Path Compatibility). *A symbolic path sp is compatible with a symbolic path sp', denoted by $sp \prec sp'$, if and only if $In(sp) \sqsubseteq In(sp')$, where for $In(sp) = C_1 C_2 \ldots C_n$ and $In(sp') = C_1' C_2' \ldots C_n'$, $In(sp) \sqsubseteq In(sp')$ holds if and only if $C_i \subseteq C_i'$ for $1 \leq i \leq n$.*

Definition 8. *Two expressions φ and φ' are equivalent over a set of inputs $X \in \mathcal{P}(D_I)$, denoted by $\varphi \overset{X}{\equiv} \varphi'$, if and only if $\forall x \in X \bullet \varphi[x] = \varphi'[x]$. If $X = D_I$, then φ and φ' are equivalent which is denoted by $\varphi \equiv \varphi'$.*

Example. Consider symbolic paths $sp_1 \in SymPath(\mathcal{S}_{PPC}^*)$ and $sp_1' \in SymPath(\mathcal{T}_{PPC}^*)$, defined as follows. sp_1' is not compatible with sp_1 as $In(sp_1') \not\sqsubseteq In(sp_1)$ and therefore $sp_1' \not\prec sp_1$.

$sp_1 = \bar{s}_0 \, (\{a \leq 300\}, \bar{s}_1)(\{a \leq 300\}, \bar{s}_1); In(sp_1) = (\{a \leq 300\})(\{a \leq 300\})$

$sp_1' = \bar{t}_0 \, (\{a \leq 200\}, \bar{t}_0)(\{200 < a \wedge a - b < 300\}, \bar{t}_1); In(sp_1') = (\{a \leq 200\})(\{200 < a \wedge a - b < 300\})$ □

Definition 9 (Symbolic Path Containment). *A symbolic path sp is contained in a symbolic path sp', denoted by $sp \preceq sp'$, if and only if $sp \prec sp' \wedge Out(sp) \equiv Out(sp')$, where for $Out(sp) = \varphi_1 \varphi_2 \ldots \varphi_n$ and $Out(sp') = \varphi_1' \varphi_2' \ldots \varphi_n'$, $Out(sp) \equiv Out(sp)$ holds if and only if $\varphi_i \overset{C_i}{\equiv} \varphi_i'$ for $1 \leq i \leq n$, where $In(sp) = C_1 C_2 \ldots C_n$.*

Herein, the main issue is to find out whether two expressions are equivalent. It is not always possible to evaluate and compare two expressions for all the input values, for example when inputs are infinite. To overcome this issue, we introduce and define *n-uniformity* between two functions (expressions), which is defined w.r.t. the set of inputs on which they are both defined.

Definition 10 (n-Uniformity). *Let $f : D_f \to D_O$ and $g : D_g \to D_O$ be two functions where $D_f, D_g \in \mathcal{P}(D_I)$. Then, f and g are n-uniform over $D_f \cap D_g$, denoted by $f \approx_n g$, if and only if n is the smallest number for which the following statement holds.*

$(\forall 0 \leq i \leq n \, \exists x_i \in D_f \cap D_g \bullet (\forall 0 \leq j \leq n \bullet i \neq j \implies x_i \neq x_j) \wedge f(x_i) = g(x_i)) \implies f \overset{D_f \cap D_g}{\equiv} g.$

The degree of uniformity between f and g is n, if $f \approx_n g$.

Corollary 1. *Let $f : D_f \to D_O$ and $g : D_g \to D_O$ be two functions where $D_f, D_g \in \mathcal{P}(D_I)$ and $f \approx_n g$. Then $n < |D_f \cap D_g|$.*

Accordingly, if the degree of uniformity between output functions in two symbolic paths is determined, it is possible to find out if those paths are compatible or not and this could be done with a finite number of values. This is explained by the following lemma.

Lemma 1. *Let $\mathcal{S}^* = (\bar{S}, \bar{s}_0, \bar{\delta}_s, \bar{\lambda}_s, V, D)$, $\mathcal{T}^* = (\bar{T}, \bar{t}_0, \bar{\delta}_t, \bar{\lambda}_t, V, D)$, $sp \in SymPath(\mathcal{S}^*), sp' \in SymPath(\mathcal{T}^*)$. Then, $sp \preceq sp'$ if and only if*

1. $sp \prec sp'$
2. φ_i and φ'_i, $1 \le i \le n$, produce the same output for $d_i + 1$ distinct input values, where $Out(sp) = \varphi_1 \varphi_2 \ldots \varphi_n$ and $Out(sp') = \varphi'_1 \varphi'_2 \ldots \varphi'_n$ and $\varphi_i \approx_{d_i} \varphi'_i$.

Using the above lemma, for any pair of symbolic paths sp and sp', we can find the minimum number of distinct sequences of inputs required to determine if $sp \preceq sp'$ or not. This number, denoted by $DistDeg(sp, sp')$, can be calculated regarding the n-uniformity between the output functions associated to these paths.

Example. Consider symbolic paths $sp \in SymPath(\mathcal{S}^*_{\mathcal{PPC}})$ and $sp' \in SymPath(\mathcal{T}^*_{\mathcal{PPC}})$. $In(sp') \sqsubseteq In(sp)$ and hence $sp' \prec sp$. The output functions in these models (φ and φ') are polynomials of degree one, therefore $\varphi \approx_1 \varphi'$ and $DistDeg(sp, sp') = 2$: we can determine if $sp' \preceq sp$ with two sequences of inputs.

$sp = \bar{s}_0$ $(\{a \le 300\}, \bar{s}_1)(\{a \le 300\}, \bar{s}_1)$; $In(sp) = (\{a \le 300\})(\{a \le 300\})$, $Out(sp) = \varphi = (b = a)(b = a)$
$sp' = \bar{t}_0$ $(\{a \le 200\}, \bar{t}_0)(\{a \le 200\}, \bar{t}_0)$; $In(sp') = (\{a \le 200\})(\{a \le 200\})$, $Out(sp') = \varphi' = (b = a)(b = a)$ $\qquad\qquad\square$

Although *n-uniformity* is an abstract concept, as the above example suggests, in many practical cases, it can be determined by statically analysing the model/program expressions.

4   Conformance Testing for SRSMs

This section formalises conformance testing in the context of this work and the introduced formal model.

4.1   Test Case and Test Suite

A test case, defined below, specifies a sequence of inputs and their corresponding expected set of outputs according to the specification.

Definition 11 (Test Case and Test Suite).

1. *A test case tc is a tuple* (in_{seq}, out_{seq}), *where*
   - in_{seq} *is a finite sequence of inputs* $c_1 c_2 \ldots c_k$ *such that* $c_i \in D_I$ *for* $1 \le i \le k$, *and*
   - out_{seq} *is a set of finite sequences of outputs* $\{O_1, O_2, \ldots, O_n\}$ *where* $O_i = o_{i,1} \ldots o_{i,k}$ *such that* $o_{i,j} \in D_O$, *for* $1 \le i \le n$ *and* $1 \le j \le k$.
   By definition, $In(tc) = c_1 c_2 \ldots c_k$ *and* $Out(tc) = \{O_1, O_2, \ldots, O_n\}$.
2. *A test suite is a finite set of test cases.*

In the context of this work, test cases are executed to a system, one by one: the inputs are given to the system and the outputs are observed. The comparison of the observed behaviour with the expected behaviour determines the test verdict (pass/fail).

Definition 12 (Test Case Execution). *Execution of a test case tc on an SRSM S^*, denoted by $Exec(tc, S^*)$, gives the sequence of outputs specified by the concrete path $cp \in Path(S^*)$ such that $In(cp) = In(tc)$ and then, $Exec(tc, S^*) = Out(cp)$. If there is no such concrete path the test case is not applicable on the model which is denoted by $Exec(tc, S^*) = \bot$.*

Definition 13 (Test Verdict).

1. *An SRSM S^* passes a test case tc, denoted by $Pass(S^*, tc)$, if and only if it is applicable on S^* and $Exec(tc, S^*) \in Out(tc)$.*
   If S^* does not pass a test case tc, it fails, denoted by $Fail(S^*, tc)$.
2. *An SRSM S^* passes a test suite TS, denoted by $Pass(S^*, TS)$, if and only if $\forall tc \in TS \bullet Pass(S^*, tc)$.*
   If S^* does not pass a test suite TS, it fails, denoted by $Fail(S^*, TS)$.

4.2   Complete Test Suite

An ideal test suite should specify all possible behaviours of a system and its specification. Such a test suite is called *complete*. However, this is not possible in most practical cases. A common and typical approach to address this issue is to restrict the power of a test suite to only detecting conformance or only detecting non-conformance (i.e., soundness and exhaustiveness in [6]).

We define *completeness* in the context of our proposal in that we generate a test suite specifically enriched for testing a particular implementation such that

1. there would be no uncovered symbolic behaviour in any of the models (*coverage*),
2. none of the test cases fails, if the implementation conforms to the specification (*soundness*), and
3. for any non-conformant behaviour in the implementation, there is a specific test case which discovers that behaviour (*relative exhaustiveness*).

Accordingly, a *complete* test suite is the one that satisfies *test coverage*, *soundness*, and *relative exhaustiveness*.

Definition 14 (Test Coverage). *A test suite TS covers an SRSM S^* if and only if $\forall sp \in SymPath(S^*) \; \exists tc \in TS \bullet In(tc) \in In([\![sp]\!])$.*

Definition 15 (Soundness). *A test suite TS is sound w.r.t. an SRSM S^* if and only if $\forall T^* \bullet T^* \; conf \; S^* \implies \forall tc \in TS \bullet Pass(T^*, tc)$.*

Definition 16 (Relative Exhaustiveness). *A test suite TS is exhaustive relative to SRSMs S^*, the reference model, and T^*, the model to be tested, if and only if the following statements hold.*

1. $\forall sp \in SymPath(S^*) \; \forall sp' \in SymPath(T^*) \bullet In([\![sp]\!]) \cap In([\![sp']\!]) \neq \emptyset \implies \exists tc \in TS \bullet In(tc) \in In([\![sp]\!]) \cap In([\![sp']\!])$.
2. $\forall sp \in SymPath(S^*) \; \exists Part(sp) \bullet \exists p \in Part(sp) \bullet In([\![p]\!]) \cap In(Path(T^*)) = \emptyset \implies \exists tc \in TS \bullet In(tc) \in In([\![p]\!]) \wedge Fail(T^*, tc)$.

3. $\forall sp \in SymPath(T^*) \; \exists Part(sp) \bullet \exists p \in Part(sp) \bullet In(\llbracket p \rrbracket) \cap In(Path(S^*)) = \emptyset \implies \exists tc \in TS \bullet In(tc) \in In(\llbracket p \rrbracket).$

In the next section, our proposed testing strategy to generate a complete test suite is presented.

5 Gray-Box Conformance Testing

In this section, we define the *transition composition* of two SRSM models which provides an integrated view of the transitions of both models in one model, regardless of their outputs. We then use this model to generate the target test suite.

5.1 Transition Composition

Intuitively, the transition composition is a (sub-)product of the models in that the transition function is defined based on the intersection of transitions.

Definition 17 (Transition Composition). Let $S^* = (\bar{S}, \bar{s}_0, \bar{\delta}_s, \bar{\lambda}_s, V, D)$ and $T^* = (\bar{T}, \bar{t}_0, \bar{\delta}_t, \bar{\lambda}_t, V, D)$ be two SRSMs with the same I/O variables. $\mathcal{M}^* = (\bar{M}, \bar{m}_0, \bar{\delta}, \emptyset, V, D)$ is the transition composition of S^* and T^*, denoted by $\mathcal{M}^* = trComp(S^*, T^*)$, where

- $\bar{M} \subseteq (\bar{S} \cup \{err_s\}) \times (\bar{T} \cup \{err_t\}),$
- $\bar{m}_0 = (\bar{s}_0, \bar{t}_0),$
- $\forall \bar{m} = (\bar{s}, \bar{t}) \in \bar{M}, C \in \mathcal{P}(D_I) \bullet \bar{s} \in \bar{S} \wedge \bar{t} \in \bar{T} \implies$

$$\bar{\delta}(\bar{m}, C) = \begin{cases} (\bar{s}', \bar{t}') & : \bar{s}' \in \bar{S} \wedge \bar{t}' \in \bar{T} \wedge \exists C', C'' \in \mathcal{P}(D_I) \bullet \bar{\delta}_s(\bar{s}, C') = \bar{s}' \\ & \wedge \bar{\delta}_t(\bar{t}, C'') = \bar{t}' \wedge C' \cap C'' \neq \emptyset \wedge C = C' \cap C'' \\ (\bar{s}', err_t) & : \bar{s}' \in \bar{S} \wedge \exists C' \in \mathcal{P}(D_I) \bullet \bar{\delta}_s(\bar{s}, C') = \bar{s}' \\ & \wedge (\exists C_e \subseteq C' \bullet \forall \bar{t}' \in \bar{T}, C'' \in \mathcal{P}(D_I) \bullet \\ & \bar{\delta}_t(\bar{t}, C'') = \bar{t}' \wedge C_e \cap C'' = \emptyset) \wedge C = C_e \\ (err_s, \bar{t}') & : \bar{t}' \in \bar{T} \wedge \exists C' \in \mathcal{P}(D_I) \bullet \bar{\delta}_t(\bar{t}, C') = \bar{t}' \\ & \wedge (\exists C_e \subseteq C' \bullet \forall \bar{s}' \in \bar{S}, C'' \in \mathcal{P}(D_I) \bullet \\ & \bar{\delta}_s(\bar{s}, C'') = \bar{s}' \wedge C_e \cap C'' = \emptyset) \wedge C = C_e \end{cases}$$

- $\forall \bar{m} = (\bar{s}, err_t) \in \bar{M}, C \in \mathcal{P}(D_I) \bullet \bar{s} \in \bar{S} \implies$
  $\bar{\delta}(\bar{m}, C) = (\bar{s}', err_t)$ if $\bar{s}' \in \bar{S} \wedge \exists C' \in \mathcal{P}(D_I) \bullet \bar{\delta}_s(\bar{s}, C') = \bar{s}' \wedge C = C',$ and
- $\forall \bar{m} = (err_s, \bar{t}) \in \bar{M}, C \in \mathcal{P}(D_I) \bullet \bar{t} \in \bar{T} \implies$
  $\bar{\delta}(\bar{m}, C) = (err_s, \bar{t}')$ if $\bar{t}' \in \bar{T} \wedge \exists C' \in \mathcal{P}(D_I) \bullet \bar{\delta}_t(\bar{t}, C') = \bar{t}' \wedge C = C'.$

In a transition composition, the outgoing transitions on each state are defined based on the intersection of the valid input domains of the transitions of the components. The specific symbols err_s and err_t identify situations in which there is a set of inputs defined in one model but not in the other. Note that we keep tracking states involving err_s and err_t as we do not want to lose any possible transition in any of the models.

Corollary 2. *Let* $\mathcal{S}^* = (\bar{S}, \bar{s}_0, \bar{\delta}_s, \bar{\lambda}_s, V, D)$, $\mathcal{T}^* = (\bar{T}, \bar{t}_0, \bar{\delta}_t, \bar{\lambda}_t, V, D)$, $\mathcal{M}^* = (\bar{M}, \bar{m}_0, \bar{\delta}, \emptyset, V, D)$, *and* $\mathcal{M}^* = crComp(\mathcal{S}^*, \mathcal{T}^*)$. *Then for all* $\bar{m}, \bar{m}' \in \bar{M}$ *and* $C \in \mathcal{P}(D_I)$ *such that* $\bar{\delta}(\bar{m}, C) = \bar{m}'$ *the following two statements hold*

- $\exists \bar{s}, \bar{s}' \in \bar{S}, C' \in \mathcal{P}(D_I)$ • $\bar{m} \in \{\bar{s}\} \times (\bar{T} \cup \{err_t\}) \wedge \bar{m}' \in \{\bar{s}'\} \times (\bar{T} \cup \{err_t\}) \wedge$
  $\bar{\delta}_s(\bar{s}, C') = \bar{s}' \implies C \subseteq C'$
- $\exists \bar{t}, \bar{t}' \in \bar{T}, C' \in \mathcal{P}(D_I)$ • $\bar{m} \in (\bar{S} \cup \{err_s\}) \times \{\bar{t}\} \wedge \bar{m}' \in (\bar{S} \cup \{err_s\}) \times \{\bar{t}'\} \wedge$
  $\bar{\delta}_t(\bar{t}, C') = \bar{t}' \implies C \subseteq C'$

Example. Figure 2 shows a part of the transition composition of the models in Fig. 1a and b.

The transition composition of two SRSM models has two main properties which allow generating a complete test suite. First, according to Definition 18, it covers both of its underlying models (Theorem 1). Second, all the symbolic paths in the transition composition is at least compatible with a symbolic path in one of the underlying models indicating that the transition composition does not have any extra behaviour (Theorem 2).

Definition 18 (Model Coverage). *An SRSM* $\mathcal{S}^*$ *covers an SRSM* $\mathcal{T}^*$ *if and only if* $\forall sp \in SymPath(\mathcal{T}^*) \exists sp' \in SymPath(\mathcal{S}^*)$ • $sp' \prec sp$.

Theorem 1. *Let* $\mathcal{S}^*$ *and* $\mathcal{T}^*$ *be two SRSMs and* $\mathcal{M}^* = trComp(\mathcal{S}^*, \mathcal{T}^*)$. *Then* $\mathcal{M}^*$ *covers* $\mathcal{S}^*$ *and* $\mathcal{T}^*$.

Theorem 2. *Let* $\mathcal{S}^*$ *and* $\mathcal{T}^*$ *be two SRSMs and* $\mathcal{M}^* = trComp(\mathcal{S}^*, \mathcal{T}^*)$. *Then*

- $\forall sp \in SymPath(\mathcal{M}^*)$ • $(\forall \bar{m} \in State(sp)$ • $\bar{m} \in \bar{S} \times (\bar{T} \cup \{err_t\})) \implies$
  $\exists sp' \in SymPath(\mathcal{S}^*)$ • $sp \prec sp'$.
- $\forall sp \in SymPath(\mathcal{M}^*)$ • $(\forall \bar{m} \in State(sp)$ • $\bar{m} \in (\bar{S} \cup \{err_s\}) \times \bar{T}) \implies$
  $\exists sp' \in SymPath(\mathcal{T}^*)$ • $sp \prec sp'$.

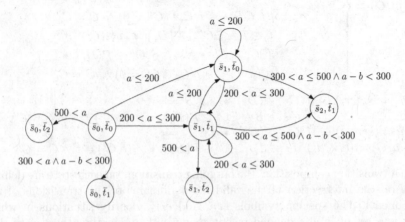

Fig. 2. An excerpt of the transition composition of $\mathcal{S}^*_{\mathcal{PPC}}$ and $\mathcal{T}^*_{\mathcal{PPC}}$.

5.2 Test Suite Generation

Having defined the transition composition of two SRSMs, we next generate a complete test suite. First, we define the test cases for each symbolic path in the transition composition, which are then accumulated in the final and complete test suite.

Definition 19. *Let S^* be the specification model, T^* be the implementation model, and $M^* = trComp(S^*, T^*)$ be the transition composition. For each $sp \in SymPath(M^*)$, $TC(sp)$ is a set of test cases to examine the compatibility between the two symbolic paths in T^* and S^* in which sp is contained, and defined as follows.*

1. *If there exists $sp' \in SymPath(S^*)$ and $sp'' \in SymPath(T^*)$ such that $sp \prec sp'$ and $sp \prec sp''$, then $TC(sp)$ is a set of test cases $\{tc_1, \ldots, tc_k\}$, where $k = DistDeg(sp', sp'')$, such that $In(tc_i) \subseteq In(\llbracket sp \rrbracket)$ and $Out(tc_i)$ is determined the output(s) produced by S^* for $In(tc_i)$, $1 \leq i \leq k$.*
2. *If there exists $sp' \in SymPath(S^*)$ such that $sp \prec sp'$ and there is no $sp'' \in SymPath(T^*)$ such that $sp \prec sp''$, then $TC(sp)$ contains only one test case tc such that $In(tc) \subseteq In(\llbracket sp \rrbracket)$ and $Out(tc)$ is the output(s) produced by S^* for $In(tc)$.*
3. *If there exists $sp' \in SymPath(T^*)$ such that $sp \prec sp'$ and there is no $sp'' \in SymPath(S^*)$ such that $sp \prec sp''$, then $TC(sp)$ contains only one test case tc such that $In(tc) \subseteq In(\llbracket sp \rrbracket)$ and $Out(tc) = \bot$ (i.e., undefined). Note that such a test case observes the behaviours not specified in the specification.*

Definition 20 (Composition-based Test Suite). *Given the specification model S^*, the implementation model T^*, and their transition composition M^*, a composition-based test suite, denoted by $C_{omp}TS(S^*, T^*)$, is defined as follows.*

$$C_{omp}TS(S^*, T^*) = \bigcup_{sp \in SymPath(M^*)} TC(sp)$$

The following theorem demonstrates that a composition-based test suite satisfies test coverage, soundness and exhaustiveness properties.

Theorem 3. *Let S^* be the specification model, T^* be the implementation model, and $M^* = trComp(S^*, T^*)$. Then, $C_{omp}TS(S^*, T^*)$ is a sound and exhaustive test suite and covers S^* and T^*.*

6 Experimental Results

In order to check the effectiveness of our approach, we use our method in the context of a well-known example from the *European Train Control System (ETCS)*, namely the *Ceiling Speed Monitor (CSM)* module which monitors the speed of a train and triggers the required actions if the maximal speed is exceeded. A complete description of the system can be found in [17]. We applied our method in testing six different (faulty) implementations of the CSM module and compared the outcomes with random testing and the equivalence class testing introduced in [16]. Implementations are mutants of a correct implementation of the CSM module. In the first implementation (IUT_1) the faults are related to boundary values (e.g., $<$ replaced by $\leq$). In the next four implementations (IUT_2, IUT_3, IUT_4, and IUT_5), the faults are in the guard condition, but they are not related to boundary values. Moreover, in IUT_4 and IUT_5, the difference between the sets of inputs defined by the correct condition and the wrong condition is too narrow (i.e., for limited number of input values the difference could be discovered). The last implementation (IUT_6) contains a fault in an output function associated to one of the transitions.

In the experiment, we mainly investigated the question whether our method observed the faults or not. We also considered the number of test cases generated by each method. Additionally, in order to have an approximation of the overhead associated with our method, we considered the time required to generate the transition composition. This time is computed based on the number of basic computation steps in generating the composition (assuming that all steps consume a constant amount of time, this time is proportional to the number of steps).

In random testing, test cases are created by generating random values in the appropriate data ranges. For equivalence class testing, we considered a refinement of the initial coarsest input equivalence class partitioning (IECP) that reflects all case distinctions visible in guard conditions of the CSM model, which implies the fault model for this testing method. Note that the number of test cases generated by IECP is the same for all the six cases. We used the test data provided in [18], for the number of generated test cases by IECP. For random testing, in each case, a random test suite of the same length as our method's, was selected and used for comparison.

Table 1 summarises the results of this experiment. Basically, the results show that our method performs better than random testing with the same number of test cases. They also show that in cases the behaviour of the IUT lies outside the fault domain of the IECP testing, in particular when the input equivalence classes are narrow, our approach performs better than IECP. This is because, in such cases, the desired input values have very low probabilities to be chosen. Therefore, in both random testing and IECP, an increase in the number of test cases has limited effect on their testing strength. The IECP testing could not kill IUT_4 and IUT_5 which are outside its fault domain and have narrow equivalence classes. IUT_2 and IUT_3 are both out of the fault domain and the set of inputs to discover their faults is not narrow (i.e., a proper input values could be chosen by random input selection). However, only IUT_3 was killed by IECP. Finally, the time required to generate the transition composition and the number of test cases could be an indication of the efficiency of our method.

Nevertheless, this experiment provides a preliminary result. In particular, having treated only one type of case study is a threat to the validity of our results. To remedy this, we plan to carry out more testing experiments considering different kinds of cases. To address the efficiency and scalability question

Table 1. Experimental results

IUT	Random Testing		IECP		Our Method		
	Killed	No. TCs	Killed	No. TCs	Killed	No. TCs	No. steps
1	✗	24	✓	186	✓	24	18
2	✗	30	✗	186	✓	30	19
3	✗	25	✓	186	✓	25	19
4	✗	37	✗	186	✓	37	22
5	✗	24	✗	186	✓	24	21
6	✓	21	✓	186	✓	21	16

more thoroughly, in addition to more case studies, we need to collect additional information from other methods to have a valid comparison between methods, such as the time required to transform the original test model into the desired formalism.

7   Conclusions and Future Work

In this paper, we presented a gray-box model-based testing strategy in that test suites are generated considering both the specification and an abstraction of the IUT. Specifications and implementations abstraction are modelled as *Symbolic Reactive State Machines (SRSMs)*, which are finite state machines with symbolic input and output. Given the SRSMs of a specification and an IUT, test cases are generated based on the *transition composition* of these models. We considered models with infinite input domain and then introduced the notion of *n-uniformity* which allows us confining the number of test cases for each symbolic path. We studied and proved coverage, soundness, and relative exhaustiveness of the proposed approach.

As for future work, we plan to roll out more testing experiments to investigate the applicability of the proposed strategy (in particular, the notion of *n-uniformity*) in different situations and discover its limitations. Moreover, we plan to study models with infinite set of symbolic paths and, then, how to select a finite subset of paths sufficient to generate a complete test suite, according to the regularity hypothesis [3]. Finally, we would like to work on efficient algorithms for generating the *transition composition* (e.g., adapting bi-simulation algorithms) and also for determining *n-uniformity*.

Acknowledgements. This work was partially supported by ELLIIT, the strategic research area funded by Swedish government. The work of M.R. Mousavi has also been supported by the Swedish Research Council (Vetenskapsrådet) with award number 621-2014-5057, and the Swedish Knowledge Foundation in the context of the AUTO-CAAS project.

References

1. Walkinshaw, N., Taylor, R., Derrick, J.: Inferring extended finite state machine models from software executions. Empir. Software Eng. **21**, 811–853 (2016)
2. Cassel, S., Howar, F., Jonsson, B., Steffen, B.: Active learning for extended finite state machines. Formal Asp. Comput. **28**(2), 233–263 (2016)
3. Gaudel, M.-C.: Testing can be formal, too. In: Mosses, P.D., Nielsen, M., Schwartzbach, M.I. (eds.) CAAP 1995. LNCS, vol. 915, pp. 82–96. Springer, Heidelberg (1995). doi:10.1007/3-540-59293-8_188
4. Chow, T.S.: Testing software design modeled by finite-state machines. IEEE TSE **4**(3), 178–187 (1978)
5. Petrenko, A., von Bochmann, G., Yao, M.Y.: On fault coverage of tests for finite state specifications. Comput. Networks ISDN Syst. **29**(1), 81–106 (1996)
6. Tretmans, J.: Model based testing with labelled transition systems. In: Hierons, R.M., Bowen, J.P., Harman, M. (eds.) Formal Methods and Testing. LNCS, vol. 4949, pp. 1–38. Springer, Heidelberg (2008). doi:10.1007/978-3-540-78917-8_1
7. Petrenko, A., Yevtushenko, N., Bochmann, G.: Fault models for testing in context. In: Gotzhein, R., Bredereke, J. (eds.) Formal Description Techniques IX. IFIP AICT, pp. 163–178. Springer, Boston (1996)
8. Kicillof, N., Grieskamp, W., Tillmann, N., Braberman, V.: Achieving both model and code coverage with automated gray-box testing. In: A-MOST 2007, pp. 1–11. ACM (2007)
9. Giantamidis, G., Tripakis, S.: Learning Moore machines from input-output traces. In: Fitzgerald, J., Heitmeyer, C., Gnesi, S., Philippou, A. (eds.) FM 2016. LNCS, vol. 9995, pp. 291–309. Springer, Cham (2016). doi:10.1007/978-3-319-48989-6_18
10. Lee, C., Chen, F., Rosu, G.: Mining parametric specifications. In: ICSE 2011, pp. 591–600. ACM (2011)
11. Ernst, M.D., Cockrell, J., Griswold, W.G., Notkin, D.: Dynamically discovering likely program invariants to support program evolution. IEEE TSE **27**(2), 99–123 (2001)
12. Grieskamp, W., Tillmann, N., Campbell, C., Schulte, W., Veanes, M.: Action machines - towards a framework for model composition, exploration and conformance testing based on symbolic computation. In: QSIC 2005, pp. 72–29. IEEE (2006)
13. Frantzen, L., Tretmans, J., Willemse, T.A.C.: A symbolic framework for model-based testing. In: Havelund, K., Núñez, M., Roşu, G., Wolff, B. (eds.) FATES/RV-2006. LNCS, vol. 4262, pp. 40–54. Springer, Heidelberg (2006). doi:10.1007/11940197_3
14. Petrenko, A., Simao, A.: Checking experiments for finite state machines with symbolic inputs. In: El-Fakih, K., Barlas, G., Yevtushenko, N. (eds.) ICTSS 2015. LNCS, vol. 9447, pp. 3–18. Springer, Cham (2015). doi:10.1007/978-3-319-25945-1_1
15. Petrenko, A.: Checking experiments for symbolic input/output finite state machines. In: IEEE ICSTW 2016, pp. 229–237 (2016)
16. Huang, W.-L., Peleska, J.: Complete model-based equivalence class testing. Int. J. Softw. Tools Technol. Transf. **18**(3), 262–283 (2016)
17. Braunstein, C., Peleska, J., Schulze, U., Hübner, F., Huang, W., Haxthausen, A., Vu, H.L.: A SysML test model and test suite for the ETCS ceiling speed monitor: Technical report, Work Package 4. Technical University of Denmark (2014)

18. Hübner, F., Huang, W., Peleska, J.: Experimental evaluation of a novel equivalence class partition testing strategy. In: Blanchette, J.C., Kosmatov, N. (eds.) TAP 2015. LNCS, vol. 9154, pp. 155–172. Springer, Cham (2015). doi:10.1007/978-3-319-21215-9_10

Model Checking of Concurrent Software Systems via Heuristic-Guided SAT Solving

Nils Timm[✉], Stefan Gruner, and Prince Sibanda

Department of Computer Science, University of Pretoria, Pretoria, South Africa
{ntimm,sgruner}@cs.up.ac.za

Abstract. An established approach to software verification is SAT-based bounded model checking where a state space model is encoded as a Boolean formula and the exploration is performed via SAT solving. Most existing approaches in SAT-based model checking rely on general-purpose solvers that do not exploit the structural features of the encoding. Aiming at a significantly better runtime performance in such settings, we show in this paper that SAT algorithms can be specifically tailored w.r.t. the structure of the Boolean encoding of the model checking problem to be solved. We define a state space encoding of concurrent software systems that preserves control flow information. This allows to modify the solver such that the number of SAT decision levels can be significantly reduced by assigning a set of atoms at each level. Such set assignment always characterises a location in the control flow of the encoded system. Moreover, we introduce heuristics that guide the SAT search into directions where a violation of the property of interest may be most likely detected. The heuristic approach enables to quickly discover errors while keeping the actually explored part of the state space small.

1 Introduction: Motivation and Related Work

In SAT-based bounded model checking (BMC) [1] the state space of a system to be verified is encoded as a propositional logic formula, and the state space exploration happens via satisfiability (SAT) solving. Thereby, each satisfying assignment of the formula characterises an error path, whereas an unsatisfiability result implies the correctness of the system under consideration. The advantage of BMC in comparison to explicit-state approaches is that the encoding yields a more compact symbolic state space representation, and that the capability of efficient solvers can be exploited to solve the encoded verification tasks. In BMC most existing approaches rely on general-purpose solvers that do not exploit the specific structure of the propositional logic encoding or any other available knowledge about the underlying verification task. In this paper we show that SAT algorithms can be specifically tailored towards solving encodings of verification tasks, which enables a significantly better solving performance. Here we focus on the verification of reachability properties (e.g. deadlocks, mutual exclusion violation) of concurrent software systems. We define a propositional logic state space encoding that can be directly constructed for a given input

Published by Springer International Publishing AG 2017. All Rights Reserved
M. Dastani and M. Sirjani (Eds.): FSEN 2017, LNCS 10522, pp. 244–259, 2017.
DOI: 10.1007/978-3-319-68972-2_16

system. The encoding preserves control flow information that can be utilised to accelerate the SAT solving procedure. SAT solving algorithms are typically based on a systematic search for a satisfying assignment of the input formula by incrementally selecting an unassigned atom, assigning it by either 1 or 0, and propagating the resulting constraints to all clauses of the formula. In case the solver's decisions lead to an unsatisfied sub formula, the solver tracks back to a previous decision level and continues its search from that point in a different branch of the search tree until a satisfying assignment is found or until the search tree is exhaustively explored [2]. We introduce an enhanced SAT algorithm that exploits the structure of our encodings in order to reduce the computational effort for solving the encoded verification task. In our approach the *number of decision levels* can be significantly narrowed down by instantiating a *set* of atoms at each level. Such a set instantiation always characterises a location in the control flow of the encoded system. Based on a simple query on whether such location is an *admissible successor location* of the current location, the *number of branches* that actually have to be explored can considerably reduced. Moreover, we show that the additional employment of heuristic guidance allows for a further enhancement of the solving performance. For this, we adapt the concept of *directed model checking* [5] which had been introduced for the exploration of explicit-state models, but was not yet considered for SAT-based model checking. We demonstrate that heuristics based on the property to be verified allow to guide the SAT search into directions where a property violation may be most likely detected. We prototypically implemented our encoding and our enhanced SAT approach with *set assignments* and *heuristic guidance* on top of the solver Sat4J [6]. Preliminary experiments show promising performance results.

Our technique is related to a number of existing approaches. In [8] we find an overview of principles of using SAT solvers as model checkers, including atom ordering strategies. It is assumed that the encoding is constructed based on an already given state space model – *not* based directly on the system to be verified. In [9] an algorithm is given to predict a beneficial ordering of the atoms before the SAT search descends into the tree. Performance improvement is achieved by knowing the *unsatisfiable core* of the $(b-1)$-bounded encoding which the solver explored in a previous iteration of incremental BMC [9]. A survey of *directed model checking* can be found in [5]. The focus in [5] is on the algorithmic techniques directed model checking approaches, including a classification of such techniques into categories like guided search, explicit-state directed model checking, and directed model checking based on binary decision diagrams. However, no approach for a directed search in SAT-based BMC is proposed. In [4] a heuristic-guided tool based on the model checker SPIN is described. The used heuristics are tuned w.r.t specific characteristics of SPIN's input language PROMELA. Thus, the directed state space exploration algorithm assumes an explicit state space model rather than a symbolic encoding. SAT-based model checking of *concurrent* systems is also the topic of [10] which is based on the insight that concurrent executions cannot drive arbitrary values through the system, and thus it is not necessary to encode how the computation operates on all values, but rather just on the values that actually arise in such executions. On the basis of an *event graph* representation of the systems behaviour a SAT problem is constructed and solved in an iterative process of modelling, solving, and re-modelling. The idea of this approach is to use the solver to encode the execution, not the system. *Conflict-directed clause learning* (CDCL) is the topic of [11] which deals with the question of how to design a predictive measure of learnt clauses pertinence. The authors were able to show the relationship between the overall decreasing of decision levels and the performance of the solver. Thereby, a good learning schema should add explicit links between independent blocks of propagated literals, which should be beneficial for reducing the number of decision levels in the remaining computation. In our work we reduce the number of decision levels based on semantic dependencies of the literals (control flow information). In [13] a heuristic improvement of the Java PathFinder is described: To find errors faster, it is important to explore parts of the state space whose possibility of containing errors is higher than others, whereby heuristic techniques prioritise potential solution candidates according to particular efficiency considerations. The authors propose a depth-first search which can be applied to verification of LTL properties of Java bytecode. With regard to heuristic model checking, the authors of [12] evaluated the resulting search behaviour on a number of models from the BEEM database within the HSF-SPIN explicit-state model checker. The technique of [12] applies a distance function to estimate the distance from a given state to an error state, and explores states with the shortest estimated distance first. Guided by the distance function, error paths can often be found after exploring only a small part of the overall state space.

2   Concurrent Software Systems

We start with an introduction to the systems we consider. A concurrent software system *Sys* consists of a fixed number of possibly non-uniform processes $P_1 \parallel \ldots \parallel P_n$, in parallel composition. Inter-process communication is assumed to happen via global variables in shared memory. In $Var = Var_s \cup \bigcup_{i=1}^{n} Var_i$ the set Var_s contains the shared variables whereas $Var_1 \ldots Var_n$ are sets of local variables associated exclusively with the processes $P_1 \ldots P_n$. Moreover, we assume that *Boolean predicate abstraction* [3] has been applied, which results in a system where all variables are *Boolean* variables, or more specifically, replaced by Boolean predicates over the original variables. Hence, in our approach variables and predicates are synonymous. Predicate abstraction is a well-established technique in software model checking to reduce the state space complexity of a verification task. In our approach we use the tool 3Spot [14] to transfer a concrete input system into an abstract system defined over predicates. 3Spot formally represents (abstracted) processes P_i as *control flow graphs* (CFGs) $G_i = (Loc_i, \delta_i, \tau_i)$ where $Loc_i = \{0, \ldots, |Loc_i|\}$ is a finite set of control locations given as binary numbers, $\delta_i \subseteq Loc_i \times Loc_i$ is a location transition relation, and $\tau_i : Loc_i \times Loc_i \to Op$ is a function labelling location transitions with operations from a set Op. The *set of operations Op* on the variables form $Var = \{v_1, \ldots, v_m\}$ consists of all statements of the form $assume(e) : v_1 := e_1, \ldots, v_m := e_m$ in which

$e, e_1, \ldots, e_m$ are Boolean expressions over Var. Thus every operation consists of a guard and a list of assignments. For convenience we sometimes just write e instead of $assume(e)$. Moreover, we omit the guard if it is just $true$.

A concurrent software system given by n single control flow graphs $G_1, \ldots, G_n$ can be modelled by one compound control flow graph $G = (Loc, \delta, \tau)$ where $Loc = Loc_1 \times \cdots \times Loc_n$, $\delta \subseteq Loc \times Loc$ and $\tau : Loc \times Loc \to Op$. G is the product graph of all single CFGs. We assume that initially all processes of a system at location 0. Moreover, we assume that a deterministic initialisation of the variables is given by an assertion over Var. Now, a computation of a concurrent system corresponds to a sequence where in each step one process is non-deterministically selected and the operation at its current location is attempted to be executed. In case the execution is not blocked by the guard, the variables are updated according to the assignment part, and the process advances to the consequent control location. Note that a CFG is a formal representation of a system but not a state space model. The state space over Var corresponds to the set S_{Var} of all type-correct valuations of the variables. Given a state $s \in S_{Var}$ and an expression e over Var, then $s(e)$ denotes the valuation of e in s. The overall state space S of a concurrent system corresponds to the set of states over Var combined with the possible locations, i.e.: $S = Loc \times S_{Var}$. Thus each state in S is a tuple $\langle l, s \rangle$ with $l = (l_1, \ldots, l_n) \in Loc$ and $s \in S_{Var}$. An example for a system where each process is represented by a control flow graph is shown in Fig. 1. We represent the truth value t by $\mathbf{1}$, and f by $\mathbf{0}$. In the example we have two uniform processes operating on the shared Boolean variables p and q. The initial state of the system is $\langle (00, 00), p = \mathbf{1}, q = \mathbf{1} \rangle$. The system implements a solution to the dining philosophers problem where each philosopher process continuously attempts to acquire the two exclusive resources p and q. Once a process has acquired both resources it releases them in a single step and attempts to acquire them again. The order in which the resources are requested is non-deterministically determined, which makes as deadlock possible: G_1 has acquired p and is waiting for q while G_2 has acquired q and is waiting for p.

CFGs allow us to model the *control flow* of a concurrent system. Checking properties of a system requires to explore a corresponding *state space* model. Typically, *Kripke structures* are used as state space models. A *Kripke structure* (KS) over a set of atomic predicates AP is a tuple $M = (S, s_0, R, L)$ where

- S is a finite set of states and $s_0 \in S$ is the initial state,
- $R \subseteq S \times S$ is a state transition relation with $\forall s \in S : \exists s' \in S : R(s, s')$,
- $L : S \times AP \to \{\mathbf{1}, \mathbf{0}\}$ is a labelling function that associates a truth value with each predicate in each state.

A path π of a KS M is a sequence of states $s_0 s_1 s_2 \ldots$ with $R(s_i, s_{i+1})$. π_i denotes the i-th state of π, whereas π^i denotes the i-th suffix $\pi_i \pi_{i+1} \ldots$ of π. By Π_M we denote the set of all paths of M starting in the initial state. All paths of a KS have to be explored in order to determine whether certain error states are reachable. Let $p \in AP$ be a predicate that characterises error states. Then an error state is reachable in M if and only if $\bigvee_{\pi \in \Pi_M} \bigvee_{i \in \mathbb{N}} L(\pi_i, p)$ holds.

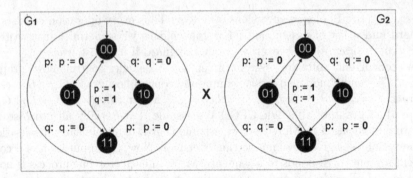

Fig. 1. Concurrent system over the Boolean variables $Var = \{p, q\}$ given by the single control flow graphs G_1 and G_2, whereby initially $p = 1$ and $q = 1$.

Verifying such conditions for a given KS is known as *model checking*. As defined in [14] a concurrent system $Sys = \|_{i=1}^{n} P_i$ given by a set of CFGs G_1 to G_n can be translated into a KS M over $AP = Var \cup \{(l_i = j) \mid i \in [1..n], \ j \in Loc_i\}$ where the predicate $(l_i = j)$ denotes that the process P_i is currently at control location j. The number of states of a KS corresponding to a given system is exponential in the number of its locations and variables. For instance, a KS corresponding to our simple example system has already 64 states. State space explosion is the major challenge in model checking. Beside the aforementioned predicate abstraction, a common approach to cope with state space explosion is to use a symbolic and therefore more compact representation of the KS. In SAT-based bounded model checking [1] all possible path prefixes up to a bound $b \in \mathbb{N}$ are encoded in a propositional logic formula $Init_0 \wedge T_{0,1} \wedge \ldots \wedge T_{b-1,b}$. The formula is then conjuncted with an encoding $Error_b$ of the error property to be checked. In case the overall formula is satisfiable, the satisfying assignment characterises an error path of length b in the state space of the encoded system. Next, we define such a propositional logic encoding for concurrent systems given by abstract control flow graphs and for errors that can be expressed as reachability properties.

3   Propositional Logic Encoding

We now describe how a propositional logic encoding $Init_0 \wedge T_{0,1} \wedge \ldots \wedge T_{b-1,b} \wedge Error_b$ can be directly constructed for a concurrent system given by control flow graphs $G_i = (Loc_i, \delta_i, \tau_i)$, $1 \leq i \leq n$ and for a given error property with $b \in \mathbb{N}$ being the *bound* of the encoding. This saves us the expensive construction of an explicit state space model. The encoding is defined over Boolean atoms. Since a state of a system is a tuple $\langle l, s \rangle$ where $l \in Loc$ is a compound location and s is a valuation of all Boolean variables in Var, we encode l and s separately.

A composite location $(l_1, \ldots, l_n) \in Loc$ is a list of single locations $l_i \in Loc_i$ where $Loc_i = \{0, \ldots, |Loc_i|\}$ and i is the identifier of the associated process P_i. Each l_i is a binary number from $\{[0]_2, \ldots, [|Loc_i|]_2\}$. We assume that all these numbers have d_i digits where d_i is the number required to binary represent the max. value $|Loc_i|$. Then, for each P_i, we introduce d_i Boolean atoms, each of which refers to a distinct digit along the binary representation of its locations: $LocAtoms := \{l_i[j] \mid i \in [1..n], \ j \in [1..d_i]\}$. Then l_i can be encoded as:

$$enc(l_i) := \bigwedge_{j=1}^{d_i} ((l_i[j] \wedge l_i(j)) \vee (\neg l_i[j] \wedge \neg l_i(j)))$$

where $l_i(j)$ is a function evaluating to 1 if the j-th digit of l_i is 1, and to 0 otherwise. A composite location $l = (l_1, \ldots, l_n)$ can subsequently be encoded as:

$$enc(l) := \bigwedge_{i=1}^{n} enc(l_i)$$

Because the function $l_i(j)$ evaluates to 1 or 0, a location encoding $enc(l_i)$ can be always simplified to a conjunction of literals over $LocAtoms$. In our example the initial location $(00, 00)$ will be encoded to $\neg l_1[1] \wedge \neg l_1[2] \wedge \neg l_2[1] \wedge \neg l_2[2]$.

Next we encode the variable (resp. predicate) part of states. For $s \in S_{Var}$, where $Var = \{v_1, \ldots, v_m\}$ is the set of Boolean variables over which the concurrent system is defined, we introduce $VarAtoms := \{v[j] \mid v_j \in Var\}$. Hence, each variable v_i is encoded by an atom $v[i]$, which allows a straightforward encoding of arbitrary logical expressions e over Var. For instance, $enc(v_1 \wedge \neg v_2) := v[1] \wedge \neg v[2]$. The initial state $\langle (00, 00), p = 1, q = 1 \rangle$ of our example system can now be encoded as $Init = \neg l_1[1] \wedge \neg l_1[2] \wedge \neg l_2[1] \wedge \neg l_2[2] \wedge p \wedge q$. Since in our simple example the variables p and q are not subscripted, we also omit the index values for the identically named atoms p and q.

For encoding the transition relation of a concurrent system we construct a formula $Init_0 \wedge T_{0,1} \wedge \ldots \wedge T_{b-1,b}$ that exactly characterises path prefixes of length $b \in \mathbb{N}$ in the systems state space. Because we consider states as parts of such prefixes, we have to extend the encoding by index values $k \in \{0, \ldots, b\}$ where k denotes the position along a path prefix. For this we introduce the notion of *indexed* encodings. Let F be a propositional logic formula over $Atoms = LocAtoms \cup PredAtoms$ and the constants 1 and 0. Then F_k abbreviates the substitution $F[a/a_k \mid a \in Atoms]$. Our overall encoding will be thus defined over $Atoms_{[0,b]} = \{a_k \mid a \in Atoms, 0 \leq k \leq b\}$. Since all execution paths start in the system's initial state, we extend the initial state encoding by the index 0: $Init_0 = \neg l_1[1]_0 \wedge \neg l_1[2]_0 \wedge \neg l_2[1]_0 \wedge \neg l_2[2]_0 \wedge p_0 \wedge q_0$. The encoding of all possible state space transitions from position k to $k+1$ is defined as follows. Let $Sys = \|_{i=1}^{n} P_i$ over Var be a concurrent system given by the single control flow graphs $G_i = (Loc_i, \delta_i, \tau_i)$ with $1 \leq i \leq n$. Then all possible transitions for position k to $k+1$ can be encoded in propositional logic as follows:

$$T_{k,k+1} := \bigvee_{i=1}^{n} \bigvee_{(l_i, l_i') \in \delta_i} (enc(l_i)_k \wedge enc(l_i')_{k+1} \wedge \bigwedge_{i' \neq i} idle(i')_{k,k+1} \wedge enc(\tau_i(l_i, l_i'))_{k,k+1})$$

where $idle(i')_{k,k+1} := \bigwedge_{j=1}^{d_{i'}} (l_{i'}[j]_k \leftrightarrow l_{i'}[j]_{k+1})$

and $enc(\tau_i(l_i, l_i'))_{k,k+1} := enc(e)_k \wedge \bigwedge_{j=1}^{m} ((enc(e_j)_k \leftrightarrow enc(v_j)_{k+1})$

assuming that $\tau_i(l_i, l_i') = assume(e) : v_1 := e_1, \ldots, v_m := e_m$.

Thus, we iterate over the system's processes P_i and over the processes' control flow transitions $\delta_i(l_i, l_i')$. Now we construct the k-indexed encoding of a source location l_i and conjunct it with the $(k + 1)$-indexed encoding of a destination location l_i'. This gets conjuncted with the sub formula $\bigwedge_{i' \neq i} idle(i')_{k,k+1}$ which encodes that all processes different to P_i are idle, i.e. do not change their control flow location, while P_i proceeds. The last part of the transition encoding concerns the operation associated with $\delta_i(l_i, l_i')$: The sub formula $enc(\tau_i(l_i, l_i'))_{k,k+1}$ evaluates to $\mathbf{1}$ for assignments to the atoms in $Atoms_{[k,k+1]}$ that characterise pairs of states s and s' over Var where the guard of the operation $\tau_i(l_i, l_i')$ is $\mathbf{1}$ in s and the execution of the operation in s results in the state s'. Otherwise $enc(\tau_i(l_i, l_i'))_{k,k+1}$ evaluates to $\mathbf{0}$. Our transition encoding requires that an operation $\tau_i(l_i, l_i')$ assigns to all Boolean variables. Thus, if a $v \in Var$ is not modified by the operation we implicitly assume that $v := v$ is part of the assignment list. The encoding of the control flow transition $\delta_1(00, 01)$ of our example system with $\tau_1(00, 01) = (assume(p) : p := \mathbf{0})$ yields the following:

$$
\begin{array}{ll}
enc(00)_k & = \neg l_1[1]_k \wedge \neg l_1[2]_k \\
\wedge & \wedge \\
enc(01)_{k+1} & = l_1[1]_{k+1} \wedge l_1[2]_{k+1} \\
\wedge & \wedge \\
idle(2)_{k,k+1} & = (l_2[1]_k \leftrightarrow l_2[1]_{k+1}) \wedge (l_2[2]_k \leftrightarrow l_2[2]_{k+1}) \\
\wedge & \wedge \\
enc(\tau_1(0, 1))_{k,k+1} & = p_k \wedge ((\mathbf{0} \leftrightarrow p_{k+1}) \wedge (q_k \leftrightarrow q_{k+1}))
\end{array}
$$

The encoding of the operation only evaluates to $\mathbf{1}$ for assignments to the atoms in $Atoms_{[k,k+1]}$ that characterise the control flow transition $\delta_1(00, 01)$ with idling G_2, the variable state s at position k with $s(p) = \mathbf{1}$ and a state s' at $k + 1$ with $s'(p) = \mathbf{0}$, and moreover, $s(q) = s'(q)$. All other assignments yield $false$ indicating that corresponding pairs of states do not characterise valid transitions.

The previous definitions now allow us to construct a formula $Init_0 \wedge T_{0,1} \wedge \ldots \wedge T_{b-1,b}$ that characterises all possible path prefixes of length $b \in \mathbb{N}$ in the state space of the encoded system. Each assignment $\alpha : Atoms_{[0,b]} \to \{\mathbf{1}, \mathbf{0}\}$ that satisfies the formula characterises such a prefix. Next, we introduce the encoding of the property to be checked for the concurrent system. In general, want to verify whether a state is reachable that satisfies a particular predicate. Such a predicate can be an arbitrary Boolean expression over Loc and Var. For our example system, a $deadlock$ circular-wait situation can be described by

$$((l_1 = 01) \wedge \neg q \wedge (l_2 = 10) \wedge \neg p) \vee ((l_1 = 10) \wedge \neg p \wedge (l_2 = 01) \wedge \neg q)$$

which can be straightforwardly encoded into a propositional logic formula

$$
\begin{array}{l}
Error := (\neg l_1[1] \wedge l_1[2] \wedge \neg q \wedge l_2[1] \wedge \neg l_2[2] \wedge \neg p) \\
\quad \vee (l_1[1] \wedge \neg l_1[2] \wedge \neg p \wedge \neg l_2[1] \wedge l_2[2] \wedge \neg q)
\end{array}
$$

over Boolean atoms. Finally we index such an *Error* formula with a search-bound $b \in \mathbb{N}$ and conjunct it with our system's state space encoding, yielding $F_{[0,b]} := Init_0 \wedge T_{0,1} \wedge \ldots \wedge T_{b-1,b} \wedge Error_b$, such that each assignment satisfying this formula witnesses a path prefix of length b ending in an error state in the state space of the encoded system. Hence the propositional logic encoding allows us to model check a system of interest via SAT solving, without the intermediate construction of an explicit Kripke structure. SAT-based BMC is typically performed incrementally by increasing the bound b until an error state or a threshold is reached. State-of-the-art SAT solvers e.g. [6] can be used for the satisfiability checks. In the remainder of this paper we introduce our enhanced SAT solving concepts that are tailored towards solving our propositional logic encodings of verification tasks for concurrent systems. For the sake of illustration, we present our approach based on a simple SAT solving algorithm that implements our enhanced concepts but not all features of modern solvers like conflict-driven clause learning [2], conflict clause minimisation [16] etc. Nevertheless, our concepts can be straightforwardly integrated into any state-of-the-art solver and combined with the advancements used in such solvers. For instance, our tool that we later present is implemented on top of the solver Sat4J [6].

4 Enhanced SAT Solving for Encoded Verification Tasks

Modern SAT solvers are based on a systematic search for a satisfying assignment of the input formula in conjunctive normal form (CNF) by incrementally selecting unassigned atoms, assigning them by either **1** or **0**, and propagating the resulting constraints to the clauses of the formula. In case the solver decisions lead to an unsatisfied clause, the solver tracks back by revising a former assignment decision and continuing the search from this point until a satisfying assignment is found or the search space is entirely explored [2]. While general-purpose solvers do not make any assumption about the structure of the input formula, our enhanced SAT solving approach exploits the structure of our encoding $F_{[0,b]}$ and control flow information about the considered concurrent system. We will see that this enables us to reduce the number of recursive calls of the SAT algorithm. We reduce both the number of decision levels as well as the number of branches to be explored which enables to significantly improve the efficiency of SAT-based BMC in our chosen area of application. First, the structure of $F_{[0,b]}$ allows us to transform the conjuncted parts of the formula separately into CNF:

$$cnf(Init_0) \wedge cnf(T_{0,1}) \wedge \ldots \wedge cnf(T_{b-1,b}) \wedge cnf(Error_b)$$

which can be done via the Tseytin transformation [15]. From now on we just write $F_{[0,b]}$ when we refer to the CNF-equivalent of the formula. The atoms of the encoding $F_{[0,b]}$ can be divided into disjoint sets: $Atoms(F_{[0,b]}) = \bigcup_{k=0}^{b} LocAtoms_k \cup VarAtoms_k$ where $LocAtoms_k$ resp. $VarAtoms_k$ refers to the set of location resp. variable atoms with position index k. Our encoding has the useful property that the application of an assignment $\alpha : LocAtoms_k \rightarrow \{0, 1\}$ results in a formula $\alpha(F_{[0,b]})$ where all $a \in VarAtoms_k$ (i.e. all k-indexed variable atoms) occur in unit clauses. Hence, the subsequent application of unit propagation [17] will immediately assign truth values to all atoms in $VarAtoms_k$. This allows us to solely consider location atoms as branching atoms, since all variable atoms will be automatically assigned under unit propagation.[1]

General-purpose SAT algorithms choose a single atom a as the branching atom at each decision level and then branch for $(a, \mathbf{0})$ (a is assigned by $\mathbf{0}$) and $(a, \mathbf{1})$ (a is assigned by $\mathbf{1}$). In our enhanced algorithm we choose the *set* $LocAtoms_{k+1}$ at each decision level k. (The use of *unit propagation* [17] will ensure that all atoms with index $k' \leq k$ will be already assigned at level k.) Now instead of branching for each possible assignment to the atoms in $LocAtoms_{k+1}$, the structure of our encoding together with knowledge about the control flow allows us to reduce the number of assignments (i.e. branches) to *admissible* ones. Note that an assignment $\alpha : LocAtoms_{k+1} \rightarrow \{0, 1\}$ characterises a location $l' \in Loc$ in the overall control flow graph $G = (Loc, \delta, \tau)$ representing the system under consideration. An assignment α is only admissible if it characterises a location l' such that $\delta(l, l')$ holds, where l is the location characterised by the assignment decision at the previous decision level k. Hence, the consideration of the control flow of the encoded system allows us to narrow down the number of branches at each level. Moreover, the number of levels gets reduced to b – the bound of the encoding. Our new algorithm BMCSAT that implements such a decision level reduction and branch reduction is depicted below.

Beside the formula F and a decision level $k \in \mathbb{N}$ the recursive algorithm takes a location $l \in Loc$ of the encoded system as input. and eventually returns an assignment $\alpha : Atoms(F) \rightarrow \{0, 1\}$ satisfying F or an unsatisfiability result. The assignment α is constructed *incrementally*. Hence, until the algorithm has terminated α may be a partial assignment for F, i.e. its domain may not necessarily contain all atoms of the input formula. The incremental construction of the overall assignment happens via the concatenation of partial assignments with disjoint domains: $\alpha \circ \alpha'$. We write $\alpha(F)$ to refer to the formula F under the assignment α. For instance, the partial assignment $\alpha = \{(a_1, \mathbf{1})\}$ for the formula $\neg a_1 \vee a_2$ yields $\alpha(\neg a_1 \vee a_2) = \mathbf{0} \vee a_2$, which gets simplified to a_2.

In Line 2 of the algorithm, *unit propagation* [17] is applied to the input formula: If a clause of F is a unit (single-literal) clause it can only be satisfied by assigning the underlying atom such that the literal is $\mathbf{1}$. This assignment will be then propagated to the remaining clauses, the formula will be simplified, and unit propagation will be repetitively applied as long as there exist further unit clauses with unassigned atoms. The application of unit propagation yields a (possibly partial) assignment α. In case α already satisfies F, BMCSAT returns α as a satisfying assignment and terminates (Line 3). In case α makes the formula $\mathbf{0}$ the algorithm terminates with an unsatisfiability result (Line 4). In every other case,

---

[1] The Tseytin CNF transformation introduces a number of auxiliary atoms for each sub formulae $T_{k-1,k}$. The assignment to all k-indexed location atoms by our enhanced algorithm and the subsequent application of unit propagation will also immediately assign truth values to the auxiliary atoms. Hence, the presence of auxiliary atoms does not affect our approach.

Algorithm 1. BMCSAT(F, k, l)

Data: CNF formula F, decision level $k \in \mathbb{N}$, control flow location $l \in Loc$
Result: assignment $\alpha : Atoms(F) \rightarrow \{0, 1\}$ satisfying F, or UNSAT

```
1  begin
2  |   α := unit-propagate(F)
3  |   if α(F) = 1 then
4  |   |   return α
5  |   else if α(F) = 0 then
6  |   |   return UNSAT
7  |   else
8  |   |   A := {α' : LocAtoms_{k+1} → {0, 1} | δ(l, α')}
9  |   |   while A ≠ ∅ do
10 |   |   |   choose α' ∈ A
11 |   |   |   A := A\{α'}
12 |   |   |   if α'' := BMCSAT((α ∘ α')(F), k + 1, α') ≠ UNSAT then
13 |   |   |   |   return α ∘ α' ∘ α''
14 |   |   return UNSAT
```

$LocAtoms_{k+1}$ is identified as the set of atoms that will be assigned at the next decision level (Line 8). Moreover, the set of possible assignments to $LocAtoms_{k+1}$ is computed and then restricted to admissible ones by the condition $\delta(l, \alpha')$. Note that since such assignments α' always characterise control flow locations $l \in Loc$, we can also use them as arguments of the transition relation δ of the underlying control flow graph. In the Lines 9 to 13, BMCSAT is recursively called resulting in a branch for each admissible assignment. The result of the calls is then concatenated with the so far partial assignment. SAT solvers do not generally explore all possible branches. Commonly, one branch is explored at a time until a satisfiability result can be obtained or until the branch turns out to be inexpedient. In the latter case conflict-driven clause learning with non-chronological backtracking [2] is performed and an alternative branch is explored. An excerpt of the branching tree for BMCSAT $(F_{[0,2]}, 0, (00, 00))$ where $F_{[0,2]}$ is the 2-bounded encoding of our example verification task is depicted below.

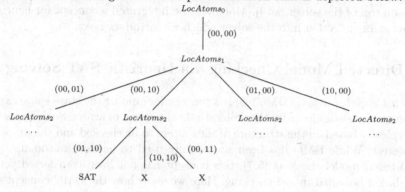

The sub formula $Init_0$ of $F_{[0,2]}$ is a conjunction of unit clauses over $LocAtoms_0$ and $VarAtoms_0$. Hence, the first application of unit propagation will yield an assignment $\alpha : LocAtoms_0 \cup VarAtoms_0 \rightarrow \{0,1\}$ that characterises the initial system state encoded in $Init_0$. The control flow location $l = (00, 00)$ is part of this initial state. Subsequently, BMCSAT will identify $LocAtoms_1$ as the set of location atoms that are assigned next. Based on the transition relation δ of the control flow graph $G = (Loc, \delta, \tau)$ the set of admissible assignments (i.e. direct successor locations of $(00, 00)$ in G) is determined: $\{(00, 01), (00, 10), (01, 00), (10, 00)\}$. For each admissible assignment BMCSAT is recursively called. The branch corresponding to the assignment $(00, 10)$ has three further branches at decision level 1. The corresponding assignments are $(01, 10)$, $(10, 10)$ and $(00, 11)$. Choosing the assignment $(01, 10)$ for $LocAtoms_2$ and the subsequent application of unit propagation immediately yields a satisfying assignment for $F_{[0,2]}$ and therefore proves that within two steps an error state is reachable in the encoded system. Thus, our BMCSAT only requires two decision levels in order to accomplish this SAT-based verification task, whereas a general-purpose SAT solving algorithm would require at least $|LocAtoms_1| + |LocAtoms_2|$ decision levels. The reduction of decision levels in our branching tree comes at the cost of an increase of branches at each level. However, our concept of admissible assignments (i.e. branches) allows us to reduce the number of branches that actually have to be explored – based on the exploitation of control flow information. In our example at decision level 0 the admissible assignment concept allows us to reduce the number of branches to be explored from 16 to only 4, and at level 1 each node of the search tree now only has 3 instead of 16 branches. The extent to which branch reduction is generally possible depends on the number of transitions in the CFG G. In case G is a complete digraph with $|Loc|^2$ transitions (i.e. all pairs of locations are bi-directionally connected via direct transitions), then our branch reduction will not have any effect and at each decision level we have to consider $|Loc|$ branches. However, for most realistic software systems represented as CFGs the number of transitions is substantially smaller than $|Loc|^2$. For the verification of such systems the application of branch reduction can enable computational savings of orders of magnitude, which we just exemplified based on our example. We implemented our enhanced concepts, that we illustrated here based on BMC-SAT, on top of the solver Sat4j. Moreover, we integrated a concept for heuristic guided error detection into the solver which we introduce next.

5   Directed Model Checking via Heuristic SAT Solving

Directed model checking (DMC) [5] is a concept for guiding the state space exploration via heuristics in order to accelerate the detection of errors. Such heuristics are typically based on the structure of the system to be checked and the property of interest. While DMC has been successfully used to improve automata- and BDD-based model checking [5,7], this concept has not been transferred yet to SAT-based bounded model checking. Here we show how the DMC concept can be integrated into our SAT-based bounded model checking approach such that the performance of SAT solving algorithm profits from heuristic guidance.

Heuristic model checking algorithms exploit useful information to guide the search. This information is given as an evaluation function $h : S \rightarrow \mathbb{N}_\infty$ that estimates the distance from the current state $\langle l, s \rangle \in S$ to an error state where S is the overall set of states. This is known as best-first search. The heuristic function h is precomputed before the search starts. In [4] a concept for computing such a h based on the system and the property to be checked is introduced and it is shown that based on h the exploration of an explicit state space model can be guided. Here we show that h can be also straightforwardly computed based on our verification tasks and then used in order to guide the SAT solver.

The evaluation function of [4] combines distances in the control flow and property-based heuristics. Our system under consideration is given as a composite CFG G composed of single CFGs $G_i = (Loc_i, \delta_i, \tau_i)$ for each process. Thus, we can easily compute a local distance function $d_i : Loc_i \times Loc_i \rightarrow \mathbb{N}_\infty$ for each process that returns the shortest directed path in G_i for a pair of its control flow locations. Now the global distance function is defined as $d(l, l') := \sum_{i=1}^n d_i(l_i, l'_i)$ where $l, l' \in Loc$ and $l = (l_1, \ldots, l_n)$. Remember that in our encoding-based approach each l can be expressed by an assignment $\alpha : LocAtoms \rightarrow \{0, 1\}$. Hence, we can also use assignments α as arguments of the distance functions, as long as the assignments characterise actual locations. Since the control flow distance does not incorporate constraints induced by variable values, the function d gives us an under-approximation of the length of a shortest path in the actual state space. From [4] we also get a property-based evaluation function that extends the distance-based one. Our property is the characterisation of an error state given as an arbitrary propositional logic expression $Error_b$ over the b-indexed atoms. For the computation of the evaluation function it is sufficient to consider the non-indexed equivalent $Error$. In our running example we had $Error :=$

$$(\neg l_1[1] \wedge l_1[2] \wedge \neg q \wedge l_2[1] \wedge \neg l_2[2] \wedge \neg p) \vee (l_1[1] \wedge \neg l_1[2] \wedge \neg p \wedge \neg l_2[1] \wedge l_2[2] \wedge \neg q)$$

We now can adapt the property-based evaluation function for our SAT-based approach as follows. Let $Error$ over $Atoms = LocAtoms \cup VarAtoms$ be a formula characterising an error state. Let F and G be arbitrary sub formulae of $Error$ and $a \in VarAtoms$. Let $enc(l_i)$ be a sub formula of $Error$ characterising a location $l_i \in Loc_i$. Then $h_{Error} : \mathcal{A} \rightarrow \mathbb{N}_\infty$ (where $\mathcal{A}$ is a set of assignments characterising states of the encoded system) is inductively defined as follows:

$$
\begin{aligned}
h_{true}(\alpha) &:= 0 \\
h_{false}(\alpha) &:= \infty \\
h_a(\alpha) &:= \text{if } \alpha(a) = \mathbf{0} \text{ then } 1 \text{ else } 0 \\
h_{\neg a}(\alpha) &:= \text{if } \alpha(a) = \mathbf{1} \text{ then } 1 \text{ else } 0 \\
h_{F \vee G}(\alpha) &:= min\{h_F(\alpha), h_G(\alpha)\} \\
h_{F \wedge G}(\alpha) &:= h_F(\alpha) + h_G(\alpha) \\
h_{enc(l_i)}(\alpha) &:= d_i(\alpha, l_i)
\end{aligned}
$$

With our running example we illustrate how h can guide the search of the SAT solving algorithm BMCSAT in the right direction: We assume that at decision level 0 the atoms of $LocAtoms_1$ have been assigned by $(00, 10)$ and we are currently at decision level 1. Hence, the atoms of $LocAtoms_2$ will be assigned next. The execution of Line 8 of our algorithm will yield the set $\mathcal{A} = \{(01, 10), (10, 10), (00, 11)\}$ of admissible assignments. For our heuristically enhanced approach, we *replace* Line 10 of BMCSAT by the following statement:

$$\alpha' := select\text{-}min(\mathcal{A}, h_{Error})$$

such that the branch resp. assignment $\alpha' \in \mathcal{A}$ with the heuristically estimated shortest distance to an error state is selected for further expansion. For our three candidates from $\mathcal{A}$ we thus get:

$$h_{Error}((01, 10)) := min\{0 + 0, 3 + 3\} = 0$$
$$h_{Error}((10, 10)) := min\{3 + 0, 0 + 3\} = 3$$
$$h_{Error}((00, 11)) := min\{1 + 2, 1 + 2\} = 3$$

Consequently $(01, 10)$ is heuristically chosen as the assignment for $LocAtoms_2$. At the next level the application of unit propagation will immediately return a satisfying assignment for the encoding $F_{[0,2]}$ and thus prove that an error state is reachable within two steps. Our heuristic guidance has thus avoided the exploration of fruitless branches associated with the other admissible assignments. Thus we now have two new concepts for tuning SAT solving for model checking:

– the introduction of *set assignments* and *admissible assignments* in BMCSAT shrinks the total number of branches to be explored, and
– the *heuristic function* h additionally guides the search into fruitful branches

Our heuristic function does not yet incorporate the variable atoms, since all $\alpha' \in \mathcal{A}$ only assign values to location atoms. For each $a \in VarAtoms$, $\alpha'(a)$ is *undefined*, and consequently $h_a(\alpha')$ yields 0. Thus, in our current approach any costs associated with variable atoms are ignored. A straightforward way to incorporate those atoms would be to compute the assignment $\alpha_{Var} := unit\text{-}propagate((\alpha \circ \alpha')(T_{k,k+1}))$ for each $\alpha' \in \mathcal{A}$, such that α_{Var} would extend α' to all variable atoms with index $k + 1$. In such a manner the costs associated with an $a \in VarAtoms$ would then be estimated by $h_a(\alpha' \circ \alpha_{Var})$.

6   Implementation and Experiments

We have prototypically implemented our SAT-based bounded model checker with heuristic guidance on top of the solver Sat4j [6]. Our tool builds abstract CFGs for a given concurrent system Sys and a set of predicates $Pred$. It supports almost all control structures of the C language as well as *int, bool, semaphore* as data types. Based on the CFGs and an input $Error$ property (e.g. mutual exclusion violation, deadlock) defined over locations and predicates, our tool automatically constructs an encoding F of the corresponding verification task. The checker now iterates over the bound b starting with $b = 0$, until a the reachability of an *Error* state can be proven or a predefined threshold for b is reached. In each iteration the encoding is processed by an solver instance of Sat4j. We have modified the solver such that it implements our proposed concepts of *set assignments, admissible assignments* and *property-based heuristic guidance* of the SAT search. For this, the heuristic function that estimates the distance from the current state to an *Error* state is precomputed based on the abstract CFGs and the *Error* property. In experiments we compared the performance of our heuristic-guided solver with the performance under the general-purpose solving of Sat4j. As input systems we used the *concurrent Boolean program benchmark collection* of the CProver project[2]. The programs of the collection implement device drivers with multiple threads i.e. processes. We checked for the reachability of states with particular combinations of program locations which we henceforth denote as *error states*. The experimental results are summarised below.

Benchmark		General-purpose	Heuristic-guided
ib700wdt	Reachable	11.3 s	2.7 s
	Unreachable	27.6 s	39.2 s
sc1200wdt	Reachable	306 s	35.7 s
	Unreachable	124 s	143 s
i8xx_tco	Reachable	807 s	122 s
	Unreachable	201 s	163 s
Machzwd	reachable	97.0 s	31.6 s
	Unreachable	11.3 s	10.7 s

The experiments were conducted on a 2.6 GHz Intel Core i5 with 8 GB. All benchmark items consist of a *set* of concurrent programs. We checked all programs individually. For some programs of each item the outcome of verification was the *reachability* of the error state, whereas for other programs an *unreachability* result was obtained. In the table we consider verification tasks with a reachability result and those with an unreachability result separately. The displayed times denote the average runtime of all reachability resp. all unreachability cases of each benchmark item. Our experiments revealed that our heuristic approach significantly enhances the solving performance of verification tasks where the reachability of an error state can be finally proven, whereas verification tasks with an unreachability outcome can be typically solved equally efficient with the general-purpose and the heuristic approach. Hence, our new approach is particularly useful for detecting errors in concurrent systems, while it does not introduce any drawbacks in case no error can be detected. Our enhanced concepts allow us to guide the SAT search into directions where errors will be most likely detected.

---

[2] www.cprover.org/boolean-programs.

7 Conclusion

We presented a new approach for accelerating SAT-based model checking. We defined a propositional logic state space encoding of concurrent systems that preserves control flow information. Moreover, we designed an enhanced SAT algorithm that exploits the structure of our encodings in order to reduce the computational effort for solving the encoded verification task. The concepts *set assignments* and *admissible assignments* allow to narrow down the number of decision levels and branches to be explored. Furthermore, we introduced a heuristic based on the property to be verified, which enables to guide the SAT search into directions where a property violation will be most likely detected. The heuristic approach facilitates further computational savings. We implemented our state space encoding and integrated our enhanced SAT concepts into the solver Sat4j. Our tool allows to perform guided SAT-based BMC with a considerably faster error detection compared to BMC via general-purpose SAT solving.

References

1. Biere, A., Cimatti, A., Clarke, E.M., Strichman, O., Zhu, Y.: Bounded model checking. In: Handbook of Satisfiability, pp. 457–481 (2009)
2. Biere, A., Heule, M., van Maaren, H., Walsh, T.: Conflict-driven clause learning SAT solvers. In: Handbook of Satisfiability, pp. 131–153 (2009)
3. Clarke, E., Kroening, D., Sharygina, N., Yorav, K.: SATABS: SAT-based predicate abstraction for ANSI-C. In: Halbwachs, N., Zuck, L.D. (eds.) TACAS 2005. LNCS, vol. 3440, pp. 570–574. Springer, Heidelberg (2005). doi:10.1007/978-3-540-31980-1_40
4. Edelkamp, S., Lafuente, A.L., Leue, S.: Directed explicit model checking with HSF-SPIN. In: Dwyer, M. (ed.) SPIN 2001. LNCS, vol. 2057, pp. 57–79. Springer, Heidelberg (2001). doi:10.1007/3-540-45139-0_5
5. Edelkamp, S., Schuppan, V., Bošnački, D., Wijs, A., Fehnker, A., Aljazzar, H.: Survey on directed model checking. In: Peled, D.A., Wooldridge, M.J. (eds.) MoChArt 2008. LNCS (LNAI), vol. 5348, pp. 65–89. Springer, Heidelberg (2009). doi:10.1007/978-3-642-00431-5_5
6. le Berre, D., Parrain, A.: The Sat4J library, release 2.2. J. Satisfiability Boolean Modeling Comput. **7**, 59–64 (2010)
7. Reffe, F., Edelkamp, S.: Error detection with directed symbolic model checking. In: Wing, J.M., Woodcock, J., Davies, J. (eds.) FM 1999. LNCS, vol. 1708, pp. 195–211. Springer, Heidelberg (1999). doi:10.1007/3-540-48119-2_13
8. Shtrichman, O.: Tuning SAT checkers for bounded model checking. In: Emerson, E.A., Sistla, A.P. (eds.) CAV 2000. LNCS, vol. 1855, pp. 480–494. Springer, Heidelberg (2000). doi:10.1007/10722167_36
9. Wang, C., Jin, H., Hachtel, G.D., Somenzi, F.: Refining the SAT decision ordering for bounded model checking. In: DAC, pp. 535–538. ACM (2004)
10. Demsky, B., Lam, P.: SATCheck: SAT-directed stateless model checking for SC and TSO. In: ACM SIGPLAN Notices, pp. 20–36. ACM (2015)
11. Audemard, G., Simon, L.: Predicting learnt clauses quality in modern SAT solvers. In: IJCAI, pp. 399–404 (2009)

12. Andisha, A.S., Wehrle, M., Westphal, B.: Directed model checking for PROMELA with relaxation-based distance functions. In: Fischer, B., Geldenhuys, J. (eds.) SPIN 2015. LNCS, vol. 9232, pp. 153–159. Springer, Cham (2015). doi:10.1007/978-3-319-23404-5_11

13. Maeoka, J., Tanabe, Y., Ishikawa, F.: Depth-first heuristic search for software model checking. In: Lee, R. (ed.) Computer and Information Science 2015. SCI, vol. 614, pp. 75–96. Springer, Cham (2016). doi:10.1007/978-3-319-23467-0_6

14. Schrieb, J., Wehrheim, H., Wonisch, D.: Three-valued spotlight abstractions. In: Cavalcanti, A., Dams, D.R. (eds.) FM 2009. LNCS, vol. 5850, pp. 106–122. Springer, Heidelberg (2009). doi:10.1007/978-3-642-05089-3_8

15. Tseytin, G.S.: On the complexity of derivation in propositional calculus. In: Studies in Constructive Mathematics and Mathematical Logic, pp. 115–125. Steklov Mathematical Institute (1970)

16. Gelder, A.: Improved conflict-clause minimization leads to improved propositional proof traces. In: Kullmann, O. (ed.) SAT 2009. LNCS, vol. 5584, pp. 141–146. Springer, Heidelberg (2009). doi:10.1007/978-3-642-02777-2_15

17. Zhang, H., Stickel, M.: An efficient algorithm for unit-propagation. In: 4th International Symposium on Artificial Intelligence and Mathematics, pp. 166–169 (1996)

Author Index

Printed in the United States
By Bookmasters